Paraphernalia!

The Victorian era is famous for the collecting, hording, and displaying of things; for the mass production and consumption of things; for the invention, distribution, and sale of things; for those who had things, and those who did not. For many people, the Victorian period is intrinsically associated with paraphernalia.

This collection of essays explores the Victorians through their materiality and asks how objects were part of being Victorian; which objects defined them, represented them, were uniquely theirs; and how reading the Victorians, through their possessions, can deepen our understanding of Victorian culture. Miscellaneous and often auxiliary, paraphernalia becomes the 'disjecta' of everyday life, deemed neither valuable enough for museums nor symbolic enough for purely literary study. This interdisciplinary collection looks at the historical, cultural, and literary debris that makes up the background of Victorian life: Valentine's cards, fish tanks, sugar plums, china ornaments, hair ribbons, dresses, and more. Contributors also, however, consider how we use Victorian objects to construct the Victorian today; museum spaces, the relation of Victorian text to object, and our reading – or gazing at – Victorian advertisements out of context on searchable online databases.

Responding to thing theory and modern scholarship on Victorian material culture, this book addresses five key concerns of Victorian materiality: collecting; defining class in the home; objects becoming things; objects to texts; and objects in circulation through print culture.

Helen Kingstone is Lecturer in Victorian Studies at the University of Glasgow. Her research addresses the relationship between memory and history in the nineteenth century, focusing on how writers in different genres and forms approached contemporary history. Her monograph *Victorian Narratives of the Recent Past: Memory, History, Fiction* was published by Palgrave Macmillan in 2017. Other publications include articles on fin-de-siècle utopian fiction in *English Literature in Transition, 1880–1920* and in *Utopias and Dystopias in the Fiction of H. G. Wells and William Morris*, ed. Emelyne Godfrey (Palgrave, 2016), and others on literature and scientific ideas of progress in *Nineteenth-Century Contexts* and in *Historicising Humans*, ed. Efram Sera-Shriar (University of Pittsburgh Press, 2018).

Kate Lister is Lecturer in English Literature at Leeds Trinity University and columnist for *The Independent*. Kate has published in the medical humanities, Victorian and contemporary medievalism, and most recently on nineteenth-century media constructions of the 'fallen woman' for *The Routledge Companion to Sex, Sexuality and the Media*. Her first monograph on Victorian women authors and the Arthurian mythology is with the University of Wales Press, and she is currently editing an International collection of essays on the History Channel's series, *Vikings*. Kate is a board member of the International Sex Work Research Hub and she is the curator of the online research project, Whores of Yore.

The Nineteenth Century Series

Series editor: Joanne Shattock, Professor Emeritus

University of Leicester, UK

The series focuses primarily upon major authors and subjects within Romantic and Victorian literature. It also includes studies of other nineteenth-century British writers and issues, where these are matters of current debate: for example, biography and autobiography; journalism; periodical literature; travel writing; book production; gender; non-canonical writing.

Recent in this series:

Life Writing and Victorian Culture
Edited by David Amigoni

Pre-Raphaelite Masculinities
Edited by Amelia Yeates and Serena Trowbridge

Thackeray in Time
History, Memory and Modernity
Edited by Richard Salmon and Alice Crossley

Paraphernalia!
Victorian Objects
Edited by Helen Kingstone and Kate Lister

Paraphernalia!
Victorian Objects

Edited by
Helen Kingstone and Kate Lister

Routledge
Taylor & Francis Group
New York London

First published 2018
by Routledge
52 Vanderbilt Avenue, New York, NY 10017

and by Routledge
2 Park Square, Milton Park, Abingdon, Oxon OX14 4RN

First issued in paperback 2020

*Routledge is an imprint of the Taylor & Francis Group, an
informa business*

Library of Congress Cataloging-in-Publication Data
CIP data has been applied for.

ISBN 13: 978-0-367-66721-4 (pbk)
ISBN 13: 978-0-8153-8781-7 (hbk)

Typeset in Sabon
by codeMantra

MIX
Paper from
responsible sources
FSC   FSC® C013985
www.fsc.org

Printed in the United Kingdom
by Henry Ling Limited

Contents

List of Figures

Acknowledgements

The chapters in this collection are based on the papers and discussions of a colloquium of the same name held at Leeds Trinity University in 2015. We would like to thank the British Association for Victorian Studies, whose conference funding scheme helped us to hold the event, and Leeds Centre for Victorian Studies, especially its then Director, Rosemary Mitchell, for all their support in enabling and encouraging our work.

We have enjoyed working with our contributors both in person at that colloquium, and since then through a long process of email correspondence. Particular thanks to Rohan McWilliam for his helpful comments and pointers on our draft introduction. We are also grateful to Michelle Salyga and Tim Swenarton at Routledge for their generous and flexible support in bringing this collection to fruition.

Acknowledgements

List of Contributors

Anne Anderson (FSA) is Honorary Associate Professor at the University of Exeter and a Course Director at the V&A Learning Centre, covering the Arts and Crafts and Art Nouveau. Anne was a senior lecturer at Southampton Solent University for fourteen years, where she specialized in the Aesthetic Movement, Arts and Crafts, Art Nouveau and Modernism. During 2009–2010, Anne worked on 'Closer to Home', the reopening exhibition at Leighton House Museum, Kensington; she also curated 'Under the Greenwood: Picturing the British Tree' for St Barbe Museum and Gallery, Lymington in 2013. Anne has held four fellowships in the United States, most recently the Last Fellowship in Material Culture at the American Antiquarian Society, Worcester, MA.

Odile Boucher-Rivalain is Professor of Victorian Literature and Culture at the University of Cergy-Pontoise. As a specialist on nineteenth century fiction she has published articles on the critical reception of Dickens, Collins, the Brontës, and George Eliot. She is the editor of an anthology of reviews in Victorian periodicals, *Roman et Poésie en Angleterre au XIXe Siècle* (L'Harmattan, 2001). She has also published a book on Harriet Martineau prefaced by Rosemary Mitchell, *Harriet Martineau, une Victorienne Engagée* (Michel Houdiard Editeur, 2012).

Julia Courtney is an independent scholar, having retired from the Open University where she served as an administrator, research fellow and Associate Lecturer, latterly in the Post Graduate Literature programme. Julia's PhD was on the novelist Charlotte M Yonge and she has published on this author as well as recent/forthcoming articles in *Women: A Cultural Review*, *English Review* and *the Journal of William Morris Studies*. Taxidermy is a 'second string' which is rapidly taking over Julia's research interests, especially given the current widespread academic work being done in Animal Studies. She has given numerous conference papers on the subject and has published in *Hampshire Studies* (2011).

Alice Crossley is a Senior Lecturer in English Literature at the University of Lincoln, where she is Programme Leader. She has published articles and chapters on youth and masculinity in the nineteenth century, dandyism, schoolboy bodies in fiction and the serialised novels of William Makepeace Thackeray. She recently edited a special issue of *Nineteenth-Century Gender Studies* on 'Age and Gender: Aging in the Nineteenth Century' (2017). Alice's monograph *Male Adolescence in Mid-Victorian Fiction* (forthcoming with Routledge) focuses on the work of W.M. Thackeray, George Meredith and Anthony Trollope, and she is co-editor with Dr Richard Salmon of *Thackeray in Time: History, Memory and Modernity* (Routledge 2016). She is currently working towards a new project on aging and speech/dialogue in Victorian fiction, as well as working on valentine cards in the nineteenth century.

Silvia Granata is tenured Lecturer at the University of Pavia. She is the author of two monographs: *The Dear Charities of Social Life. The Work of Anna Laetitia Barbauld* (2008), and *Take Every Creature in, of Every Kind: Continuity and Change in Eighteenth-Century Representations of Animals* (2010). She has published articles on animals in Victorian literature and culture, late-Victorian detective fiction, and the relationship between literature and science in the eighteenth and nineteenth centuries. She is currently working on a book-project concerning Victorian aquaria.

Heather Hind is an AHRC-funded PhD student in English at the Universities of Exeter and Bristol. She completed her MA in English Literary Studies at the University of York and her undergraduate degree at Lucy Cavendish College, Cambridge. Her thesis, provisionally titled 'Hairwork in Nineteenth-Century Literature and Culture', explores the relationship between the art of hairwork and its representation in fiction, women's magazines and craft manuals. She is currently writing on the intersections between the Brontë sisters' hair jewellery and their writings.

Helen Kingstone is Lecturer in Victorian Studies at the University of Glasgow. Her research addresses the relationship between memory and history in the nineteenth century, focusing on how writers in different genres and forms approached contemporary history. Her monograph *Victorian Narratives of the Recent Past: Memory, History, Fiction* was published by Palgrave Macmillan in 2017. Other publications include articles on fin-de-siècle utopian fiction in *English Literature in Transition, 1880–1920* and in *Utopias and Dystopias in the Fiction of H. G. Wells and William Morris*, ed. Emelyne Godfrey (Palgrave, 2016), and others on literature and scientific ideas of progress in *Nineteenth-Century Contexts* and in *Historicising Humans* ed. Efram Sera-Shriar (University of Pittsburgh Press, 2018).

Kate Lister is a Lecturer in English Literature at Leeds Trinity University and columnist for *The Independent*. Kate has published in the medical humanities, Victorian and contemporary medievalism, and most recently on nineteenth-century media constructions of the 'fallen woman' for *The Routledge Companion to Sex, Sexuality and the Media*. Her first monograph on Victorian women authors and the Arthurian mythology is with the University of Wales Press, and she is currently editing an International collection of essays on the History Channel's series, *Vikings*. Kate is a board member of the International Sex Work Research Hub and she is the curator of the online research project, Whores of Yore.

Thad Logan is Lecturer in English at Rice University, USA. She is the author of *The Victorian Parlour: A Cultural Study* (Cambridge University Press, 2001) and the material culture entry in *The Wiley-Blackwell Encyclopedia of Victorian Literature,* as well as articles and presentations on domestic interiors. Her current research focuses on Dante Gabriel Rossetti and the representation of material things in art and literature.

Rohan McWilliam is Professor of Modern British History at Anglia Ruskin University, Cambridge. In 2012–2015, he was President of the British Association for Victorian Studies. His published works include *Popular Politics in Nineteenth-Century England* (1998) and *The Tichborne Claimant: A Victorian Sensation* (2007). He is the editor (with Kelly Boyd) of *The Victorian Studies Reader* (2007), (with Jonathan Davis) of *Labour and the Left in the 1980s* (2018) and (with Sasha Handley and Lucy Noakes) of *New Directions in Social and Cultural History* (2018). He has written articles on subjects including melodrama, Elsa Lanchester and Jonathan Miller. He is also the editor of two book series, Becoming Modern: New Nineteenth Century Studies (University Press of New England) and New Directions in Social and Cultural History (Bloomsbury), which is organized on behalf of the Social History Society. He serves on the editorial board of the Journal of Victorian Culture where he is reviews editor. At present, he is at work on a two-volume history of the West End of London.

Ralph Mills is a historical archaeologist researching the recent and contemporary past. In 2017 he was awarded a PhD by Manchester Institute for Research and Innovation in Art and Design (MIRIAD), Manchester School of Art. His research into 'Objects of Delight' continues: he is investigating what mass-produced miniature objects, focusing on artefacts displayed in domestic contexts in the Old and New Worlds, can tell us about the material culture of nineteenth century working-class people.

Sophie Ratcliffe is Fellow and Tutor in English at Lady Margaret Hall and Associate Professor in Nineteenth-Century Literature at the University of Oxford. She has published books and articles on a variety of nineteenth- and twentieth-century writers, and has special interests in questions of material culture, affect, and ethics. She is currently working on a book about material culture and medicine.

François Ropert is a senior Lecturer in English studies at the University of Cergy-Pontoise (France). He is a fellow of the Cergy-based research centre AGORA, formerly 'Centre for Comparative Identities, Cultures and Civilisations' (CICC). His research interests range across late Victorian and modernist poetry and criticism. His work is mainly concerned with poetical figurations of authority and modernity in times of crisis. He has published articles on Matthew Arnold, Algernon Charles Swinburne, Oscar Wilde, and T. S. Eliot. He also has research and teaching interests in the French translations and adaptations of Victorian children's verse and prose fiction.

Valerie Sanders is Professor of English at the University of Hull. She has published widely on Victorian women writers, with books including *The Private Lives of Victorian Women: Autobiography in Nineteenth-Century England* (1989), *Eve's Renegades: Victorian Anti-Feminist Women Novelists* (Macmillan, 1996), *The Brother-Sister Culture in Nineteenth-Century Literature* (Palgrave, 2002) and *The Tragi-Comedy of Victorian Fatherhood* (Cambridge University Press, 2009), as well as editing many volumes, most recently of the works of Margaret Oliphant. She is currently writing a volume on Oliphant for the Key Popular Women Writers series to be published by Edward Everett Root.

Peter Yeandle is Lecturer in History at the University of Loughborough. His monograph *Citizenship, Nation, Empire: The Politics of History Teaching* was published by MUP in February 2015, and he is co-editor with Kate Newey and Jeffrey Richards of *Politics, Performance and Popular Culture: Theatre and Society in Nineteenth-Century Britain* (2016). His essay is part of a wider project examining the overlaps of imperial imagery and consumer culture in late-Victorian and Edwardian Britain.

Introduction

'It's a Victorian Thing'

Helen Kingstone and Kate Lister

As Freddie Mercury once said, 'I want to lead the Victorian life, surrounded by exquisite clutter.'[1] Victorian culture does indeed have a reputation for 'exquisite clutter,' perhaps beautiful, but also cumbersome, excessive and in the way. While the material remains of the Victorian period in the twenty-first century are too multifarious to allow for any easy distillation, they can perhaps be summed up under the heading of 'paraphernalia.' The Victorians are famous for the collecting, hoarding, and displaying of things; for the mass production and consumption of things; for the invention, distribution, and sale of things; for those who had things, and those who did not. For many people, as Freddie Mercury's comment epitomizes, the Victorian period is intrinsically associated with paraphernalia.

The term paraphernalia carries implications of the miscellaneous; of being an auxiliary to a greater part. It thus becomes the 'disjecta' of everyday life, neither valuable enough for museums nor symbolic enough for purely literary study. This collection looks at the historical, cultural and literary debris that makes up the background of Victorian life: Valentines cards, fish tanks, figs, china ornaments, hair ribbons, dresses, and more. Contributors also consider how we use Victorian objects to construct the Victorian today, through museum collections, the relation of Victorian text to object, and our reading – or gazing at – Victorian advertisements, in and out of their original contexts. Their discussions encompass both the objects that have survived the intervening century and more, and those that we can only access through documentary references, in text or illustrations. The paraphernalia of the Victorian era makes it the perfect venue for a material culture analysis.

This popular association of the Victorian era with paraphernalia is by no means false. Objects are visible wherever you turn in Victorian literature: the auction in *Vanity Fair* (1848); the jewellery Dorothea denies herself in *Middlemarch* (1871–1872); the mantra of *Great Expectations'* (1861) Wemmick: 'Portable property!'. Even working-class homes take pride in their 'bright green japanned tea-tray', as *Mary Barton* (1848) emphasizes, even if they only have six teacups and need extra visitors to bring their own. The Victorian enthusiasm for the material is, perhaps, understandable given the design and production possibilities brought about by the seemingly unstoppable march of industry, capitalism, and the expansion of the British Empire, and epitomized in that hymn to productivity, the 1851 Great Exhibition. The revolution in production and marketing techniques made many formerly luxurious items available to the working class for the first time. The Empire and expanding trade routes brought the exotic to British shores as the bourgeoisie clambered to own something of India, China and Japan. Of course, not all the artefacts collected in Britain were brought with the full blessing of those who had been relieved of their treasures. Following Lord Elgin's removal of the Parthenon marbles in 1801–1805, later British Imperial military campaigns, like the punitive Third Anglo-Ashanti War in 1873–1874, saw the Ashanti's treasures taken from the royal mausoleum in Kumasi and brought to the British Museum.

This imperial appropriation also had a more localized – and democratizing – effect. An 1851 leaflet 'The Illustrated Exhibitor' highlights what a novelty it was for the 'working man' to be able to see objects such as the Indian Koh-I-Noor diamond in their own neighbourhood.

> For a sight of a single one of these stones an adventurous voyager traversed enormous distances two centuries ago, and by dint of extraordinary influence, audacity, and fortune was enabled to record himself as the only European who had ever succeeded in the attempt. That stone is now in Hyde-park, and may be seen by any working man in the country for a shilling.[2]

This leaflet combines an ostensible celebration at the might of the British Empire (George Cruikshank's famous engraving of the Great Exhibition set the Crystal Palace 'hubristically at the top of the globe') with an unsettling democratization.[3] Something was lost through this relocation: the exotic tamed becomes the everyday, only 'worth a shilling.' As Isobel Armstrong reminds us, under the stark daylight of the Crystal Palace, the Koh-I-Noor 'lost its aura' in visual terms too, and 'people complained' that 'it might as well have been glass.'[4]

The guide and this object thus gesture towards another kind of democratization, encapsulated in the second of the pair of engravings George Cruikshank made for Henry Mayhew's story about the Exhibition. As Armstrong highlights, these myriad and ill-assorted 'humanly made' but now 'animate' objects 'begin to ask questions about the substantivizes, the materiality, of things.'[5] Charlotte Brontë wrote to her father of the Great Exhibition that 'it is a wonderful place – vast, strange, new and impossible to describe. Its grandeur does not consist in one thing, but in the unique assemblage of all things.'[6] How things change their meanings when they come into new configurations – and become configurations – is the central topic of this volume.

This zeal for producing, consuming, and cataloguing all this stuff became, however, a hostage to fortune. The modernist backlash against all things Victorian seized vociferously on such objects as a visible symbol of all it rejected. In 1934, the architectural critic A. E. Richardson wrote that 'Victorian decoration, in its tenacity, resembles the smother of ivy on ancient walls.'[7] Victorian architecture came to be reviled as cumbersome, excessive and embarrassingly dated; a shift in aesthetic taste that led to the demolition of once-celebrated buildings.[8] P.G. Wodehouse quipped, 'whatever may be said in favour of the Victorians, it is pretty generally admitted that few of them were to be trusted within reach of a trowel and a pile of bricks.'[9] The Bloomsbury Group were particularly savage and influential in their indictment of Victoriana. In *Orlando*, Virginia Woolf ridiculed the Victorian obsession with 'things' as 'indecent... hideous and... monumental', and caustically characterized the Victorian experience as:

A conglomeration of the most heterogeneous and ill-assorted objects, piled higgledy-piggledy in a vast mound where the statue of Queen Victoria now stands! Draped about a vast cross of fretted and floriated gold were widow weeds and bridal veils; hooked on to other were crystal palaces, bassinettes, military helmets, memorial wreaths, wedding cakes, cannon, Christmas trees, telescopes, extinct monsters, globes, maps, and mathematical instruments [...] The incongruity of the objects, the association of the fully clothed and partly draped, the garishness of the different colours and their plaid-like juxtaposition afflicted Orlando with a most profound dismay.[10]

That clutter (perhaps not so exquisite in Woolf's portrayal) is to Orlando the antithesis of freedom and beauty. The very 'incongru[ous]... juxtaposition' demonstrates a lack of judgement about what is important. In many ways, for the Modernists at least, Victorian aestheticism became symbolic of the lumbering, imposing, outdated world views that they were bent on challenging. As we show in this collection, the kind of consumer culture Woolf so reviles gained new manifestations in the bazaars of the Victorian West End, but we also show how for many Victorian consumers, their choices about which objects to purchase, collect and display were nonetheless significant ones.

In the decades since the publication of Asa Briggs' *Victorian Things* (1990), Victorian Studies – and the Humanities more generally – has gradually taken something of a 'material turn.' Studies such as Andrew H. Miller's *Novels Behind Glass* have teased out Victorian anxieties that their moral world was in danger of being reduced to little more than a 'warehouse of goods and commodities', reading literature as a register of how Victorian senses of self were influenced by commodities.[11] Since Bill Brown's seminal *A Sense of Things* (2003), the study of things as things has gained further ground.[12] Thing theory distinguishes between objects – made by people for people, constructs of commodity culture, owned and used – and 'things', the grubby matter of which objects are made, but which precedes and exceeds them. Brown's work teases out a distinction between objects and things and moves away from understanding material objects in terms of commodity, to terms rather of signs and signifiers. He draws on a dichotomy between World and Earth to capture this object/thing dichotomy, and David Trotter (2008) expands on that opposition to envisage things as 'Earth/Matter hidden within World/History.'[13] Brown's exemplar case is the scenario in which objects break, or are used beyond their intended purpose, transforming at that moment into things: the spoons hung up as an art installation, forming a mobile of metal shapes, are no longer spoons.[14]

For John Plotz (2008), the matter is more complex again, as he probes what lies between categories, remaining unclassifiable, and refusing to sit still. Expanding on and filling the gap between literary studies and anthropology, Plotz suggests adding 'a third term' between existing ideas of 'abstract commodity' and 'autochthonous thing': 'portable property.'[15] This term usefully characterizes those objects that shift between 'fungibility' and 'sentimental attachment', between exchange-value and a use-value that often consists mainly of possession: for what is the 'use' of objects such as the Eustace Diamonds or the Moonstone? Mary Poovey (2003) has argued that Victorians began to 'measure their worth' by 'a form of value that was always deferred.'[16] This evokes not only Jacques Derrida's 'différance', but also that doubleness of objects that concerns Plotz: this object/thing *could* be circulated and take on commodity value, but for the moment will stay here. In corollary, any object/thing *could* potentially become the focus of sentiment, even if right now it is merely being sold.[17] As Valerie Sanders will show, objects can have both sentimental and practical value when seen as things, taken out of their original context and set within new contexts over which possessors, or appropriators, exercise their imagination.

One risk of the material turn is that it risks reducing Victorian culture down to two competing approaches; one embracing literary theory and playing with an eternally ineffable object/thing slippage; and the other taking a zealously historicist and even literal approach, 'relegat[ing] literature, or the literariness of the literary, to the periphery' as Bill Brown describes the practice championed by Elaine Freedgood.[18] Freedgood makes a central distinction between 'weak metonymic readings', which turn things into symbols, effectively reading them as basic thematic metaphors (e.g., mahogany = wealthy), and the 'strong metonymic readings' she champions, which take things literally, and step sideways into their past and context.[19] By contrast, as Bill Brown characterizes his thing theory practice, it follows Adorno in 'granting the physical world its alterity [as] the very basis for accepting otherness as such.'[20] Brown and those inspired by his approach embark on literary, more awe-struck readings of texts, trying to restore to things their 'excess' of meaning.

These two approaches within Literary Studies can be more easily placed side by side when we recognise that the 'things' Freedgood and Brown have in mind are not necessarily the same things. Both seek to give back to objects/things their history, and both grant them a new centrality. But while Freedgood takes a longstanding historicist methodology to its logical conclusion, Brown seeks instead to break out of the framework in which 'objects' exist only in their relation to us, in a one-way relationship we impose upon them. Instead, in thinking about objects that do not or cannot do the job we demand of them, he insists on taking us off our omnipotent pedestal and revealing our true status as a thing among things.

An approach that takes more inspiration from archaeology and branches out beyond it to examine both objects that have survived, and depictions and references to those that have not, is that of material culture. Attentive examinations of objects – particularly within homes – from Amanda Vickery's *Behind Closed Doors: At Home in Georgian England* (2009) to Jane Hamlett's *Material Relations* (2010) has enhanced our understanding of the social relationships in families. Particularly rich for our study has been Isobel Armstrong's *Victorian Glassworlds* (2008), which as one reviewer describes it, 'implicitly reverses the terms of the phrase 'material culture' by exploring the culture of a material.'[21] Armstrong's book puts the human dimension of the material front and centre, in a way that influences many of the chapters in this volume.

The relationship between material and culture is always in question in material culture studies. The area has gained a new wealth of material and expansive perspective in Frank Trentmann's work, and in *Empire of Things* (2016) (an emphatically global journey going back to fifteenth-century China), he insistently views consumption as something that is not merely 'the outcome of historical forces' but that 'also changed states, societies and daily life.'[22] Evoking William James's concept of the 'material self' (as integral as our social and spiritual selves), he suggests that industrialization gave people new opportunities to express and shape their selves through political institutions such as consumer boycotts and co-operatives. Trentmann thus sees the nineteenth century as an era when – far from becoming alienated from objects – people's innate investment in objects was able to take moral and social form. Whether or not you see this as a positive or enriching development, the most significant ramification of Trentmann's work is to bring into play a broader set of agencies – individuals and groups far beyond 'advertizers' and 'brands' – in shaping people's consumption needs, desires and expectations.[23] As Rohan McWilliam shows in this collection, for instance, one driver beyond the opening of the first major West End bazaar was the Napoleonic Wars, particularly its creation of war widows who needed a respectable and low-risk means to make a living.

As this demonstrates, this book takes a broad and interdisciplinary look at how paraphernalia manifested itself in Victorian culture and society, and how it has been treated, collected, and interpreted since. Thus, while an admirable recent collection edited by Jonathon Shears and Jen Harrison focused on Victorian literary manifestations of 'bric-à-brac', the present volume offers a panoptical view of Victorian obsession with literary, physical and theoretical 'things'. We also provide a humanising perspective on that teeming population that, nonetheless, still appears in popular culture as an edifice: the Victorians. Peter Andersson calls for more attention to '"backstage" Victorian culture' and 'discourses other than civility and discipline', and this book does that, but it also brings together such 'backstage' sources with those 'literary' sources that Andersson suggests are too often funnelled through narrowly Foucauldian approaches.[24] In this way, we recognise 'the coexistence of restrained and expansive behaviours', and seek to join rather than divide them.[25] We put things back, perhaps not in their place, but in their multifarious contexts: the exceptional and the ordinary, and on many occasions (through antique collection, online curation, and children's games among others) out of their original context altogether.

This collection sets out to cover many different types of paraphernalia, as expressed through the material and textual survivals of the Victorian past. The collection moves broadly in five parts: (I) 'A Magic Cave': Collecting Objects; (II) Ornaments: Defining Class at Home; (III) Decentring Meaning: Objects Becoming Things; (IV) Object or Text? Reading the Body; (V) Objects in Circulation: Print Culture.

Part I examines a key question for understanding Victorian paraphernalia: Why do we collect and keep things? Brown suggests that we do so to help us negotiate a relationship with the past. Collecting serves perhaps 'to keep the past proximate... or... to make the past distant, to objectify it (as an idea in a thing) in an effort to arrest its spectral power.'[26] This comes most clearly into relief when we consider the Victorian relationship with another kind of distance, the geographical – and cultural – distance of the colony and metropole. As Plotz emphasizes, the kind of two-type value placed on objects in his analysis of Victorian literary texts show a clear 'asymmetry': 'the flow of culture-bearing objects from core to periphery is not counterbalanced or interrupted by a flow in the opposite direction.' For him, this is a 'crucial component' of the power of the British Empire, as indeed any empire.[27] It also gave an additional piquancy to the objects that its citizens took out to the colonies. Mementoes such as springs of heather 'gained their power only in motion', since back at home they would signify nothing special. As McWilliam reminds us, however, objects from across the Empire *did* enter Britain and take on the cachet of exoticism through bazaars. In the opening chapter, he argues that bazaars in the early nineteenth century provided the model for later department stores and turned shopping into a form of entertainment.

Victoria's reign also saw the founding of what would eventually become the Victoria and Albert Museum, which the first Director, Sir Henry Cole, described as 'a refuge for destitute collections.'[28] In the second chapter, Anne Anderson examines antique-collecting through diaries and autobiographical travelogues, to show how they can help us understand the Victorian obsession with things, as commemorations of moments and memories. In the final chapter of the section, Thad Logan examines the collection of objects amassed by Dante Gabriel Rossetti at Tudor House, taking seriously Walter Pater's notion that Rossetti 'kn[ew] no region of spirit which shall not be sensuous also, or material.'[29] While Rossetti, like many painters of the time, almost always painted from life, Logan shows how he was particularly dependent on the literal presence of people and things – old fabric, pieces of metalwork, wood carvings – in order to produce images of them.

Attitudes to paraphernalia are also heavily inflected by class, as we show in Part II, 'Ornaments: Defining Prosperity at Home.' Just as different classes' relationship to money, purchasing power and the objects it purchases will necessarily be different, the notion of 'portable property' does not apply equally or evenly. Was there a correlation in Victorian Britain, or in the colonies, between one's position on the class scale, and the number of objects in one's possession? We might find a closer correlation if we replace 'number of objects' with 'monetary value of', but even here it is a more complex picture than we might expect. As Silvia Granata, Julia Courtney and Ralph Mills will show, some fashions of collection or display – of aquaria, of taxidermy, and of antiques – were of course particularly attractive to the upper classes, but they also suggest that these were most eagerly and attentively taken up by middle-class or even working-class aspirants. All these types of collection, and indeed a general excess of paraphernalia, came to be most archetypally associated with the Victorian middle-class home.

As Plotz views it, however, this is not merely a blind accruing of objects, but instead a way of bolstering – and proving – middle-class identity. What holds back inescapably working-class characters like Mrs Tulliver in George Eliot's *The Mill on the Floss* (1860), or spells the ultimate doom of the aristocracy in nineteenth-century realist (middle-class) novels, is the way they fetishize their objects. Thomas Richards has argued that consumer culture developed as an affirmation of middle class values; he describes the Great Exhibition as 'an abundance achieved by middle class means, sanctioned by middle-class representatives, and aimed at the middle class.'[30] While this might lead us to expect the bourgeoisie and nouveau riche to care only for the monetary value of objects, Plotz suggests that they demonstrate a distinctive doubled relationship with their possessions, by at once deploying a canny commercial eye, and at other moments holding onto their working-class Tulliver instinct, or perhaps copying their 'betters' – by revealing sentimental attachments.[31] Miller reads an ambivalence towards commodity culture in Victorian literature and traces a 'menacing material culture' throughout canonical nineteenth-century novels. Miller proposes that the Victorian obsession with things led to a reactionary obsession with frugality; 'expenses must be watched and kept low, consumption thoughtfully restrained, the cost of clothing learned and its purchase regulated.'[32]

New research reveals just how important, and how treasured, objects also were in working-class households. Alastair Owens et al have highlighted the centrality – and sometimes surprising abundance – of 'routine' objects in working-class London: even poor families had, and threw away, clay pipes, teapots, and even ornaments.[33] This is a point that we expand upon through Ralph Mills' showcase of one particular Holborn mantelpiece. As Owens et al highlight, 'object-driven' studies can risk 'replac[ing] narratives of deprivation and disadvantage with ones of material affluence and self-improvement.'[34] This kind of analysis can make us dismiss poverty, or at least deny 'the existence of class relationships and class struggles.'[35] As Mills shows, however, the mantelpieces of the Holborn poor do have class significance, whether that be as a sign of conformity to aspirational mores, or as a badge of working-class solidarity against the different tastes of the middle class. A similar risk of undermining poverty is run by the kind of studies that Peter K. Andersson advocates as he throws down the gauntlet by asking 'How Civilized Were the Victorians?' (2015). He suggests that a genuine examination of material culture reveals Victorian people to have had, and been (or seemed?), more fun than we even now attribute to them. While this is a useful corrective to persistent accounts of the Victorian era through solely Foucauldian lenses of 'anxiety' and 'repression', it can also distort by concealing poverty under a façade analogous to Orlando's 'draped' veils and wreaths. We might be circling around a similar cultural problem to that recently outlined in a 2015 report commissioned by the Rowntree Trust on what constitutes a 'socially acceptable standard of living' in the UK.[36] As a *Guardian* newspaper response argued, that inability to afford a television licence, or a broadband internet connection, can prevent people from 'participat[ing] in society.'[37] The fact that people can own possessions and still be crippled by poverty is one we need to remember when examining Victorian objects as well as twenty-first-century ones.

In the chapters of Part II, Granata, Courtney, and Mills all examine how Victorian householders used objects to ornament their house and demonstrate their class status, but taking very different contexts. Granata focuses on the aquarium in the upper-class Victorian home, with its tension between being a commodity (and class signifier) and being a host for living creatures who could not survive without it. Courtney shows how the Victorian fashion for taxidermy arose from a multitude of different motivations, and while it could be used by upper-class practitioners as a hobby, it could be a scientific practice for middle-class naturalists, or as a glimpse of the Empire for boys at school. And finally, Ralph Mills uses George Godwin's sketch of a Holborn chimney piece to excavate the kind of ornamental objects bought and displayed in working-class households, and the self-presentation behind those choices. As he shows, the mantelpieces of even quite poor families in the mid-century were bedecked with mass-produced plaster cats, parrots, and even Napoleons.

Part III, 'Decentring Meaning: Objects Becoming Things', goes to the heart of current debates about the relationship of object and thing. These essays consider how what objects mean can shift as their use changes and they become 'things' in Brown's sense. Valerie Sanders shows how, following Lewis Carroll, children in popular Edwardian stories by Edith Nesbit and Frances Hodgson Burnett take objects out of their intended usage, bringing their inventive instincts into play in real or imagined emergencies. Sanders suggests that while the children try to manipulate objects, they are ultimately often worsted by them, and obliged to concede the stronger object powers of adults. François Ropert examines how Swinburne and Wilde employ devotional objects in figurative ways, arguing that these poets decentre these objects' primary religious meaning by using them in aestheticized and even iconoclastic ways. In his analysis, these devotional objects can thus become readable as signifiers of decadence in the late Victorian era. As the readings undertaken by Plotz and Freedgood demonstrate, convention encourages us to focus on certain objects at the expense of others. Sanders' and Ropert's readings interrogate that hierarchy. As we see again in Peter Yeandle's essay that closes this collection, we face a methodological issue in the prominence of the *unusual*, the aberrant and the exotic in the historical record, and the notability to our eyes of those elements of Victorian culture that most strikingly jar with our own. Sanders and Ropert draw attention to the way in which quite ordinary objects can take on new significance, and sanctified things can be revealed as merely objects.

Developing that type of slippage, Part IV highlights the power of texts to act as objects, and indeed of objects to act as texts. The archetypal example of this is the Bible. In Elizabeth Gilbert's neo-Victorian *The Signature of All Things* (2013) (in which the female protagonist comes up with a theory of evolution by natural selection simultaneously with Darwin and Russell Wallace), in Tahiti 'the natives... believed that the Bible [the gentle old missionary] carried was, in fact, his god.' As this missionary describes the paradox in a neat analysis of the Christian slippage between fetish and portal,

> They found it most disturbing that I carried my god so casually tucked under my arm, or that I left my god sitting unattended on the table, or that sometimes I lent my god to others! I tried to explain to

them that my god was everywhere, you see. They wanted to know, 'Then why can we not see him?' I said, 'Because my god is invisible,' and they said, 'Then how do you not trip over your god?' and I said, 'Verily, my friends, sometimes I do!'[38]

This echoes Joseph Gurney's (1832) *Hints on the Portable Evidence of Christianity* (probably, Plotz suggests, the first book title to use the term metaphorically), which highlights 'the portable evidence of Christianity' and describes the Bible as 'a portable book.'[39] This means, of course, both that it as material object can be lent and borrowed, exchanged and shared, and that its message is transferable across cultures and races: the central legitimating logic of missionary work.

This idea of the potential *power* of the book as physical object takes its first real leap beyond association with the Bible itself in Thomas Carlyle's lecture 'Hero as Man of Letters' (1841), which he argues that 'the thing we called "bits of paper with traces of black ink" is the purest embodiment a Thought of man can have. No wonder it is, in all ways, the activest and noblest.'[40] Books are 'runes', full of 'magic' power to build St Paul's Cathedral and accomplish 'miracles.'[41] This celebration of books' self-sufficient power is a sentiment echoed two decades later by Miss Clack in Wilkie Collins' *The Moonstone*: her recurrent characteristic is to deposit tracts and volumes of sermons around people's houses, in the hope that they may do what she cannot, namely transform them into pious, godly beings. Perhaps even if people do not read them, sheer proximity to these tracts as objects might have the power of conversion.

As Heather Hind shows in this volume, even hair can tell a story. In fact, as she shows through tracing locks of hair as textual objects in literary texts by Mary Elizabeth Braddon and Alfred, Lord Tennyson, they can even be made to lie, yielding readily to verbal reworkings by the characters who attempt to read them. Meanwhile, Sophie Ratcliffe takes up the obverse scenario, to show how when periodicals are torn up into hair-curling papers, stories can also turn into hair accessories. She teases out the anxieties within texts themselves that this may be their fate. In an era when writers were hesitantly, but increasingly, defining themselves as professionals, a book was, as Plotz reminds us, 'no amulet' but a 'combination of its material and its textual properties': part of its intrigue for writers and buyers alike.[42]

The final section, Part V, moves to thinking about what happens when objects start moving. When the words and images that depict them start circulating in print, how does that change the way we think about them? Odile Boucher-Rivalain considers the debates over women's dress in Victorian England, highlighting the financial risks and health hazards of fashions such as the crinoline. She shows how Harriet Martineau denounced such impractical fashions in her periodical articles, and provocatively suggested causal links between hooped skirts, rheumatism and even untimely deaths. Alice Crossley demonstrates the long and diverse history of Victorian Valentines, showing how they were used as occasions for mischievous tricks as well as for more expected romantic purposes, and how fully the emerging market catered for such subversive uses. Peter Yeandle investigates the interrelationships between popular imperialism, advertising and consumption of the exotic, calling for famous adverts to be put back in their original contexts alongside the news, and in the process questioning the orthodoxy of popular enthusiasm for empire. The rise of digital ways of viewing Victorian periodicals, he argues, disrupts the analogue way these texts and images flowed into and fed off each other, and can contribute to that distorted view of the Victorians as diametrically opposed to us 'moderns' and 'postmoderns' in aesthetics, ethics, and attitudes. On the contrary, nineteenth-century critiques of imperialism need to be reabsorbed into our picture of the era, even if they are less eye-catching than its jingoism.

Our own time is, of course, arguably just as concerned with paraphernalia, but the online revolution has forced a new relationship with it. We find ourselves in an age of virtual things with no physical original: email, text, and instant messaging have replaced letters and telegrams; contactless cards, online banking, bitcoin, and mobile phones have replaced hard cash; kindle may be in the process of replacing books; music is made, bought, and listened to online; an array of social networking sites allow users to socialize online rather than face to face; the online has become the new public sphere. But what happens to all these 'things' when the power is switched off? What kind of electronic information will be preserved for future generations? How do we preserve emails, text messages, and the produce of social media platforms? The fact that we are still surrounded by Victorian clutter is a poignant counterpoint to the paucity of what our digital age will leave behind for future generations, and a reminder of the richness of what still remains to be explored.

Notes

1 Don Rush, 'The Queen Tapes', *Circus Magazine* (17 March 1977), accessed 3 November 2017, http://queenarchives.com/qa/03-17-1977-circus-magazine.
2 'The Illustrated Exhibitor: Guide to the Great Exhibition,' *The British Library*, accessed 13 October 2016, www.bl.uk/collection-items/the-illustrated-exhibitor-guide-to-the-great-exhibition.
3 Isobel Armstrong, *Victorian Glassworlds: Glass Culture and the Imagination 1830–1880* (Oxford and New York: Oxford University Press, 2008), 218.
4 Ibid., 229.
5 Ibid., 219, 220.
6 Charlotte Brontë, *The Letters of Charlotte Brontë: With a Selection of Letters by Family and Friends*, ed. Margaret Smith, vol. 3 (Oxford: Oxford University Press, 2004), 230–31.

7　A. E. Richardson, 'Architecture,' in *Early Victorian England, 1830–1865*, ed. G. M. Young, vol. 2 (Oxford: Oxford University Press, 1934), 235.

8　See Gavin Stamp, *Lost Victorian Britain: How the Twentieth Century Destroyed the Nineteenth Century's Architectural Masterpieces* (London: Aurum Press, 2010).

9　P. G. Wodehouse, *Summer Moonshine* (London: Arrow Books, 2008), 23.

10　Virginia Woolf, *Orlando*, ed. Rachel Bowlby (Oxford: Oxford University Press, 2000), 221–22.

11　Andrew H. Miller, *Novels behind Glass: Commodity Culture and Victorian Narrative* (Cambridge: Cambridge University Press, 1995), 7.

12　Bill Brown, *A Sense of Things: The Object Matter of American Literature* (Chicago: University of Chicago Press, 2003).

13　David Trotter, 'Household Clearances in Victorian Fiction,' *19: Interdisciplinary Studies in the Long Nineteenth Century* 0, no. 6 (1 April 2008): 16, doi:10.16995/ntn.472.

14　Bill Brown, 'Thing Theory,' *Critical Inquiry* 28, no. 1 (2001): 1–2.

15　John Plotz, *Portable Property: Victorian Culture on the Move* (Princeton, New Jersey: Princeton University Press, 2008), 17.

16　Mary Poovey, ed., *The Financial System in Nineteenth-Century Britain* (Oxford and New York: Oxford University Press, 2002), 2.

17　Plotz, *Portable Property*, xiv.

18　Brown, *A Sense of Things*, 17.

19　Elaine Freedgood, *The Ideas in Things: Fugitive Meaning in the Victorian Novel* (Chicago: University of Chicago Press, 2006), 2, 4.

20　Brown, *A Sense of Things*, 18; Theodor Adorno, *Negative Dialectics Trans. E. B. Ashton (New York: Continuum, 1997)*, trans. E. B. Ashton (New York: Continuum, 1997), 193.

21　Elsa B. Michie, 'Victorian Glassworlds: Glass Culture and the Imagination 1830–1880, by Isobel Armstrong,' *Victorian Review* 38, no. 1 (Spring 2012): 226.

22　Frank Trentmann, *Empire of Things: How We Became a World of Consumers, from the Fifteenth Century to the Twenty-First* (London: Allen Lane, 2016), 10–11.

23　Trentmann, *Empire of Things*, 11.

24　Peter K. Andersson, 'How Civilized Were the Victorians?,' *Journal of Victorian Culture* 20, no. 4 (2 October 2015): 450, 443.

25　Ibid., 451.

26　Brown, *A Sense of Things*, 12.

27　Plotz, *Portable Property*, 2.

28　'100 Facts about the V&A,' *Victoria and Albert Museum*, 1 August 2013, www.vam.ac.uk/content/articles/0-9/100-facts-about-the-v-and-a/.

29　Walter Pater, 'Dante Gabriel Rossetti,' in *Appreciations: With an Essay on Style* (London, 1883), 221.

30　Thomas Richards, *The Commodity Culture of Victorian England: Advertising and Spectacle, 1851–1914* (Stanford, California: Stanford University Press, 1991), 5.

31　Plotz, *Portable Property*, 9–10.

32　Miller, *Novels behind Glass: Commodity Culture and Victorian Narrative*, 221.

33　Alastair Owens et al., 'Fragments of the Modern City: Material Culture and the Rhythms of Everyday Life in Victorian London,' *Journal of Victorian Culture* 15, no. 2 (1 August 2010): 220.

34　Ibid., 221–22.

35 James Symonds, 'The Poverty Trap? Abject and Object Perspectives on the Lives of Slum Dogs and Other Down-and-Outs' (Poverty In-Depth: New International Perspectives Symposium, York, 2 July 2009). See also James Symonds, 'The Poverty Trap: Or, Why Poverty Is Not About the Individual,' *International Journal of Historical Archaeology* 15, no. 4 (December 2011): 563–71, doi:10.1007/s10761-011-0156-8.

36 Matt Padley, Laura Valadez, and Donald Hirsch, 'Households below a Minimum Income Standard' (Loughborough; Joseph Rowntree Foundation, January 2015).

37 Patrick Wintour, '40% of British Families "too Poor to Play a Part in Society"' *Guardian*, 19 January 2015, www.theguardian.com/society/2015/jan/19/british-families-poor-society-income-level-cost-of-living-benefit-cuts.

38 Elizabeth Gilbert, *The Signature of All Things* (London: Bloomsbury, 2013), 377.

39 Joseph John Gurney, *Hints on the Portable Evidence of Christianity* (London, 1832), v–vi.

40 Thomas Carlyle, *Thomas Carlyle: Selected Writings*, ed. Alan Shelston (Harmondsworth: Penguin, 1971), 245.

41 Ibid., 240.

42 Plotz, *Portable Property*, 7.

Works Cited

"100 Facts about the V&A." *Victoria and Albert Museum*, 1 August 2013. www.vam.ac.uk/content/articles/0-9/100-facts-about-the-v-and-a/.

Adorno, Theodor. *Negative Dialectics*. Translated by E. B. Ashton. New York: Continuum, 1997.

Andersson, Peter K. "How Civilized Were the Victorians?" *Journal of Victorian Culture* 20, no. 4 (2 October 2015): 439–52.

Armstrong, Isobel. *Victorian Glassworlds: Glass Culture and the Imagination 1830–1880*. Oxford and New York: Oxford University Press, 2008.

Briggs, Asa. *Victorian Things*. Harmondsworth: Penguin, 1990.

Brontë, Charlotte. *The Letters of Charlotte Brontë: With a Selection of Letters by Family and Friends*. Edited by Margaret Smith. 3 vols. Oxford: Oxford University Press, 2004.

Brown, Bill. *A Sense of Things: The Object Matter of American Literature*. Chicago: University of Chicago Press, 2003.

———. "Thing Theory." *Critical Inquiry* 28, no. 1 (2001): 1–22.

Carlyle, Thomas. "Hero as Man of Letters". 1841. *Thomas Carlyle: Selected Writings*. Edited by Alan Shelston. Harmondsworth: Penguin, 1971.

Freedgood, Elaine. *The Ideas in Things: Fugitive Meaning in the Victorian Novel*. Chicago: University of Chicago Press, 2006.

Eliot, George. *The Mill on the Floss*. London: William Blackwood and Sons, 1860.

Gilbert, Elizabeth. *The Signature of All Things*. London: Bloomsbury, 2013.

Gurney, Joseph John. *Hints on the Portable Evidence of Christianity*. London, 1832.

Hamlett, Jane. *Material Relations: Domestic Interiors and Middle-Class Families in England, 1850–1910*. Manchester: Manchester University Press, 2010.

Michie, Elsa B. "Victorian Glassworlds: Glass Culture and the Imagination 1830–1880, by Isobel Armstrong." *Victorian Review* 38, no. 1 (Spring 2012): 226–27.

Miller, Andrew H. *Novels behind Glass: Commodity Culture and Victorian Narrative*. Cambridge: Cambridge University Press, 1995.

Owens, Alastair, Nigel Jeffries, Karen Wehner, and Rupert Featherby. "Fragments of the Modern City: Material Culture and the Rhythms of Everyday Life in Victorian London." *Journal of Victorian Culture* 15, no. 2 (1 August 2010): 212–25.

Padley, Matt, Laura Valadez, and Donald Hirsch. "Households below a Minimum Income Standard." Loughborough; Joseph Rowntree Foundation, January 2015.

Pater, Walter. "Dante Gabriel Rossetti." In *Appreciations: With an Essay on Style*, 220. London: Macmillan, 1883.

Plotz, John. *Portable Property: Victorian Culture on the Move*. Princeton, New Jersey: Princeton University Press, 2008.

Poovey, Mary, ed. *The Financial System in Nineteenth-Century Britain*. Oxford and New York: Oxford University Press, 2003.

Richards, Thomas. *The Commodity Culture of Victorian England: Advertising and Spectacle, 1851–1914*. Stanford, California: Stanford University Press, 1991.

Richardson, A. E. "Architecture." In *Early Victorian England, 1830–1865*, edited by G. M. Young, 2 vols., 179–247. Oxford: Oxford University Press, 1934.

Rush, D. The Queen Tapes. *Circus Magazine*. Accessed 3 November 2017. http://queenarchives.com/qa/03-17-1977-circus-magazine. 1977.

Stamp, Gavin. *Lost Victorian Britain: How the Twentieth Century Destroyed the Nineteenth Century's Architectural Masterpieces*. London: Aurum Press, 2010.

Symonds, James. "The Poverty Trap? Abject and Object Perspectives on the Lives of Slum Dogs and Other Down-and-Outs." presented at the Poverty In-Depth: New International Perspectives Symposium, York, 2 July 2009.

———. "The Poverty Trap: Or, Why Poverty Is Not About the Individual." *International Journal of Historical Archaeology* 15, no. 4 (December 2011): 563–71. doi:10.1007/s10761-011-0156-8.

"The Illustrated Exhibitor: Guide to the Great Exhibition." *The British Library*. Accessed 13 October 2016. www.bl.uk/collection-items/the-illustrated-exhibitor-guide-to-the-great-exhibition.

Trentmann, Frank. *Empire of Things: How We Became a World of Consumers, from the Fifteenth Century to the Twenty-First*. London: Allen Lane, 2016.

Trotter, David. "Household Clearances in Victorian Fiction." *19: Interdisciplinary Studies in the Long Nineteenth Century* 0, no. 6 (1 April 2008). doi:10.16995/ntn.472.

Vickery, Amanda. *Behind Closed Doors: At Home in Georgian England*. New Haven: Yale University Press, 2009.

Wintour, Patrick. "40% of British Families 'too Poor to Play a Part in Society.'" *Guardian*, 19 January 2015. www.theguardian.com/society/2015/jan/19/british-families-poor-society-income-level-cost-of-living-benefit-cuts.

Wodehouse, P. G. *Summer Moonshine*. London: Arrow Books, 2008.

Woolf, Virginia. *Orlando*. Edited by Rachel Bowlby. Oxford: Oxford University Press, 2000.

Part I

'A Magic Cave'

Collecting Objects

1 The Bazaars of London's West End in the Nineteenth Century

Rohan McWilliam

> ...the best exhibitions in this modern Babylon of ours are those which cost nothing, and amongst these gratuitous shows none are more attractive, varied and fascinating than the shops.
>
> Henry Mayhew[1]

The Poetics of the Bazaar

In *Letters from England* (1807), the poet and social critic Robert Southey (employing the unlikely Spanish alias of Don Manuel Alvarez Espriella) described his walk home in London from Charing Cross down the Strand:

> It took me through a place called Exeter Change, which is precisely a Bazar [sic], a sort of street under cover, or large long room, with a row of shops on either hand, and a thoroughfare between them; the shops being furnished with such articles as might tempt an idler, or remind a passenger of his wants – walking-sticks, implements for shaving, knives, scissors, watch-chains, purses, etc.

Southey was also intrigued by the menagerie upstairs and by the spectacle of 'a pair of shoes in one window floating in a vessel of water, to show that they were water-proof.' In what seems to have been an impulse buy, he purchased a 'travelling caissette' [sic], a useful collection of shaving and writing material for a gentleman of leisure.[2]

The *Oxford English Dictionary* holds this to be the first use of the term 'bazaar' in English (in the sense of 'a fancy fair in imitation of the Eastern bazaar'). Exeter Change, which Southey visited, was really an arcade but the word 'bazaar' was coming into more frequent use in the early nineteenth century to describe an innovation in shopping.[3] Less than a decade after Southey, at least sixteen London shops, mostly dotted around the West End, described themselves (or a section of their interior) as a 'bazaar'.[4] These seems to have been emporia featuring stalls with an assortment of different objects on display, as opposed to speciality shops which dealt in one group of items. Bazaars became dream worlds of consumption. Where the customer would formerly have been served by one shop assistant, there was now the possibility of different assistants to serve multiple kinds of need. The bazaar therefore prefigured both the department store and the shopping mall.

This study examines three West End bazaars: the Soho Bazaar, the Pantheon on Oxford Street, and the Lowther Bazaar on the Strand. As we will see, they offered contrasting examples of the bazaar, a term seldom deployed in a strict way at the time. Arcades could be described as 'bazaars' (as Southey did); sometimes a speciality shop could be described in that way. A bazaar is defined here as a building which contains rows of stalls under one roof offering diverse kinds of goods. This contrasts with an arcade which is usually made up of a series of speciality shops in a private street under a glass roof.[5]

Charles Knight defined bazaars as a 'mingled assemblage of sundry wares rather than wares of one kind'.[6] They offered mostly non-essential fancy goods and aroused desire. Tammy Whitlock argues that bazaars were innovative in placing such fancy goods centre stage in shops rather than on the periphery.[7] This was why it was significant that London's West End developed a number of bazaars. Their cultural work assisted in the creation of the West End as a pleasure district.

The stores described here were commercial bazaars. They contrast with charity bazaars and fetes which became ubiquitous opportunities for fundraising in the nineteenth century and which continue to serve as opportunities for community building. Both commercial and charity bazaars seem to have begun in the years between 1813 and 1816.[8] The commercial bazaar may have proved particularly attractive to female shoppers as it invoked a device that middle-class women were employing for fundraising and philanthropy.

The mid-nineteenth century is usually thought to have enjoyed a retail revolution with the coming of the department store.[9] Department stores offered vital landmarks for the middle classes in nineteenth-century cities around the globe: palaces of consumption where the purchase of prestige goods was only one part of the experience. Shopping for non-essential goods became a matter of lifestyle and entertainment: big stores were places to meet and to be seen. Department stores allowed women access to the big city, offering a safe and respectable environment where it was also possible to find refreshments and ladies' lavatories.[10]

But histories of consumerism now show that the department store did not come from nowhere. It had its roots in the exchanges of Elizabethan and Stuart London (Exeter Change on the Strand, which Southey visited, was built in 1673). These extended luxury shopping beyond the aristocracy to the middling sort.[11] In the early nineteenth century, the experience of middle-class shopping changed. The manufacture, storage, and display of goods came to require different spaces, requiring innovations in retail. Bartering was rejected in favour of cash and clear, non-negotiable prices. This was the moment that saw the creation of arcades and bazaars with their stylish forms of consumerism.

What the commercial bazaar represented was the spectacle of nineteenth-century abundance – at least for the middle classes. This was a world from which the working classes were excluded except as shop assistants and as manufacturers of the products sold. A reformatory school, for example, set 'outcast boys' to work making 'fancy boxes' for sale at the Soho Bazaar.[12] The nineteenth century produced a profusion of 'things': objects reeking of conspicuous consumption that described a lifestyle.[13] Identities could be created through artefacts intended to adorn the home. We need, in particular, to reclaim the world of the nineteenth-century mantelpiece with its *objets d'art*, curiosities, knick-knacks, ornately decorated Chinoiserie, and (later) photographs of loved ones.[14]

Bazaars and arcades made objects into forms of performance. One of the reasons the West End developed as a pleasure district was because its shops offered goods and experiences that were more various than could be obtained closer to home, were of guaranteed quality, and were displayed in sumptuous surroundings. As London grew, West End shops not only served those who lived close by but people from the suburbs and out of town. Displays in the West End came to possess forms of theatricality that gained from their proximity to actual theatres and museums. They also anticipated events like the Great Exhibition. Henry Mayhew grasped this dimension to London shops as a whole:

> Without doubt, the shops of London are by far the most attractive exhibition to that enlightened class denominated in newspapers advertisements 'Visitors from the country'. You may take them to a picture-gallery, and they will stare with all the vacancy of *en-nui*; induce them to visit a flower show, and they will be bored; go with them to a play or a pantomime, and they will return but half-amused. But turn them loose, so to speak, amongst the shops, and they will find an endless source of pleasure which seems never to weary, but presents one ever-changing kaleidoscope of fancy and amusement.[15]

These last terms – 'kaleidoscope', 'fancy', and 'amusement' – express some of the appeal of the bazaar idea in the nineteenth century.

The bazaar was a device for promoting mass retail and commercial society. It stood for the celebration of commodities but also conferred an identity on consumers. The bazaar assumed a shopper who had time to browse and was open to curiosity and distraction. It was distinctive as a form of retail as it brought goods closer to the customer, making them more available for inspection and comparison without the shop assistant necessarily intervening (until the moment of purchase). Shop assistants could reinforce the identities of those who came to buy: their deference and politeness suggested shoppers were people of discernment, able to appreciate quality goods; alternatively, they could view customers with suspicion, trying to spot potential shoplifters. Well before the coming of the department store, bazaars and arcades created new worlds of female shopping. Shop assistants were also often female, creating a space that contrasted with the masculine sites of shopping and recreation.[16] Significantly, bazaars also sold toys and thus became open to children, offering them a fantasy space and point of entry into the world of the big city. Part of the cultural work of the bazaar was to entwine consumption and enchantment.

There were many bazaars in central London after 1800, evidence of the format becoming popular in the late Georgian period. The Pantechnicon on Belgrave Square sold large furniture, carriages, and piano fortes. Baker Street had a bazaar whose highlights included a 'Padorama', simulating the experience of a railway journey for a public still not used to this new technological innovation (it was also the original home of Madame Tussaud's waxworks).[17] In addition to the Pantheon, Oxford Street had the Queen's Bazaar (which employed a diorama to pull in customers) while a bazaar was in Portman Square to its immediate north. The Egyptian Hall in Piccadilly recreated itself as a bazaar in 1831. Twenty years later, the Prince of Wales's Bazaar opened on Regent Street. Charity bazaars proved a vehicle for elite women both to organize and to show off arts and crafts. In the Spring of 1845, the Anti-Corn Law League took over the Covent Garden Theatre, which it transformed into a Tudor Hall and held a bazaar. It raised £250,000 in six weeks selling goods associated with the northern manufacturing districts for which it acted as spokesperson.[18] There is even a suggestion that the Covent Garden bazaar may have inspired Thackeray to call his great 1847–1848 novel *Vanity Fair*, premised as it is on society as a kind of fancy fair where anything (and anybody) could be bought.[19]

Bazaars took their inspiration and imaginative framing from eastern shopping marts with a wide range of goods laid out for the delectation of customers. They offered a form of shopping shaped by the values of Romanticism. Theirs was an orientalist structure of feeling though their wares were often simple household objects. By this means, the domestic could be proclaimed as exotic. As Gary Dyer argues, the term 'bazaar' drew on the simultaneous fascination with, and fear of, the Turkish and Arab world.[20] In a self-advertising tract for the Soho Bazaar, a father explains the word 'bazaar' to his children:

> ...the term Bazaar is given by the Turks and Persians to a kind of Market or Exchange, some of which are extremely magnificent; that of Ispahan, in Persia, surpasses all the other European exchanges, and yet that of Tauris exceeds it in size. There is the old and the

new Bazaar at Constantinople, the former is chiefly for arms, and the latter for different articles belonging to goldsmiths, jewellers, furriers, and various other manufactures.[21]

Bazaars thrived on a fascination with the commercial life and customs of other countries. At the same time, they evoked the Middle Ages. Charles Knight claimed that:

> If we go back to the time of Fitz-Stephen, who wrote in the twelfth century, we find that the *bazaar* system was much more extensively adopted in London than at the present day; that is, that the member of one trade were wont to congregate at one spot, which thence became known as the mart for that particular kind of goods. The system is well known to be prevalent in the East, where at Constantinople, Smyrna, Cairo, and other large towns, most of the retail shops are assembled in this manner.[22]

Mediaevalist, orientalist, imperial, global, commercial, domestic: if we appreciate these multiple registers, then we grasp something of the bazaar idea.

The Soho Bazaar

The first major bazaar in the West End was the Soho Bazaar which opened in 1816 at 4–6 Soho Square. Crucially, it had an entrance on Oxford Street which was already establishing itself as one of the major shopping thoroughfares in London. The Soho Bazaar was never simply a commercial enterprise. It was based upon the remarkable vision of its owner John Trotter.

Trotter was a relentless polymath who developed a universal language (similar to notes in music), made his own pedometer, and developed schemes to improve the nation's finances.[23] He made a fortune as an army contractor during the Napoleonic Wars when he employed the buildings at 4–6 Soho Square as a warehouse. At the end of the war, there was no obvious use for these buildings so he came up with the idea of turning them into a bazaar. Stalls would be offered to respectable women, particularly widows and daughters of soldiers who had died in the war and who were destitute. For a daily fee (to pay for the building's heating, lighting, and taxes), they could then sell fancy goods and keep the profits. It prevented women having to open a shop that might be unsuccessful: the Soho Bazaar managed the risk. This was a very new idea and typical of his mindset. Trotter had initially approached the government to fund the initiative but, when this did not work out, went ahead himself. Trotter's bazaar was based upon the principles of philanthropy. Applicants for stalls were assured that 'respectability, moral character and good temper, are not only essential, but *indispensable*, to the prosperity of all those persons who may sit in the Bazaar.'[24] Character references were therefore important, not least to establish links to fallen soldiers (though women of proven respectability were also allowed stalls).

An enthusiast, the Reverend Joseph Nightingale, saw the building as a real breakthrough in retail. In a pamphlet arguing that Trotter's enterprise was worthy of emulation, he wrote: 'The word Bazaar is a word given in Persia, and other eastern countries, to public markets, or daily fairs. Its application to the establishment in Soho Square is sufficiently appropriate and novel.'[25] No foreign wares could be sold in Trotter's emporium except by special permission; the idea was to encourage domestic manufacture. Goods were to be sold for the cheapest price possible. There was to be no use of credit: all goods had to be exchanged for ready money. An exemplary paternalist, Trotter set the opening hours of the bazaar as ten to six. This was deliberate as it meant that the women of the bazaar could go home and not be exposed to the temptations of the city at night (many London shops stayed open later). There were a number of male beadles who officiated at the store (offering a model of male protection) but it was otherwise a female enterprise. However, whilst women ran the stalls, the rental might be paid for by men. For example, Mary Ann Garratt ran an umbrella stall but the stall itself was in the name of her father.[26]

Nightingale estimated 2,500 people shopped there on a daily basis and the enterprise proved lucrative from the start.[27] There were two floors and stalls were arranged in aisles. Shop assistants (who paid two or three shillings as a daily fee) were subject to considerable discipline. Charles Knight recorded that

> Some of the rules of the establishment are very stringent. A plain and modest style of dress, on the part of the young females who serve at the stalls, is invariably insisted on, a matron being at hand to superintend the whole; every stall must have its wares displayed by a particular hour in the morning, under penalty of a fine from the renter; the rent is paid day by day, and if the renter be ill, she has to pay for the services of a substitute, the substitute being such an one as is approved by the principle of the establishment.[28]

When a Miss Butler discovered a lost twenty-pound note in the bazaar, she handed it in. Trotter advertised its loss and, when no one claimed it after six months, gave it to Miss Butler as a reward for honesty.[29] This performance of trustworthiness and probity alerts us to the way the bazaar worked.

The respectability of Trotter's bazaar was such that it enjoyed royal patronage. Within a year of opening, Queen Charlotte visited and was shown round with a wheel chair following in case she needed to rest.[30]

Other royal visitors included Prince Frederick of Prussia in 1830 and Prince Amadeus of Savoy in 1865.[31] According to Charles Knight, 'in the height of "the season", the long array of carriages drawn up near the building testifies to the extent of the visits paid by the high-born and the wealthy to this place'.[32] The Soho Bazaar became a major London landmark. A nearby cake shop, for example, in Soho Square advertised itself as being suitable for people visiting the Soho Bazaar.[33] Trotter's enterprise was adept at self-publicity. There were songs about the bazaar.[34] A promotional pamphlet told the story of a visit to the Soho Square which made it clear that the bazaar had something for all the family.[35]

But what did people buy in the bazaar? Goods had to be relatively light so that they could be brought to the bazaar and carried away by customers (or their servants). The focus was particularly on items of dress and adornment for women and children. Gloves and hosiery were associated with the store but the bazaar always went beyond that. Some goods were essential whilst others were decorative. Shoppers purchased gauze, coloured paper, bugles, knitting needles, shuttlecocks, and fiz-gigs (fireworks).[36] Smith's Gold Reliever (which promised to freshen up old gilt frames) was available to purchase.[37] Items of dress were displayed but so were sewing patterns which were cheaper here than elsewhere, an important consideration for London dressmakers who patronized the store.[38] Like many such stores, the Soho Bazaar was particularly well patronized at Christmas as a good place to purchase gifts.[39]

These were goods, then, that serviced a middle-class lifestyle. The bazaar came to include a registry for governesses and an agency for female servants.[40] It offered ways of imagining the rooms of the bourgeois household.[41] There were card racks, paper screens with gold ornamentation, and prints of King John signing Magna Carta whilst every kind of stationery was available to service the needs of female letter writers.[42] These goods therefore played an active role in constructing shoppers in particular ways, defining their lifestyles and aspirations. The Soho Bazaar manufactured cultural capital. Upper-class patronage reinforced the idea that the goods of the Soho Bazaar satisfied the demands of fashion and philanthropy.

The material culture of middle-class childhood could be purchased in the forms of toys and nursery decorations. The Soho Bazaar proclaimed the role of women as mothers and guardians of the household through its distinctive female space. As the comic paper *Judy* noticed, men were strangely redundant if they dared to enter the premises: 'The first sensation of a timid male stranger visiting the Soho Bazaar alone, and for the first time, is that he will be probably asked what he wants there, and be ordered out again.'[43]

Royal patronage and its presence in the West End marked out the Soho Bazaar as a conservative institution. However, it was also shaped by the values of nineteenth-century liberalism, standing for self-help and rigid work discipline. There was always a paternalist dimension to the Soho Bazaar not only in terms of its care of women but in the causes it promoted. At the time of the Lancashire Cotton Famine in 1862, warm clothing was sent to people suffering unemployment.[44] In 1870 a stall was created to benefit refugees from the Paris Commune.[45] Three years later, a stall was created to sell sewing by poor women. This was a scheme initiated by Lady Victoria Lambton, who chaired the committee that ran it. Poor women could pay an annual subscription of ten shillings and then display lacework, knitting, crochet, and pinafores for children.[46]

A different vantage point for the Soho Bazaar comes through the records of shoplifting. These tell us something about the objects in the store but also the social practices that came with the shopping experience.[47] As always, we only know about those who were apprehended in the act of stealing; it is more difficult to write about the successful shop lifter who, of course, got away with it. These cases reveal that shopping involved the gaze of the shop assistant who would inform on anyone seen taking goods without payment. In 1826, Louisa Tappy identified Charlotte Williams as having taken a reticule from an adjoining stall and (as with many female shoplifting cases) hidden it under her shawl. When the bazaar's officer apprehended Williams, she claimed she had a child at home and took the reticule 'for want' though she then said she intended to pay for it and there had been a misunderstanding. She was transported for seven years.[48] Four years later, Elizabeth Holder was spotted by a female inspector apparently stealing an inkstand. When apprehended, she was made to open a bag round her waist in which were found silver thimbles, miniature glasses, card cases, pocket-books, pen knives, smelling bottles with silver tops, sealing wax, needle cases, tweezers, and scissors.[49] Five years later, 'Mary Allen' (the report assumes her name is fictitious) was caught stealing a muslin collar from the bazaar. A police constable found on her person a package of seventy-two silk laces, a gilt thimble, a prayer book with silver clasps, a jet bracelet, a jet necklace, a caddy spoon, and some fancy toilet articles which had been stolen from various shops. The judge expressed 'regret at seeing a person of so respectable appearance, and who appeared to have moved in good society, so degraded by her own vicious propensities....' She too was transported for seven years.[50]

Speculations on the motivations for stealing these goods is dangerous without more evidence. Shoplifting was often defined in the nineteenth century as a peculiarly female pathology, not least because the goods stolen were often not essential. 'Kleptomania' became a standard explanation around mid-century, referring particularly to women who developed an obsessive desire to steal even though they had no material need to do so.[51] It involved a construction of femininity in which women were imagined as susceptible to temptation: another 'female malady' like fainting, hysteria, and insanity.[52] When Mary-Anne Bartholomew, wife of a West End tradesman, was arrested for stealing a packet of needles and two bottles of pomade (hair oil) from the bazaar in 1863, Mr Lewis for the defence said, 'The prisoner was well connected, and had no need to commit these petty pilferings; but it was one of those irresistible passions, for which she herself, as she stated, could not account. The accused was labouring under a severe domestic affliction'.[53] She was given three months hard labour.

The bazaar, as we have seen, was associated with the goods that made possible the tasks of the middle-class home: sewing, letter writing, haircare. Some of the goods that were stolen were tempting because they were small and so could be easily hidden away. This also suggests something of the way mundane household goods become objects of desire and even of fetishism. Many London shops had problems with shop lifting but the openness of the bazaar may have made it particularly attractive. In the hurly-burly atmosphere with so many transactions happening at once, the feeling was encouraged that no one would be looking as the pilfering went on. More, with so many goods on display, there may have been a feeling that no one would notice when an item went missing. What we learn from these cases is that the vigilant gaze of the shop assistant was such that items were often immediately missed.

One critic claimed in 1867 that the Soho Bazaar 'seems intended for the diffusion of things that nobody can ever manage to want.'[54] This was likely a man writing. Clearly, the bazaar did produce things that people wanted to consume in their homes. It lasted until 1889 when the publishers A and C. Black bought the premises but maintained the distinctive mahogany counters.[55]

The Pantheon on Oxford Street

Of the three bazaars described here, the Pantheon, which opened on Oxford Street in 1834, is the one that most anticipated the department store. It did not have the separate departments or window displays that characterized such shops from the *Bon Marché* in mid-century Paris onwards, but it did mark another shift away from speciality shops which had been the norm in retail up to that point. It was, however, shaped by visual spectacle and offered a space for sociability. The Pantheon experience was about more than the purchase of goods. To put the Pantheon in context, we should note that it coincided with the development of what we would now see as embryonic department stores. High streets had begun to boast emporia with multiple forms of goods and purposes. In 1830, Bainbridge's in Newcastle and Kendal, Milne, and Faulkener in Manchester opened as drapery shops which expanded beyond their traditional stock. Two years later in Manchester a bazaar opened in Deansgate.[56] A wider trend in retail thus manifested itself on Oxford Street in 1834.

The Pantheon illustrates some of the juxtapositions between mass entertainment, exhibitions, and retail that made the West End distinctive and anticipated the department store of the later nineteenth century. The Queen's Bazaar, opposite on Oxford Street, was actually turned into the Princess's Theatre in 1839. The Pantheon did the reverse, moving from being a theatre to a bazaar. As a space it continued to possess a distinctive theatricality: it was intended for different kinds of performance and display. Yet it was a building that had never quite worked. It had originally opened on Oxford Street in 1772 with a design by the architect James Wyatt: a grand rotunda and dome that evoked Santa Sofia in Istanbul (an orientalist trope) and was meant to provide entertainment for the elite. Entrance was initially dependent on knowing the right people. There were balls, masquerades, and concerts. It failed to pay its way and in 1789 the Italian Opera Company moved there when its home in the Kings Theatre on the Haymarket burned down. Mozart was even invited to become the house composer.[57] The Company had barely completed a season when the Pantheon itself burnt down in 1792. Rebuilt shortly afterwards, it returned to its role of providing miscellaneous entertainments for the Georgian glitterati but closed in 1814.

In 1833–1834, the Pantheon was reopened as what was called a 'bazaar'. There was a huge refit by the architect Sidney Smirke which cost between £25,000 and £60,000 (accounts vary).[58] John Timbs described the sight once a visitor ascended the staircase decorated with Haydon's painting *Death of Lazarus*:

> ...the great Basilical Hall or Bazaar... is 116 feet long, 88 feet wide, and 60 feet high; it is mostly lighted from curved windows in the roof, which is richly decorated, as are the piers of the arcades, with arabesque scrolls of flowers, fruit and birds; the ornaments of *papier-maché* by Bielefield. The style of decoration is from the loggias of the Vatican. The galleries and the floor are laid out with counters, and promenades between. From the southern end of the hall is the entrance to an elegant conservatory, and aviary, mostly of glass, ornamented in Saracenic style.[59]

Isobel Armstrong interprets the Pantheon as 'a glass fantasia, a fecund romanticized space.' The glass roof, the conservatory and the fish swimming behind glass created hypnotic forms of transparency.[60] The conservatory also had its own fountain.[61] This feeling of transparency may have made for a perfect shopping area: everything could be seen with clarity. The customer was less likely to be sold shoddy goods which made it a comforting space.

The galleries upstairs were seen as a great opportunity for modern artists to make a living. The Pantheon did not have the feel of an exclusive art gallery. Paintings were displayed to be sold with the gallery taking a ten per cent commission on sales. It provided a way for paintings to filter down to a middle-class public. The number of painters living in London had increased by a remarkable seventy per cent between 1840 and 1845, evidence of an increasing art market that went beyond the elite.[62] The bohemian writer and social commentator George Augustus Sala treated the Pantheon's art works with disdain, holding that it featured 'twentieth-rate masters': 'The place seems haunted by the ghosts of bygone pictorial mediocrities. It is the lazar-house of painting – an hospital of incurables in art'.[63]

There was also an aviary: the Pantheon was the place to buy a parrot. Birds as pets were an important adornment to the home. Other goods for sale were various: fancy glass, wax figures, pencil cases, china, silverware, music.[64] Toys included India rubber balls, drums, hares-and-tabors, and Noah's arks.[65] Sala found their price at the Pantheon 'ruinously expensive' which suggests that the bazaar focussed its attention on the well-off, middle-class consumer. It was not cheap and nasty.

The Pantheon established its patriotic credentials on its opening day when it placed on top of its portico a huge pyramid to celebrate William IV's birthday. The pyramid was over fifty feet high and on the base were the king's initials with a crown sporting a laurel leaf and stars around. It was lit in such a way that it could be seen from miles away.[66] Queen Adelaide visited the Pantheon the following year and was much impressed by the experience.[67] These episodes fit with a pattern of royal patronage but also suggest something of the conservative cultural politics of the Pantheon: royal approval became an important part of the West End shopping experience.

Shop girls at the Pantheon dealt differently with customers on the basis of gender. Women were treated 'with great affability' whilst men were treated 'with condescension that mingled with a reserved dignity that awes the boldest spirit.'[68] Men clearly made purchases but the Pantheon (like the Soho Bazaar and later the department stores) was constructed as a space where women had agency.

The store became a distinctive London landmark. It included a refreshment counter which sold arrow-root cakes and thus was a place to meet people. Young people were also known to meet and flirt in the conservatory. In evoking this world of young people at the Pantheon, Sala expressed their networks and sociability largely thorough the objects that could be found in the store:

> The world is as yet a delightful Pantheon, full of flowers – real, wax, and artificial, and all pleasant – sandal-wood fans, petticoats with worked edges, silk stockings, satin shoes, white kid gloves, varnished broughams, pet dogs, vanilla ices, boxes at the opera, tickets for the Crystal Palace, tortoise-shell card-cases, enamelled visiting-cards, and scented pink invitation notes, with '*On dansera*' in the left-hand

bottom corners, muslin slips, bandoline, perfumes, ballads and polkas with chromolithographed frontispieces, and the dear delightful new novels from Mudie's with uncut leaves, and mother-o'-pearl paper knives with coral spring handles to cut them withal.[69]

The Pantheon provided a network and a set of attractive objects: items of entertainment and courtship for the sons and daughters of the well off. Many of these objects were gendered female and could become associated with romance and sentimentality. The artist Henrietta Ward recalled:

> It was a splendid building in form and colour. Under its imposing dome everything that was useful and decorative was sold. I was in the habit of shopping there constantly, and found an additional attraction in the aviary which contained the most beautiful parrots and all kinds of birds. There was also an Aquarium, with performing fishes and a large diving bell which I could never make up my mind to enter, The Pantheon being the first large enterprise of the kind was well patronized and appreciated, and one was sure of meeting friends there.[70]

The Pantheon lasted until 1867 when it was turned into a depot by the wine merchants W. and A. Gilbey. The site is now the 'Oxford Street Pantheon' branch of Marks and Spencer.

The Lowther Bazaar

In contrast to the other bazaars described here, the Lowther Bazaar on the Strand was essentially a large shop with one owner but which sold a variety of fancy goods. The frontage on the Strand, next to a shirt shop, while grand, was not obtrusive. It did, however, employ the techniques of theatre and showbusiness to draw people in, anticipating the ways in which shopping would become a form of spectacle divorced from actual need.

Opening around 1833, the bazaar lasted until 1857. It was built on the other side of the Strand from the better known Lowther Arcade, which became one of the main locations to buy toys in the West End.[71] Barely had the Lowther Bazaar been created than it featured as a location in a pantomime at the Adelphi Theatre across the road: *Harlequin and Margery Daw, or the Saucy Slut and the See-Saw.*[72] Thomas Graves, the owner (who had been in the hosiery trade) made his bazaar a place of enticement.[73] He created a 'Wheel of Fortune'. Customers could purchase a ticket which they gave to the woman who spun the wheel. A voucher would then be issued, according to where the wheel landed, which could be exchanged for goods of that value in the store. The practice led to Graves ending up in Bow Street Magistrate's Court for contravening the laws on gaming by running what was in effect a lottery. There were also suggestions that the Wheel of Fortune was rigged. A customer complained that he had paid seven shillings for seven spins of the wheel but had got a sixpenny voucher back each time.[74] Attempts to fine Graves were unsuccessful. He later sought additional publicity by employing Nina Lassave, accomplice of Giuseppe Fieschi, the would-be assassin of King Louis Philippe of France, to spin the Wheel in 1836.[75] This is ironic as Louis Philippe would later become a devotee of the Lowther Bazaar when he sought exile in London after he was deposed in 1848.[76]

The great attraction at the bazaar was the Magic Cave. This was a cosmorama, an exhibition of grand paintings enhanced through lenses and special lighting effects to provide greater scenic realism. The practice emerged in Paris in 1808 and was soon imitated in London. It was thus part of a tendency at bazaars to include panoramas or dioramas with their enhanced pictures on a vast scale. Bazaars celebrated gigantism. Admission was sixpence and it was said to have brought in £1,500 a year.[77] The entrance was below ground with opening hours from ten in the morning to ten at night. There were usually eighteen cosmoramic paintings by artists on display. Views included Ehrenbreitstein, Amsterdam, Mayence, Melrose Abbey, St Peter's at Rome, the valley of Piedmont, and the wreck of the *Isabella*. There was also the Hall of Battles in the Palace in Versailles. The cosmorama offered an easy alternative to foreign tourism: a Grand Tour accessed through the Strand. In 1842 it was said that 25,000 people had visited the Magic Cave.[78]

Beyond these diversions, the Lowther Bazaar was a place to buy a range of goods. There were items aimed at both men and women though there seems to have been a focus on men's toiletries. For eleven shillings and sixpence gentlemen could purchase a dressing case tooled in Russian leather. It contained a pair of razors, a comb, tooth and shaving brushes, together with boxes for soap and tooth powder. There were also rosewood and mahogany desks for sale.[79] Like the Lowther Arcade opposite, the bazaar was associated with the sale of children's toys. Other fancy items in the bazaar included ink stands, work boxes, tea caddies, cake and card baskets, vases, tea trays, cigar cases, bagatelle tables, *papier-mâché* pole and hand screens, work boxes, and envelope cases.[80] The prevalence of items made from *papier-mâché* is worth noting. Although the technique dated back to the ancient world, it had come into greater use in the eighteenth century. It lent itself to fancy goods and decorative objects.

The Lowther Bazaar reopened with a substantial refit in 1841.[81] Whilst, as is obvious from the objects sold, women were among the customers, the bazaar may have been a more obviously male space than the other two places described here. *Lloyd's Weekly Newspaper* captured its flavour when it noticed that it was 'thronged with weak gents, who spend their two pence on steel pens, and think themselves fine fellows by affecting to flirt with the flaxen amiabilities who attend'.[82] This was a place for well-off men to ogle the shop girls. For that reason, the Lowther Bazaar was about the arousal of sensory appetites and the male gaze. Shop girls were part of the display. The spectacle of the cosmorama was juxtaposed with the appeal of shop assistants.

To understand the Lowther Bazaar, we need to understand that it offered a shopping experience that was juxtaposed with other sites of diversion that became the hallmark of London's West End. The district offered a cornucopia of exhibitions, curiosities, strange objects, spectacles, and panoramas.[83] The idea of a 'Magic Cave', found beneath the shop, would have been inviting as a source of mystery and imagination. The West End shopping experience was about spectacle.

The Meanings of the Bazaar

Is the only thing that links the three examples discussed here the word 'bazaar'? Clearly the word allowed for disparate forms of shopping and consumption.

What connects the three bazaars is that they helped turn shopping into a practice that was more than just functional. It could involve aesthetic pleasure, fashion, and sociability. The bazaars offered a distinctive form of cultural capital but also operated in different ways: the philanthropic impulse of the Soho Bazaar contrasted with the vulgarity of the Lowther Bazaar. The bazaar, the arcade, and (later) the department store hailed customers with the message that they lived to shop, to consume objects. The fancy and frivolity of some of the objects purchased should lead us to reject any notion that the Victorians were killjoys. Some objects were functional (cutlery, for example) but there was a pleasure in the decorative and the fun. Spectacular shops helped turn town and city centres (such as London's West End) into distinctive pleasure districts.

These were spaces where it was possible to enter and not feel obliged to purchase. The gaze of the shop girl might catch the occasional shoplifter but the multiple stalls prevented the guilt induced by entering a small shop where, under the gaze of the counter staff, one felt obliged to buy. Here was a shopping experience which appeared to empower the consumer. Another experience that contrasted with the speciality shop was that of entering to purchase one item and finding one's attention grabbed by something completely different. The bazaar was premised on the impulse buy. What one cannot capture from the sources unfortunately is the sound of the bazaars. A single shop with only a small number of customers would not have enjoyed the boisterous hubbub of the bazaar experience. The poetics of the bazaar involved both an assemblage of goods blended with a profusion of voices and transactions. This was a cacophonous soundscape that early nineteenth-century consumers would have associated with fairs and with markets like Covent Garden. The bazaar was part of a transition in retailing that led from the street market to the department store.

The deployment of the term 'bazaar' also flattered the act of consumption. The name suggested a form of imaginative fancy dress but without the necessity of the haggling and bargaining associated with eastern bazaars. Its orientalist frame meant that the mundane act of shopping could become exotic, even mysterious, open to possibilities. The use of the 'Magic Cave' with its cosmoramic views of foreign places played into this script. So too did the fact that bazaars featured women as part of the display.

This kind of atmosphere became the signature of London's West End and other pleasure districts. There is a sense in which the West End was actually made from the fancy objects that people purchased: prestige stationery, fans, *papier-maché* screens, kitchenware, the best china. These goods were constructed as offering finery and the badge of respectability but were also fetishized through the power that the idea of the bargain exerted on the imagination. They were the paraphernalia with which the middle-class domestic interior was assembled. Bargain hunting became one of the tactics of city life. Knick-knacks helped make the West End.

The commercial bazaar described here was mainly replaced by the department store in the later nineteenth century although many shops even today employ a bazaar format: it anticipated the supermarket, for example. The charitable bazaar has been more enduring, though giving way to the jumble sale in the twentieth century (the first use of the term 'jumble-sale', according to the Oxford English Dictionary, was in 1898).

According to Deborah Cohen, the cluttered Victorian domestic interior was the product of the later nineteenth century.[84] However, it is clear that London shops from at least the early nineteenth century were feeding a middle-class public eager for decorative goods. Spectacular shops offered a lifestyle. The bazaars discussed here were liminal spaces that blurred the division between the shop, the theatre, and the exhibition site, turning shopping into a form of entertainment.

Notes

1 Henry Mayhew (ed.), *The Shops and Companies of London and the Trades and Manufactories of Great Britain* (London: Strand, 1865), 5.

2 [Robert Southey], *Letters from England: By Don Manuel Alvarez Espriella* (London: Longman, Hurst, Rees, Orme and Brown, 1807), vol. 1, 82–83.

3 On bazaars, see Frank K. Prochaska, *Women and Philanthropy in Nineteenth-Century England* (Oxford: Clarendon Press, 1980), 47–72; Tammy

C. Whitlock, *Crime, Gender and Consumer Culture in Nineteenth-Century England* (Aldershot: Ashgate, 2005), 41–69; Gary R. Dyer, "The 'Vanity Fair' of Nineteenth-Century England: Commerce, Women, and the East in the Ladies' Bazaar," *Nineteenth Century Literature* 46 (1991): 196–222; Annette Shiell, *Fundraising, Flirtation and Fancywork: Charity Bazaars in Nineteenth Century Australia* (Cambridge: Cambridge Scholars, 2012).

4 Joseph Nightingale, *The Bazaar: Its Origin, Nature, and Objects Explained and Recommended as an Important Branch of Political Economy* (London: privately published, 1816), 67–68.

5 This is a companion piece to my article, "Fancy Repositories: The Arcades of London's West End in the Nineteenth Century" (forthcoming). Both feed into the history of the West End of London that I am writing.

6 Charles Knight (ed.), *London* (London: Charles Knight, 1841–1843), vol. 5, 395.

7 Whitlock, *Crime, Gender and Consumer Culture*, 52.

8 Prochaska, *Women and Philanthropy*, 49.

9 Geoffrey Crossick and Serge Jaumain (eds.), *Cathedrals of Consumption: The European Department Store, 1850–1939* (Aldershot: Ashgate, 1999); Bill Lancaster, *The Department Store: A Social History* (Lancaster: Lancaster University Press, 1995).

10 Erika Diane Rappaport, *Shopping for Pleasure: Women in the Making of London's West End* (Princeton: Princeton University Press, 2000).

11 Linda Levy Peck, *Consuming Splendour: Society and Culture in Seventeenth-Century England* (Cambridge: Cambridge University Press, 2005).

12 *Daily News*, July 26, 1858, 3.

13 The classic work on Victorian material culture remains Asa Briggs, *Victorian Things* (Stroud: Sutton, 2003 [1988]).

14 I explored some of this territory in "The Theatricality of the Staffordshire Figurine," *Journal of Victorian Culture* 10 (2005): 107–14.

15 Mayhew (ed.), *The Shops and Companies of London*, 5.

16 Pamela Cox and Annabel Hobley, *Shopgirls* (London: Arrow, 2014).

17 Whitlock, *Crime, Gender and Consumer Culture*, 58.

18 Peter Gurney, *Wanting and Having: Popular Politics and Liberal Consumerism in England, 1830–1870* (Manchester: Manchester University Press, 2015), 220–56.

19 Dyer, "The 'Vanity Fair' of Nineteenth-Century England", 214.

20 Ibid., 201.

21 Anon, *A Visit to the Bazaar* (London: J. Harris, 1818), 3.

22 Knight (ed.), *London*, vol. 5, 386.

23 William Jerden, *The Autobiography of William Jerden* (London: Arthur Hall, Virtue and Co., 1852), vol. 2, 220–21.

24 Nightingale, *The Bazaar*, 9 (italics in original).

25 Ibid., 6.

26 This is made clear in the trial of Charlotte Williams: *Old Bailey Proceedings Online* (www.oldbaileyonline.org, version 7.2, 11 July 2016), October 1826, trial of CHARLOTTE WILLIAMS (t18261026-89).

27 Nightingale, *The Bazaar*, 16.

28 Knight (ed.), *London*, vol. 5, 396.

29 *The Morning Post*, February 5, 1827, 3.

30 *The Bury and Norwich Post: Or, Suffolk, Norfolk, Essex, Cambridge, and Ely Advertiser* May 28, 1817, 2.

31 *The Morning Post*, June 26, 1830, 3; *The Morning Post*, October 7, 1865, 5.

32 Knight (ed.), *London*, vol. 5, 396.

33 *The Morning Chronicle*, January 11, 1831, 1.

34 Anon, *The Bazaar, a Popular Song Arranged to a Popular Air* (London: T. Holloway, c.1825); Charles Hindley, *The Life and Times of James Catnach* (London: Reeves and Turner, 1878), 194.

35 Anon, *A Visit to the Bazaar*.

36 *Royal Cornwall Gazette, Falmouth Packet & Plymouth Journal*, June 8, 1822, 4.

37 *The Morning Post*, June 16, 1859, 1.

38 *The Morning Chronicle*, October 31, 1850, 5.

39 *The Standard*, January 11, 1871, 6.

40 *The Morning Post*, November 19, 1868, 7.

41 Jane Hamlett, *Material Relations: Domestic Interiors and Middle-Class Families in England, 1850–1910* (Manchester: Manchester University Press, 2010).

42 Anon, *A Visit to the Bazaar*, 63–67.

43 quoted in *Manchester Times* February 21, 1874, supplement, 8.

44 *Daily News*, November 19, 1862, 3.

45 *The Morning Post*, November 17, 1870, 5.

46 *The Morning Post*, May 22, 1873, 5.

47 On shoplifting, see Whitlock, *Crime, Gender and Consumer Culture*, 127–52; Elaine S. Abelson, *When Ladies Go A-thieving: Middle-Class Shoplifters in the Victorian Department Store* (New York: Oxford University Press, 1989); William M. Maier, "Going on the Hoist: Women, Work and Shoplifting in London, c. 1890–1940," *Journal of British Studies* 50 (2011): 410–33.

48 *Old Bailey Proceedings Online* (www.oldbaileyonline.org, version 7.2, 11 July 2016), October 1826, trial of CHARLOTTE WILLIAMS (t18261026-89).

49 *The Morning Post*, December 6, 1830, 4.

50 *The Standard*, November 13, 1835, 4; *The Standard*, November 14, 1835, 4; *The Morning Post*, November 17, 1835, 4.

51 Whitlock, *Crime, Gender and Consumer Culture*; Patricia O'Brien, "The Kleptomania Diagnosis: Bourgeois Women and Theft in late Nineteenth-Century France," *Journal of Social History* 17, (1983): 65–77.

52 Elaine Showalter, *The Female Malady: Women, Madness and English Culture* (London: Virago, 1987).

53 *Daily News*, March 26, 1863, 7.

54 *The Hampshire Advertiser*, July 13, 1867, 7.

55 F.H.W Sheppard (ed.), *Survey of London* vol. 33 (London: Athlone Press, 1966), 59.

56 Whitlock, *Crime, Gender and Consumer Culture*, 32; Bill Lancaster, *The Department Store*, 7, 9.

57 Judith Milhous, Gabriella Dideriksen and Robert D. Hume, *Italian Opera in Late Eighteenth-Century London* vol. 2: *The Pantheon Opera and its Aftermath, 1789–1795* (Oxford: Clarendon Press, 2000), 51.

58 *The Morning Post* October 26, 1833, 3; *The Morning Post* December 9, 1833, 3.

59 John Timbs, *Curiosities of London; Exhibiting the Most Rare and Remarkable Objects of Interest in the Metropolis* (London: J. S. Virtue, 1867 [1855]), 41. The detail about Haydon's painting is from *The Morning Post*, December 21, 1867, 3.

60 Isobel Armstrong, *Victorian Glassworlds: Glass Culture and the Imagination, 1830–1880* (Oxford: Oxford University Press, 2008), 140.

61 George Augustus Sala, *Twice Around the Clock; Or the Hours of the Day and Night in London* (Leicester: Leicester University Press, 1971 [1858]), 182.

62 Thomas M. Bayer and John R. Page, *The Development of the Art Market in England* (London: Pickering and Chatto, 2011), 153.

63 Sala, *Twice Around the Clock*, 175.

64 *The Morning Post*, October 18, 1865, 7; *The Morning Post*, July 16, 1842, 7; *The Morning Post*, February 12, 1844, 7; *The Morning Chronicle*, August 7, 1844, 8.

65 Sala, *Twice Around the Clock*, 180.

66 *The Morning Chronicle*, May 29, 1834, 2.

67 *The Morning Post*, October 14, 1835, 3.

68 Sala, *Twice Around the Clock*, 181.

69 Ibid., 182.

70 (Mrs.) E. M. (Henrietta) Ward, *Memories of Ninety Years* (London: Hutchison, 1924), 30.

71 I discuss the Lowther Arcade at length in 'Fancy Repositories'.

72 *The Morning Post*, December 27, 1833, 3.

73 Graves is identified as a hosier in *The Post Office London Directory* (London: Lowe and Harvey, 1832), 163.

74 *The Morning Chronicle*, September 14, 1833, 4.

75 *Jackson's Oxford Journal*, April 16, 1836, 4.

76 *The Hampshire Advertiser*, December 9, 1871, 7.

77 John Timbs, *Curiosities of London*, 41.

78 *The Morning Chronicle*, November 13, 1840, 2; *The Morning Post*, May 20, 1842, 1; *The Morning Post*, April 14, 1840, 1; *Magic Cave* handbill (London: Star Press 1840): John Johnson Collection: Dioramas 3 (44).

79 *The Morning Post*, April 14, 1840, 1.

80 *The Morning Post*, April 14, 1840, 1; *The Morning Post*, December 9, 1842, 1.

81 *The Mirror of Literature, Amusement and Instruction*, December 25, 1841, 403.

82 *Lloyd's Weekly Newspaper*, January 4, 1857, 8.

83 Richard D. Altick, *The Shows of London* (Cambridge, MA: Belknap Press/Harvard University Press, 1978).

84 Deborah Cohen, *Household Gods: The British and their Possessions* (New Haven and London: Yale University Press, 2006), 34.

Works Cited

Anon. *A Visit to the Bazaar*. London: J. Harris, 1818.

Anon. *The Bazaar, A Popular Song Arranged to a Popular Air*. London: T. Holloway, c.1825.

Abelson, Elaine S. *When Ladies Go A-thieving: Middle-Class Shoplifters in the Victorian Department Store*. New York: Oxford University Press, 1989.

Altick, Richard D. *The Shows of London*. Cambridge, MA: Belknap Press/Harvard University Press, 1978.

Armstrong, Isobel. *Victorian Glassworlds: Glass Culture and the Imagination, 1830–1880*. Oxford: Oxford University Press, 2008.

Bayer, Thomas M., and John R. Page. *The Development of the Art Market in England*. London: Pickering and Chatto, 2011.

Briggs, Asa. *Victorian Things*. Stroud: Sutton, 2003 [1988].

Cohen, Deborah. *Household Gods: The British and Their Possessions*. New Haven and London: Yale University Press, 2006.

Cox, Pamela, and Annabel Hobley. *Shopgirls*. London: Arrow, 2014.

Crossick, Geoffrey, and Serge Jaumain, eds. *Cathedrals of Consumption: The European Department Store, 1850–1939*. Aldershot: Ashgate, 1999.

Dyer, Gary R. "The 'Vanity Fair' of Nineteenth-Century England: Commerce, Women, and the East in the Ladies' Bazaar," *Nineteenth Century Literature* 46, (1991): 196–222.

Gurney, Peter. *Wanting and Having: Popular Politics and Liberal Consumerism in England, 1830–1870*. Manchester: Manchester University Press, 2015.

Hamlett, Jane. *Material Relations: Domestic Interiors and Middle-class Families in England, 1850–1910*. Manchester: Manchester University Press, 2010.

Hindley, Charles. *The Life and Times of James Catnach*. London: Reeves and Turner.

Jerden, William. *The Autobiography of William Jerden*. London: Arthur Hall, Virtue and Co., 1852.

Knight, Charles, ed. *London*, 6 vols. London: Charles Knight, 1841–1843.

Lancaster, Bill. *The Department Store: A Social History*. Lancaster: Lancaster University Press, 1995.

Maier, William M. "Going on the Hoist: Women, Work and Shoplifting in London, c. 1890–1940." *Journal of British Studies* 50, (2011): 410–33.

Mayhew, Henry, ed. *The Shops and Companies of London and the Trades and Manufactories of Great Britain*. London: Strand, 1865.

McWilliam, Rohan. "The Theatricality of the Staffordshire Figurine." *Journal of Victorian Culture* 10, (2005): 107–14.

Milhous, Judith, Gabriella Dideriksen, and Robert D. Hume. *Italian Opera in Late Eighteenth-Century London* vol. 2: *The Pantheon Opera and Its Aftermath, 1789–1795*. Oxford: Clarendon Press, 2000.

Nightingale, Joseph. *The Bazaar: Its Origin, Nature, and Objects Explained and Recommended as an Important Branch of Political Economy*. London: Privately Published, 1816.

O'Brien, Patricia. "The Kleptomania Diagnosis: Bourgeois Women and Theft in late Nineteenth-Century France." *Journal of Social History* 17, (1983): 65–77.

Peck, Linda L. *Consuming Splendour: Society and Culture in Seventeenth-Century England*. Cambridge: Cambridge University Press, 2005.

Prochaska, Frank K. *Women and Philanthropy in Nineteenth-Century England*. Oxford: Clarendon Press, 1980.

Rappaport, Erika D. *Shopping for Pleasure: Women in the Making of London's West End*. Princeton, NJ: Princeton University Press, 2000.

Sala, George A. *Twice Around the Clock; Or the Hours of the Day and Night in London*. Leicester: Leicester University Press, 1971 [1858].

Sheppard, F.H.W., ed. *Survey of London*. London: Athlone Press, 1900, 50 vols.

Shiell, Annette. *Fundraising, Flirtation and Fancywork: Charity Bazaars in Nineteenth Century Australia*. Cambridge: Cambridge Scholars, 2012.

Showalter, Elaine. *The Female Malady: Women, Madness and English Culture*. London: Virago, 1987.

Southey, Robert. *Letters from England: By Don Manuel Alvarez Espriella*. London: Longman, Hurst, Rees, Orme and Brown, 1807, 3 vols.

Timbs, John. *Curiosities of London; Exhibiting the Most Rare and Remarkable Objects of Interest in the Metropolis*. London: J. S. Virtue, 1867 [1855].

(Mrs.) E. M. (Henrietta) Ward, *Memories of Ninety Years*. London: Hutchison, 1924.

Whitlock, Tammy C. *Crime, Gender and Consumer Culture in Nineteenth-Century England*. Aldershot: Ashgate, 2005.

2 The Bric-à-Bracquer's Étagère or Whatnot

Staging 'Artistic' Taste in the Aesthetic 'House Beautiful'

Anne Anderson

Upon first entering an Aesthetic era (c.1870–1890) drawing room, the visitor's eye would inevitably be drawn to the étagère, an elaborate piece of furniture often positioned above the fireplace. This essential paraphernalia, its central mirror surrounded by dainty shelves, was intended for the display of precious and valuable objects. However, by the 1870s the étagère had become a battleground on which the notion of good taste was contested. Carrying mementoes, souvenirs, and memorabilia, each telling a story about the homeowner, the étagère became a sort of household shrine; upon it, a narrative of personal relationships and self-discovery could be materialized in 'things.' We should not dismiss such displays as mere 'clutter', as these things carried emotional resonance.[1] As mnemonic objects mementoes and souvenirs memorialized loved ones and places visited. Bill Brown has argued objects are 'congealed actions, passionate acts of seeking, selecting and situating.'[2] Once transformed into 'moments' things can materialize memories creating a sentimental world of recall. For Remy Saisselin, mementoes and souvenirs construct the dream world of the bourgeois, an 'intimate escape from the world of material cares.'[3]

However, for many homeowners the selection and arrangement of things on an étagère transcended sentimental associations; here one could express one's taste. This demanded knowledge as well as intuition; the étagère allowed one to materialize personal preferences, to create a harmonious composition based on colour and form, and to exercise connoisseurial skills. Freedom of expression was paramount; Oscar Wilde (1854–1900), a self-appointed arbiter of taste, decreed a home was 'to bear the impress of a distinct individuality' and 'should express the feelings of those who live in it.'[4] As the étagère was not bound by any rules it offered the perfect site for self-expression; through selection and arrangement, a unique statement could be made. For the novelist Henry James, writing in the preface to *The Spoils of Poynton* (1897), art was 'all discrimination and selection.'[5] The heroine of the novel, Fleda Vetch, displays her intuitive taste by creating an artful arrangement at 'Ricks', the house to which Mrs Gereth has withdrawn: 'It's your extraordinary genius; you make things "compose" in spite of yourself.'[6]

In the 'arrangement and effect of everything' Fleda's hand is infallible; the drawing room has been transformed into a carefully composed work of art, one that also conveys a soul, a story, a life. Fabricating a personal style through interior décor signalled originality, which lay at the heart of the bourgeois cult of Individuality.[7]

Although writer and novelist Grant Allen (1848–1899) shunned the 'stereotyped notions of the professional decorator' in favour of individual choice, selection was not solely driven by personal tastes. Aesthetes, a socio-economic coterie defined by Walter Hamilton as 'the union of persons of cultivated taste to define and decide upon what is to be admired', fabricated a collective identity.[8] Those who did not accept their ruling were deemed Philistines and there was no hope for them. Admittance into their exclusive circle was not based on wealth, as Hamilton claimed 'riches without taste are of no avail, whilst taste without money, or with very little, can always effect much.'[9] Although aesthetic tastes were initially shaped by the likes of Dante Gabriel Rossetti (1828–1882) and James McNeil Whistler (1834–1903), by the 1880s they were indelibly linked with Wilde's self-accessorising preference for lilies, sunflowers, and peacock feathers. Although Wilde insisted that 'every home should wear an individual air in all its furnishings and decorations', his so-called 'broad principles' encouraged a fashion for 'Old Blue' china, Persian rugs, seventeenth-century brass sconces, and Morris & Co. wallpapers.[10] Alongside personal dress, a beautiful home became the most effective way of expressing one's cultural capital.

With class consciousness, as well as artistic expression, inscribed and constructed through an assemblage of objects the étagère became central to the House Beautiful, an epithet derived from Clarence Cook's domestic advice manual published in 1877. However, as 'taste was a commodity that set its possessor apart' such demonstrations caused some anxiety.[11] Wilde capitalized on the public's insecurity in matters of taste proffering advice through his lecture tour of America (1882) and Britain (1883). Wilde suggested an over-mantle built up to the ceiling 'with little shelves on which you may place your rare china or ornaments'; at its centre a space might be left for a little circular mirror, whose beauty lay in its capacity to 'concentrate light in a room.'[12] According to Allen there had to be some kind of ornament above the mantelpiece 'which will rivet the eye, and so vindicate the claims of the hearth to be the central place.'[13] His ideal solution was an 'unpretentious ebonized étagère mirror, portioned into compartments by a little balustrade and with three shelves dividing it horizontally, for small vases and other knick-knacks.'[14]

As its name suggests, the étagère, derived from *estagiere* (shelf, stage, or storey, meaning floor), was French in origin; similar to the English 'What-not', it consists of a series of stages or shelves. The glass fronted curio cabinet or vitrine is related to the étagère; these forms could be merged into one piece of furniture. Many étagères have a glass fronted cabinet lodged in the centre of its framework. Sometimes these doors are solid, facilitating panels of painted decoration or providing a framework for painted tiles. The étagère could also be merged with a mirror to form an over-mantel, its galleried shelves and compartments providing the decorator with plenty of scope. Whether floor standing or wall-hung shelving, all these variants served the same purpose, namely the display of ornaments or other small articles often defined as 'knick-knacks' or '*bric-à-brac*.' Appearing at the end of the eighteenth century, during the reign of Louis XVI, designs often reflected the fashion for *Chinoiserie*, the European imitation and interpretation of Chinese, Japanese, and East Asian artistic traditions, as they were frequently used for the display of Oriental porcelains. A hundred years later their primary function was still for the display of precious porcelains alongside other *objets de vertu*.

The étagère was intimately connected with the emergence of collecting as a hobby. Allen recommended a 'few pieces of Venetian glass, a Vallauris vase or two, a bit of hawthorn-pattern porcelain and a couple of tiny, low specimen vases, with a bright flower or two or a sprig of maidenhair, to liven up the whole.'[15] This would form an 'exceedingly pretty centre-piece to the picture' and give 'free scope to individual taste and fancy instead of merely reflecting the stereotyped notions of the professional decorator.'[16] This was the art of the 'personal touch', using a diverse range of carefully selected items to make a unique statement.[17] Alicia Warden, the heroine of Frank Frankfort Moore's *The Collector* (1898), who scorns a house 'furnished as ten thousand other houses', put her faith in antiques as 'unique articles.'[18] Romantically defined by Henry James as 'the material odds and ends of the more labouring ages', antiques attain their value outside the standard circulation of commodities.[19] Chippendale chairs, Sèvres porcelain, and Venetian glass were now deemed artistic, not just because they were old but because they were handmade; individuality was thus assured. Alicia informs her fiancé Reggie Gathorne, 'Individuality, individuality – that is the true note of all art, whether it be the art of writing, as you do, or the art of furnishing a house properly, as we women do.'[20] Quaint and charming, antiques recalled a bygone age of refinement and elegance. The past offered a form of sanctuary; as Desmond Coke conceded, in *Confessions of an Incurable Collector* (1928), 'Old things seem to me the only refuge that the human soul can find from this new tyranny. They give leisure, they bring peace.'[21] Antiques offered a 'divertissement' or release from a degraded present into an idealized past.

The search for the 'Old Beautiful' promoted a new craze dubbed *Bricàbracomania* by the popular press.[22] A *bric-à-bracquer* was a 'gentlemanly' amateur, a 'dabbler', who collected for pleasure; 'a hobby rather than a career, a way to occupy leisure time rather than a way to make money.'[23] A virtuoso, who privileged beauty as well as age and historical associations, his choices were based on personal sympathies, a highly subjective view of ancient times and other cultures. American journalist James Grant Wilson claimed the *bric-à-bracquer* was drawn to the quaint, everyday things that appealed to the heart rather than the mind.[24] Anything might catch the eye; instincts would be aroused, the *bric-à-brac* hunter drawn to any object which made a personal appeal. As literary scholar Talia Schaffer asserts, each discovery was 'mystified into a moment of aesthetic and sentimental affirmation', becoming a means to demonstrate individual taste and inscribe a personal history.[25] Every object commemorates a discovery, thereby enshrining an experience, Brown's 'moment', in a material thing: valuable works of art now became souvenirs and mementoes enabling the production of an 'object-based historiography.'[26] Such discoveries would be commemorated in a new literary genre: Major Herbert Byng Hall's *The Bric-à-Brac Hunter or Chapters on Chinamania* (1875) was the first in a long line of autobiographical travelogues recording adventures 'antiquing.' *Bric-à-brac* hunting empowered the 'free spirit', while unorthodox antiques embodied liberated sensibilities. Although deemed 'junk' by many, *bric-à-brac* had many advantages – it was cheap, cheerful, and individualistic. As keen collector Arthur Hayden observed, 'variety is the key-note to the fascinating hobby of collecting.'[27]

Chinamania, as it was dubbed by the *Punch* cartoonist George Du Maurier, was central to the new sport of *bric-à-brac* hunting. Porcelains and pottery lost their utilitarian purpose, as tea or dinner wares, moving into the category of *objet d'art*, being 'viewed from an aesthetic standpoint where the object appears to have no other function than visual enjoyment or satisfaction.'[28] Valued for their tactile and visual qualities, ceramics were 'available for creating decorative visual displays.'[29] Displays clustered around the mantelpiece which was second only to the 'fire-place as the centre of family life – the spiritual and intellectual centre.'[30] For poet Rosamund Marriott Watson (1860–1911), the chimney piece set the standard for the whole house; it was the 'ideal altar(s)' for 'blue china, for silver or bronze candelabra, for the Chelsea Nymph, the Empire clock;... they nobly fulfil the first duty of their kind by forming majestic and distinctive *leit-motif* for their neighbouring plenishing, an example for the whole of the house.'[31] Architect Colonel Sir Robert William Edis (1839–1927) warned the mantel shelf had to be sufficiently broad for the 'various ornaments, useful or otherwise, which are wanted':

> with perhaps a central panel for a good portrait or subject picture... round it on either side might be plain panelling carried up to the ceiling line, with recesses for sculpture or bronzes or tiers of shelves for those whose tastes lie in china or other *bric-à-brac*...[32]

The *bric-à-bracquer's* accomplishments lay not only in his astute acquisitions, but also in the art of composition: his ability to create a harmonious whole from disparate parts, fashioning a 'gesamtkunstwerk' or 'total art work.'[33] As designer Lewis F. Day (1845–1910) observed, 'even the little knick-knacks in a room should go together; they should not look as though they had met by accident.'[34] Within the House Beautiful, the étagère was a 'total art work.' Through domestic advice manuals, it can be shown that the étagère became essential paraphernalia for the home decorator. Its popularity is also revealed through contemporary furniture catalogues, photographs, and paintings of the parlour and drawing room. Such sources also specify the most popular items selected, especially by those homeowners who aspired to aesthetic or artistic credentials.

Étagère: The Taste for 'Black and Gold' Furniture

E. W. Godwin's design for an Anglo-Japanese drawing room, published in a catalogue issued by the cabinet maker William Watt in 1877 (National Art Library), shows the fireplace framed by hanging shelves. The fireplace itself is topped by an elaborate over-mantel, its superstructure providing individual shelves for *objets de vertu*. Godwin's interior breaks with the 'ponderous Gothic of the previous generation', his 'lightness of form' being attributed to the newly awakened interest in Japanese art.[35] After a protracted period of isolation, trading links with Japan were reopened as a result of Commander Perry's successful expedition in 1853–1854. The British public encountered Japan at the 1862 International Exhibition; Rutherford Alcock, British Consul in Tokyo, exhibited his diverse collection of ceramics, metalwork, lacquer and textiles.

The impact on artistic circles was profound: Rossetti and Whistler competed for specimens of blue and white 'Nankin China' or 'Old Blue' china, as Chinese porcelains were popularly dubbed.[36] At Kelmscott House, Hammersmith, William Morris's Old Blue china plates were carefully arranged on purpose built white shelves, designed by Philip Webb, while at Kelmscott Manor, his summer retreat near Lechlade, he created a china closet.[37] At Standen House, East Grinstead, Webb set the Old Blue china against green panelling, following Rossetti's preference. Henry Treffry Dunn's *Dante Gabriel Rossetti and Theodore Watts - Dunton in the Sitting Room at 16 Cheyne Walk* (1882, NPG, London) enshrines the artist's taste: 'One of the prettiest and most curiously furnished old-fashioned parlours that I had ever seen.'[38] Rossetti led the fashion for bedecked over-mantels; this description of his bedroom fireplace from Dunn notes a medley of unusual things:

> A massive panelled oak mantelpiece reached from the floor to the ceiling, fitted up with numerous shelves and cup-board like recesses, all filled with a medley of brass repoussé dishes, blue china vases filled with peacock feathers, oddly-fashioned early English and foreign candlestick, Chinese monstrosities in bronze and various other curiosities, the whole surmounted by an ebony and ivory crucifix. The only modern thing I could see anywhere in the rooms was a Byrant and May's match box.[39]

The fireplace in his 'sitting room' at Cheyne Walk was 'a most original compound of Chinese black-lacquer panels, bearing designs of birds, animals, flowers and fruit in gold relief, which had a very good effect.'[40] For Watson old lacquer threw out the 'dim suggestions of romance'; 'The rich colours, the peculiar sheen of old lacquer cannot be successfully simulated, neither can the modern occidental designer recapture the feeling of lines and curves traced far away and long ago.'[41] This taste for Oriental lacquer created a vogue for black and gold furniture. Thomas Jeckyll (1827–1881), who is credited with conceiving some of the earliest Anglo-Japanese furniture, designed a spectacular fireplace and over-mantel étagère for the drawing room of 1 Holland Park, the Ionides's home. This was specifically for the display of the 'obligatory collection of blue and white porcelain.'[42] Jeremy Cooper claims this was the first of its kind, 'a precedent thereafter poorly imitated throughout suburban London.'[43] Mass production brought the étagère' into disrepute; as Watson warned,

> Unless you can be very sure of something absolutely harmonious and good in the way of a superstructure, it is better by far to refrain. Above all, to eschew the maddening machine-made arrangements, pitiful in their triviality and lack of purpose, of little shelves and little timid pillars, and little balconies enshrining little bits of looking glass; often they are ebonized, sometimes they are of natural wood, hardly ever are they to be encouraged.[44]

While architects and designers like Godwin, Jeckyll and Christopher Dresser (1834–1904) tried to capture the spirit of Japan, commercial manufacturers simply exploited the vogue for black and gold furniture that emulated lacquer. Unusual variants were intended to attract a public always on the lookout for novelties. Regent Street retailers Howell and James, who according to Cooper remained 'committed to the avant-garde', offered their clients an étagère fitted with a clock; designed by the architect Thomas Harris they were fashionably labelled 'Jacobean' and 'Queen Anne.'[45]

Henry William Batley (1846–1932) also designed an ebonized étagère/clockcase for Howell and James in a Gothic-Japanese style. Batley is often dismissed as an imitator of Bruce James Talbot (1831–1881) and Thomas Edward Collcutt (1840–1924), the principal designer for the London cabinetmakers Collinson & Lock.[46] Batley, whose furniture designs for James Shoolbred & Co. were displayed at the 1878 Paris Exposition Universelle, gathered ten years work on interior design into his *Series of Studies for Furniture, Decoration etc.* (1883). Plate 6 illustrated a design for a drawing-room mantelpiece in satinwood, inlaid and carved, exhibited at Paris; balustrades of turned spindles are used to create individual compartments, each filled with beautiful *objets d'art* such as precious Venetian glass and Oriental ceramics (Figure 2.1).

Figure 2.1 Henry William Batley (1846–1932) Plate 6 from *Series of Studies for Furniture, Decoration etc.* Designed and etched by H. W. Batley, London: Sampson Low, Marston, Searle & Rivington, 1883. Credit: Anne Anderson.

Edis also favoured 'good splayed Venetian glasses' as they lightened up the room and reflected the ornaments.[47] Batley's structure culminates in a convex mirror, an iconic object thanks to Rossetti's predilection for old mirrors: standing in Rossetti's sitting room, Dunn remarked 'whichever way I looked I saw myself gazing at myself'.[48]

According to Harry Quilter (1851–1907), art critic for *The Spectator*, black and gold furniture had become passé by the 1880s. Quilter railed against Aesthetic dogma as it was imposing a straightjacket on the home decorator. It irked him that the *'cant of a certain set'* decreed there was only one way to decorate a room; 'one which requires blue china and sage green paint and tinted ceilings and black and gold furniture.'[49] It would have been 'better that England were full to the brim with ugliness... than that it should be an upholsterers' paradise of blue china and black and gold étagère.'[50] Charlotte Gere concludes 'Aesthetic schemes, though apparently eclectic, always seem to follow a set of unwritten but inviolable rules that span cultures.'[51] They also spanned continents, decorative schemes for American houses bearing striking similarities to those found in English homes.

The House Beautiful: Picturing the Étagère

The bourgeoisie enjoyed images of themselves that celebrated the concept of the home. There is little doubt that these images perpetuated social norms, casting women as the eponymous domestic goddess or 'Angel in the Home.' However, this role now extended to home decorating; creating an ideal environment in which to care for her husband and raise a family was now a woman's duty according to John Ruskin (1819–1900). She was to secure the 'order, comfort, and loveliness' of the home.[52] In *Art in the House* (1878), German scholar Jakob von Falke deemed it a 'woman's aesthetic mission' to create a beautiful home.[53] Ladies were deemed to be intuitively artistic due to their sensitive and refined nature, even though the high arts of painting, sculpture and architecture were considered too physically and intellectually demanding for them:

> It has been said with truth that taste, or, in other words, the sense of beauty, that is the faculty of distinguishing the beautiful from the ugly, is intuitive, and it is customary to attribute it more especially to the female sex.[54]

Apparently, a woman's artistic taste was 'part of her essential gender identity.'[55]

However, according to Ruskin women were not destined for 'invention or creation but for sweet ordering, arrangement and decision.'[56] The home she ordered and arranged was a 'sacred place, a vestal temple, a temple of the hearth...And wherever a true wife comes, this home is always round her....'[57] Woman's true place and power was in the home; in effect she was Home. In the 'House of Art', where the Useful and the Beautiful were to lie down together, woman was both artificer and priestess.[58] Artist's naturally responded by situating women in their preordained surroundings. Invariably confined to the domestic realm, women artists were complicit in perpetuating this mythology. Nancy A. Sabine Pasley's *A Game of Cards* (1887–1891 Geffrye Museum) is dominated by an ebonized over-mantel étagère; a carefully orchestrated display of ceramics features a matching pair of moon flask vases and figurines. Along the standard white chimney piece, which has been artfully concealed by an embroidered velvet runner, are matching pairs of blue bottle vases. Old Blue china is suspended from the walls. This artful arrangement, akin to the composition of a painting through its harmonious juxtaposition of shapes and colours, demonstrates the sophisticated, fashionable tastes of the occupants.

Henry Dunkin Shephard's painting *Home Sweet Home* (1887, private collection), which centres on a domestic angel at the piano, features an over-mantel largely laden with Old Blue china and Japanese Imari porcelains. In *Home and Garden: Paintings and Drawings of English, middle-class, urban domestic spaces 1675–1914* (2003), David Dewing concludes this careful selection of furniture and ornaments is meant to suggest a 'refined, cultivated ambience, with educated and accomplished inhabitants, who have an awareness of modern taste. *Home Sweet Home* is… an essay in taste and style and a commentary on the meanings of home.'[59]

This display appears to echo Clarence Cook's advice, as we can see gathered on the mantel a 'few beautiful and chosen things – the most beautiful the family purse can afford.'[60] Their purpose was to 'lift us up, to feed thought and feeling, things we are willing to live with, to have our children grow up with, and that we never can become tired of, because they belong alike to nature and to humanity.'[61] 'Great things', an engraving or picture, might be flanked by a plaster cast of some lovely masterpiece ordered from London, Paris, or Berlin. There should still be room for 'pleasant little things'; a bit of Japanese bronze, or the Satsuma cup, or the Etruscan vase, or the Roman lamp, or the beautiful shell, or the piece of English or Venetian glass.[62] Space should be made for the tumbler filled with roses, the quaintly painted gourd or the wreath of autumn leaves. Echoing Watson, there should be 'real candlesticks, with real candles to be lighted at twilight…in the hour of illusion and of pensive thought, casting a soft wavering gleam…bringing a few moments of poetry to close the weary working day.'[63]

Hints on Household Taste: Charles Locke Eastlake on Forming a Museum

As home decorating became a female prerogative, fearing the worst a plethora of domestic manuals appeared inevitably penned by men who considered themselves authorities due to their superior intellect and education. In *Hints on Household Taste* (1869), considered the first guidebook of its kind, Charles Locke Eastlake (1836–1906) concluded ladies were uneducated, lured by visual appearance rather than quality and often led astray by duplicitous shopkeepers who were drawn from the lower classes.[64] In Moore's *The Collector* (1898) Alicia, who favours the antique over the modern, also blamed the retailers, especially department stores and trade catalogues:

> And poor Lil and her husband thought it all so highly artistic, including the dreadful over-mantel with its fussy shelves and nooks and Japanese fans, and the etchings chosen by the two thousand on the

judgement of the proprietors of Spinder's Stores, Limited. Oh Reggie, I think I should die if you were to ask me to live in a house furnished as ten thousand other houses are furnished annually by Spinders.'[65]

It was the intention of writers as diverse as Eastlake, Rev. W. J. Loftie, Grant Allen, Mrs Mary Eliza Haweis and William Morris to 'set the crooked straight.' Haweis noted that 'most people are now alive to the importance of beauty as a refining influence. The appetite for artistic instruction is even ravenous....*objets de vertu* from all countries are within everybody's reach, all that is lacking is the cool power of choice.'[66] Although taste was intuitive, it apparently needed cultivating and refining.

Eastlake scorned 'knick-knacks'; by that expression he meant 'the heterogeneous assemblage of modern rubbish, which under the head of "china ornaments" and various other names, finds its way into the drawing-room or boudoir.'[67] But Eastlake did not wish to discourage the collection of really good specimens of art-manufacture, arguing the senses could be refined by assembling a 'little museum':

> the smallest example of rare old porcelain, ivory carvings, of ancient metalwork and enamels, of Venetian glass, of anything which illustrates good design and skilful workmanship, should be acquired whenever possible and treasured with the greatest care...An Indian ginger-jar, a Flemish beer-jug, a Japanese fan, may each become in turn a valuable lesson in decorative form and colour...[68]

Those who possessed such things should associate and group them together as much as possible thus forming a very picturesque feature in the room.[69] A mantelpiece with 'a capital set of narrow shelves' raised over a mirror would be ideal for specimens of old china: 'The plates should be placed upright on their edges, and may be easily prevented from slipping off by a shallow groove sunk in the thickness of each shelf. A little museum may thus be formed, and remain a source of lasting pleasure to its possessors, seeing that "a thing of beauty is a joy forever".'[70] Eastlake also favoured wooden brackets, which could be obtained in a wide variety of shapes, even though they were often weak in construction and of very inferior design (Figure 2.2).

In *A Plea for Art in the House* (1877), Rev. William Loftie, commended the wise father who encouraged his children to 'make a collection'; as adults these young men and women had gained:

> a love for something which would serve as an amusement and relaxation for leisure hours. Such people have no occasion for card-playing or gambling to pass a long evening. To them a spare hour is not an enemy to be killed. Satan finds no mischief for their idle hands to do. They wonder how anybody can complain of *ennui*, for their time is fully occupied, and life is only too short for what they want to get into it.[71]

Mantel-piece Shelves,
executed from a Design by Charles L. Eastlake.

Figure 2.2 "Mantel-piece Shelves executed from a design by Charles L. Eastlake," Charles Locke Eastlake, *Hints on Household Taste in Furniture, Upholstery, and Other Details*, 122, London: Longmans,
Green & Co., 1869. Credit: Anne Anderson.

However, Loftie did not condone 'private museums': 'I think houses
which are ugly and badly furnished and uncomfortable as none the
better for being filled with curiosities.'[72] Above all, it was a moral duty
to provide a beautiful home:

> Except for people who are actually artists, much that goes to
> make home beautiful must of necessity be obtained by judicious
> collecting…it is the duty of everyone who is so fortunate as to
> possess a home and to be the head of the family, to endeavour,

so far as he can, to make his family happy by making his home beautiful....Too many men collect only for their own private gratification.[73]

One should strive to have the best, whether ancient or modern. Moreover, there was satisfaction to be gained from knowing that

> what I have will sell for as much as I gave, or more, even after a few years wear; and that it is pretty to look at and pleasant to live in the house with; and that moreover I have had a lot of fun buying it... buying things that are pretty and good, is the only way I know by which you can both eat your cake and have it too.[74]

The House Beautiful: Clarence Cook on the Étagère

Clarence Chatham Cook (1828–1900), author of *The House Beautiful* (1877), arguably the most influential advice manual after Eastlake's *Hints on Household Taste*, was an early and influential supporter of American antiques, seeing the 'resuscitation of 'old furniture' and revival of old simplicity' as denoting improving taste, rather than merely the outcome of 'centennial mania.'[75] *In Pursuit of Beauty Americans and the Aesthetic Movement*, Marilynn Johnson observes that by the 1870s 'writers equated owning American antiques with having taste':

> Possession of the antique suggested not only learning and background but a special talent, a refined eye that set one apart. Money was important- one could after all, hire advice. But only the man or woman of taste possessed an instinct for the trea-sure hidden amid trash, and so joined those select, or better still elect, few who were destined to walk with the apostles of the new aestheticism.[76]

Cook, who advocated mingling 'things old and new', recognised the benefits of the étagère: 'If there be space enough in the living-room to permit it, an étagère – the fine name which we have given to a set of shelves – will gave us an opportunity to display pretty things in the way of bric-a-brac of which we may be the possessor.'[77] Cook provided specific examples; a 'Chinese étagère with Cupboard' from Mr Sypher's which was as 'fine a black as ebony' (Figure 2.3).[78]

The disposition of the shelves was worthy of comment:

> observe that no one of them extends entirely across the space to be shelved, nor is there any upright partition dividing the shelves themselves. The object of the irregular arrangement is first...to avoid

monotony, but it finds a better excuse in the accommodation it gives to articles of different sizes and shapes.'[79]

This visual variety was informed by Japanese aesthetics, notably the art of asymmetric ordering. Asymmetry was carefully balanced, creating a harmonious arrangement akin to a musical composition with individual objects acting as 'key notes': 'there were places for little things and places for larger things, and each is at home in its own compartment, and being somewhat isolated…does not suffer by having its beauty interfered with by that of its neighbour.[80] Cook defines the étagère as the 'ornamental upholder of the ornamental.'[81]

As space in the American home was limited Cook recommended 'pretty hanging shelves or étagère', their little cupboards ideal for 'frail objects of curiosity, or beauty, or both' which needed to be 'kept under lock and

Chinese Étagère, with Cupboard.
No. 35.

Figure 2.3 'Chinese étagère with Cupboard' No. 35 from Clarence Cook, *The House Beautiful, Essays on Beds and Tables, Stools and Candlestick*, 95, New York: Scribner, Armstrong and Co., 1877. Credit: Anne Anderson.

key.'[82] The example illustrated, 'stained a rich black', was designed by Cottier & Co.; it resembles Godwin's Anglo-Japanese design as illustrated in Watt's catalogue.[83]

Cook hoped this advice would facilitate clearing the drawing room which was all too often crowded beyond capacity. Overcrowding was uncomfortable; it also destroyed the usefulness of many articles of furniture. Things were bought from pure whim or 'because the buyer doesn't know what to do with her money' as the 'temptation to New York rich people is to be all the time buying things for show.'[84] Conversely filled with 'Indian porcelain and Venice glass' topped with a 'great platter of old blue', the effect of Cottier's étagère was 'brilliant' . Echoing Eastlake, for Cook the étagère was a means to an end:

> An artist's eye would leave all for the colour of the pots and bits of glass that are arranged on the shelves. Such a cabinet might be made a museum for the preservation of all the curiosities and pretty things gathered in the family walks and travels. The bubble-bottle of old Roman glass stirred in walking by one's own foot in the ruined palace of the Caesars, and not bought in a shop; the Dutch drinking glass, with the crest of William of Orange; the trilobites found in a Newburgh stone-wall, or the box of Indian arrow-heads, jasper, and feldspar, and quartz, picked up in a Westchester County field; bits of nature's craft and man's gathered in one of these pendant museums, may make a collection of what were else scattered and lost, and which though of little intrinsic value, and of small regard to see, will often find its use in a house of wide-wake children.[85]

Bric-a-brac now commanded serious consideration; when well chosen, and having beauty of form and colour or workmanship, such things had a 'distinct use and value as educators of certain senses – the sense of colour, the sense of touch, the sense of sight.'[86] Cook commended Japanese ivory and wood carving, specifically Netsuke, a button-like toggle, which although modest was poetically or wittily conceived. Made to be clasped or rolled in the palm, they had been developed by necessity. Such 'toys' would inform a child's taste and delicacy of perception; 'our senses are educated more by these slight impressions than we are apt to think; and *bric-à-brac*, so much despised by certain people, and often justly so, may have a use that they themselves might not unwillingly admit.'[87]

The aesthete, who valorized all five senses (sight, touch, hearing, smell, and taste), experienced beauty through arresting artefacts. Spectacular *objets d'art* enhanced experience enabling the aesthete to live in the 'moment.' Art critic and philosopher Walter Pater maintained 'each object is loosed into a group of impressions – colour, odour, texture – in the mind of the observer...for that moment only.'[88] With choice determined subjectively, governed by the 'observer', 'value is aesthetically (that is, sensuously yet suprasensuously) determined.'[89]

Conclusion

As a household shrine, the spiritual and intellectual heart of the home, the mantelpiece étagère encapsulated the world view of the homeowner. Combining the works of man with those of nature, its displays were intended to refine the senses, especially the appreciation of colour and form. While objects gathered far and wide offered a means of self-culture, they also carried emotional value. For Mrs Gereth, in *The Spoils of Poynton*, old things have a personality of their own : 'Ah the little melancholy tender tell-tale things: how can they *not* speak to you and find a way to your heart?'[90] For Fleda Vetch, Mrs Gereth's 'pupil', old things are analogous to ghosts, 'for what they were and what they are'; they created a 'presence, a perfume, a touch. It's a soul, a story, a life. There's ever so much more here than you and I.'[91] A 'thing' becomes a life, standing in for people both present and past; through possession the soul of the owner passes into the object endowing it with personality. Over time an object absorbs many personalities. When Dorelia McNeill, artist Augustus John's muse, chose an object or a colour it became 'mystically endowed with a part of her own beauty and incorporated in the living work of art that was her home.'[92] In *Two Flamboyant Fathers*, Nicolette Devis observed 'Objects in the house had a quality of character and an intrinsic beauty of their own; they were admired and loved as people were; for their personality.'[93]

Embodying memories, old things could evoke a distant past while simultaneously inducing more personal recollections. Hartford collector Henry Wood Erving declared, 'old china is fascinating stuff and one's imagination can create all sorts of histories and romances connected with it.'[94] It was the 'romance' of old china, its sentimental associations as well as its aesthetic appeal, which provoked the scouring of curio shops and attics at home and abroad. The lure of the chase, the chance discovery, and the satisfaction of possession offered a seductive means of recounting one's life through things. 'Being possessed by possessions' was not just about accumulation; the process facilitates 'fashioning an object-based historiography and anthropology.'[95] Moreover, the accumulation of antiques created the illusion of hereditary aristocratic sensibility rather than bourgeois brash, vulgar newness. The étagère became a stage upon which social or class 'distinction' could be enacted. Freedom of expression was guaranteed as no two would ever be alike. Its fashioning came down to individual choice; it was a 'total art work' in miniature, a gesamtkunstwerk. Once selected and arranged into a harmonious whole, such specimens and *objet d'art* induced thoughtfulness; as Wilde suggested 'the mission of the aesthetic movement is to lure people to contemplate – not to lead them to create.'[96] The 'Life Beautiful' freed one, as far as possible, 'from mundane responsibility allowing the "reflective elements" in human nature to be occupied by "things of the mind".'[97] The étagère offered many objects of reflection.

Notes

1 Stana Nenadic, "Romanticism and the urge to consume in the first half of the nineteenth century" in *Consumers and Luxury: Consumer Culture in Europe 1650–1850*, ed. Maxine Berg and Helen Clifford (Manchester: Manchester University Press, 1999), 209.

2 Bill Brown, *A Sense of Things the Object Matter of American Literature* (Chicago and London: The University of Chicago Press, 2003), 146.

3 Remy Saisselin, *The Bourgeois and the Bibelot* (New Brunswick, New Jersey: Rutgers University Press, 1984), 71.

4 Oscar Wilde, "The House Beautiful" in *Collins Complete Works of Oscar Wilde, Centenary Edition* (Glasgow: Harper Collins, 1999), 914.

5 Henry James, "Preface," *The Spoils of Poynton, A London Life, The Chaperone* (New York: Charles Scribner's Sons, 1908), v.

6 James, *The Spoils of Poynton*, 249.

7 Alan S. Kahan, *Liberalism in Nineteenth Century Europe: The Political Culture of Limited Suffrage* (London: Palgrave Macmillan, 2003), 160.

8 Walter Hamilton, *The Aesthetic Movement in England* (London: Reeves and Turner, 1882), vii.

9 Ibid.

10 Wilde, "The House Beautiful," 914.

11 Charlotte Gere with Lesley Hoskins, *The House Beautiful Oscar Wilde and the Aesthetic Interior* (London: Lund Humphries and the Geffrye Museum, 2000), 77.

12 Wilde, "House Beautiful," 920.

13 Grant Allen, "The Philosophy of Drawing-Rooms" in *The Cornhill Magazine*, 41, March 1880, 321.

14 Ibid.

15 Ibid.

16 Ibid.

17 Karen Halttunen, "From Parlor to Living Room: Domestic Space, Interior Decoration and the Culture of Personality," in *Consuming Visions: Accumulation and Display of Goods in America, 1880–1920*, ed. S. J. Bronner (New York and London: W.W. Norton & Company, 1989), 185.

18 F. Frankfort Moore, "The Collector" in *The Woman At Home, Annie S. Swan's Magazine*, Vol. V, October to September 1898: 978, 981.

19 James, "Preface," *Spoils of Poynton*, ix. See Brown, *A Sense of Things*, 157.

20 Moore, "The Collector," 978.

21 Desmond Coke, *Confessions of an Incurable Collector* (London: Chapman and Hall, 1928), 4.

22 Thomas Rohan, *Old Beautiful* (London: Mills and Boon, 1926). See Anne Anderson, "Transatlantic Bric-à-Brac Hunters: the Pleasures of Antiquing c. 1870–1930," *Symbiosis: A Journal of Transatlantic Literary and Cultural Relations*, 19:1 (April 2015): 75–95.

23 Talia Schaffer, *The Forgotten Female Aesthetes: Literary Culture in Late Victorian Britain* (Charlottesville and London: University of Virginia Press, 2000), 79.

24 James Grant Wilson, "About Bric-à-brac," *Art Journal*, Vol. 46, October 1878 (New York: Appleton & Co., 1878), 314.

25 Schaffer, *Forgotten Female Aesthetes*, 82.

26 Brown, *A Sense of Things*, 5.

27 Arthur Hayden, *By-Paths in Curio Collecting*, (London: T. Fisher Unwin Ltd., 1919), 26.

28 Moira Vincentelli, *Women and Ceramics: Gendered Vessels* (Manchester: Manchester University Press, 2000), 109.

29 Ibid.

30 Clarence Cook, *The House Beautiful, Essays on Beds and Tables, Stools and Candlestick*, (New York: Scribner, Armstrong and Co., 1877), 121.

31 Watson, *The Art of the House*, 37–38.

32 Robert W. Edis, *Decoration and Furniture of Town Houses A Series of Cantor Lectures Delivered before the Society of Arts, 1880, Amplified and Enlarged* (New York: Scribner and Welford, 1881), 122.

33 A German word, meaning a synthesis of the arts, making use of many media, now accepted in English as an aesthetic term.

34 Lewis F. Day, *Every-day Art: Short Essays on the Arts Not Fine* (London: Batsford, 1882), 213.

35 Jeremy Cooper, *Victorian and Edwardian Furniture and Interiors from the Gothic Revival to Art Nouveau* (London: Thames and Hudson, 1987), 117.

36 Anne Anderson, "*Chinamania*: Collecting Old Blue for the House Beautiful c. 1860–1900" in *Material Cultures, 174–1920: The Meanings and Pleasures of Collection*, eds. John Potvin and Alla Myzelev (Aldershot: Ashgate, 2009): 109–128.

37 Anne Anderson, "Coming out of the China Closet? Performance, identity and sexuality in the House Beautiful.", *Oriental Interiors*, ed. John Potvin (Aldershot: Ashgate), 136.

38 Henry Treffry Dunn, *Recollections of Dante Gabriel Rossetti and His Circle (Cheyne Walk Life)*, edited and annotated by Gale Pedrick (London: Elkin Mathews, 1904), 17–18.

39 Ibid., 36.

40 Ibid., 18.

41 Rosamund Marriot Watson, *The Art of the House* (London: George Bell & Sons, 1897), 90.

42 Cooper, *Victorian and Edwardian Furniture and Interiors*, 118.

43 Ibid., Figure 314, 138.

44 Watson, *The Art of the House*, 47.

45 Ibid., 150.

46 Susan Weber Soros, "Rediscovering H. W. Batley (1846–1932), British Aesthetic Movement Artist and Designer," *West 86th: A Journal of Decorative Arts, Design History and Material Culture*, 6:2, Spring-Summer 1999, 2–41.

47 Edis, *Decoration and Furniture of Town Houses*, 123.

48 Dunn, *Recollections*, 17–18.

49 Harry Quilter, "ART: *The Cornhill* on Drawing-Rooms," *The Spectator*, No. 2698, 13 March 1880, 335–36.

50 Ibid.

51 Charlotte Gere, *Nineteenth Century Decoration: the Art of the Interior* (New York: Harry N Abrams, 1989), 308.

52 John Ruskin, "Of Queen's Gardens" in *Sesame and Lilies* (London: Collins, 1910), 110.

53 Jacob von Falke, *Art in the House, Historical, Critical and Aesthetical Studies on the Decoration and Furnishing of the Dwelling*, translated

from the third German edition by Charles C. Perkin (Boston: L Prang and Company, 1878), 311.

54 Ibid., 318.

55 Schaffer, *Forgotten Female Aesthetes*, 76.

56 Ruskin, "Of Queen's Gardens," 91.

57 Ibid., 92.

58 Falke, *Art in the House*, 314–15.

59 David Dewing, *Home and Garden: Paintings and Drawings of English, Middle-class, Urban Domestic Spaces 1675–1914* (London: Geffrye Museum, 2003), 196.

60 Cook, *The House Beautiful*, 121.

61 Ibid.

62 Ibid., 123.

63 Ibid.

64 Charles Locke Eastlake, *Hints on Household Taste in Furniture, Upholstery and Other Details*, London: Longmans, Green & Co., 2nd edition, 1869), 138–44.

65 Moore, "The Collector," 978.

66 Mrs H. R. Haweis, (Mary Eliza) *The Art of Decoration* (London: Chatto and Windus, 1881), 3.

67 Eastlake, *Hints on Household Taste in Furniture*, 121.

68 Ibid.

69 Ibid.

70 Ibid.

71 Rev. William Loftie, *A Plea for Art in the House* (London: Macmillan & Co., 1877), 97–98.

72 Ibid., 22.

73 Ibid., 20.

74 Ibid., 27.

75 Cook, *The House Beautiful*, 187.

76 Marilynn Johnson, "Art Furniture Wedding the Beautiful to the Useful," in *In Pursuit of Beauty: Americans and the Aesthetic Movement*, ed. D. Bolger Burke et al., exhibition catalogue (New York: Metropolitan Museum of Art, 1987), 164.

77 Cook, *The House Beautiful*, 96.

78 Ibid., 95–96.

79 Ibid., 96.

80 Ibid., 96–97.

81 Ibid., 97.

82 Ibid., 98.

83 Ibid., 99–100.

84 Ibid., 100.

85 Ibid., 101.

86 Ibid., 102.

87 Ibid., 103.

88 Walter Pater, *The Renaissance, Studies in Art and Poetry* (Oxford and New York: Oxford University Press, 1990), 151–52.

89 Brown, *A Sense of Things*, 154.

90 James, *The Spoils of Poyton*, 248.

91 Ibid., 249–50.

92 Virginia Nicholson, *Among the Bohemians Experiments in Living 1900–1939* (London: Penguin, 2003), 118.

93 Nicholette Devas, *Two Flamboyant Fathers* (London: Hamish Hamilton Ltd., 1967) quoted ibid, p.118 .

94 Henry Wood Erving, "The Random Recollections of an Early Collector," *The Twenty-fifth Anniversary Meeting of the Walpole Society*, Walpole Society, 1935, 31.
95 Brown, *A Sense of Things*, 5.
96 Wilde, "The Artist as Critic," 1147.
97 Geoffrey Squire, "The Union of Persons of Cultivated Taste," in *Simply Stunning: The Pre-Raphaelite Art of Dressing*, ed. Geoffrey Squire (Cheltenham: Cheltenham Art Gallery and Museums, 1996), 11.

Works Cited

Allen, Grant. "The Philosophy of Drawing-Rooms," *Cornhill Magazine* 41 (March, 1880): 312–26.

Anderson, Anne "*Chinamania*: Collecting Old Blue for the House Beautiful c. 1860–1900." In *Material Cultures, 174–1920: The Meanings and Pleasures of Collection*, edited by John Potvin and Alla Myzelev, 109–28. Aldershot: Ashgate, 2009.

———. "Transatlantic Bric-à-Brac Hunters: The Pleasures of Antiquing c. 1870–1930," *Symbiosis: A Journal of Transatlantic Literary and Cultural Relations* 19, no. 1 (April 2015): 75–95.

———. "Coming out of the China Closet? Performance, identity and sexuality in the House Beautiful." In *Oriental Interiors*, edited by John Potvin, 127–44. Aldershot: Ashgate, 2015.

Batley, William Henry. *Series of Studies for Furniture, Decoration etc.* Designed and etched by H. W. Batley. London: Sampson Low, Marston, Searle & Rivington, 1883.

Brown, Bill. *A Sense of Things: The Object Matter of American Literature.* Chicago and London: The University of Chicago Press, 2003.

Coke, Desmond. *Confessions of an Incurable Collector.* London: Chapman & Hall, 1928.

Cook, Clarence. *The House Beautiful, Essays on Beds and Tables, Stools and Candlestick.* New York: Scribner, Armstrong and Co., 1877.

Cooper, Jeremy. *Victorian and Edwardian Furniture and Interiors from the Gothic Revival to Art Nouveau.* London: Thames and Hudson, 1987.

Day, Lewis F. *Every-day Art: Short Essays on the Arts Not Fine.* London: Batsford, 1882.

Devas, Nicholette. *Two Flamboyant Fathers.* London: Hamish Hamilton Ltd., 1967.

Dunn, Henry Treffry. *Recollections of Dante Gabriel Rossetti and His Circle (Cheyne Walk Life)*, edited and annotated by Gale Pedrick. London: Elkin Mathews, 1904.

Eastlake, Charles Locke. *Hints on Household Taste in Furniture, Upholstery and Other Details.* London: Longmans, Green & Co., 1869.

Edis, Robert W. *Decoration and Furniture of Town Houses a series of Cantor Lectures Delivered before the Society of Arts, 1880, Amplified and Enlarged.* New York: Scribner and Welford, 1881.

Erving, Henry Wood. "The Random Recollections of an Early Collector," *The Twenty-fifth Anniversary Meeting of the Walpole Society*, 27–43. Walpole Society, 1935.

Falke, Jacob von. *Art in the House, Historical, Critical and Aesthetical Studies on the Decoration and Furnishing of the Dwelling*, translated from the third German edition by Charles C. Perkins. Boston: L Prang and Company, 1878.

Gere, Charlotte. *Nineteenth Century Decoration: the Art of the Interior*. New York: Harry N Abrams, 1989.

Gere, Charlotte with Lesley Hoskins. *The House Beautiful Oscar Wilde and the Aesthetic Interior*. London: Lund Humphries and the Geffrye Museum, 2000.

Hall, Herbert Byng. *The Bric-à-Brac Hunter or Chapters on Chinamania*. London: Chatto and Windus, 1875.

Halttunen, Karen. "From Parlor to Living Room: Domestic Space, Interior Decoration and the Culture of Personality." In *Consuming Visions: Accumulation and Display of Goods in America, 1880–1920*, edited by S. J. Bronner, 157–90. New York and London: W.W. Norton & Company, 1989.

Hamilton, Walter. *The Aesthetic Movement in England*. London: Reeves and Turner, 1882.

Haweis, Mrs H.R. (Mary Eliza). *The Art of Decoration*. London: Chatto and Windus, 1881.

Hayden, Arthur. *By-Paths in Curio Collecting*. London: T. Fisher Unwin Ltd 1919.

Home and Garden: Paintings and Drawings of English, Middle-class, Urban Domestic Spaces 1675–1914. Exhibition catalogue edited by David Dewing. London: Geffrye Museum, 2003.

James, Henry. *The Spoils of Poynton, A London Life, The Chaperone*, 1–266. New York: Charles Scribner's Sons, 1908.

———. "Preface" in *The Spoils of Poynton, A London Life, The Chaperone*, v–xxiv. New York: Charles Scribner's Sons, 1908.

Johnson, Marilynn. "Art Furniture Wedding the Beautiful to the Useful." In *In Pursuit of Beauty: Americans and the Aesthetic Movement*. Exhibition catalogue edited by D. Bolger Burke *et al.*, 142–75. New York: Metropolitan Museum of Art, 1987.

Kahan, Alan S. *Liberalism in Nineteenth Century Europe: The Political Culture of Limited Suffrage*. London: Palgrave Macmillan, 2003.

Loftie, Rev William. *A Plea for Art in the House*. London: Macmillan & Co., 1877.

Moore, F. Frankfort. "The Collector," *The Woman At Home, Annie S. Swan's Magazine*, 5 (October 1897–September 1898): 974–987.

Nenadic, Stana. "Romanticism and the Urge to Consume in the First Half of the Nineteenth Century." In *Consumers and Luxury: Consumer Culture in Europe 1650–1850*, edited by Maxine Berg and Helen Clifford, 208–27. Manchester: Manchester University Press, 1999.

Nicholson, Virginia. *Among the Bohemians Experiments in Living 1900–1939*. London: Penguin, 2003.

Pater, Walter. *The Renaissance, Studies in Art and Poetry*. Oxford and New York: Oxford University Press, 2003.

Quilter, Harry. "ART: *The Cornhill* on Drawing-Rooms," *The Spectator*, No. 2698 (13 March 1880): 335–36.

Rohan, Thomas. *Old Beautiful*. London: Mills and Boon, 1926.

Ruskin, John. "Of Queen's Gardens," *Sesame and Lilies*, 95–158. London: Collins, 1910.

Saisselin, Rémy. *The Bourgeois and the Bibelot*. New Brunswick, New Jersey: Rutgers University Press, 1984.

Schaffer, Talia. *The Forgotten Female Aesthetes: Literary Culture in Late Victorian Britain*. Charlottesville and London: University of Virginia Press, 2000.

Soros, Susan Weber. "Rediscovering H. W. Batley (1846–1932), British Aesthetic Movement Artist and Designer". *West 86th: A Journal of Decorative Arts, Design History and Material Culture*, 6:2, Spring-Summer 1999: 2–41.

Squire, Geoffrey. "The Union of Persons of Cultivated Taste." In *Simply Stunning: The Pre-Raphaelite Art of Dressing*, edited by Geoffrey Squire, 7–12. Cheltenham: Cheltenham Art Gallery and Museums, 1996.

Vincentelli, Moira. *Women and Ceramics: Gendered Vessels*. Manchester: Manchester University Press, 2000.

Watson, Rosamund Mariott. *The Art of the House*. London: George Bell and Sons, 1897.

Wilde, Oscar. "The House Beautiful", *Collins Complete Works of Oscar Wilde, Centenary Edition*, 913–25, Glasgow: Harper Collins, 1999.

———. "The Critic as Artist," *Collins Complete Works of Oscar Wilde, Centenary Edition*, 1108–55. Glasgow: Harper Collins, 1999.

Wilson, James Grant. "About Bric-à-brac." *Art Journal*, 46, New York: Appleton & Co (October 1878): 313–15.

3 Rossetti's Things

The Artist and his Accessories

Thad Logan

Dante Gabriel Rossetti was famous during his lifetime, and in the first decades after his death in 1882, for his unique collection of curious things, and for paintings of women on which, in the words of biographer Henry Currie Marillier, he

> lavished... all the wealth of his fine imagination... surrounding them with quaint and beautiful accessories in the way of stamped leather or tapestry backgrounds, richly embroidered robes, inlaid pieces of furniture, jewels, vases, ornaments and flowers such as he alone knew how to select and paint.[1]

In his life and in his art, Rossetti had an intense relationship with material things, a relationship that was both like and unlike that of other Victorian householders and other Victorian artists. This essay investigates that relationship. I begin with a detailed look at the things Rossetti gathered around himself at Tudor House (also sometimes known as Queen's House), his home in Chelsea, then move to consider the 'accessories' in his artwork, creating an inventory of specific items in paintings and drawings and attempting to identify originals of some virtual objects. I go on to show how Rossetti's treatment of things differs from that of other Victorian painters and conclude by discussing what the things represented by Rossetti actually do in and for his art.

In 1862 Rossetti assumed the lease of 16 Cheyne Walk, Chelsea, and turned, as Elizabeth Helsinger has observed, to 'the task that was to absorb much of his time and money for the rest of the decade: furnishing and decorating the large house.'[2] It might be fairly said that he originated the genre of the 'artistic home,' which would be popularized after his death.[3] Contemporaries were impressed, or disturbed, by the sense of entering an intensely personal and visually elaborate space, an effect created by the multiplicity of old and unusual things that had obviously not been acquired through the usual pathways in which consumer goods circulated in Victorian Britain.[4] In his study of Rossetti's art, Ford

Madox Hueffer explained 'that he had for many years a quite charming delight in anything rich and strange,' and that 'at the fine house in Chelsea, Rossetti... let his enthusiasms have full scope.'[5]

Perhaps the most compelling witness to the extraordinary world of Tudor House was Henry Treffry Dunn, who as a young man came to work as Rossetti's studio assistant. Dunn recalled that on his first visit he was 'ushered into one of the prettiest, and one of the most curiously-furnished and old-fashioned sitting rooms that it had ever been my lot to see.'[6] Dunn noticed, among other things, 'mirrors of all shapes, sizes, and designs,' a mantelpiece he described as 'a most original compound of Chinese black-lacquered panels, bearing designs of birds, animals, flowers and fruit in gold relief,' and 'an old English china cupboard, inside of which was displayed a quantity of Spode ware.' Moving among blue and white china, mirrors, mandolins, and dulcimers, Dunn seems to have been particularly impressed by chests, boxes, and cabinets, noting, for instance, 'a well-stocked Chippendale bookcase,' William's 'special tobacco box,' and 'a massive panelled oak mantelpiece... fitted up with numerous shelves and cupboard-like recesses, all filled with a medley of brass repoussée dishes, blue china vases filled with peacock feathers, oddly-fashioned early English and foreign candlesticks, Chinese monstrosities in bronze, and various other curiosities.'[7]

Rossetti was ahead of his time in amassing what we would now call antiques. As Marillier noted, 'Bric-a-brac was not of much account in England when Rossetti first began rummaging in the dealers' shops for old and battered cabinets, Chippendale chairs, carved oak panels, "hawthorn" jars, and an infinite variety of brass implements, chandeliers, sconces, mirrors, and vases of antique and comparatively neglected types.'[8] According to Rossetti's brother William,

> in early youth Dante Rossetti had not any habit of buying artistic articles of furniture, or attractive bric-a-brac of any kind; in fact, he had no money to spend for such purposes... [but] as the time was approaching for removing to Cheyne Walk, he launched out upon purchasing things here and there to a large extent... He found in Buckingham Street, Strand, an old gentleman named Minister... who had a really big stock of really capital old-fashioned furniture... Rossetti regarded him as a 'Minister of Grace,' and bought a number of things from him. Hence he proceeded to further purchases; and soon the house began to fill with Chinese tables and chairs, Dutch tiles, Flemish and oriental and African curtains and draperies, looking-glasses and mirrors of the seventeenth and eighteenth centuries, a chandelier here and another there, and numerous knick-knacks of whatever kind. He had a particular liking for convex round-shaped mirrors.[9]

In his journal, William recalls a visit made with his brother to 'old and out of the way shops' in Antwerp in 1863, where they 'bought a good number of things: brass pots, gold ornaments as worn by peasants, a large pot with blue figures of birds, etc., a Dutch Bible with old prints, [and] some valence for a bed.' At about this time, Rossetti began his famous collection of blue and white china; according to William, 'he formed a very fine display... which made his big sunlit drawing room a sight to see.'[10]

At the end of the 1860s, Rossetti described himself as having once had 'a mania for buying bric-a-brac' and the rooms of Tudor House were indeed full of the things he acquired during this decade.[11] After his death in 1882, auctioneers T.G. Wharton, Martin & Co. held a sale of his effects that went on for three days; the catalogue they prepared listed 680 lots and is one of the best sources we have of the extraordinary array of objects in Rossetti's collection.[12] Perhaps the most interesting part of the catalogue for those who are interested in how Rossetti's things appear in his artwork are the lists of jewellery and ornamental objects to be sold on the second day of the auction. There are 37 lots of the former and 72 of the latter (some lots containing more than one item). Here is a sample of some of the objects stored in the cabinets and drawers of Tudor House:

Fine gold neck chain in velvet lined morocco case
Indian carved comb, Chinese ditto, and Indian salad fork
Bronze spoon, items for chatelaine, a rosary, antique brass purse
Small German prayer book with silver clasps and corners, and amber box
Silver gilt scent case inlaid with turquoise and precious stones, formerly the property of the Countess of Blessington
Egyptian armlets and a gold pin
Seven Indian necklaces, gold, silver and coral, and Chinese fan
Velvet girdle, metal chains, and Indian brass spice box
Sundry finger rings and various items
Brass urn, mounted with elephant handles
Plated 3-light candelabra, fitted with serpentine branches
A 17 in. marble figure of an Egyptian mummy
A suit of armour
A 16 in. copper bowl, on claw feet and griffin head handles
Blue china dish, and a jug mounted with curiously shaped handles
A very curious old steel water bottle of about the time of Cromwell
A silver mounted highly ornate yataghan, in rich silver sheath
Small Irish harp (18th century)
An antique lute, and an Indian musical instrument.

Julie Codell has cogently argued that in its formidable array of old and unusual objects, Tudor house was very different from the ordinary middle-class home.[13] Certainly, there was nothing quite like it in Rossetti's lifetime, at least, and we can tell from the responses of contemporaries that it did not represent mainstream taste. On the other hand, for middle- and upper-middle-class Victorian households, the acquisition of a large number of furnishings and ornaments was by no means unusual, as I've noted elsewhere.[14] Even authorities associated with design reform, who critiqued the thoughtless amassing of consumer goods, believed in a 'more is more' approach to domestic decoration. Lucy Orrinsmith, for instance, tells her audience that '"what shall be added next?" should be a constantly recurring thought,' and goes on to suggest 'a Persian tile, an Algerian flower-pot, an old Flemish cup, a piece of Nankin blue, an Icelandic spoon, a Japanese cabinet, a Chinese fan... each in its own way beautiful and interesting.'[15] Rossetti's evident delight in filling his home with things – even an eclectic jumble of them – did not necessarily distinguish him from other reasonably affluent Victorians, who also were concerned to 'fill up every corner with something,' as Hueffer said of Rossetti with reference to his 'medieval' watercolours.[16]

It is Henry Dunn who reminds us that there was a utilitarian aspect to the artist's habit of laying up treasures for himself on earth, noting that 'anything... Rossetti saw in his rambles that might be of possible use to him for a picture he would buy.'[17] Among Dunn's descriptions of his early visit to Tudor House, one stands out because it shows us the collector actively engaging with his things, and thus reminds us that they were often put to use in his creative work:

> Rossetti was hastily pulling out drawer after drawer from an old cabinet that stood in one of the recesses of the room. He was searching for something suitable to paint round the neck of the girl in his picture *The Loving Cup*, and before him lay a rare store of necklaces, featherwork, Japanese crystals, and knick-knacks of all kinds, sufficient to stock a small window.[18]

Some years later, when Rossetti was spending time alone, or in the company of Jane Morris, at Kelmscott Manor (jointly rented with William Morris from 1872 to 1874), he frequently wrote to Dunn asking that things be sent to him there. These letters tell us how important his things were to Rossetti and what a good memory he seems to have had for exactly where individual items were located in his not-particularly-tidy home. In one letter, for instance, Dunn was asked to pack up 'one of the two low folding firescreens covered with peacock feathers under glass,' 'that large purple blue jar which Emma broke,' 'a sort of blue green garden pillar of glazed ware which I fancy may be lying in the lower part of the corner cupboard in the studio,' and '[a] little blue green pot with black stand which is on the drawers in the first floor bedroom.'[19] The postscript to this letter, written early in 1874, reads 'As a kernel to the parcel please introduce a candlestick which is somewhere I think in the drawing room.'

What seems to be an obsession with having objects sent to him at Kelmscott may in part be traced to habits formed long before, when, as a member of the Pre-Raphaelite Brotherhood, Rossetti (along with William Holman Hunt and John Millais) determined to draw and paint from life rather than follow the schematized conventions of academic art. And of course, it would have been standard practice for Victorian artists to have what were commonly known as props, as well as live models, in their studios, to which they made continual visual references as they worked. Even so, Rossetti's insistence on having the thing itself literally present to him seems particularly pronounced and can perhaps only be explained with reference to a profound psychic need to fill the space around him with material things of his own choice.

Roger Frye, writing on the watercolours of the 1850s for *The Burlington Magazine*, noticed how important the paraphernalia of his romantic visions were to Rossetti, and went so far as to argue that it was in painting these material things, rather than human figures, that his real genius for visual design appeared. As a modernist, Frye was most concerned with the formal aspects of the art object, and to his eye

> Rossetti's form became clear, definite and truly expressive almost exactly in proportion as he was concerned with the accessories of his drama...Take, for instance, 'The Chapel before the Lists.' It is clear that... the drama gained for him intensely in value from the fact that his lovers were surrounded by all the objects of mediaeval chivalry. One can see with what delight he has dwelt on all the possible furniture of such a scene, with what love he has elaborated and embroidered every nook and corner.[20]

> Frye refers later in his article to 'all the little figures and objects with which [Rossetti's] fancy loved to play': not only do we see these make their appearance in his art well before the 1860s, but – and this will be no surprise to those familiar with the Pre-Raphaelite love of visual detail – they are already very much a part of his earliest work as a Pre-Raphaelite brother.

To begin a closer look at the things in Rossetti's artwork, let us consider two versions of *Dante Drawing an Angel on The First Anniversary of the Death of Beatrice*. The first, a pen and ink drawing made in 1848–1849, is signed 'Dante G. Rossetti P.R.B.,' and was given to Millais (Figure 3.1).

Figure 3.1 Dante Gabriel Rossetti, *First Anniversary of the Death of Beatrice*, 1849. Pen and Ink, 15 3/4 × 12 7/8 in. Photo © Birmingham Museums Trust.

It shows Dante at home, drawing an angel and presumably thinking of Beatrice, when he is surprised by sympathetic visitors. Quite a few accessories are part of the composition, including a musical instrument, an hourglass, a crucifix, a carved wooden chair, fabric hangings at the door and window, and what appears to be a necklace on the principal

Figure 3.2 Dante Gabriel Rossetti, *Dante drawing an Angel on the Anniversary of Beatrice's Death*, 1853. Watercolour, 16 1/2 × 24 in. Image © Ashmolean Museum, University of Oxford.

visitor. The more elaborate watercolour version of 1853 adds to these a lemon tree in a ceramic pot, a water cistern, basin, and hand towel, some kind of cabinet with inlaid metal fittings, glass bottles with coloured liquids, a metal fixture on the wall by Dante's table, and an unusual convex mirror (Figure 3.2).

A list of objects that appear in Rossetti's work throughout his career is shown below; it is perhaps surprising to see that nearly all these things are represented in the two versions of *Dante Drawing an Angel*.

Bells
Blue and White 'Pots'
Books
Bottles
Boxes
Broom
Brush and/or Comb
Cabinet with Metal Fittings
Candleholders
Carved Wooden Furniture
Censers

Decorative Ceramics
   Dark Blue or Green Round/Hexagonal pot
   Large pots for fruit trees
Fabric/Drapery
Hourglasses
Jewels/Jewellery
Mirrors
Musical Instruments
   Lute, Harp, Violin, Dulcimer, etc.
Oil Lamps
Plates
Statuary/Figures
Tiles
Trays
Vases (Glass and Ceramic)
Water Ewer (Cistern) and Basin

While this is not an exhaustive list of all things in all paintings, a general inventory of the types of objects that appear and reappear can help us move toward a more specific understanding of what these objects are and how and when they appear. Such an inventory can be useful, for instance, in paradigmatic analyses that track objects in Rossetti's work over time. An early version of this kind of analysis is Marillier's account of the distinctive spiral-shaped pearl ornament which first appeared in *Princess Sabra Drawing the Lot* (1861).[21] We could also observe, if only in passing, that a cylindrical glass vase figures in *The Girlhood of Mary Virgin* (1849), *Hist, Said Kate the Queen* (1849–1851), and *The Blue Silk Dress* (1866). Carved wooden furniture also appears in multiple works, from among the earliest (*Girlhood*) to the oil version of *Mariana* (1870). A low, Middle Eastern style oil lamp that is prominent in *Prosperpina* (1874) is one of the very few accessories in *The Annunciation* (1849–1853). Most strikingly, perhaps, a water basin (usually with a cistern above it and a hand towel nearby) can be seen in the 1853 *Dante Drawing an Angel*, the pen and ink version of *Mariana in the South* (1856–1857), *Lucrezia Borgia* (1860), two versions of *Washing Hands* (1865), *The Roman Widow* (1864), and *La Bella Mano* (1875).

   We can't, of course, know what led Rossetti to return again and again to certain objects, or kinds of object, or to certain colours or shapes of things, or what led him to choose a clear glass vase over a ceramic one (or vice versa). Perhaps an item provided a needed element of design, evoked a certain sensory experience, suggested a culturally shared meaning, or had some purely idiosyncratic appeal.[22] We can, however, investigate whether the objects acquired, stored, and displayed at Tudor House became part of the virtual collection in the paintings and drawings. As it turns out, the relationship between things in Rossetti's art and things in his life is a complex and sometimes surprising one. Many of the accessories in his early works were in fact drawn not from life but from the work of other artists, in particular those of northern Renaissance masters Albrecht Dürer and Jan Van Eyck.

Many scholars have noted the importance of these painters to the Pre-Raphaelites in general and to Rossetti in particular.[23] In her biography of Rossetti, Jan Marsh writes that he bought and studied etchings by Dürer, and that for the watercolour version of the *First Anniversary of the Death of Beatrice* 'he copied background details of a water urn, towel and brush from Dürer's *Birth of the Virgin* (1503–1504).'[24] In fact, what Marsh calls an urn is actually a round cistern affixed to the wall above a basin, and what we see here is the first iteration of a motif which will recur many times in Rossetti's work, as noted above. A close look at the print will show many other details that will also become part of Rossetti's repertoire, including candleholders, books, a bottle, a pitcher, and a wooden chest with metal fittings.

There are several other 'Flemish Primitive' works that Rossetti saw during his trip to the continent with William Holman Hunt in 1849 that made a deep impression on him. For instance, there was the Van der Weyden *Annunciation* (1434) in the Louvre, whose details include a bottle of clear liquid, what appears to be a blue and white pot with lilies, several interesting pieces of metalwork, carved wooden furniture, a wooden cabinet with metal fittings, and two oranges. Van Eyck's Ghent altarpiece (1432), which Rossetti would have seen on his trip to Belgium with William Holman Hunt, depicts magnificent brocade fabrics, jewels (including many pearls), and elaborate, figural woodcarving, as well as blue and white tiles. Memling's diptych *Virgin and Child with Maarten van Nieuwenhove* (1487) appears to have been the source of the dark, oval-shaped convex mirror in the 1853 version of First Anniversary of the Death of Beatrice.[25] Of course there is a great deal more that might be said about the influence of these fifteenth-century paintings on the young artists who formed the Pre-Raphaelite Brotherhood, but my point is that the objects Rossetti saw in them, along with those in the Dürer prints he had access to, formed the basis of a certain vocabulary of things that stayed remarkably consistent throughout his life, despite dramatic changes in his style – from the early 'angular' works, to the small, jewel-like watercolours, to the larger works in oil. It is this vocabulary that he begins to use in 1849. This explains the fact, noted above, that a list of accessories in the two versions of *The First Anniversary of the Death of Beatrice* constitutes a nearly complete inventory of the kinds of things that appear in all the later paintings.

To make this claim, however, is not to deny that real objects also were models for those in Rossetti's artwork; we have, as I've indicated above, indisputable evidence that Rossetti found it of enormous importance, especially in the 1860s and 1870s, to have things literally in front of him as he worked. Many of these came from the collection at Tudor House, and since we have an inventory of at least some of this collection in the auction catalogue, as well as other textual (and some visual) documentation of it, it is possible to identify many of the objects Rossetti painted. Much fine work has been already been done in this way by comparing the jewels in the paintings to those listed in the catalogue compiled for the sale of Rossetti's effects, or to those in the May Morris bequest to the Victorian and Albert Museum, which contains pieces given to Jane Morris by Rossetti.[26] Matching other kinds of virtual objects with their real-life counterparts is more challenging, for reasons I'll discuss in a moment, but we can make some positive or at least probable identifications.

The plates shown reflected in a round mirror in *La Bella Mano*, for instance, as well as those lined up behind the central figure in *The Loving Cup* (1867), are almost certainly those kept in Rossetti's bedroom. These were described by Dunn in his *Recollections*, we may recall, as 'a medley of brass repoussé dishes' which, with 'various other curiosities,' filled 'a massive panelled oak mantelpiece.'[27] We also have a sketch by Dunn of this part of the room, including the bed and its antique hangings, that is replicated in almost exact detail in the mirrored image seen in *La Bella Mano*.[28] It seems quite likely that the casket seen in Rossetti's *Pandora* (1868–1871) was based on the 'brass ecclesiastical casket, inlaid with stones, surrounded by figures in recess,' that is part of lot 397, and that the lamp in *Mnemonsyne* (1880) is the 'Indian oil lamp that is included in lot 432 along with a 'Pair of brass candlesticks... a drinking cup, an incense casket, and a pyx.' The unusual box we see on the mantelpiece in *Marigolds* (1873) might well have been adapted from the 'very finely-designed bronze Chinese casket supported on four pillars, the top surmounted by a bronze griffin' (lot 281), and we can probably be more certain that the lady in *Fazio's Mistress* (1863) sits in a chair modelled on that described in lot 101 (from the master bedroom) as 'a high backed easy chair upholstered in stamped green velvet.' While it is not mentioned in the catalogue, the extraordinary owl-feather fan wielded in *Monna Vanna* (1866) and also seen in *Veronica Veronese* (1872) can be identified as that in the watercolour that Dunn made of Rossetti's sitting room at Tudor House.

The letters to Dunn, always a valuable source for an investigation of Rossetti's things, also highlight the challenges involved. Even Dunn, who presumably knew the collection as well as anyone, frequently irritated his employer by mistaking the item that was requested. In a letter from July of 1873, for instance, Rossetti snaps 'You have now sent me an old rag of a figured silk counterpane. I asked distinctly for a linen Indian counterpane covered with a light yellowish or brownish pattern in embroidery.' In fact, he had actually written 'I want something of a spotted russet colour – somewhat like an Indian "bandana" handkerchief...

something yellow and red and amounting to a sort of russet.'[29] The point here is not that Rossetti was extraordinarily demanding in these matters – although this was, in fact, the case and he bombarded not only Dunn but Charles Howell and Murray Marks with requests – but that material things are often surprisingly difficult to describe in a language in such a way as to preclude confusion with similar things. This, it seems to me, is one of the difficulties in matching items in the auction catalogue with their representations in paintings. For instance, there are in the paintings several versions of a round object made of pierced metalwork that seems to be an incense burner, but is this the 'perforated brass casket' of lot 433, the 'incense burner' in the same lot, the 'incense casket' of lot 432, or one of the pair of 'fine brass incense burners' in lot 380. Or perhaps none of the above?

Even if we had photographs of all the objects in the Tudor House, there is another potential source of confusion. Despite Rossetti's insistence on having the thing itself on hand in the studio, he was perfectly content to make changes in his representation of an object when it suited him. Thus the censer in *Joan of Arc* (1863), though clearly very similar to that in *Fazio's Mistress* and *Sybilla Palmifera* (1866), seems to sit on taller legs. We know that the ornate Chinese hair ornaments that appeared in *The Beloved* (1865–1866) were in fact not red but green and blue, and, moreover, that the model for the young African girl in attendance was actually an African boy.[30] The following anecdote about the making of *La Bella Mano* offers compelling evidence of Rossetti's inconsistency in terms of drawing or painting from life. I have taken it from *Murray Marks and his Friends*, as cited by Virginia Surtees in her *Catalogue Raisonée* of the works of Rossetti.

> The toilet caster [on the table to the left of the lady] was also lent by [Marks]. He said it was silver, but Rossetti insisted, greatly to his indignation, in having it gilt. He tried to persuade him it was quite easy to paint it as a golden one though it was silver, and that it would not only be a waste of money to have it gilt, but would lessen the value of the castor itself. Rossetti appeared to agree to this idea, but one day, when Marks went to the studio, he found to his annoyance that the castor had been gilded...The golden basin... was brass, although Rossetti has painted it as though it were gold.[31]

If Rossetti could paint a brass basin as though it were gold, why could he not have done the same with the silver caster? The curious workings of Rossetti's psyche are beyond the scope of this essay, of course; my point is simply that identifying objects in his paintings is complicated by several factors. We can't necessarily be sure, first of all, that they were drawn from life rather than from other artworks, we can't always easily match verbal descriptions in the letters or the auction catalogue with specific items they refer to, and we can rarely say with absolute certainty that a given object in the real world has found its way untransformed onto the canvas.

Shortly after Rossetti's death, Sidney Colvin wrote of his large works in oil: 'For the combination of keen and flashing intensity with mystery and delightfulness of quality, his paintings of tissues and jewels and flowers at this period stands, it is no extravagance to say, alone in art.'[32] Brilliant as Rossetti's treatment of such things was, he was hardly the only Victorian to lavish attention upon objects. There are significant differences, however, between Rossetti's things and those of other Victorian painters. Take, for example, Frederick Leighton, who was also associated with the aesthetic movement. Leighton, both in style and subject matter, invoked classicism, which in its various incarnations discourages attention to detail in favour of attention to the overarching design. (Hence John Ruskin's attempt to 'rescue' the detail appears under the sign of classicism's opposite, the Gothic.[33]) From their earliest days, the Pre-Raphaelite Brotherhood insisted on the importance of the detail in painting, thus forcing a break with the neo-classical principles codified by Sir Joshua Reynolds – and winning Ruskin as their champion. While Leighton's paintings can be compared with Rossetti's work in the mid-1860s, insofar as both are producing images of beautiful women for those images' sake, it is only Rossetti who, within those canvases, pays real attention to material things as things in themselves, giving them almost equal time with the figures he represents. In fact, as more than one critic has pointed out, the figure/ ground distinction can become destabilized in Rossetti's work. Nicolette Gray, for instance, noted as early as 1945 that 'the separation of his figures [from their backgrounds] has been an arbitrary convenience: both pictorially and imaginatively they form a unity.'[34]

It might be argued that the more appropriate artists to consider here, in relation to the representation of things, are Victorian genre painters such as William Powell Frith and Robert Martineau, who took great pains to produce detailed images of objects as part of their panoramic or anecdotal representations of Victorian life. In contrast to these painters, however, Rossetti was never interested in the everyday life of a Victorian household, whether that life was lived in the palaces of the very wealthy, the cluttered and comfortable nests of the middle classes, or the idealized cottages of agricultural labourers. Just as most of Rossetti's literary works are a world away from the mimetic realism of Dickens or George Eliot, so the representations of objects in his paintings do not hold a mirror up to the world of ordinary things, unless we conceive that mirror to be a magic one. Furthermore, while his subjects often bear some relation to figures of myth, legend, or romance, Rossetti's works ultimately have little narrative content. Unlike things in the works of Martineau, Frith, Hunt, Augustus Egg, and others, Rossetti's things are not deployed to help tell a story.

To say this is also to argue that iconographic readings of Rossetti's things are problematic. As a young man, of course, he clearly was fascinated, along with Hunt and Millais, by the way common objects could appear in quattrocento paintings as signs pointing to moral or spiritual truths. Using either traditional Christian iconology or a Victorian language of flowers to read later works, however, should be met with some scepticism. It seems to me unlikely, for instance, that the lemon tree and iris surrounding the sumptuous beauty in *La Bella Mano* as she chooses her jewellery are really, as has been suggested, symbols of the virgin. And indeed we have William Michael Rossetti's word, in *Dante Gabriel Rossetti as Designer and Writer*, that his brother 'had no sympathy with any downright allegory.'[35]

Two other Victorian artists, Frederick Sandys and William Holman Hunt, also paint things with the kind of fascinated attention that we find in Rossetti; I would argue that it is just what those two have in common – an abiding interest in the emblematic or symbolic resonance of objects – that makes their things quite different from Rossetti's. Hunt was famous for his use of 'natural' symbols and his conscious attempt to present spiritual realities through a realistic presentation of the material world.[36] For Hunt, obsessive attention to the precisely detailed material thing was part of his commitment to truth. In his discussion of Hunt's *Finding Christ in the Temple at Jerusalem* (1860), George Frederic Stephens notes approvingly that Hunt 'not only actually went to Jerusalem to obtain the best models for a Scriptural subject, and get the true character of costume and accessories from the best available source, but studied with earnestness all the history and recorded facts that bore, even indirectly, upon his subject.... We should need to write a bulky volume to illustrate fully all the recondite and diversified labours which the artist has brought to bear upon the accessories of this work.'[37] In fact, Hunt's things, in painting after painting, work exactly as Ford Madox Brown had argued they should do, to create a kind of reality effect through their informed representation of 'the character of the times and the habits of the people.'[38] Now, whatever Rossetti's obsessions with obtaining exactly the right fabrics, flowers, and castors, I think we can agree that the note struck here is a very different one: for Rossetti, what mattered about objects was visual and emotional, not archaeological.

I would argue, in fact, that many critics, Victorian and contemporary, who talk of Rossetti's sensuality have not taken it seriously – or literally – enough: the term has been used as a euphemism for eroticism, but in fact, it's sensory perception itself and the things (including bodies) that trigger or evoke it, that are important to Rossetti as an artist. Claims that what really mattered to Rossetti was mental or ideational are difficult to sustain, at least in his visual work. The *Rossetti Archive*, for instance, in its introduction to the pictures, approvingly cites T. Martin Wood to the effect that what Rossetti wanted most was 'to attain in art not an imitation of life but an expression of his ideas about it.'[39] The question of imitating life is, of course, a thorny one, but to say that what he most wanted to express were 'ideas' seems to me finally wrong-headed. It was Walter Pater, after all, who summed up Rossetti's achievement by saying that 'like Dante, he knows no region of spirit which shall not be sensuous also, or material.'[40] This is not to say that connotations, associations, and even a certain kind of symbolism do not attend upon the objects depicted in his drawings, paintings, and watercolours. It is only to say that Rossetti's art does not have the kind of paraphrasable meaning that is implied in the notion that it was a vehicle for the expression of ideas. Wood himself, read in context, follows Pater and makes the following point:

> in his art things seem to have about them the meaning lent them by an imagination that spiritualized objective things so that they seem there in essence only and rendered with a sympathy that shows how alive to the significance of outward beauty Rossetti was, and how his own time and every-day surroundings were fused and blent with his most far-reaching imaginings.[41]

The works create an intense sensory experience for the viewer and imply that the artist was himself engaged in some version of such an experience.[42] Yet even in the large oil paintings of the 1860s, in which objects frame the face and torso of the central figure, and in which flowers and mirrors and *objets d'art* function almost as jewels to enhance that figure, things are not merely what William Rossetti called 'adjuncts.'[43] They are, perhaps, something like charms, however.[44] In his discussion of Rossetti's sonnet on Giorgione's *Venetian Pastoral*, George Landow speaks of the 'bliss of the moment's beauty,' and it's to help create such moments – replete and intense, but not reducible to a 'meaning,' that Rossetti marshals his extensive visual vocabulary of things.[45] And if Rossetti's images of things give us a purely formal pleasure in arrangements of shape and colour, line and volume, as Roger Frye understood, we do not have to sacrifice another kind of pleasure, that of recognizing the images as representations of particular objects, with all the associations they trail in their wake as well as the sensory experiences they evoke: the tang of a lemon, say, or the softness of a feather. Like the 'kissed mouth' of Fanny Cornforth as immortalized in *Boca Baciata* (1860) that 'loses not its sweetness,' these curious and lovely things are not used up but offer themselves again and again.[46]

Rossetti's things work visually to create potent images, and in doing so they often create a mood of what Charles Baudelaire, in 'L'Invitation au Voyage,' called 'luxe, calme, et volupté.'[47] I am hardly the first to think of Baudelaire in connection with Rossetti, but I will conclude with an idea suggested by his poem 'Correspondences,' in which Baudelaire explores the potential of material things to transmit a powerful yet untranslatable meaning.[48] The symbolic potential of objects to speak to the spirit is one which Rossetti teases out as well, yet his work is obviously very different from that of a Symbolist painter like George Watts, who once said 'I paint ideas, not things.'[49] Rossetti painted things, not ideas, but those things can seem strangely rich and mysterious, with a kind of 'arduous fullness' like that of his sonnets. Bruno Latour, among others involved in what has been called the New Materialism (including Jane Bennett in *Vibrant Matter*), has mounted a persuasive case against a worldview in which there is a constitutive and unbridgeable divide between inert matter on the one hand and mind or spirit on the other.[50] It is no surprise that Rossetti, who more or less gave us William Blake, intuitively grasped the 'vibrancy' of matter, and created artworks in which his things, like his figures, seem to have a secret inner life, an interiority that we can just glimpse, but never fully enter into, nor possess.

Notes

1 Henry Currie Marillier, *Dante Gabriel Rossetti: An Illustrated Memorial* (London: George Bell and Sons, 1904), 131.
2 Elizabeth Helsinger, *Poetry and the Pre-Raphaelite Arts* (New Haven and London: Yale University Press, 2008), 180.
3 See Mary Eliza Joy Haweis, *Beautiful Houses: Being a Description of Certain Well-known Artistic Houses* (London: Sampson, Low, Marston, Searle, and Rivingon, 1882), and Frederic George Stephens, *Artists At Home, Photographed by J.P. Mayall* (New York: Appleton, 1884).
4 Henry James, for one, was not amused, writing to Charles Eliot Norton that

> the rarest hour of all perhaps, or at least the strangest, strange verily to the pitch of the sinister, was a vision ... of D. G. Rossetti in the vernal dusk of Queen's House Chelsea, among his pictures, and his poetry, and his whole dainty 'esthetic.'
> Henry James, *Autobiography*, ed. Frederick W. Dupree
> (New York: Criterion Books, 1956), 515

5 Ford Madox Hueffer, *Rossetti: A Critical Essay on His Art* (London: Duckworth, 1902), 59. For an excellent discussion of Tudor House and Rossetti's things in life and in art, see Jessica Feldman, "Modernism's Bric-a-brac," *Modernism/Modernity* 8, no. 3 (2001), 453–70.
6 Henry Treffry Dunn, *Recollections of Dante Gabriel Rossetti and His Circle (Cheyne Walk Life)*, ed. Gale Pedrick (London: Elkin Matthews, 1904), 17–18.
7 Ibid., 18–24, 35.
8 Marillier, *Dante Gabriel Rossetti: An Illustrated Memorial*, 80.
9 William Michael Rossetti, *Some Reminiscences of William Michael Rossetti*, Vol. I (New York: Charles Scribner's Sons, 1906), 275–76.
10 William Michael Rossetti, *Dante Gabriel Rossetti: His Family Letters, With a Memoir*, Vol. I (London: Ellis and Elvey, 1895), 263. For a thorough

and provocative discussion of blue and white china, see Anne Anderson, "'Fearful Consequences ... of Living Up to One's Teapot,'" *Victorian Literature and Culture* 37, no. 1 (2009), 219–54.

11 Letter to George Rae, 21 August 1869. *The Correspondence of Dante Gabriel Rossetti*, Vol. 4, ed. William E. Fredeman (Cambridge: D.S. Brewer, 2002), 241.

12 T.E. Wharton, Martin & Co., *16 Cheyne Walk, Chelsea: The Valuable Contents of the Residence of Dante Gabriel Rossetti, (Deceased), To Be Sold By Auction* (London: T.E. Wharton, Martin & Co., 1882).

13 See Julie Codell's argument that Rossetti's domestic space constituted a critique of commodity culture. "Displaying Aestheticism's Bric-a-Brac: Rossetti's Material and Virtual Goods," *Palaces of Art: Whistler and the Art Worlds of Aestheticism*, Lee Glazer and Linda Merrill, eds. (Washington, DC: Smithsonian Institution Scholarly Press, 2013), 119–31. See also "Rossetti as a Collector" in Julien Treuherz, Elizabeth Prettejohn, and Edwin Becker, eds. *Dante Gabriel Rossetti* (Zwolle, Amsterdam, and Liverpool: Wanders Publishers, the Van Gogh Museum, the Walker Museum, 2003), 229–32.

14 Thad Logan, *The Victorian Parlour: A Cultural Study* (Cambridge: Cambridge University Press, 2001).

15 Lucy Orrinsmith, *The Drawing Room: Its Decorations and Furniture* (London: Macmillan, 1878), 132–3.

16 Hueffer, 34.

17 Dunn, 29. William Rossetti also observed that his brother made purchases with an eye to using them the paintings. *Some Reminiscences*, Vol. I, 275–76.

18 Dunn, 27.

19 Henry Dunn lived for many years at Tudor House: after his death, a number of his letters passed into the hands of Mrs. Theodore Watts Dunton, and eventually from her estate to the National Art Library at the Victoria and Albert Museum. As reproduced, with commentary, by Gale Pedrick in *No Peacocks Allowed: Dante Gabriel Rossetti and His Circle* (Carbondale IL: Southern Illinois University Press, 1964) the letters give us a unique look at Rossetti's things. My examples are taken from Pedric, 171.

20 Roger Frye, "Rossetti's Water Colours of 1857," *The Burlington Magazine* 29, no.129 (1916), 100.

21 Marillier, 132.

22 For a discussion of objects in Pre-Raphaelite paintings see Marcia Werner, *Pre-Raphaelite Painting and Nineteenth-Century Realism* (Cambridge: Cambridge University Press, 2005).

23 For more on the influence of Northern Renaissance artists on the PRB and on Rossetti in particular, see Alison Smith, "Revival and Reformation: The Aims and Ideals of the Pre-Raphaelite Brotherhood," in *Pre-Raphaelite Painting Techniques 1848–1856*, Joyce H. Townsend, Jacqueline Ridge, and Stephen Hackney, eds. (London: Tate Publishing, 2001). Elizabeth Helsinger also discusses this topic at length in "Acts of Attention," Chapter 2 of *Poetry and the Pre-Raphaelite Arts*.

24 Jan Marsh, *Dante Gabriel Rossetti, Painter and Poet* (London: Weidenfeld and Nicolson, 1999), 168.

25 See George Landow, Dante Gabriel Rossetti's "For a Virgin and Child, by Hans Memling," from *Replete with Meaning: William Holman Hunt and Typological Symbolism*, online at *The Victorian Web* www.victorianweb.org/painting/whh/replete/hans.html.

26 Important discussions of jewellery and accessories in Rossetti's work include Shirley Bury, "Rossetti and His Jewellery," The Burlington Magazine 118,

no. 875 (1976), 94 + 96–102, "Dante Gabriel Rossetti and 'Pre-Raphaelite' Fashion," in Charlotte Gere and Geoffrey C. Munn, *Pre-Raphaelite to Arts and Crafts Jewellery* (Woodbridge, Suffolk: Antique Collectors Club, 1996), and Julie Codell, "Dress and Desire: Rossetti's Erotics of the Unclassifiable and Working-Class Models," in J. De Young, ed., *Fashions in European Art: Dress and Identity, Politics and the Body 1775–1925* (London: I.B. Tauris, 2017).

27 Dunn, 35.

28 Dunn, illustration facing page 35, "Bed in Which Rossetti was Born."

29 Pedrick, 161, 160.

30 See William Michael Rossetti, *Dante Gabriel Rossetti as Designer and Writer* (London: Cassell and Company, 1889), 51.

31 C. G. Williamson, *Murray Marks and His Friends* (London and New York: John Lane, 1919), 82. Cited in Virginia Surtees, *The Paintings and Drawings of Dante Gabriel Rossetti (1828–1882): A Catalogue Raisonnée* (Oxford University Press, 1971), 138.

32 Sidney Colvin, "Rossetti as a Painter," *The Magazine of Art* 6 (1883), 183.

33 John Ruskin, "The Nature of Gothic," Chapter 6, *The Stones of Venice* Vol. II (London: Smith, Elder, and Company, 1851–1853).

34 Nicolette Gray, *Rossetti, Dante, and Ourselves* (London: Faber and Faber, 1945), 29. Helsinger has also argued that "attempts to 'read' the iconic significance of objects or their visual components are countered by the extent to which these are embedded in patters that refuse to privilege the readable or symbolic elements." *Poetry and the Pre-Raphaelite Arts*, 178.

35 William Michael Rossetti, *Designer and Writer*, 108.

36 See Landow, *Replete With Meaning*.

37 Fredric George Stephens, *William Holman Hunt and His Works: A Memoir of the Artist's Life with Description of His Pictures* (London: James Nisbit and Co., 1861), 56–57, 69.

38 See Ford Madox Brown, "On the Mechanism of a Historical Picture," *The Germ*, no. 2 (1850), 70–73.

39 T. Martin Wood, *Drawings of D.G. Rossetti* (London: George Newnes, 1907), 10.

40 Walter Pater, *Selected Works*, ed. Richard Aldington (New York: Duell, Sloan, and Pearce, 1883), 91.

41 Wood, 11.

42 Helsinger speaks at length of Rossetti's art as concerned with sensuous attention, and uses the phrase "lyrical knowledge" to describe what his poems and paintings offer. *Poetry and the Pre-Raphaelite Arts*, 52. See also Laurence Roussillon-Constanty, "From the *House of Life* to the *Decorative Arts*: Dante Gabriel Rossetti and Ceramics," *Miranda* 7 (2012), 6: "Despite the true-to-nature representation of individual objects the overall sense is that Rossetti is using motifs, patterns and textures to highlight the pleasures derived from the senses of touch, sight and hearing."

43 William Michael Rossetti referred to his brother's paintings of the 1860s as "beautiful women with floral adjuncts." *Dante Gabriel Rossetti: His Family Letters, With a Memoir*, Vol. I (London: Ellis and Elvey, 1895), 203.

44 Feldman similarly speaks of "magical objects" ("Aestheticism's Bric-a-Brac," 466). See also Codell's insightful discussion of "uncanny things" in Rossetti's paintings that escape conventional categories of signification both in themselves and in their unexpected, de-contextualized juxtapositions, in "Dress and Desire: Rossetti's Erotics of the Unclassifiable and Working Class Models," *Palaces of Art: Whistler and the Art Worlds of Aestheticism*, Lee Glazer and Linda Merrill, eds. (Washington, DC: Smithsonian Institution Scholarly Press, 2013), 101–104.

45 See Jessica Simmons, "For a Venetian Pastoral by Giorgione (In the Louvre)": "Life Touching Lips with Immortality," 2004, *The Victorian Web*, www. victorianweb.org/authors/dgr/simmons5.html.

46 Rossetti inscribed a passage from Boccacio's *Decameron* on the back of the canvas: "Bocca baciate non perda ventura, anzi rinova come fa la luna." The painting is held by the Museum of Fine Arts, Boston: their website translates the Italian as "The mouth that has been kissed loses not its freshness; still it renews itself even as does the moon," www.mfa.org/collections/object/ bocca-baciata-lips-that-have-been-kissed-34360.

47 Charles Baudelaire, "L'Invitation au Voyage," *Les Fleurs Du Mal* (Paris: Georges Crès, 1917), 92–93.

48 Ibid., 17.

49 Quoted in Edward Lucie-Smith, *Symbolist Art* (London: Thames and Hudson, 1972), 47.

50 See Bruno Latour, *We Have Never Been Modern* (Cambridge MA: Harvard University Press, 1993) and Jane Bennett, *Vibrant Matter* (Durham NC: Duke University Press, 2010).

Works Cited

Anderson, Anne. "'Fearful Consequences... of Living Up to One's Teapot': Men, Women, and 'Cultchah' in the English Aesthetic Movement c. 1870–1900." *Victorian Literature and Culture* 37, no. 1 (2009), 219–54.

Baudelaire, Charles. *Les Fleurs du Mal*. Paris: Georges Crès, 1917.

Bennett, Jane. *Vibrant Matter: A Political Ecology of Things*. Duke University Press, 2010.

Brown, Ford Madox. "On the Mechanism of a Historical Picture." *The Germ*, no. 2 (February 1850), 70–73.

Bury, Shirley. "Rossetti and His Jewellery." *The Burlington Magazine* 118, no. 875 (February 1976), 94 + 96–102.

Codell, Julie. "Displaying Aestheticism's Bric-a-Brac: Rossetti's Material and Virtual Goods." *Palaces of Art: Whistler and the Art Worlds of Aestheticism*, edited by Lee Glazer and Linda Merrill, 119–31. Washington, DC: Smithsonian Institution, Scholarly Press, 2013.

———"Dress and Desire: Rossetti's Erotics of the Unclassifiable and Working-Class Models." *Fashion in European Art: Dress and Identity, Politics and the Body 1775–1925*. Edited by J. De Young. London: I.B. Tauris, 2017.

Colvin, Sidney. "Rossetti as a Painter." *The Magazine of Art* 6 (1883), 181–83.

Dunn, Henry Treffry. *Recollections of Dante Gabriel Rossetti and His Circle (Cheyne Walk Life)*, edited by Gale Pedrick. London: Elkin Matthews, 1904.

Feldman, Jessica. "Modernism's Victorian Bric-a-Brac." *Modernism/Modernity* 8, no. 3 (2001): 453–70.

Fredeman, William E. *The Correspondence of Dante Gabriel Rossetti*. Vol. 4. Cambridge: D.S. Brewer, 2002.

Frye, Roger. "Rossetti's Water Colours of 1857." *The Burlington Magazine* 29, no. 159 (June 1916), 100–101 + 104–105 +108–109.

Gere, Charlotte, "Dante Gabriel Rossetti and 'Pre-Raphaelite' Fashion." *Pre-Raphaelite to Arts and Crafts Jewellery*, edited by Charlotte Gere and Geoffrey C. Munn. Woodbridge, Suffolk: Antique Collectors Club, 1996.

Gray, Nicolette. *Rossetti, Dante, and Ourselves*. London: Faber and Faber, 1945.

Haweis, Mary Eliza Joy. *Beautiful Houses: Being a Description of Certain Well-Known Artistic Houses.* London: Sampson, Low, Marston, Searle, and Rivington, 1882.

Helsinger, Elizabeth. *Poetry and the Pre-Raphaelite Arts.* New Haven and London: Yale University Press, 2008.

Hueffer, Ford Madox. *Rossetti: A Critical Essay on His Art.* London: Duckworth, 1902.

James, Henry. *Autobiography.* Edited and introduced by Frederick W. Dupree. New York: Criterion Books, 1956.

Landow, George. *Replete With Meaning: William Holman Hunt and Typological Symbolism. Victorian Web.* www.victorianweb.org/painting/whh/replete/contents.html.

Latour, Bruno. *We Have Never Been Modern.* Cambridge, MA: Harvard University Press, 1993.

Logan, Thad. *The Victorian Parlour: A Cultural Study.* Cambridge: Cambridge University Press, 2001.

Lucie-Smith, Edward. *Symbolist Art.* London: Thames and Husdon, 1972.

Marillier, Henry Currie. *Dante Gabriel Rossetti: An Illustrated Memorial,* third edition. London: George Bell and Sons, 1904.

Marsh, Jan. *Dante Gabriel Rossetti: Painter and Poet.* London: Weidenfeld and Nicolson, 1999.

Orrinsmith, Lucy. *The Drawing Room: Its Decorations and Furniture.* London: Macmillan, 1878.

Pater, Walter. *Selected Works,* edited by Richard Aldington. New York: Duell, Sloan, and Pearce, 1883.

Pedrick, Gale. *No Peacocks Allowed: Dante Gabriel Rossetti and His Circle.* Carbondale, IL: Southern Illinois University Press, 1964.

Rossetti, William Michael. *Dante Gabriel Rossetti as Designer and Writer.* London: Cassell and Company, 1889.

———. *Dante Gabriel Rossetti: His Family Letters, With a Memoir.* Volume I. London: Ellis and Elvey, 1895.

———. *Some Reminiscences of William Michael Rossetti,* Vol. I. New York: Charles Scribner's Sons, 1906.

Roussillon-Constanty, Laurence. "From the *House of Life* to the *Decorative Arts*: Dante Gabriel Rossetti and Ceramics." *Miranda* [Online] 7 (2012) doi:10.4000/miranda.4436.

Ruskin, John. *The Stones of Venice.* London: Smith, Elder, and Company, 1851–1853.

Simmons, Jessica, "'For a Venetian Pastoral by Giorgione (In the Louvre)': 'Life Touching Lips with Immortality.'" *The Victorian Web,* 2004. www.victorianweb.org/authors/dgr/simmons5.html.

Smith, Alison. "Revival and Reformation: The Aims and Ideals of the Pre-Raphaelite Brotherhood." In *Pre-Raphaelite Painting Techniques 1848–1856,* edited by Joyce H. Townsend, Jaqueline Ridge, and Stephen Hackney. London: Tate Publishing, 2001.

Stephens, Frederic George. *Artists at Home, Photographed by J.P. Mayall.* New York: Appleton, 1884.

———. *William Holman Hunt and His Works: A Memoir of the Artist's Life with Description of His Pictures.* London: James Nisbit and Co., 1861.

Surtees, Virginia. *The Paintings and Drawings of Dante Gabriel Rossetti: A Catalogue Raisonnée.* Oxford: Clarendon Press, 1971.

Treuherz, Julien, Elizabeth Prettejohn, and Edwin Becker, eds. *Dante Gabriel Rossetti.* Zwolle, Amsterdam, and Liverpool: Wanders Publishers, The Van Gogh Museum, The Walker Museum, 2003.

Werner, Marcia. *Pre-Raphaelite Painting and Nineteenth-Century Realism.* Cambridge University Press, 2005.

Wharton, T. E. Martin & Co. *16 Cheyne Walk, Chelsea: The Valuable Contents of the Residence of Dante Gabriel Rossetti (Deceased), To Be Sold by Auction.* London: T.E. Wharton, Marton, & Co., 1882.

Williamson, C. G. *Murray Marks and His Friends.* London and New York: John Lane, 1919.

Wood, T. Martin. *Drawings of D.G. Rossetti.* London: George Newnes, 1907.

Part II

Ornaments

Defining Prosperity at Home

4   The Dark Side of the Tank
The Marine Aquarium in the Victorian Home

Silvia Granata

Among the many objects that filled Victorian homes, the aquarium was central in two different ways. It often occupied a prominent place in the house, being displayed to be admired and discussed by family members and guests alike; but it was also central from a less material point of view, as a *locus* of encounter between technological, scientific, and cultural trends. This chapter briefly discusses some of these trends, looking at the multiple reasons for the so-called *aquarium craze* of the 1850s and early 1860s. While it is partially true, as noted by David Allen, that 'aquaria were not expressive of Victorianism', since we still have them today,[1] I suggest that the way in which Victorians enjoyed and conceptualized the marine tank was deeply imbricated with various aspects of coeval culture, reflecting the beliefs, assumptions, and preoccupations of its owners.[2] I thus investigate what early aquarists saw in the tank, but also what they *wanted* to see, in order to better understand the way they experienced it, which was rich, impressively multi-layered, and culturally specific.

Yet, there were also darker sides to the Victorian aquarium, which eventually contributed to the fading of the vogue. In the second part of this essay, I consider some of the difficulties inherent in a hobby that could involve a significant amount of commitment, dedication, and expense. In particular, by looking at James Shirley Hibberd's *The Book of the Aquarium* (1856, 1860), I explore the tension between the aquarium's status as a commodity and its ambiguous nature as an object whose purpose was to contain living (and particularly fragile) beings.[3] Hibberd's text significantly deviates from the approach adopted by other manuals published in the same period. While most authors tended to frame the hobby as a follow-up of zoological studies, with a strong emphasis on information about the anatomy and behaviour of sea creatures, Hibberd discussed it mostly as a domestic ornament.[4] Although he made some concessions to the trend of stressing the aquarium's educational purpose, he also made it very clear that there was no need for a thorough study of marine biology, or for time-consuming, expensive collecting trips, as the tank could provide a perfectly respectable and rewarding pastime even without them. From the very beginning he remarks that he 'never intended to treat the subject in a strictly scientific manner,' thus addressing readers who were not necessarily much interested in science, but clearly wanted to participate in the latest fashion, and considered the tank mostly as an object of décor.[5] Therefore, practical matters such as the tank's placement in the room, cleaning, or choosing and arranging internal fittings, which were often marginalized in other texts, are here foregrounded. This approach offers a unique source of information on the material aspects of Victorian tank-keeping, allowing us to better understand what the hobby really was, but also what kind of implications its success (or failure) entailed for its early enthusiasts.

'The Latest Object of Fashion and Wonder'

The invention itself was made possible by recent discoveries: tanks exploited the properties of Wardian Cases, named after Nathaniel Bagshaw Ward (1791–1868), an East End doctor and botanist; he came upon the principle of the closely glazed case in 1829, when he saw ferns and mosses growing from mould in a covered jar where he had placed a moth; he understood that the evaporating moisture condensed and was again deposited on the soil, thus keeping a constant level of humidity. Ward soon began to make experiments and publicly announced his discovery to the British Association in 1837.[6] Wardian cases were soon adopted for collections of ferns and tropical plants; the 1845 repeal of glass duties eventually made them more affordable, allowing for widespread use.[7] The survival of marine creatures inside the tank depended on a better understanding of the photosynthetic process, which was achieved thanks to the growing focus of research on chemical cycles.[8] Railway transport too was instrumental in the diffusion of the hobby, as it allowed more people to reach and enjoy the seaside, but also offered an easy and fast means to take sea creatures back to the city.

As Victorian commentators emphatically noted, the marine aquarium represented a condensed version of the age's scientific and technical excellencies made available to the wider public, something to enjoy and also to be proud of. The aquarium thus had an indubitable appeal as a marvel of modernity, which intersected with the growing scientific interest in the sea and its inhabitants.[9] Such interest, though, did not remain circumscribed to scientific circles but was disseminated among the wider public by a thriving market of popularizing books and magazines. In this period, more and more people took on hobbies related to natural history, which often merged with the ongoing expansion of tourism, the passion for collecting and the typically Victorian impulse towards an acquisitive appreciation of nature.[10] Hence, beside enclosing a piece of the sea, the aquarium could also enclose a whole experience, drawing together travel, the enjoyment of the seaside, an interest in science, and a passion for collecting, but also the technical knowledge required to build the tank and make it work. Due to this felicitous combination the marine tank, initially devised as a tool for research, rapidly became a widespread ornament in Victorian homes, and people began to cultivate the hobby with the help of a fast-increasing number of manuals and magazine articles that provided detailed practical instructions.

Indeed, keeping a marine aquarium was by no means an easy task. The very first ones were handmade and hand-filled: in the first place, the would-be aquarist had to travel to the seaside to collect his own specimens. Aquarium books gave detailed instructions on how, and what, to collect, including advice about the right moment in the day (obviously at low tide) and proper season, the tools needed (which may include a geological hammer, chisel, scalpel, baskets, nets, jars, and water-boots), and the choice of the fittest animals and plants. Unlike other kinds of natural-history collections like shells, pressed flowers, or insects, the aquarium required that the specimens stayed alive; this involved greater care in extracting them from their environment, but also in preparing them for their journey. For instance, collectors should avoid putting together animals that would eat each other. Each species needed a particular treatment, but all had to reach their new home as comfortably and quickly as possible. Seawater too – at least at the beginning of the vogue – had to be procured: aquarists could ask incoming ships to deliver it, paying a small sum for the service. Very soon though, specialized shops began to sell seawater by the gallon, and chemically produced saltwater also entered the market. The tank itself had, in the early stages of the vogue, to be built by the collector or commissioned to a manufacturer. Even later, when ready-made tanks became available for purchase, most books suggested a do-it-yourself approach: they argued that, for the true aquarist, this was part of the pleasure, allowing him not only to prove his technical skills, but also to create the tank of his own liking. After all, the ability to indulge the owner's idiosyncrasies was one of the key features of the hobby.[11] Unlike today's aquaria, Victorian ones often displayed remarkably ornate designs, in tune with the rest of the furniture.

The construction of a proper tank, though, entailed a wide range of problems. First of all, it had to be the right size and shape for the creatures it was meant to hold; then, the aquarist also had to be very careful in the choice of materials. Tanks usually consisted of glass, cement, slate, and wood; green or blue paper was used to shade the water from direct light and heat. Most importantly, materials that may damage the collection (such as rocks containing metallic substances that might poison the water) had to be avoided. Various accessories could then be added according to the use intended (as a decorative object, as a tool for the study of sea creatures, or as a combination of both) and to the aquarist's financial means.

A look at the catalogue published by Alford Lloyd, the owner of the most popular aquarium shop in London, provides a very vivid idea of the amount and variety of equipment that could be involved (he even included a form with frequently asked questions; customers could fill it in and send it back to the shop for advice). He sold everything, including live specimens of animals and plants, seawater (both natural and artificial), rockwork, sand and shingles, various models of tanks and vessels, tables and stands, and a wide range of accessories such as thermometers, hydrometers, lenses and jars, nets, sponge-sticks to clean the tank, and syringes for aeration (*A List, with Descriptions,* 1858). Of course, not all these things were strictly necessary. One of the reasons for the hobby's popularity was its adaptability; it could meet different needs, from both a cultural and social point of view, and it could be adjusted to different incomes. Once the tank was ready, a particular attention should be devoted to its placement in the room, as it had to receive enough light and heat, but not too much. Finally, the aquarist also had to furnish it, in order to offer each specimen a fit environment (some marine animals burrow in the sand, others need to climb out of water or to hide behind stones). Internal décor though, as the tank's general appearance, was also supposed to express the good taste of the aquarist in recreating a beautiful and elegant miniature sea. Decorative features typical of mid-Victorian gardening were often adapted for aquaria; rockeries, grottoes, and arches in particular were deemed very desirable, as they offered a touch of the picturesque. Algae too, required to maintain the healthy balance of the collection, could provide a scenic feature, being arranged according to colour and shape as in an underwater version of landscape painting. Therefore, the tank's form, its position in the room, the arrangement of its internal landscape and the choice of specimens had to meet requirements that were both technical and aesthetic.

The home aquarium had a complex nature as a kind of domestic zoo, or live-collection, and as a very particular piece of furniture. If successful, it provided the satisfaction of having your own miniature world, which could be constantly improved. It offered a piece of the exotic – and still largely unknown – submarine environment in the home, participating in the wider desire to enclose, or domesticate, wild nature. But the home tank was also meant to be an ornament: it usually enjoyed pride of place in the parlour or in the drawing room, that is, in the most public room of the house.[12] It was meant to function as a display of selfhood, showcasing the wealth, the taste, and the interests of the owners. In particular, as other kinds of private collections, it also reflected the growing interest for natural history, which became charged in this period with a wealth of new implications. Displaying a rich and ordered collection of pressed flowers, seaweeds, insects, or fossils testified to the owner's interest in science, but also to the capacity to appreciate nature, which came to be considered a sign of refined sensibility.[13] Moreover, a well-cared collection also attested to habits of industry and order, much valued by Victorians even when pastimes and leisure activities were concerned.[14] In fact, all popular texts on the aquarium insistently underlined that the successful aquarist must be observant (great stress was given to the capacity for trained vision and attention), precise, patient, and – above all – persevering. The relation between tank-keeping and moral virtues may seem surprising nowadays, but for Victorians this was a significant aspect of the hobby, as I discuss below in relation to Hibberd's book.

The Book of the Aquarium

James Shirley Hibberd (1825–1890) is now mostly remembered as a prominent personality in the world of Victorian gardening. After a brief commitment to the Vegetarian Society in the 1840s, he worked as a public lecturer and scientific journalist; in the same period, he started to grow a city garden (still a rather unusual activity in the early 1850s). He published extensively on his own horticultural experiments, and eventually became the editor of some of the most popular gardening magazines of his time, including *The Floral World and Garden Guide*, *The Gardener's Magazine*, and *Amateur Gardening*, which is still published today. Throughout his career, he promoted gardening as an activity that should not be limited to the parks and gardens of the very wealthy, but rather as a way for the people to enjoy nature and all the benefits it could bestow.

This can be seen very clearly in his *Rustic Adornments*, a book devoted to fashionable adornments for the house and the garden, including the aquarium, fern cases, floral ornaments, caged birds, and apiaries.[15] Its success was mostly due to the fact that 'it persuaded people that none of these operations was beyond them and that through its self-help instructions they could create a home that would be a credit to both their status and their taste.'[16] The whole text was a celebration of domesticity, national pride, and progress, its basic assumption being that embellishing one's house and garden should be both a pleasure and a duty, as the dwelling reflects the inner qualities of the owner:

> in a certain sense the Home is the outside of a man; it is an external vesture, and more or less, but always in some degree, a visible embodiment of his mental character. The man of intellect and taste will impress on everything about him an air of usefulness or elegance, and will make the best of the roughest materials that fate may cast in his path.[17]

Crucially, the correspondence between the house and its owner also works the other way around, as the owner is inevitably influenced by its dwelling and what it contains. In fact, if ordinary residences were constructed in accordance with correct principles of taste, the dwellers in them would attain a higher status in mind and morals, for the character is powerfully impressed for good or evil by what surrounds it permanently.[18]

The Book of the Aquarium, first published in 1856, adopts the same perspective.[19] At once aspirational, advertorial, and cautionary, it addresses readers who, albeit not necessarily affluent, have some leisure time, some money to invest in recreational pursuits, and – most importantly – who strive after *style*. Hibberd insistently argues that this fashionable hobby should not be circumscribed to the mansions of the upper classes, and could be enjoyed, perhaps on a smaller scale, even with a modest investment. This suggests a household whose members did care about social standing and wanted their house to reflect the latest fashions. Yet, for these readers, taste could be a rather slippery concept, as testified by the fact that, besides warnings against technical mistakes, Hibberd often provides guidance on aesthetic matters. In particular, he repeatedly cautions his audience not to overdo it, as they would thus incur in the worst danger for the socially aspiring, that of looking ridiculous. As an example, he states that 'when the "Aquarium mania" broke out, it was common enough to see tanks containing fishes, reptiles, insects, blocks of coral, nameless structures coloured with red sealing-wax, with perhaps a model of a frigate on the top, "becalmed and lifeless".' Quite significantly, such ugliness and confusion also mean inefficiency, and the author humorously notes that in those tanks

> gold fishes had their flesh gnawed away by carnivorous larvae, lizards got out and crept under ladies' dresses to be trodden on; and sometimes a huge beetle would take wing, and go round the room and through the flame of the candle with a horrible buzz, which from that moment brought the aquarium into disrepute, at least with the gentler members of the family.[20]

A further clue on Hibberd's intended public is provided by the remarkable attention devoted to issues of budget. He gives plenty of advice on what to buy, and where, and often suggests various options for different budgets. For instance, he observes that 'Dr. Badham and Gosse were giving manufacturers perplexing orders for blown tanks, which cost from fifteen to twenty shillings each', but 'a better kind of vessel was to be found in every horticultural glass warehouse.' He then suggests using a propagating glass (a small glass vase, usually bell-shaped, commonly employed by gardeners to grow herbs). Discussing Mr Hall's idea for a cheap tank, which could be placed in a window, mounted on a deal box, he states that this

simple trick of creating a cheap and elegant tank did more to popu-
larize the Aquarium than all the exhibitions and all the books that
have been written on the subject, for it enabled thousands to enjoy
a delight which had previously been confined to the wealthy few.[21]

Hibberd then provides the names of manufacturers who sell it on his
own design. He evidently wrote for people who had some money to
spare, but not to throw away.

The aquarium, then, was not only a tool to observe what was inside
by looking through its transparent glass walls, but an elegant piece of
furniture to be looked at and admired. Although it could provide a window on the miniature sea inside, its function was more that of a mirror
reflecting the taste of its owner, which could be a very serious matter for
such class-conscious readers. For this reason, every choice regarding the
tank had to be made very carefully, as you would naturally do for any
kind of investment that matters, from both a social and a financial point
of view.

Money Matters

Hibberd's text is indeed pervaded by a meticulous preoccupation with
money, both his own and his readers'. Since he grounds his advice on
his own aquarium experience, he often gives detailed accounts of his
expenses. Moreover, he makes it very clear that his work too has a cost:
in one of his frequent harangues against plagiarism, he forcibly explains
that his know-how has a value that is not just *intellectual*, since he invested money to acquire it: 'as the instructions here given are the result
of personal observation and experiment, including no small expenditure
of time and money, I here put up the notice which appears in the preface
to the other portion of the work – *Pirates Beware*.'[22]

But he is also very attentive when it comes to his readers' spending.
Unlike other authors, who treated tank-keeping as closely related to sea-
shore collecting, he frames his readers as consumers, rather than collectors. Notwithstanding a passing remark on the fact that 'the true lover
of nature will collect his specimens rather than purchase them,' he soon
proceeds to guide (and encourage) the would-be aquarist's purchases,
framing them as a *necessity*.[23] For instance, he states that 'much valuable information' may be gathered from Lloyd's catalogue, adding that
'no keeper of an aquarium should be without it.'[24] Contradicting the initial (and customary) praise of seaside rambles, Hibberd underlines that,
for its readers at least, buying, rather than collecting, is the safest option:
in almost intimidating terms, he observes that 'no one should attempt to
set up an Aquarium without first paying him [Lloyd] a visit. He is ready
to give counsel as well as to take money.'[25] The authority of Lloyd is so
unquestionable that, while dissuading beginners from even attempting

to keep a particularly delicate species of actinia, Hibberd remarks that 'Mr. Lloyd refuses to sell it, in order that its death may bring no blame upon him.'[26] This presents Lloyd as the ultimate authority, but also as a man of the utmost integrity, a reliable and wholly honest businessman, whom prospective customers can implicitly trust.

It must be noted that almost all aquarium authors had some kind of connection with Lloyd's shop,[27] but Hibberd's insistent endorsement is far more pervasive than the scattered references found in other manuals. Readers evidently suspected an agreement, and he replied that the author 'has not recommended in these pages any particular trader or trading interest, and has no interest of that sort of his own to promote.'[28] Yet, he foregrounds the commercial aspect of the pursuit in a way that amounts to a proper, although unofficial, advertisement. Many of the items mentioned are followed by their price, and the publicity effect is further increased when the price accompanies an illustration, as in a commercial catalogue. In discussing both tanks and specimens, he often underlines their cheapness, their durability (a quality much emphasized in advertisements of goods), and the ease with which they can be procured.[29]

Thus, on the one hand, the author stresses that even those who lack competence (or even interest) in science can participate in this exciting novelty. On the other hand, though, he also underlines that such participation is necessarily limited: his suggestions aim at avoiding mistakes, but they also reinforce the boundary between hobbyist and researcher, a boundary that his reader should not dare to trespass. While other texts presented the aquarium as a tool for zoological studies, thus foregrounding the contiguity between experts and amateurs by depicting them as members of the same community of students of nature,[30] Hibberd repeatedly marks the distance, for instance by suggesting different options for each category.[31] The underlying principle seems to be that, while for researchers making mistakes is a potential source of knowledge, for hobbyists it only entails a loss of time and money. His readers therefore must proceed by relying on other people's expertise.

Most importantly, he is careful to acknowledge, and sanction, the commercial aspect of the hobby. He admits that 'after all it is most likely that a majority of those who keep Aquaria, will purchase rather than collect their stock', and adds that 'it is a fortunate circumstance that it can be purchased, for we are not all so circumstanced that we can take train whenever the whim suits us, and erratic as crabs, suit our movements to tides, seasons, winds, and changes of the moon.'[32] This comment reveals the tension between the author's desire to retain – at least formally – the aquarium's connection with zoological studies and the acknowledgement that his readers may have neither the time nor the money to invest in collecting expeditions to the seaside. By ironically casting collectors as 'erratic crabs', he pictures them as *privileged*, free to follow their whims, while implicitly framing his readers as serious, hard-working people, who probably do not enjoy such liberty of movement or expense.

This is particularly significant since such an approach was by no means common in aquarium books. Most manuals insistently portrayed an interest in natural history as positively colliding with monetary interests.[33] At the very beginning of *Glaucus*, Charles Kingsley opposes an imaginary 'London merchant' to his 'douce and portly head clerk' who humbly cherishes an interest in natural history: while the latter is able to both notice and appreciate nature even in its humblest forms, the former is described as blind, seeing the collection as an assemblage of 'useless moths.'[34] Natural history is presented as an antidote to the dangerous tendency of the age, dominated by a 'self-seeking and Mammonite generation, inclined to value everything by its money price, its private utility.'[35] The opposition between the entomologist and the merchant was reframed a couple of years later by Henry Noel Humphreys within a discussion of trained vision. The 'astute merchant deciphers at a glance the precise state of the most intricate accounts', but 'of the thousand interesting and wonderful things concerning the little beetle that crosses his path in his country walk, he is incapable of seeing any single particle.' The entomologist instead recognises that 'there are things well worthy of investigation beyond the region of money-making, and the attractive but narrow circle distinguished by the fascinating characters, £. s. d.'[36]

Perhaps in response to these unflattering comments, which could possibly offend or humiliate his intended audience, Hibberd argues that

> we know already that the luxuries of refinement are no longer monopolized by the wealthy, that the merchant is not rendered sordid by commerce, but that he can delight in the strength of Angelo and the grace of Raphael; the ledger does not dwarf the trader's soul below the appreciation of Titian's lights or Rembrandt's shadows; and the persevering plodder, who from four to six does battle with armies of statistics, can retire to his suburban villa to rejoice as a happy soul in the midst of his family, or fondle his tame birds with the affection of a child.[37]

For Hibberd, a proper concern for money (both earned and spent) is not something to be ashamed of, and not below gentility. It is rather the sign of a healthy, responsible attitude. Moreover, there is nothing wrong in admitting that the hobby has a commercial side, as this does not in the least diminish its value or significance.

Death in the Tank

By the time Hibberd published his text, the aquarium had indeed become a commodity. However, due to its amphibious nature, it was also a remarkably fragile one: its purpose was to host life, but – if something went wrong – it could easily host death. Of course, at this stage, tank keeping was still quite difficult, and most texts warned readers against common mistakes, but the general tendency was to emphasize that difficulties could be overcome. Hibberd instead decidedly foregrounds the warning approach, since 'to set up a tank and manage it in accordance with sound principles, is not such an easy matter as some writers have represented it.' This is what distinguishes his book from similar texts:

> some writers, otherwise estimable and able men, have laboured assiduously to describe the various forms of life to which the Aquarium introduces us, and have said little or nothing on the system to be pursued to render those forms of life amenable to the conditions under which the aquarian desires to observe them.[38]

Yet, the result of his approach is that references to the death of marine creatures are omnipresent.

Hibberd warns his readers that many things can go wrong from the very beginning, starting with the wrong choice of specimens; for instance, the inexperienced collector 'will be tempted to bag some specimens of oarweed, (*Laminaria*,) on account of their attractive appearance [...] They are, however, useless, for they soon perish in confinement, and render the water turbid with their putrescence.'[39] The book is punctuated by references to species that may easily die and turn poisonous for other tank guests. Moreover, marine creatures collected on the shore could also suffer death by travel, and the author duly reminds his readers that 'the transit must be quickly performed, or many of the specimens will perish.'[40] Even worse, the aquarium itself can turn into a deathly trap: aquarists should avoid old, ill-constructed tanks, otherwise 'we shall consign to a tomb every item of marine stock committed to it. Instead of preservatories such tanks are sepulchres; river fishes may need no better, but marine zoophytes soon perish in them.'[41] In some instances, tanks can be so wrong that fish do not just die, but kill themselves, as in the case of the 'vessels with four sides of glass', which 'admit a vast deal too much light; the consequence is that some of the inhabitants commit suicide, and the vegetation, instead of doing its work in an orderly way, becomes rampant and unmanageable.'[42] And the aquarium itself can *die*: 'the walls should be of plate glass, for, though stout common glass may last a long while, one night's frost may at last cause an explosion and the consequent loss of the stock, and great destruction of furniture.'[43] In the worst possible scenario, the tank can even become a danger to the aquarist himself:

These slate tanks are very heavy, and it is not desirable, unless a house is built expressly to receive them, to increase the weight by piling up rockwork inside them. In my case any serious addition to the combined weight of tank and water might cause the whole affair to subside from the study at the top of the house to the bed-room immediately below it, which would be an unpleasant circumstance, especially if it happened at night.[44]

Furthermore, the inexperienced aquarist may involuntary kill specimens through a wrong placement in the room; as in Byron's poem, 'darkness is death', but 'light from all sides' might also be fatal.[45] Then, special attention should be devoted to predatory species: 'crabs sprawl over anemones and torment them, and anemones entangle fishes with their barbed threads and destroy them'; starfish 'are given to the practice of absorbing molluscs out of their shells.'[46] Quite significantly, Hibberd remarks that not only the inexperience, but also the *moral* flaws of the aquarist may have murderous outcomes, and he regretfully admits he lost 'the whole stock in a tank of forty gallons this spring' because 'in a moment of injudicious haste, I set it to work again, and next morning it was a deadhouse.'[47] Inattention, haste, and greed inevitably bring about their own punishment, usually in the guise of the death of specimens, or – in the worst cases – of the demise of the whole collection. In fact, if bad things happen to the aquarium, 'it must be concluded that it has been either unskilfully stocked or injudicially managed.'[48]

This pervasive preoccupation with death, though, does not only stem from a concern for the lives of marine creatures. Throughout his career, Hibberd showed a remarkable interest in animal welfare: he denounced the cruelties perpetrated in Smithfield market and commented on the need to make up – with extra care and affection – for the deprivation of liberty suffered by pets.[49] Yet, from the way in which he talks about death in the tank, it is evident that he does not see it as an occasion for mourning.[50] On a simpler level, death is in this case an economic damage. For instance, the aquarist would be 'paying heavy penalties in the use of tanks made wholly of glass.'[51] The old-fashioned tanks, 'on which I wasted my money years ago,' are mainly blamed as a financial loss. He even warns the aquarist not to *invest* in creatures unfit for captivity, suggesting 'not to *speculate* largely on any of the shell-fish' [emphasis mine].[52] But this does not mean that the tank and its inhabitants only have an economic value: dead creatures also represent a failure of the aquarium itself. The failure reflects on the owner, not as a bad scientist (which he is not meant to be), but as a bad manager. While positive qualities are attributed to the successful aquarist, a bad result is often blamed on his personal flaws.

Thus, the aquarium is a commodity, that is, something with an economic value, but its value is not limited to the economic sphere.[53] As observed by Freedgood, 'our sense of value is constrained into a small number of distinct categories, the aesthetic, the economic, the personal – whole disciplines are now deployed to maintain the distinctions between what we hope are incommensurable realms of worth and worthiness.'[54] It was not yet so for Victorians, and the aquarium provides a very good example: in it, economic value overlaps with other values that were subjective, but also historically and culturally specific. Such overlapping can help us understand the reasons and significance of Hibberd's emphasis on death, which patently clashes with his often-quoted definition of the aquarium as 'a thing of beauty and a joy for ever.'[55]

When the aquarium does not work, it turns – as any other object – into a thing: in Brown's words, 'we begin to confront the thingness of objects when they stop working for us [...] The story of objects asserting themselves as things, then, is the story of a changed relation to the human subject.' In fact, 'the thing really names less an object than a particular subject-object relation.'[56] In this case, due to the multifaceted investment of Victorian aquarists (in terms of status, and of the skills, virtues and taste supposedly required to keep it working) the effect is not only that the owner begins to 'confront' the material item; he also confronts his own failure. It is within this frame that we should interpret Hibberd's constant preoccupation. He repeatedly foregrounds the aquarium's aesthetic value; yet, if pollution invades the tank, the object itself becomes useless, because its very purpose (and much of the appeal it exerted on Victorians) obviously depends on its transparency. Moreover, if the inhabitants die, not only will the aquarist be left with a tank containing dead fish, which is certainly not a nice sight, but he may even end with a glass tank full of overgrown algae and putrefying animals. From a 'thing of beauty' it will turn into a thing disgusting, and probably in the room of the house that most represented the owner.

But Hibberd also insists – as all early aquarists did – that the proper aquarium should be self-sustaining and that, once set in motion, it should last, thus reproducing the balance providentially established by nature in the sea.[57] This eagerly desired stability of the aquarium is also one of the aspects that align it with any other material good. Yet, the aquarium may refuse to behave like a commodity, and from a 'joy forever' it could turn into a very short-lived thing and a waste of money. Indeed, when the aquarium goes wrong it undermines the very relation, which is one of ownership, between subject and object. The death of the specimens makes the relation meaningless: you still own them, but when dead, they signify nothing.[58]

Hibberd himself later recognised that the fading of the vogue may in part depend on unrealistic expectations, which he had contributed to foster. In the 1857 edition of *Adornments*, he had launched into a hyperbolic description of the suburban idyll he wished his readers to achieve:

may your flowers flourish, your bees prosper, your birds love you, and your pet fishes live for ever [...] and may you find in every little thing that lives and grows a pleasure for the present hour, and a suggestion of things higher and brighter for contemplation in the future.[59]

However, in 1870 he admitted that such expectations had to be significantly downsized:

when engaged in the experiments which were the foundation of my first written essays on the aquarium, fifteen years ago, and subsequently of the 'Book of the Aquarium', [...] the grand difficulty was to determine an exact and self-sustaining balance between the various forces and influences that an aquarium brings into play. Every failure then occurring was the result of attempting too much. It is impossible to forget the waste of time, and strength, and money in attempts to domesticate the larger forms of marine algae; and how those hopes only faded out when years of watchfulness and wasted energy made it but too evident that *it was easier to dream than to do* [emphasis mine]. Small quantities of sea water enclosed in vessels in dwelling-houses are too peculiarly circumstanced to be made representative of Neptune's watery kingdom, but they may be representative of rock-pools and recesses. We may treat them as spoonfuls of water, and achieve such success as spoonfuls admit of; but we must not suppose we have the sea at our command.[60]

The death of marine creatures in the tank, then, measures the distance between the desire for a stable relationship with the object as it should be (entailing – as Victorians saw it – a confirmation of the owner's qualities) and the fact that the aquarium may elude attempts at containing it conceptually as a commodity. Hibberd's exhortations to buy ready-made items and to rely on the professional expertise of others may be interpreted as an attempt to fill the gap between desire and reality. Crucially, he tries to circumvent the fact that the aquarium is not wholly a commodity by encouraging his readers to be thoughtful consumers (haste and greed are bad qualities for an aquarist, as for a buyer). His solution is thus to buy, but to buy well.

Victorians enthusiastically embraced the aquarium also because it *reflected* them in many ways, but at times the tank could also turn into a dark mirror. Texts like Hibberd's may thus provide valuable insights on the reasons behind its success, but also on those for its quick decline, which was not only due to practical, objective difficulties.[61] Investigating the way in which the hobby was conceptualized, discussed, and imagined may shed some light on the cluster of social and moral meanings that Victorians attributed to it. Such entanglement of values, and the difficulty of matching the expectations deriving from it, is probably among the reasons why, after the initial craze, many tanks were moved from the parlour to the attic.

Notes

1 David Elliston Allen, "Tastes and Crazes," in *Cultures of Natural History*, ed. Nicholas Jardine, James A. Secord, and Emma C. Spary (Cambridge: Cambridge University Press, 1996), 405–406. Allen remarks that, unlike other typically Victorian objects like ferneries, the aquarium 'had no discernible stylistic associations or symbolical import: it seems to have been purely the product of a technical development'; thus, it was enthusiastically adopted mainly because of 'its sheer novelty and its impact as a curiosity.' Ibid., 404–405.
2 I concur with Judith Hamera, who observes that, in the case of the aquarium, 'it is not its lack of symbolic fixity but, rather, its remarkable visual and rhetorical mutability that accounts for its enduring popularity.' Judith Hamera, *Parlor Ponds: The Cultural Work of the American Home Aquarium, 1850–1970* (Ann Arbor: The University of Michigan Press, 2012), 1.
3 Hibberd published three separate books on the aquarium in 1856, devoted to the freshwater, the marine tank, and the water cabinet, respectively. In the same year they were reissued as a single volume under the title *The Book of the Aquarium and Water Cabinet; or Practical Instructions on the Formation, Stocking, and Management, in all Seasons, of Collections of Fresh-Water and Marine Life*. The book, published by Groombridge & Sons, sold very well, and a new edition, 'revised and enlarged', followed in 1860. The 1860 edition was divided into two parts, *The Freshwater Aquarium* and *The Marine Aquarium*, with page numbering restarting from page 1 in each section. Unless otherwise stated, I refer here to this edition.
4 Such approach also informs the illustrations: while other texts mostly depict animals and plants as if they were in the sea, or grouped according to species as in zoological texts, Hibberd's are more focused on aquaria themselves, describing in detail various models of tanks, accessories, and implements.
5 Hibberd, *Book of the Aquarium*, General Preface, v.
6 Philip Rehbock, "The Victorian Aquarium in Ecological and Social Perspective," in *Oceanography: The Past*, ed. Mary Sears and Daniel Merriman (New York: Springer Verlag, 1980), 526.
7 See Allen, "Tastes and Crazes," 403; Isobel Armstrong, *Victorian Glassworlds: Glass Culture and the Imagination, 1830–1880* (Oxford: Oxford University Press, 2008), 369; Sarah Whittingham, *Fern Fever: The Story of Pteridomania* (London: Frances Lincoln, 2012), 18.
8 Rehbock, "The Victorian Aquarium," 526–29.
9 See Alain Corbin, *The Lure of the Sea. The Discovery of the Seaside in the Western World, 1750–1840*, trans. Jocelyn Phelps (London: Penguin, 1995), 97; Rebecca Stott, *Darwin and the Barnacle* (New York: W.W. Norton, 2003), xxiii.
10 Aileen Fyfe, "Natural History and the Victorian Tourist: from Landscapes to Rock Pools," in *Geographies of Nineteenth-Century Science*, ed. David N. Livingstone and Charles W. J. Withers (Chicago: University of Chicago Press, 2011), 380.
11 Hamera, *Parlor Ponds*, 4.
12 Thad Logan, *The Victorian Parlour. A Cultural Study* (Cambridge: Cambridge University Press, 2001), 27; 31.
13 Ibid., 142.

14 Ibid., 28.
15 *Rustic Adornments* was first published by Groombridge & Sons in February 1856, and sold out in six months. A second, enlarged edition followed in 1857, and a third one 'revised, corrected, and enlarged, with nine coloured plates and two hundred and thirty wood engravings' in 1870.
16 Anne Wilkinson, *Shirley Hibberd, the Father of Amateur Gardening: His Life and Works, 1825–1890* (Birmingham: Cortex Design, 2012), 68.
17 Hibberd, *Rustic Adornments*, 3rd ed., 5.
18 Ibid.
19 The information provided much resembles the chapters on aquaria of *Rustic Adornments*, which was published in the same year. However, *The Book of the Aquarium* targeted a slightly less well-to-do audience, as the author explains in the preface to the first edition:

> I have done my best to explain and illustrate the whole rationale of marine and fresh-water tanks in my lately published work, *Rustic Adornments for Homes of Taste*; but since that work, owing to the expense incurred in its production, is published at a price which every lover of the Aquarium cannot command, I have thought it no less a duty than a pleasure to treat the subject more briefly, but still practically, and I hope profitably, in a volume of less dimensions and less cost, written for another class of readers.

Hibberd, *Book of the Aquarium*, 1st ed., unnumbered page.
20 Hibberd, *Freshwater Aquarium*, in *Book of the Aquarium*, 44.
21 Ibid., 18–19.
22 Hibberd, *Marine Aquarium*, in *Book of the Aquarium*, iv.
23 Ibid., 27.
24 Ibid., 14.
25 Ibid., 44.
26 Ibid., 39.
27 The connection was mutually useful: collectors provided Lloyd with specimens and mentioned him in their books (a list of endorsements of his shop from the most popular aquarium manuals was included in his catalogue); in turn, he sold their texts alongside other necessaries for aquarists; moreover, he promoted useful contacts between researchers, fostering exchanges of specimens and information.
28 Hibberd, *Rustic Adornments*, 3rd ed., vi.
29 As noted by Wilkinson, Hibberd kept endorsing products throughout his career, 'although he frequently denied that he ever took money for mentioning names. Victorian writers and publishers were notorious for their 'puffing' of products, which eventually led to legislation designed to promote fairer advertising.' Wilkinson, *Shirley Hibberd*, 138–39.
30 On the complex politics of mid-Victorian science see Bernard V. Lightman, *Victorian Popularizers of Science: Designing Nature for New Audiences* (Chicago: University of Chicago Press, 2010).
31 See for instance Hibberd, *Marine Aquarium*, in *Book of the Aquarium*, 48; 84; 110.
32 Ibid., 44.
33 Silvia Granata, "'Let us Hasten to the Beach': Victorian Tourism and Seaside Collecting," *Lit: Literature Interpretation Theory*, 27, no. 2 (2016): 103–104.
34 Charles Kingsley, *Glaucus; Or, the Wonders of the Shore* (Cambridge: Macmillan & Co., 1855), 5.
35 Ibid., 42.

36 Henry Noel Humphreys, *Ocean Gardens: The History of the Marine Aquarium, and the Best Methods Now Adopted for Its Establishment and Preservation.* (London: Sampson Low, Son, & Co, 1857), 10–11.
37 Hibberd, *Rustic Adornments*, 3rd ed., 2.
38 Hibberd, *Marine Aquarium, in Book of the Aquarium*, iii.
39 Ibid., 34.
40 Ibid., 43.
41 Ibid., 6.
42 Ibid., 9.
43 Hibberd, *Freshwater Aquarium*, in *Book of the Aquarium*, 13–14.
44 Hibberd, *Rustic Adornments*, 3rd ed., 27–28.
45 Hibberd, Marine Aquarium, in Book of the Aquarium, 25.
46 Ibid., 47–48.
47 Ibid., 17.
48 Hibberd, *Freshwater Aquarium*, in *Book of the Aquarium*, 27.
49 See Wilkinson, *Shirley Hibberd*, 30; Christopher Hamlin, "Robert Warington and the Moral Economy of the Aquarium," *Journal of the History of Biology* 19, no. 1 (1986): 149. Such caring attitude, though, did not extend to all animals: Hibberd had a life-long antipathy to cats, which he saw as the natural enemies of both garden flowers and pet birds; he even admitted to having killed some of the cats belonging to his neighbours in 'retaliation' for the havoc they made in his property. Wilkinson, *Shirley Hibberd*, 59; 107.
50 It must be noted that marine creatures were not usually recognised as pets by this time. This was partly due to their marked otherness, and to the limited interaction allowed by the tank. See Hamera, *Parlor Ponds*, 22; 128.
51 Hibberd, *Marine Aquarium*, in *Book of the Aquarium*, 10.
52 Ibid., 18; 51.
53 Crucially, 'objects circulate in different *regimes of value* in space and time', and their value can only be understood by considering how 'they circulate in specific cultural and historical milieus.' Arjun Appadurai, ed., *The Social Life of Things: Commodities in Cultural Perspective.* (Cambridge: Cambridge University Press, 1986), 4.
54 Elaine Freedgood, *The Ideas in Things. Fugitive Meaning in the Victorian Novel.* (Chicago: University of Chicago Press, 2006), 148.
55 Hibberd, *Rustic Adornments*, 2nd ed., 122.
56 Bill Brown, "Thing Theory," *Critical Inquiry* 28, no. 1 (2001): 4.
57 Hamlin, "Robert Warington," 132; Rehbock, "The Victorian Aquarium," 533.
58 In this too, aquarium inhabitants were quite different from more usual pets like cats, dogs or birds, that were often properly buried or memorialized in various ways. See Hannah Velten, *Beastly London: A History of Animals in the City.* (London: Reaktion Books Ltd., 2013), 187.
59 Hibberd, *Rustic Adornments*, 2nd ed., 507–508.
60 Hibberd, *Rustic Adornments*, 3rd ed., 26.
61 Hamlin notes that aquarium inquiries in *Science Gossip* 'declined rapidly between 1866 and 1869; eighteen items in 1866; thirteen in 1867; two in 1868, none in 1869.' Hamlin, "Robert Warington," 132. Hibberd himself admitted in 1860 that 'the 'aquarium mania' may be considered as fairly dead', since those who had taken it on only because it was fashionable soon abandoned it: 'we rarely hear of "aquarians in trouble" now-a-days, because the thousands who set up aquaria, without the least idea that to be successful they must be managed on philosophical principles, have long ago given them up as "troublesome".' According to him, the marine tank would survive mainly as a tool for zoological or botanical studies. Shirley Hibberd,

"Management of Aquaria," *Recreative Science* 1 (1860): 73. On the end of the aquarium craze see also William H. Brock, "Glaucus: Kingsley and the Seaside Naturalists," in *Science for All: Studies in the History of Victorian Science and Education* (Aldershot, Variorum, 1996), 29.

Works Cited

Allen, David Elliston. "Tastes and Crazes." In *Cultures of Natural History*, edited by Nicholas Jardine, James A. Secord and Emma C. Spary, 394–407. Cambridge: Cambridge University Press, 1996.

Appadurai, Arjun, ed. *The Social Life of Things: Commodities in Cultural Perspective*. Cambridge: Cambridge University Press, 1986.

Armstrong, Isobel. *Victorian Glassworlds: Glass Culture and the Imagination, 1830–1880*. Oxford: Oxford University Press, 2008.

Brock, William H. "Glaucus: Kingsley and the Seaside Naturalists." In *Science for All: Studies in the History of Victorian Science and Education*. Aldershot: Variorum, 1996.

Brown, Bill. "Thing Theory." *Critical Inquiry*, 28, no. 1 (2001): 1–22.

Corbin, Alain. *The Lure of the Sea. The Discovery of the Seaside in the Western World, 1750–1840*. Translated by Jocelyn Phelps. London: Penguin, 1995.

Freedgood, Elaine. *The Ideas in Things. Fugitive Meaning in the Victorian Novel*. Chicago: University of Chicago Press, 2006.

Fyfe, Aileen. "Natural History and the Victorian Tourist: From Landscapes to Rock Pools." In *Geographies of Nineteenth-Century Science*, edited by David N. Livingstone and Charles W. J. Withers, 371–98. Chicago: University of Chicago Press, 2011.

Granata, Silvia. "'Let us Hasten to the Beach': Victorian Tourism and Seaside Collecting." *Lit: Literature Interpretation Theory*, 27, no. 2 (2016): 91–110.

Hamera, Judith. *Parlour Ponds: The Cultural Work of the American Home Aquarium, 1850–1970*. Ann Arbor: University of Michigan Press, 2012.

Hamlin, Christopher. "Robert Warington and the Moral Economy of the Aquarium." *Journal of the History of Biology*, 19, no. 1 (1986): 131–53.

Hibberd, Shirley. *Rustic Adornments for Homes of Taste, and Recreations for Town Folk, in the Study and Imitation of Nature*. 2nd ed. London: Groombridge & Sons, 1857.

Hibberd, Shirley. *Rustic Adornments for Homes of Taste. A New Edition, Revised, Corrected, and Enlarged, with Nine Coloured Plates and Two Hundred and Thirty Wood Engravings*. 3rd ed. London: Groombridge & Sons, 1870.

Hibberd, Shirley. *The Book of the Aquarium and Water Cabinet; or Practical Instructions on the Formation, Stocking, and Management, in all Seasons, of Collections of Fresh-Water and Marine Life*. London: Groombridge & Sons, 1856.

Hibberd, Shirley. *The Book of the Aquarium; or Practical Instructions on the Formation, Stocking, and Management in all Seasons, of Collections of Marine and River Animals and Plants*. A New Edition, Revised and Enlarged. Rev. ed. London: Groombridge & Sons, 1860.

Hibberd, Shirley. "Management of Aquaria." *Recreative Science*, 1 (1860): 73–77.

Humphreys, Henry Noel. *Ocean Gardens: The History of the Marine Aquarium, and the Best Methods Now Adopted for its Establishment and Preservation*. London: Sampson Low, Son, & Co., 1857.

Kingsley, Charles. *Glaucus; or, the Wonders of the Shore*. Cambridge: Macmillan & Co., 1855.

A List, with Descriptions, Illustrations, and Prices of Whatever Relates to Aquaria. W. Alford Lloyd, Aquarium Warehouse, 19, 20 and 20a, Portland Road, Regent's Park, 1858.

Lightman, Bernard V. *Victorian Popularizers of Science: Designing Nature for New Audiences*. Chicago: University of Chicago Press, 2010.

Logan, Thad. *The Victorian Parlour. A Cultural Study*. Cambridge: Cambridge University Press, 2001.

Rehbock, Philip. "The Victorian Aquarium in Ecological and Social Perspective." In *Oceanography: The Past*, edited by Mary Sears and Daniel Merriman, 522–39. New York: Springer-Verlag, 1980.

Stott, Rebecca. *Darwin and the Barnacle*. New York: W.W. Norton, 2003.

Velten, Hannah. *Beastly London: A History of Animals in the City*. London: Reaktion Books Ltd., 2013.

Whittingham, Sarah. *Fern Fever: The Story of Pteridomania*. London: Frances Lincoln, 2012.

Wilkinson, Anne. *Shirley Hibberd, the Father of Amateur Gardening: His Life and Works, 1825–1890*. Birmingham: Cortex Design, 2012.

5 'A chimney-piece in Plumtree-court, Holborn'

Plaster of Paris "Images" and Nineteenth-Century Working-Class Material Culture

Ralph Mills

Although working people formed the largest elements of the populations of nineteenth-century industrializing countries, we know relatively little about their domestic material culture.[1] This absence highlights the significance of a unique record of the ornaments on a mantelpiece encountered in a squalid mid-century Holborn alley. A group of apparently prosaic objects provides a rare opportunity to explore aspects of everyday domestic life and thinking.

Situated just south of London's Holborn Viaduct, Plumtree Court is (in 2016) a gloomy side street, shadowed on one side by the brick cliff that is the rear wall of the City Temple and on the other by the new headquarters of an investment bank. It serves merely as a pedestrian link between Shoe Lane and Farringdon Street, and as an access to an underground car park. Plumtree Court was just as gloomy in the nineteenth century, as George Godwin found when he visited 'this pestilent hole' in 1854: 'Long the haunt of fever,' he recorded, and 'a cradle of immorality and misery...the court is very narrow and the drainage very imperfect.'[2] Godwin – architect, builder, activist, and journalist – was drawing attention to the horrendous living conditions of many who experienced suffocating overcrowding and lack of sanitation in the courts and alleys of the area. In Plumtree Court, he commented, the City Medical Officer of Health found sixty-seven people squeezed into the fifteen rooms of number 9; at number 24 he discovered eighteen adults and twenty-two children in just four rooms.[3]

In the midst of his explorations of these unlikely surroundings, Godwin discovered an example of something he felt was special: 'the love of art, which we find very often exhibited in the most miserable quarters, in the shape of plaster casts and little prints.' These 'not very refined...but agreeable and cheering' objects – painted parrots and spotted cats – he described as evidence of 'a striving upwards', and he had a sketch made of 'an actual chimney-piece' (Figure 5.1) 'as a record of some well-known barbaric favourites.'[4]

A Chimney-piece in Plumtree-court, Holborn.

Figure 5.1 George Godwin, 'A chimney-piece in Plumtree-court, Holborn' (1854).

Godwin's drawing is a detailed and hugely valuable record of a rarely studied aspect of the interior lives of those he called 'the labouring classes.'[5] It reveals a mantelpiece and chimney-breast crowded with seemingly unremarkable domestic paraphernalia, some of which is utilitarian (a small mug, a clay pipe, a candlestick), some associated with faith (a crucifix, a rosary, a phial of holy water, and religious prints) surrounding a significant array of purely decorative objects. A mix of symmetry and jumble, it is possible to discern two mysterious figures (perhaps corn dollies or crocheted dolls), a pair of miniature bowls of fruit, an urn, a parrot, and three miniature cats. The smallest of the cats has its back to us, and a second is a "nodder"; its counterbalanced head suspended from a wire loop so that it moves when touched. The third leads us to the source of Godwin's "barbaric favourites," for it is recognizable as a typical *gatto lucchesi* – a plaster of Paris cat from Lucca, in Northern Italy.[6]

If, in the 1850s, you were in Shoe Lane, just around the corner from Plumtree Court, it was likely that you were in the midst of the hustle and bustle remembered by Alfred Bennett:

> "Chair-menders – 'Ornaments for your fire-stoves!' – Fly-catchers – Draught-bags – Italian images – Sham sailors – Groundsel – Baked chestnuts and potatoes – Night refreshments – Fruit and vegetable hawkers – Strawberries in pottles – Street stalls – Orange

girls – Hand-bills – Beggars with paintings – Cheap Jacks – Preachers – Waits – Workmen's paper caps – Soldiers – Sailors – Pensioners – Beadles – Lamplighters – Crossing sweepers – Shoeblacks – Undertakers"[7]

Almost hidden in the midst of that crowd, probably threading his way with care between the peddlers of draught bags and the sham sailors, Bennet had noticed a seller of "Italian images."[8] The "images" that he and his ilk hawked were miniature figures made of plaster of Paris – spotted cats, green parrots, Venuses, Shakespeares, heroes, villains, gods and goddesses, famous buildings, fake fruits, and garish flower pots.

Godwin's sketch can be regarded as an archaeological 'assemblage', a group of artefacts linked stratigraphically at a moment in time, the mantelpiece acting as the 'deposit' in which they had lain undisturbed for one hundred and fifty years. It is therefore possible to 'excavate' this deposit, which contains some eight objects that that can be defined as *miniatures*.[9] This chapter includes some of the results of that exercise.

Before the nineteenth century, 'images' were most likely to be three-dimensional objects, usually miniature statuettes.[10] The origin of the word is linked to imagination and imitation, appropriate for objects that were miniature representations of originals both real and imaginary. So it was that itinerant Italian peddlers of plaster of Paris statuettes, the *figurinai*, were known in the English-speaking world as 'image-sellers.' Contemporary illustrations, artworks and popular media, including newspapers, magazines, and even ballads, tell us that image-sellers, bearing trays of plaster statuettes on their heads, or in baskets, plied their itinerant trade throughout the nineteenth century on every continent and in every industrializing country.[11] They were to be found not only in both urban and rural Britain, but on the other side of the world on a dusty road in Bendigo, the gold rush town in Australia, or amongst dingy New York tenements, or hawking their wares in Russia, Scandinavia, France, Germany, Brazil, and New Zealand.

When Columbus first stepped foot in America, so the tongue-in-cheek story went, he was welcomed by an image-seller from Lucca, who enthusiastically attempted to interest him in his stock-in-trade.[12] In the nineteenth century, image-sellers were ubiquitous. *Figurinai* had been migrating from the impoverished province of Lucca, and principally from the small town of Coreglia Antelminelli, since the eighteenth century. They travelled first to France, then spread through Europe, then across the Atlantic to North and South America and beyond. They may have eventually even been present in Peking.[13]

In Italy, a "master" (*padrone* or *capo*) would collect together a *compagnia*, consisting of a varying but small number of men, often close relatives (*garzoni*). Small boys were 'sold' by their parents, sometimes for pitifully small sums, to the masters, to form the mainstay of the street sales forces.[14] A *compagnia* might include sculptors and mould makers or *formatori*. *Gittatori* would make the plaster casts. The process of 'throwing' (*gittatura*) the casts was not the same as throwing pottery: liquid plaster of Paris would be poured into a mould and then swirled around to ensure it entered all the crevices of the mould and create a hollow cast. The casts were often left uncoloured or sometimes painted bizarre colours by *pittori* or *decoratori*. Others were varnished or given coats of metallic paint to resemble bronze.

In the beginning, their trade was seasonal. A *compagnia* would set off from Lucca in the spring, loaded with casts, and return at the end of the summer. They began to take moulds with them and make casts on the road, using locally purchased plaster of Paris. Later, as *figurinai* spread further and further afield, what began as temporary workshops became more or less permanent. Sometimes called 'statuaries,' these workshops appeared in London, where Thomas Archer described modellers of plaster figures, wearing green tunics, blue blouses, and concertina-shaped hats working in rooms where 'grimy cupids swing disconsolately from the ceilings in a dim twilight till the gas is lighted when they vibrate like monstrous moths intent on self-destruction.'[15]

Workshops were also established in America and beyond. Newspaper accounts tell of a company in 1883 Pittsburgh that used air pressure to force plaster into zinc moulds, while another in Philadelphia utilized cheaper gelatine moulds.[16] In St Paul, Minnesota, a *formatori* explained to a journalist that they added salt to the plaster to increase its strength. We learn from the same sources that a gelatine mould would cost about $2 and would cast about 50 statuettes. Plaster of Paris cost $1 a barrel, enough to make 500 figurines. The journalist calculated that each figurine would cost about 10 cents to manufacture. These competed with better quality casts that cost about 40 cents each to make. Allowing for the time the plaster took to harden, and for trimming and varnishing, it would take two and a half hours to make a statuette, which would be sold for 50 cents.[17]

The image-sellers told journalists that certain figures always sold well ("pretty ladies," Shakespeare and Milton, Venuses) whereas others were a failure (for example, President Cleveland).[18] They also explained that they would saturate a local market, then either move on or exchange their existing moulds for new ones in order to create a fresh stock of characters.[19]

Plaster of Paris is fragile and easily damaged or broken. Plaster objects were cheap and readily discarded, and gypsum plaster does not survive in archaeological deposits. As a result, unlike the more familiar and robust ceramic decorative objects made typically in Staffordshire, most plaster 'images' have not survived and have therefore been overlooked by historians and archaeologists. During the nineteenth century, however, there were only occasional references to 'china', while plaster 'images' and 'sunburnt' image-sellers 'with flashing black eyes' captured the attention and imagination of writers and artists, who wrote about them, drew them, painted them, and eventually photographed them.[20] Image-sellers had begun to be represented at the end of the eighteenth century in crude woodcuts illustrating cheap and cheerful chap-books and children's books. They were soon so familiar that they could be used to represent the letter *I* in children's alphabet books (Figure 5.2).

Figure 5.2 'Images, very fine, very pretty. From *The Uncle's Present, a New Battledore*' (1810).

William Wordsworth noticed image-sellers early in the nineteenth century. In 1805 he wrote of:

> The Italian, as he thrids his way with care,
> Steadying, far-seen, a frame of images
> Upon his head; with basket at his breast[21]

Wordsworth also identified two of the most popular 'images' when he wrote about an 'adventurous boy', a London-bound 'Italian Itinerant', in his 1820 *Memorials of a tour on the Continent,* who would, on his head:

> ...poise a show
> Of Images in seemly row;
> The graceful form of milk-white Steed,
> Or Bird that soared with Ganymede;
> Or through our hamlets thou wilt bear
> The sightless Milton, with his hair
> Around his placid temples curled;
> And Shakspeare at his side—a freight,
> If clay could think and mind were weight,
> For him who bore the world![22]

A few years later, the lesser poet 'Upton' told us of an image-boy:

> Seduced from a land to the sciences dear,
> A poor distressed foreigner crawls about here;
> His hope and dependence for lodging and bread,
> The image, "fine image," he bears on his head:
> Pity, pity a stranger, debarred of all joy,
> A destitute, wandering Italian Boy.[23]

By the middle of the century, middle-class artists and writers were beginning to co-opt image-sellers to communicate allegory and romanticism. For example, Liverpool artist William Daniels painted himself as an image seller cradling Homer, with Shakespeare and a colourful parrot prominent on the tray he balanced on his head. James Collinson, flirting with the Pre-Raphaelites, painted image-boys in *Italian Image – Boys at a Roadside Alehouse* (1849). Another minor poet, James Smith, had romantically and informatively described 'The Image Boy' in his 1841 work that began:

> WHOE'ER has trudged on frequent feet,
> From Charing Cross to Ludgate Street,
> That haunt of noise and wrangle,
> Has seen on journeying through the Strand,

A foreign Image-vender stand
Near Somerset's quadrangle.[24]
His coal-black eye, his balanced walk,
His sable apron, white with chalk,
His listless meditation,
His curly locks, his sallow cheeks,
His board of celebrated Greeks,
Proclaim his trade and nation.[25]

Smith then contrasted the eclectic but well-founded wares of the Italian boy with lesser examples, objects that he gently scorned but which no doubt featured on many a mantelpiece: Queen Victoria with carrot-coloured hair, a poodle with a golden tail, John Wesley, a parrot, a milkmaid with a pea green pail. Significantly, amongst the 'celebrated Greeks', along with Cleopatra, Homer, Milton, Locke, Abelard, and Heloise, is listed Napoleon.[26]

Many, if not the majority, of the figures on the image-sellers' trays and in their baskets were reduced-scale copies; miniatures of classical or contemporary statues, or copies of existing figures, including moulds of Staffordshire figurines.[27] The 'designs' were therefore either archaeological artefacts (for example, the Venus de Medici and the Venus de Milo) or roughly contemporary (for example, Canova's *Shakespeare*, Sauvage's *Enfant lisant, Enfant dessinant* or Joshua Reynold's *The Infant Samuel*).[28] There was almost certainly a process of copying copies of copies, which together with the wear and tear on moulds, many of which were plaster of Paris, added to the lack of detail of some of the figures.[29]

Other figures were sculpted by anonymous sculptors and *formatori* in Italy, on the road or in the temporary or permanent workshops the image-sellers established around the world.[30] These were the cats and other animals, the buildings, the often-inaccurate figures of contemporary heroes and heroines, politicians and celebrities that the image-sellers created to meet demands, sometimes local, resulting from fame or infamy, be that short- or long-lived.

Although some plaster images were direct copies of Staffordshire originals, there were often major differences between them. The *figurinai* created scores of miniature representations of classical statues, for example. Working-class mantelpieces therefore featured many a good copy, in miniature, of Venus de Medici and Venus de Milo. Staffordshire Venuses, sculpted by anonymous potters, are lumpen by comparison.[31] Italian image-sellers hawked figurines and busts of Greek and Roman gods and goddesses: Apollo, Clytie, the Belvedere Hercules, the winged Victory, the Dying Gladiator, Psyche, and others.[32] They also copied and sold contemporary favourites, such as Powers' *Greek Slave* and Falguire's *Diana* and Clesinger's *Woman bitten by Snake*.[33] They shared with Staffordshire wares the ability to materialize fame, with a host of celebrities from Beethoven and 'Battling Nelson' (the boxer) to George Washington and the Duke of Wellington.[34] But, as Eduard Charton wrote in an 1850 edition of *Le Magazin Pittoresque*:

> Most literary and political celebrities appeared [on the image-seller's board]...soon to descend and disappear...we simply cast our admiration or our whims of the moment in plaster, as if we wanted to symbolise the fragility of the material and of what it represents...Alas! How many of these reputations even outlasted plaster! Those great men who disappeared before their busts; who became out of date before being yellowed by time! ...The moulder is a strict judge...he ruthlessly breaks the moulds of anyone who is no longer in vogue.[35]

A vein of humour runs through accounts of the activities of image makers and sellers. For example, at one point in an otherwise grim exploration of London in 1845, George Reynolds described an Italian 'statuary' who operated a 'depository' of plaster of Paris figures. Here he found:

> A strange assembly of images...heathen gods seemed to fraternize with angels, Madonnas, and Christian saints; Napoleon and Wellington stood motionless side by side; George the Fourth and Greenacre occupied the same shelf; William Pitt and Cobbett appeared to be contemplating each other with silent admiration; Thomas Paine elbowed a bishop; Lord Castlereagh seemed to be extending his hand to welcome Jack Ketch; Cupid pointed his arrow at the bosom of a pope.[36]

Reynolds mischievously paired opposing and ill-matched characters; king with criminal, bishop with anti-religious reformer, Cupid and celibate Pope, Napoleon and Wellington. But in doing so he also inadvertently demonstrates a little of the range of 'types' that people sought and bought: not only heroes but also anti-heroes, revolutionaries and reformers, royalty and rogues. The working people of the time were happy to have heathen gods or angels on their mantelpieces, and perhaps both. Each object on the mantelpiece suggests meanings and symbolisms that perhaps the purchaser was unaware of, but which formed the agency of the figure. The parrot, for example, was long associated with the exotic, with sunshine, with good luck, and with the erotic. The bowls of fruit, probably brightly coloured, again would have communicated the exotic, as well as the rarely achieved. The urn spoke of antiquity and perhaps immortality. The cats of sensuality, of companionship, of the magical.

Cats had been one of the Italian image-seller's earliest staples. Easy to sculpt and cast, and less liable to break during transport, the *gatto lucchesi* became a sort of trade mark. In Sweden, image-sellers were called *Gipskatter*, a term that eventually became one of racial abuse. Often decorated with no more than a few dots applied using a smoky lamp, plaster cats appeared on mantelpieces in the eighteenth century. This argues against those who, influenced by the rarity of Staffordshire ceramic cats, have suggested that there was little love for ornamental cats until the end of the nineteenth century.[37] It may be that the plaster cat was so popular that Staffordshire potters couldn't compete.

The market, of course, evolved. In the eighteenth century, before the 'industrial revolution', John Flaxman, father of the more well-known sculptor John Flaxman, had a shop in Covent Garden and later on the Strand where he made and sold plaster casts, and where his son learned many of the skills he was to later utilize in his career. Flaxman senior's stock, in 1759, included Niobe, the Venus de Medici, Hercules, Ajax and Achilles 'for the few'. 'Less refined and more ordinary tastes' were offered George II, Lord Howe, Admiral Hawke, General Wolfe, William Pitt, and Admiral Boscawen.[38] In those days, as the *Gentleman's Magazine* commented in 1827, 'the sale of plaster figures...was not so hackneyed a trade, as it has now become by the large importation of Italians.'[39] George Godwin, too, had remarked that the type of object on the Plumtree Court had previously 'decorated homes of greater pretence' before finding 'a resting place lower down the social scale.'[40]

But once the trade had become 'hackneyed', the low prices of the miniatures, the fact that trading took place in the street or at the door, and the poor reputation of the 'images' all point to mostly working-class customers. *The New York Times* in 1874 reported that 'their purchasers are, for the most part, among people in humble circumstances who have still something for superfluities.' This is essentially the definition of 'working class' as used in this chapter: people to whom the purchase of a non-utilitarian decorative object represented a significant part of any disposable income. That object therefore would be regarded as having value.

While image-sellers hawked their wares amongst tenements, along the busy streets of industrial districts and areas where living conditions were poor, they were generally scorned by writers on home décor, whose readers would have generally been middle class. A plaster of Paris figurine might be purchased for some specific purpose, for example a plaster Cupid for a Valentine's day decoration, but rarely recommended for general use.[41] 'Images' were to be found in humbler abodes around the world: the *Sydney Empire* noted in 1873 that many cottages had a table 'bedizened with plaster images.'[42] We learn from the *Brooklyn Daily Eagle* in 1888 that:

> The Italian image man bore upon his head figures he had moulded in clay and painted in bright colours. There was the Virgin child, the crucifix, the Madonna, St Peter's church at Rome, the Capitol at Washington, Jenny Lind, Daniel Webster, roosters, rabbits, dogs, etc. These images generally adorn the mantels of the servants' rooms.[43]

The makers of figurines were also working class.[44] This meant that they and the image-sellers benefited from short lines of communication. They drank in the same taverns, bargained in the streets with the same house-wives, and mixed with the same savoury and unsavoury individuals, all of whom were potential and actual customers.[45] They lived amongst the people they sold to, and were usually as poor, if not poorer, than many of them. That they were slightly exotic, slightly 'alien', perhaps helped also. They brought a little of 'sunny Italy' to the dull streets of grey London and chilly Baltimore, and exoticism and good taste to mining towns in the United States, South America, and Australia.

Most customers of image-sellers would have been female: 'The wife of the British workmen has one spot of which she is especially proud, and to adorn it she is willing to make some sacrifice. This is the mantelshelf over the fireplace' reported the *New York Times* in 1874. 'This favourite place is generally loaded with a variety of ornaments of the most singular description. Among them the images of the Italian vendor occupy a prominent position.'[46] Commentators detected an improvement in tastes as the century progressed. Writing in 1837, William Hone had approved of a change from 'the uncouth cat and the barbarous parrot' as evidence that 'society is improving in every direction.'[47] Two decades later, Henry Mayhew noted a 'remarkable' improvement in both 'images' and 'casts' and 'moulded productions of all kinds...from the pristine rudeness of "green parrots".' This, he wrote, was 'creditable to the taste of working people, who are the chief purchasers of the smaller articles.'[48]

Two popular 'images' demonstrate the variety of roles that miniatures performed on the stage that was the nineteenth-century working-class mantelpiece: figurines of Venus and Napoleon.

Henri Brest, French vice-consul on the Greek island of Melos, died there aged 100 in 1896. It was he who had first taken charge of the fragmentary 'Venus de Milo' after its discovery some seventy-six years earlier. By the time Brest died the sculpture was dubbed by the *Pall Mall Gazette* 'the most remunerative effigy of the goddess that the world has ever known...she has acquired a pile for many peripatetic Italian image sellers.'[49] Her fame would be easily understandable in a period of easy and rapid communications like the present, but in the early nineteenth century it demonstrated a broad and speedy spreading of knowledge and awareness amongst the working classes that is difficult to explain. Although one can understand copies of the various Venuses appearing in museums and galleries, they also stood on many mantelpieces, as William Hone noted, in working-class districts, along with Apollo and 'other beauties of ancient sculpture.'[50]

The West Australian explained eloquently in 1884:

Pause before Venus de Medici with no vulgar gaze, but with admiration at so true a conception of the goddess of love and beauty and such a model for modern times. Of course the originals are perfect, but they are beyond our reach; it would be sufficient however for us if the works of 'Phidias' were correctly modelled from the originals, and no matter where obtained whether from a statuary in the New Road, London, or from an Italian image boy in the streets.[51]

That Venus was a familiar entity in the nineteenth century, a familiarity that ignored class boundaries, was underlined by Charles Dickens, who in *Barnaby Rudge* had his character Miggs exclaim, 'I wouldn't seem to say to all male creeturs "Come and kiss me"'—and here a shudder quite convulsed her frame—'for any earthly crowns as might be offered. Worlds,' Miggs added solemnly, 'should not reduce me. No. Not if I was Wenis'. 'Well, but you ARE Wenus, you know,' said Mr Dennis, confidentially.'[52]

Although Aphrodite/Venus embodied love, sexuality, and beauty, the popular press was nevertheless able to extract humour from the goddess. In 1827 a street keeper in Walbrook had charged Andrea Giannone with offering for sale 'that there image for sale' – a sleeping Venus – which the street-keeper thought to be 'indecent, not to say indelicate.'[53] The Chief Clerk supposed that 'persons of the street keeper's delicacy will shortly seize our Apollo Belvedere' (a full-size cast of which had been placed in the Egyptian Hall by the 'Corporation Committee of Taste') 'and break it to pieces, to prove the superior purity of their ideas.' The Italian did not appear to understand English and simply laughed. The Lord Mayor telling him that it was 'no laughing matter,' let him go, advising him that if he was caught again he would be punished. The Italian was advised that he must not come again into the city unless he put 'petticoats on his figures' because 'all the taste is on the other side of Temple Bar.' The Italian 'went away laughing.' The event inspired *The Examiner* to include a piece of doggerel that poked fun at the 'sad Macaroni', the over-zealousness of the censorial public servant and the nonsensical instruction to clothe the statuette:

> The heathenish wench may be pretty;
> But unless she thinks best
> To have herself drest,
> Hang me if she comes in the City.[54]

A lighthearted piece in an 1888 edition of the *Springfield Daily Republic*, tells of the art club that sketched the Venus of Milo ('unarmed and having nothing to defend herself') 'or rather a plaster image representing that lady, who is now dead.' The writer muses that the statue 'is probably inaccurate, as it represents her as having no arms or hands' and complains that it isn't worth making a statue of 'people who become exhausted abruptly at the shoulder' and who have no funny bones to hit on the mantelpiece.[55]

This gentle humour demonstrates an important, international, commonality of knowledge, for to be able to understand the joke the reader, wherever they are in the world, has to be familiar with the details of original. For example, at the tail end of the century a journalist describes an encounter between an image-seller, a 'swarthy son of Italy', and a *Cincinnati Commercial Tribune* newspaper office wit. Having dismissed 'Napolyun ze gret' and 'Vognah, de gret moosishin', the 'sporting editor' asks about 'Venus duh Meelo' who costs 'thirty cent-a.'[56] The editor exclaims, 'Thirty cents for an old broken plaster of Paris figure? Throw it away.' The image-seller explains that the statue doesn't have arms: 'Dah nevveh fin-a da arrums.' The editor continues the jape, telling the Italian that if he made one with arms he'd pay thirty cents for it, but 'I wouldn't give you a nickel for it in that damaged condition.' The unfortunate Italian offers the Venus for a quarter ('Dat Statue de fines' in all de worl'. It ees wort millions dollas') but in the end leaves, disgusted.[57] More seriously, the *Pittsburg Dispatch* considered that 'Every home with growing children should have reproduction in some form of the Venus of Milo. It is an education in itself to be brought up with it.'[58]

Like many of the popular figurines, both female and male, cast by the image-men, Venuses were either nude or semi-naked. This miniature state of *déshabillé* inspired Thomas Hardy to write a passage in *Jude the Obscure* in which Sue comes across an image-seller and choses a Venus ('of standard pattern') and an Apollo from his stock, which included Diana, Bacchus, Mars, kings and queens, a minstrel, and Cupid. Having bought the figures for 'considerably less' than the ten shillings initially demanded, and the image-seller having gone on his way, Sue has second thoughts about her purchase, which suddenly 'seemed so very large now that they were in her possession, and so very naked.'[59] As well as Sue's mixture of enthusiasm and shame, Hardy incidentally reveals a sales ploy widely used by image sellers, who would begin negotiations by asking a ridiculously high sum and then abruptly drop the price or accept a fraction of the original without many, or any, intermediate steps. This often surprised the customer into going ahead with a purchase, just as Sue did in Hardy's novel.

Even Queen Victoria was not resistant to the charms both of image-sellers and Venus. In 1853, the *Morning Post* reported that amongst the crowd watching the Queen catch a train at Windsor station was '...a poor Italian boy, with his rude frame of images upon his head.' The Queen noticed the boy and asked that he follow her to her suite. 'The Queen gazed for a moment on the youth, and then selected from his little stock, "The Infant Samuel Praying", a "Venus', and a "Lady at the Bath".'[60]

Not all Venuses were equal. A reporter from the *St Paul Daily Globe*, who was visiting a plaster of Paris workshop in 1885, found it difficult to identify some of the figures 'that might have been the Venus of Milo or the Goddess of Liberty; at any rate they were female figures, with about as many clothes on as the females wear at some variety theaters.'[61] Lillie French, too, warns us that 'very few of the small casts of the Venus of Milo... are made from beautiful models, and I have never seen a small one that did not disappoint me.'[62] But Venus was still displaying her 'solemn majesty' in St Paul, Minnesota, in 1902 and posed 'in all her wondrous loveliness' in Erigo Guaspari's Indianapolis workshop in 1903.[63]

Napoleon Bonaparte was just as enthusiastically displayed on mantelpieces around the world. On entering a room in her South Australian home and discovering a burglary, Mrs Piesse exclaimed, 'Oh dear, not only my money is gone, but Napoleon's head is gone along with it!'[64] Mrs Piesse's distress would have been understood by many during the nineteenth century. George Shaw, who worked in Staffordshire potteries, recording his memories at the end on the nineteenth century, was puzzled by the popularity of Napoleon:

> I remember the figure of Napoleon Bonaparte was the leading article of our industry at this toy factory. These Napoleons must have been in large demand somewhere, for shoals of them were made at that time...It is curious how a man who thirty years before had been a veritable ogre and demon to the English people should now have become so popular. If all the Napoleons made at this toy manufactory could have had life given them, then England, if not invaded, would have been crowded by military Frenchmen, and of the dreaded Napoleonic type.[65]

Shaw described working people's original 'terror' of Napoleon, but throughout the world he soon became associated with a complex mix of nostalgia, nationalism, working-class identity, republicanism, and quiet resistance to the establishment.

Napoleon provided artists with opportunity for allegory. John Thomas Smith etched a diminutive, isolated figure of the recently defeated Bonaparte next to a larger bust of Wellington standing on the tray of the image-seller in his 1815 engraving *Very Fine, Very Cheap*, one of a series of illustrations of street cries. *The Fall of Napoleon* is an 1836 painting by George Wallis in Wolverhampton Art Gallery. As a work of art it is not spectacular, and indeed it was reviewed rather dismissively at the time it went on show. However, when first exhibited it caused a sensation amongst gallery visitors. It shows two sailors, one black, both presumably drunk, staggering along a pavement and tripping up (deliberately?) an unfortunate image-seller who is coming around the corner of a building. From the image-seller's tray topples a plaster figurine of Bonaparte. The use of the figurine as a visual reference to the demise of Napoleon underlines the familiarity of these objects at the time. The painting also incidentally nicely shows the arrangement of spikes or rods

Figure 5.3 'The Figure Merchant' (1852). Frontispiece for *Godey's Lady's Book*. Several Napoleon figures are present on the tray. The Italian Image Boy (1888). True Williams, *Belford's Annual* (left-hand image).

on the image-seller's board that fitted into the hollow interior of the casts he balanced precariously on his head.

Several Napoleons appear on the tray of the image-boy pictured on the frontispiece of the 1852 American publication *Godey's Women's Book* (Figure 5.3, Right) and towards the end of the century, *Belfords Annual*, another American magazine, this time for children, published an illustration of an image-seller that not only shows the continuing popularity of Napoleon, but also of cats (Figure 5.3, Left).

Through what they represented and what they meant to their owners, these miniature decorative objects provide us with evidence of their 'social function.' They are 'instruments furthering the ideological foundations of society.'[66] Plaster cats or parrots, Venuses and Napoleons not only act as 'aesthetic objects or reflections of the spirit of their times' but also allow us to reveal and examine the 'fundamental attitudes and presuppositions by which any age lives, and on which all of the institutions of every society must ultimately rest.'[67] Gowans defines 'social function' as:

> the uses of arts and artifacts in society—what they were intended for by those who commissioned them, in addition to what significance they may have for us today, either as reflections of social values in the past or as aesthetic objects in the present; in addition to whatever component of artistic expression they may have.[68]

To this I would add the uses to which they were put by those in the past who acquired them, which often differed radically from the intentions of their creators, and the ways that the objects, through their agency, influenced society (a reverse view).

Miniature 'images' can tell us much about working-class people in the recent past, their 'states of being, activities, relationships, needs, fears, hopes…they reflect beliefs of which the makers, individually or collectively (as society), were unaware or, if aware, unwilling to express openly, to verbalize.'[69] Because working people tended to live near the centres of cities or close to the industries in which they laboured, much of their infrastructure has been destroyed by subsequent developments and the clearance of 'slums.' Until quite recently, archaeologists tended to regard nineteenth-century deposits as disturbed 'overburden.'[70] Most contemporaries who wrote about 'ordinary people' focused on 'the poor' whose miseries lent melodrama to the works of novelists and fuel to the writings of Engels, Marx, Mayhew, and Booth. But for the expanding capitalist system to 'work' it was necessary that people bought the products manufactured by the new industries.

Henry Mayhew calculated that in mid-century London there would have been approximately 1.5 million workers, a further 1.5 million part-time workers, and a similar number of people who worked occasionally or were unemployed.[71] Most of these people would have been leading 'quiet respectable lives of hard work', as W.W. How, The Bishop Suffragen for East London, wrote in 1888.[72] Any member of one of these huge groups could have bought and displayed decorative objects that cost at most a few pence and often just a farthing. Multiplying these already large numbers to include the rest of Britain and the world's industrializing countries implies that the image-sellers had very many potential customers. F. S. Schwarzbach calculated that Staffordshire produced at least 1,000,000 figures each year (and that 'double or treble that amount is not an unreasonable figure').[73] Assuming that plaster of Paris figures was cheaper and more widely distributed, many millions must have been sold during the century.

These objects appear to confer no advantage or superiority on their owners. Indeed it could be said that they did the reverse, as, in the eyes of many commentators, they communicated poor or bad taste. They were nevertheless desired by very many. The culture of knick-knacks and bric-à-brac may be a conscious or unconscious grouping in opposition to the establishment, with the objects on the mantelpiece acting as badges, signals both to their owners and to any visitors from the same or different classes. That they were hugely valued is borne out by Octavia Hill's rueful account of a lady living in a gloomy basement who, when offered more salubrious accommodation, was reluctant to move because she was afraid that her 'bits of things' would look bad in better light.[74] 'The working man's home' wrote Simon Patten in 1907, 'is crowded with tawdry, unmeaning and useless objects; each pointless object is loved, however, as the mark of superiority and success, and its enjoyment energizes the possessor.'[75]

Sales of long-established favourites, the Venuses, Apollos, Napoleons, Clyties, Washingtons, and the like, depended on the public enthusiasm for these characters. As well as buying poorly moulded and bizarrely painted cats and parrots, or sentimental figures of *The Infant Samuel at Prayer*, working-class people acquired figurines of ancient Greek gods and goddesses, as well as miniature busts of Shakespeare, Milton, and Walter Scott. They had enough disposable income and enough interest and knowledge to support image-sellers throughout the industrial revolution and up to the Second World War. They invested in figures that demonstrated a wider range of awareness and taste, and probably literacy, than might be assumed. Image-sellers were often regarded as spreading knowledge and good taste: an anonymous writer in *The Penny Magazine* suggested in 1833 that 'those...venders of images, by selling for a few pence the plaster busts of great men and casts from ancient works of art, may pretend to the dignity of traders, and even have the merit of improving and propagating a taste for the fine arts.'[76]

That working people, who outnumbered their middle-class peers throughout the century, were showing signs of increasing materiality raised fears of working-class foment. In 1854 the writer George Sala satirized a publican for his enthusiasm for things 'classical', and perhaps revealed some of that middle- and upper-class unease. He wrote that:

> There wasn't an Italian image-man out of Leather Lane that came in to take a drop but he'd buy a Venus, or a Jenny Lind, or a Holy Family of; and these he'd stick up on gim-crack brackets under his tubs, and ask me with a simpering grin I didn't think it classical? Classical! What business has a license victualler with the classics?[77]

Similar anxiety had been expressed by *Punch* in a verse published in 1842 that contained the lines:

> But yet when at the bookseller's
> I call for Scott or Moore,
> Some servant buys the very same—
> Such books destroy the poor![78]

Henry Glassie wrote that 'a method based on the document is prejudiced; fated to neglect the majority of people, for they were non-literate and, within the boundaries of literacy, to neglect the majority of people, for they did not write.'[79] It can be suggested that this majority communicated through their material culture rather than writing. Carl Moritz's observation in 1782 that 'the common people of England read their English authors' rang true throughout the following century.[80] Jonathan

Rose surveyed working-class cultural literacy in the nineteenth century and suggested that 'autodidact culture flourished.'[81]

The Holborn mantelpiece may have been decorated with prosaic cats and parrots and bowls of plaster fruit but it linked to material evidence of a significant working-class cultural literacy that was uniform throughout the industrializing world of the nineteenth century. Unbeknown to those who displayed their knick-knacks on it, the mantelpiece acted as a 'node', to borrow Bjørnar Olsen's term, in a vast network that stretched from Italy, across Europe, to the New World.[82] Exploring that network linked the author to those itinerant street sellers of 'images' who were probably hawking their wares just around the corner in Shoe Lane, shouting 'Buy my images! Very pretty! Very cheap!' even as Godwin was visiting Plumtree Court.

Notes

1 Cohen, Lizabeth A. "Embellishing a Life of Labor: An interpretation of the Material Culture of American Working-Class Homes, 1885–1915," *Journal of American Culture* 3, no. 4 (1980): 752; Keith Matthews, "Familiarity and Contempt: The Archaeology of the 'Modern'," in *The Familiar Past? Archaeologies of Later Historical Britain*, eds. Sarah Tarlow and Susie West (London: Routledge, 1999), 57; Ruth Mather "The Home-Making of the English Working Class," *Many Headed Monster* blog, 2013, http://manyheadedmonster.wordpress.com/2013/07/10/ruth-mather-the-home-making-of-the-english-working-class.

2 George Godwin, *The Builder 14* (1856): 305.

3 Ibid.

4 Ibid.

5 Ibid.

6 Ibid.

7 Alfred Rosling Bennett, *London and Londoners in the Eighteen-Fifties and Sixties* (London: Unwin, 1924), 52–53.

8 William Wordsworth, *The Prelude* (London: Moxon, 1850).

9 Ralph Mills, *Miniatures in Historical Archaeology: Toys, Trifles and Trinkets Re-examined*. Master's thesis, Department of Archaeology and Ancient History, University of Leicester, 2010; Ralph Mills, "Material Culture in Miniature: The Historical Archaeology of Nineteenth Century Miniature Objects" in *The Importance of British Material Culture to Historical Archaeologies of the Nineteenth Century*, ed. Alasdair Brooks (Lincoln NA: University of Nebraska Press, 2015), 243–73.

10 In his *Dictionary* of 1785, Samuel Johnson defined "image" as: "Any corporeal representation, generally used of statues; a statue; a picture; an idol; a false god; a copy; representation; likeness; a semblance; show; appearance; an idea; a representation of any thing to the mind; a picture drawn in the fancy."

11 There are many contemporary examples of newspaper stories featuring "image-sellers." For example *The Examiner* (London) 4 November 1827; The *Bendigo Advertiser*, 14 July 1857; The *St Johnsbury Caledonian* (Vermont) 27 December 1867; the *New York Times*, 5 April 1874. Magazine examples include *Punch* (London); *Godey's Picture Book* (Philadelphia);

Belford's Annual (Canada/US) and *The Penny Magazine of the Society for the Diffusion of Useful Knowledge* (London). For ballads, see Rohan McWilliam, "The Theatricality of the Staffordshire Figurine," *Journal of Victorian Culture* 10, no. 1 (2005): 109.

12 Raniero Paulucci di Calboli, *Larmes Et Sourires De l'émigration Italienne* (Paris: Juven, 1909), 109; Janet Ross and Nelly Erichsen, *The Story of Lucca* (London: Dent, 1912), 116.

13 Renato Fucini, "La Luminara" *Cento Sonetti in Vernacolo Pisano di Renato Fucini 1870.* Biblioteca Nazionale Braidense, www.braidense.it/scaffale/fucini1.html (Accessed 17 August 2017).

14 In 1890, five little boys were sold "for a bottle of olive oil and $2 apiece" (*The Opelousas Courier*, Louisiana, 28 June 1890).

15 Thomas Archer, *The Pauper, The Thief and the Convict* (London: Groombridge, 1865), 66–67.

16 Zinc moulds: *Arizona Weekly Citizen*, 4 August 1883; gelatine moulds: *New York Times*, 5 April 1874.

17 *St Paul Daily Globe*, 29 November 1885.

18 There are many references to figurines of Shakespeare, Milton and Venus. For example *The Indianapolis Journal*, 17 March 1889 reported: "We sell more Shakespeare and Milton busts than any other kind." *The Pittsburg Dispatch*, 12 June 1892: "Every home with growing children should have reproduction in some form of the Venus of Milo." That figurines of Cleveland sold poorly is mentioned in *The Indianapolis Journal*, 17 March 1889.

19 *Arizona Weekly Citizen*, 4 August 1883.

20 George Augustus Sala, *London Up to Date* (London: Black, 1894), 228.

21 Wordsworth, *The Prelude*.

22 William Wordsworth, *Memorials of a Tour on the Continent, 1820* (London: Longman, 1822).

23 Upton, "The Italian Boy" *The Universal Songster or Museum of Mirth, Vol 3.* (London, 1826), 3.

24 Somerset House.

25 "Chalk" refers to plaster of Paris. Plaster figures were and are often (especially in North America) called "chalkware." "Celebrated Greeks" were figurines of Greek gods, heroes and mythological figures. James Smith, *Comic Miscellanies in Prose and Verse, Volume 1* (London: Colburn, 1841).

26 Ibid.

27 Anon, "Imitation is the Sincerest Form of Flattery," *Georgian Index*, 2008. www.georgianindex.net/Chalkware/chalkware.html (Accessed 17 August 2017).

28 William Hone included Venuses in his 1837 article "Nature and Art: Buy My Images" in his *Every-day Book and Table Book: Or, Everlasting Calendar of Popular Amusements. Vol II.* (London: Tegg), 308. *New York Times*, 5 April 1874. Canova's portrait of Shakespeare was the standard original for most plaster busts: Joseph Parker Norris, *The Portraits of Shakespeare* (Philadelphia: Lindsay, 1885), 67. Referring to them as "street images," Hone reported that the copies of Sauvage's two little boys (*Enfant Lisant, Enfant Dessinant*, 1781) were hugely popular in 1826 (Hone *Every-day Book*, 315). Now manufactured in resin, they can still be purchased today. *The Infant Samuel Praying*, a three dimensional copy of Joshua Reynolds' 1776 painting *The Infant Samuel*, was also a popular figure. Queen Victoria purchased one from "a poor Italian boy" at Windsor railway station (*Morning Post*, London, 21 July 1853).

29 Hone, *Every-day Book*, 311.

30 Paola Sensi-Isolani, "Italian Image Makers in France, England and the United States," in *Italian Americans Celebrate Life, the Arts and Popular Culture*, eds. Paola A. Sensi-Isolani, and Anthony Julian Tamburri, (San Francisco: Italian American Studies Association, 1990), 95–116.

31 Compare the ceramic Venuses at www.mystaffordshirefigures.com/blog/venus with the Venus de Medici being proffered for sale by Thomas Rowlandson's image-seller of 1820 (*Images*, one of *Rowlandson's Characteristic Sketches of the Lower Orders*).

32 Sensi-Isolani, 99.

33 *The Daily Dispatch* (Richmond, Virginia), 3 March 1857. *The Weekly Thibodaux Sentinel and Journal of the 8th Senatorial District*, 10 October 1896.

34 A figurine of "Battling Nelson" was reported by *The San Francisco Call*, 22 December 1904.

35 Edouard Charton, "Marchands de Figures de Plâtre," *Le Magazin Pittoresque* (Paris, 1850), 588–89 [translated by the author].

36 George W. M. Reynolds, *The Mysteries of London* (London: Vickers, 1845), 173. James Greenacre (1785–1837) was the "Edgware Road Murderer", hanged for the murder of his fiancée in 1837; William Pitt the Younger (1759–1806) was a politician and Prime Minister; William Cobbett (1763–1835) was a parliamentary reformer; Thomas Paine (1737–1809) was politician, philosopher, revolutionary and opponent of organised religion; Robert Stewart, Vicount Castlereagh (1769–1822) was a statesman; Jack Ketch (d 1686) was an infamous executioner.

37 Myrna Schkolne, *People, Passions, Pastimes and Pleasures: Staffordshire Figures 1810–1835* (Winston Salem, NC: Hot Lane Press, 2006), 230; Adrian Harding, and Nicholas Harding, *Victorian Staffordshire Figures 1835–1875. Book Four.* (Atglen, PA: Schiffer, 1998), 236.

38 *The Huddersfield Chronicle and West Yorkshire Advertiser*, 13 August 1859.

39 Simon Jacob, "Plaster Figure Makers: A Short History," *National Portrait Gallery*, 2011.
www.npg.org.uk/research/programmes/plaster-figure-makers-history.php (Accessed 17 August 2017).

40 Godwin, 305.

41 *The Sunday Oregonian*, 6 February 1910.

42 *Empire* (Sydney), 8 May 1873.

43 *Brooklyn Daily Eagle*, 27 May 1888.

44 F.S. Schwarzbach, "Twelve Ways of Looking at a Staffordshire Figurine: An Essay in Cultural Studies," *Victorian Institute Journal* 29 (2001): 47.

45 Sala, *London Up To Date*, 70. There are a number of accounts of image-sellers interacting with wives and housewives, some of whom would trade their husband's clothing for figurines. For example *The Highland Weekly News* (Ohio) 23 December 1880 tells of exchanging an Ulster overcoat for "a plaster-of-paris cat in seven colours." George Reynolds, amongst others, wrote of the often-brutal lives of image-sellers in working-class districts: George W. M. Reynolds, *The Mysteries of London* (London: Vickers, 1845), 45. The *Omaha Daily Bee*, 27 May 1888, luridly describes the miseries of "Dago Alley," where "the Italian roams about with plaster images."

46 *New York Times*, 5 April 1874.

47 Hone, *Every-day Book*, 315.

48 Henry Mayhew, *London Labour and the London Poor Volume I.* (London: Griffin, Bohn, 1861), 217.

49 *Pall Mall Gazette*, 4 August 1896.
50 Hone, *Every-day Book*, 315.
51 *The West Australian*, 30 October 1884.
52 Charles Dickens, *Barnaby Rudge* (Ware: Wordsworth Editions, 1998), 551.
53 *The Examiner*, November 4th 1827.
54 Ibid.
55 *Springfield Daily Republic*,10 March 1888.
56 "Vognah" was a mispronunciation of Richard Wagner.
57 *Sacramento Daily Union*, 4 May 1898.
58 *Pittsburg Dispatch*, 12 June 1892.
59 Thomas Hardy, *Jude the Obscure* (New York: Harper, 1895), 107.
60 *Morning Post*, 21 July 1853.
61 *St Paul Daily Globe*, 29 November 1885.
62 Lillie Hamilton French, *Homes and Their Decoration* (New York: Dodd, Mead, 1903), 367.
63 *St Paul Globe*, 25 September 1902. *The Sunday Journal*, 25 January 1903.
64 *South Australian Register*, 12 November 1856.
65 Charles Shaw, *When I was a Child: By an Old Potter* (London: Methuen, 1903).
66 Alan Gowans, *Learning to See: Historical Perspective on Modern Popular/ Commercial Arts* (Bowling Green OH: Bowling Green University Press, 1981), 4.
67 Ibid., 4.
68 Ibid., 16.
69 Mills 2015. Jules David Prown and Kenneth Haltmann, "Introduction" in *American Artifacts: Essays in Material Culture*, eds. Jules David Prown and Kenneth Haltman (East Lansing: Michigan University Press, 2000), x.
70 Keith Matthews, *The Familiar Past? Archaeologies of later historical Britain* 157.
71 Mayhew, *London Labour and the London Poor Volume I*.
72 Geoff Ginn, "Answering the 'Bitter Cry': Urban Description and Social Reform in the Late-Victorian East End," *The London Journal* 31, no. 2 (2006): 193.
73 Schwarzbach, *Victorian Institute Journal* 29 (2001): 13.
74 Octavia Hill, *Homes of the London Poor* (New York: State Charities Aid Association, 1875), 40.
75 Bill Brown, *A Sense of Things. The Object Matter of American Literature* (Chicago: University of Chicago Press, 2003), 33.
76 Anon, "Wandering Italians," *The Penny Magazine* 1 (1833), 56.
77 George Augustus Sala, "The Bottle of Hay," *Household Words*, 207 (1854): 70.
78 Anon. "The Vices of the Poor," *Punch or the London Charivari*, 2 (1842): 122.
79 Henry Glassie, *Folk Housing in Middle Virginia*. (Knoxville: University of Tennessee Press, 1976), 8.
80 Robert L. Patten, "The New Cultural Marketplace: Victorian Publishing and Reading Practices" in *The Oxford Handbook of Victorian Literary Culture*, ed. Juliet John (Oxford: Oxford University Press, 2016), 501.
81 Jonathan Rose, *The Intellectual Life of the British Working Classes* (New Haven CT: Yale University Press, 2001), 189.
82 Bjørnar Olsen, "Material Culture after Text: Re-Membering Things," *Norwegian Archaeological Review* 36, no. 2 (2003): 98.

Works Cited

Anon, "Wandering Italians," *The Penny Magazine*, (54) (1833): 42–44.

Anon, "The Vices of the Poor," *Punch or the London Charivari*, 2 (1842): 122.

Anon, "Imitation is the Sincerest Form of Flattery," *Georgian Index*, 2008. Accessed 17 August, 2017. www.georgianindex.net/Chalkware/chalkware.html.

Archer, Thomas. *The Pauper, The Thief and the Convict*, London: Groombridge, 1865.

Arizona Weekly Citizen, 4 August 1883.

The Bendigo Advertiser, 14 July 1857.

Bennett, Alfred Rosling. *London and Londoners in the Eighteen-Fifties and Sixties*, London: Unwin, 1924.

Brooklyn Daily Eagle, 27 May 1888.

Brown, Bill. *A Sense of Things. The Object Matter of American Literature*, Chicago: University of Chicago Press, 2003.

Charton, Edouard. "Marchands de figures de plâtre," *Le Magazin Pittoresque*. Paris, 1850.

Cohen, Lizabeth A. "Embellishing a Life of Labor: An Interpretation of the Material Culture of American Working-Class Homes, 1885–1915," *Journal of American Culture*, 3, no. 4 (1980): 752–75.

The Daily Dispatch, Richmond, Virginia, 3 March 1857.

Dickens, Charles. *Barnaby Rudge*, Ware: Wordsworth Editions, 1998.

Empire, Sydney, 8 May 1873.

The Examiner, London, 4 November 1827.

Fucini, Renato. "La Luminara" *Cento sonetti in vernacolo pisano di Renato Fucini 1870*. Biblioteca Nazionale Braidense. Accessed 17 August 2017. www.braidense.it/scaffale/fucini1.html.

Ginn, Geoff. "Answering the 'Bitter Cry': Urban Description and Social Reform in the Late-Victorian East End," *The London Journal*. 31, no. 2 (2006): 179–200.

Glassie, Henry. *Folk Housing in Middle Virginia*, Knoxville: University of Tennessee Press, 1976.

Godwin, George. *The Builder 14*, 1856, 305.

Gowans, Alan. *Learning to See: Historical Perspective on Modern Popular/ Commercial Arts*, Bowling Green OH: Bowling Green University Press, 1981.

Hamilton French, Lillie. *Homes and Their Decoration*, New York: Dodd, Mead, 1903.

Harding, Adrian, and Nicholas Harding. *Victorian Staffordshire Figures 1835– 1875. Book Four*, Atglen, PA: Schiffer, 1998.

Hardy, Thomas. *Jude the Obscure*, New York: Harper, 1895.

The Highland Weekly News, Ohio, 23 December 1880.

Hill, Octavia. *Homes of the London Poor*, New York: State Charities Aid Association, 1875.

Hone, William. "Nature and Art: Buy My Images," *Every-day Book and Table Book: Or, Everlasting Calendar of Popular Amusements. Volume II*, London: Tegg, 1837.

The Huddersfield Chronicle and West Yorkshire Advertiser, 13 August 1859.

The Indianapolis Journal, 17 March 1889.

Jacob, Simon. "Plaster Figure Makers: A Short History," *National Portrait Gallery*, 2011. Accessed 17 August 2017. www.npg.org.uk/research/programmes/plaster-figure-makers-history.php.

Mather, Ruth. "The Home-Making of the English Working Class," *Many Headed Monster*, 2013. Accessed 17 August 2017. http://manyheadedmonster.wordpress.com/2013/07/10/ruth-mather-the-home-making-of-the-english-working-class.

Matthews, Keith. "Familiarity and Contempt: The Archaeology of the 'Modern'," In *The Familiar Past? Archaeologies of Later Historical Britain*, eds. Sarah Tarlow and Susie West, London: Routledge, 1999.

Mayhew, Henry. *London Labour and the London Poor Volume I*, London: Griffin, Bohn, 1861.

McWilliam, Rohan. "The Theatricality of the Staffordshire Figurine," *Journal of Victorian Culture* 10, no. 1 (2005): 107–14.

Mills, Ralph. *Miniatures in Historical Archaeology: Toys, Trifles and Trinkets Re-examined*. Master's thesis, Department of Archaeology and Ancient History, University of Leicester, 2010.

Mills, Ralph. "Material Culture in Miniature: The Historical Archaeology of Nineteenth Century Miniature Objects" in *The Importance of British Material Culture to Historical Archaeologies of the Nineteenth Century*, ed. Alasdair Brooks, Lincoln NA: University of Nebraska Press, 2015.

Morning Post, London, 21 July 1853.

New York Times, 5 April 1874.

Olsen, Bjørnar. "Material Culture after Text: Re-Membering Things," *Norwegian Archaeological Review*, 36, no. 2 (2003): 87–104.

Omaha Daily Bee, 27 May 1888.

The Opelousas Courier, Louisiana, 28 June 1890.

Pall Mall Gazette, 4 August 1896.

Parker Norris, Joseph. *The Portraits of Shakespeare*, Philadelphia: Lindsay, 1885.

Patten, Robert L. "The New Cultural Marketplace: Victorian Publishing and Reading Practices" in *The Oxford Handbook of Victorian Literary Culture*, ed. Juliet John, Oxford: Oxford University Press, 2016, 501.

Paulucci di Calboli, Raniero. *Larmes Et Sourires De l'émigration Italienne*, Paris: Juven, 1909.

The Pittsburg Dispatch, 12 June 1892.

Prown, Jules David, and Kenneth Haltmann. "Introduction" in *American Artifacts: Essays in Material Culture*, eds. Jules David Prown and Kenneth Haltman, East Lansing: Michigan University Press, 2000.

Reynolds, George W. M. *The Mysteries of London*, London: Vickers, 1845.

Rowlandson, Thomas. *Rowlandson's Characteristic Sketches of the Lower Orders*, London: Leigh, 1820.

Rose, Jonathan. *The Intellectual Life of the British Working Classes*, New Haven CT: Yale University Press, 2001.

Ross, Janet and Nelly Erichsen, *The Story of Lucca*, London: Dent, 1912.

Sacramento Daily Union, 4 May 1898.

Sala, George Augustus. "The Bottle of Hay," *Household Words*, 207 (1854): 69–74.

Sala, George Augustus. *London Up to Date*, London: Black, 1894.

The San Francisco Call, 22 December 1904.

Schkolne, Myrna. *People, Passions, Pastimes and Pleasures: Staffordshire Figures 1810–1835*, Winston Salem, NC: Hot Lane Press, 2006.

Schwarzbach, F. S. "Twelve Ways of Looking at a Staffordshire Figurine: An Essay in Cultural Studies," *Victorian Institute Journal*, 29 (2001): 6–60.

Sensi-Isolani, Paola. "Italian Image Makers in France, England and the United States," in *Italian Americans Celebrate Life, the Arts and Popular Culture*, edited by Paola Sensi-Isolani, A. and Anthony Julian Tamburri, San Francisco: Italian American Studies Association, 1990.

Shaw, Charles. *When I was a Child: By an Old Potter*, London: Methuen, 1903.

Smith, James. *Comic Miscellanies in Prose and Verse, Volume 1*, London: Colburn, 1841.

The South Australian Register, 12 November 1856.

Springfield Daily Republic, 10 March 1888.

St Johnsbury Caledonian (Vermont) 27 December 1867.

St Paul Daily Globe, 29 November 1885.

St Paul Globe, 25 September 1902.

The Sunday Journal, 25 January 1903.

The Sunday Oregonian, 6 February 1910.

Upton, "The Italian Boy" *The Universal Songster or Museum of Mirth, Volume 3*, London: Fairburn, 1826.

The Weekly Thibodaux Sentinel and Journal of the 8th Senatorial District, 10 October 1896.

The West Australian, 30 October 1884.

Wordsworth William, *Memorials of a Tour on the Continent, 1820*, London: Longman, 1822.

Wordsworth, William. *The Prelude*, London: Moxon, 1850.

6 The Secret Lives of Dead Animals

Exploring Victorian Taxidermy

Julia Courtney

Stuffed mammals, birds, and fish were ubiquitous if silent observers of Victorian daily life. In museums, private collections, drawing rooms, and workshops; grouped, singly, or as dismembered body parts, they were everywhere. In Dickens' *Our Mutual Friend* (1864–1865) amongst the comfortable contents of Boffin's Bower are 'stuffed birds and waxen fruits under glass shades' while at the upper end of the social scale the royal residences at Osborne and Balmoral were adorned with deer hunt trophies.[1] This chapter premises that for much of the nineteenth and early to-mid-twentieth centuries stuffed animals or more properly, taxidermic mounts, became a means of expression for varied, even conflicting, interest groups. As natural history specimens, as decorative items, as preserved pets, and as hunting trophies, these animals served scientific, decorative, celebratory, and commemorative functions. Such categories help us to classify and understand the 'afterlives of animals' although in practice they frequently overlap, as when the hooves of a favorite horse become inkstands or a fierce bear serves as a dumb waiter.[2] But, in all these situations the animals occupy a space between the living and the dead, the sentient and the stuffed, where many feelings and meanings can enter.

Given current scholarly interest in both animal studies and material culture, it is not surprising that recent studies of taxidermy have increased, even proliferated. Amongst them, Rachel Poliquin discusses the practice under the chapter headings 'Wonder', 'Beauty', 'Spectacle', 'Order', 'Narrative', 'Allegory', and 'Remembrance'; concluding that '[t]he animals are never just cultural objects but are rather provocative animal-things imbued with both the longing to capture animal life immortally and the longing to see the living animal again.'[3] The essays collected in Samuel Alberti's *The Afterlives of Animals* (2011) offer a series of 'animal biographies', tracing 'the shifting meanings (scientific, cultural, emotional) of singular animals and their remains.' Ann Colley (2014) draws on the philosophy of Maurice Merleau-Ponty to theorize the reciprocal haptic process of contact with skins of both live and dead animals.[4] Sarah Amato includes a chapter on taxidermy at the end of her 2015 *Beastly Possessions*, and, Pat Morris' authoritative *A History of Taxidermy* (2010) provides a comprehensive overview of the subject with a range of illustrations.

This chapter draws on these, and other studies, in order to present instances of how taxidermic mounts contributed to the meaning of 'Victorian Things.'[5] Museologist Susan Pearce 'would contend that specimens of the natural world work within human society in exactly the same way as human artifactual material...They are part of the human construction of the world as single pieces...and as collections.'[6] While in general agreement with Pearce, I argue that the idiosyncratic nature of taxidermy makes it unique within 'human artifactual material.' Thanks to its liminal epistemological status, the same object is able to operate as a space for conflicting interpretation embodying different meanings for different beholders.

Mellany Robinson points out that 'these are objects which fall between the natural and the artificial...[which] cannot be controlled despite man's best efforts to contort them into familiar objects'; she notes that 'the art of taxidermy lay in its depiction of dead things as living things.'[7]

The taxidermic process arrests decomposition; and even the simplest specimen represents composition, that is putting together or combining, in both a practical and an ideological sense. In the combining of the living and the stuffed as animal objects we find a challenge to Lévi-Strauss' opposition between the raw and the cooked, which can be extended from his thesis to include a contrast between the natural and the artificial; between things which do not rot and things which decay, between putrefaction and imputrescibilty, softness and hardness, silence and noise, a refutation of the 'kind of logic [that we find] in tangible qualities.'[8] Sarah Amato, John Miller, and others rightly emphasize the commodification of animals and their dismembered parts as evidence of human denigration of animals.[9] At the same time, I suggest that nineteenth-century viewers seemed ready to negotiate the liminalities implicit in the proximity of the live and the stuffed largely because of the positive qualities they attributed to these dead animals. Certainly, the specimens were created, manipulated, and interpreted according to human rather than animal need, but favorable interpretations enabled viewers to accept and admire them.

Taxidermy, Science and the Wonders of Nature

First, the beasts served a scientific and educative function. In this enterprise the pioneer American taxidermist Charles Willson Peale gave valuable advice: 'Ask the beasts and they shall teach thee.'[10] Surviving natural history museum displays worldwide indicate that a major function of nineteenth-century taxidermy was the scientific study of animal species, undertaken by both professionals and amateurs entranced by 'the romance of Victorian Natural History' as Lynn Merrill puts it.[11] Such displays illustrated both the Victorian passion for accurate taxonomy and the educational discovery of the wonders of nature, enlisted equally to back the arguments of Darwin and to praise the works of God.

As Stephen T. Asma argues, 'If one wanted to be a Victorian naturalist of any distinction, one had to be well versed in the taxidermic arts.'[12] He points out that long before Darwin wrote *On the Origin of Species* (1859), he learned the art of taxidermy from John Edmonstone, a freed black slave who worked at the Edinburgh Museum. Darwin said that 'he gained his livelihood by stuffing birds, which he did excellently: he gave me lessons for payment, and I often used to sit with him, for he was a very pleasant and intelligent man.'[13] Asma adds, 'Some ten years later Darwin disembarked from the returning *Beagle* with over 450 stuffed birds, the now-famous Galapagos finches among them.'[14] Meanwhile, he had sent 'a vast amount of material...back to England, in particular the sad little bodies of two mocking birds, similar but not identical—the kind of thing that made him more and more sure of the mutability of species.'[15]

In contrast, Richard Owen, first superintendent of London's Natural History Museum, was no evolutionist: for this vigorous opponent of Darwin, the study of nature revealed the wonders of divinely ordered creation, a traditional, and pervasive opinion. For example, readers of Samuel Maunder's popular *Treasury of Natural History* (1848), a detailed alphabetical dictionary of natural history from Aard-Vark to Zygodactyl would begin with a quotation from Pope:

> To Thee, whose temple is all space
> Whose altar, earth, sea, skies!
> One chorus let all being raise!
> All nature's incense rise![16]

This view of the natural world persisted throughout the century, even as Darwin's work became popularized and accepted. Indeed, recent studies suggest that apart from a number of high-profile polemicists, many Victorians managed to combine notions of evolution with belief in a divine Creator.[17]

But whatever their ideological stance, for nineteenth-century naturalists, taxonomy – the collection and classification of plants and living creatures – formed what Richard Fortey has called 'the basis for naming the living world... the reference system for nature.'[18] This process could not be undertaken or illustrated without the aid of taxidermy, which preserved specimens for generations of students to study and identify. Living animals would often not survive lengthy voyages from their places of origin to European zoos, or once there often died in captivity; taxidermy might be the only method of presenting them to an interested public. Even today, nineteenth-century specimens often represent the only examples of now extinct species. Ironically, the species may well have been helped along the road to extinction by over-enthusiastic collecting.

Not only exotic creatures from distant shores were captured and listed in this way. Naturalists often collected local species, and there is evidence that taxidermy was seen as a suitable leisure pastime for those interested in natural history; 'Stuff it Yourself' manuals abounded. One early example of a manual, expressly addressed to 'the young collector' was issued as an Appendix to Maunder's *Treasury* (1848) and, by the beginning of the twentieth century, Harrods was circulating a catalogue of supplies for home taxidermy including various sizes of brain scoop.[19]

The Life and Death of Birds

'The young collector' was advised to begin by stuffing a rook. Birds are relatively easy to mount compared with mammals; and partly due to this and partly thanks to the beauty of their plumage they were amongst the first and most popular examples of taxidermy for decorative as well as for educational and scientific purposes, with beautiful exotic birds arranged under glass domes or in fire screens, often without much reference to their appearance in the wild. Earlier in the century, birds were generally mounted individually and often in poses alien to their natural stance, but increasingly as taxidermic skills progressed, narrative elements were introduced; for example, groups featuring a sparrow hawk and its luckless prey demonstrating nature literally red in beak and claw. More lyrically, Hampshire taxidermist Edward Hart specialized in producing beautifully detailed scenes of birds in their native habitats, often complete with nests and painted backdrops of village or woodland scenes.[20]

Before the availability of binoculars and fast exposure camera techniques, the only way to identify a rare bird was to shoot it first; it could then be preserved by the taxidermist's skill to prove the sighting. It was not until the end of the century, with inception of the RSPB (founded as The Plumage League in 1889) and the campaign eventually leading to the Importation of Plumage Acts, effective from 1921 onwards, that widespread concern was expressed about the loss of bird species. Edward Hart declared that had he not shot and preserved rare specimens, someone else would have killed them and they would have been lost to science.[21] A rare example of protest came from the future architect and designer Ernest Gimson, when at the age of seventeen, he 'fiercely objected to Alderman Kempson's request in *The Leicester Daily Post*, August 1882, for local huntsmen to extend the local Museum's collection of stuffed birds and animals.' Gimson attacked museums generally for waging 'a "war of extinction" against nature.'[22] At this time, the curator of the Leicester Museum was Montagu Browne, himself a noted taxidermist and author of books of practical guidance. Not until 1897 did a reviewer of his *Artistic and Scientific Modelling and Taxidermy* object:

> One thing we must regret: it is that when an amateur becomes a scientific naturalist of this description he also becomes an absolutely ruthless person with regard to the creatures he kills. To get birds in their breeding plumage, &c., he perpetrates hideous, nay, disgusting, crimes. Indeed the collector is far more destructive to species than the much-decried sportsman, who after all pays attention to close times. This the collector never dreams of doing. Mr. Browne speaks very feelingly about sea-birds, and is of course a humane man; but this study of taxidermy, of which he is such an admirable exponent, is dreadfully wasteful, and this search after perfection means hecatombs of feathered victims. But it is an admirable book, and is most comprehensive, and is also handsomely printed and illustrated (*The Spectator* 15 May 1897, 25).

In earlier years, adverse criticism of taxidermy seems to have been directed mainly towards practitioners failing to meet the exacting standards of London taxidermist Rowland Ward, Brown and their colleagues; Brown protested about 'outrages on nature' and museum holdings of 'atrociously rendered mammals, [with] a greater sprinkling of funereal and highly disreputable birds.'[23]

Birds and Boyhood: The Story of a Collection

Clearly, stuffed birds could function as both decorative and educational objects. These elements could also be overlaid by local pride (as evidenced by Browne's Leicester Museum collection) and by romantic constructions of boyhood. Maunder's 'young collector' could combine a healthy love of the outdoors, spiritually uplifting contact with the natural world, and prowess in tree climbing (in search of nests and eggs) while satisfying the adolescent urge to collect, identified by Pearce.[24] The reminiscences of famed 'white hunter' Frederick Courteney Selous (1851–1917) stressed his early interest in natural history collecting, for 'there was not a rook's nest in any one of the fine old elms or oak trees in the park in which the schoolhouse stood, from which he was not able to get the eggs' while he also 'trapped and skinned water rats and other small animals.'[25]

The story of Winchester College's collection of stuffed birds illustrates the role of taxidermy in constructing group identity. In this case a version of bucolic boyhood in natural surroundings suffused by educational ideals. In 1897, the College celebrated the 500 years since its foundation by William of Wykeham by erecting the Memorial Buildings to be used as a Museum; the structure's Italianate style invoking Renaissance ideals of art and civilization. A large proportion of the museum holdings were devoted to Natural History specimens contributed by members of the College Natural History society past and present.[26] In 1874, an old Wykehamist, Frederic Walker Joy, gave the college about a dozen cases of stuffed birds and we know that these were moved to the newly created museum in 1897. At this time the College Museum Committee called on the skills of local taxidermist William Chalkley (1842–1922) who charged £1.12.6p for 'fumigating and renovating thirteen cases of stuffed birds' which were probably Joy's donation.[27] Between 1863 and the end of the century, Chalkley himself assembled a collection of over one hundred Hampshire Birds, generally brought to him by sportsmen or members of the local public. By 1900, the collection had evidently outgrown the restricted premises above the shop which the taxidermy specimens and equipment shared with Chalkley's shop assistant, so the taxidermist offered it for sale.[28] The birds were snapped up by headmaster Dr Fearon (Headmaster 1884–1901) for the college museum, and the collection catalogue by Rev J E Kelsall carries a brief 'Introduction' by Fearon paying tribute to 'the life long devotion and poetic imagination of Mr W. Chalkley.'[29] The header text, *Benedicite omnes volucres coeli Domino,* suggests that Fearon shared the conviction of Richard Owen and Samuel Maunder that contemplation of the wonders of nature inspired praise of a benevolent creator. As well as praising God in their stuffed condition, the birds also served to praise the school and the county. Fearon's introduction stressed that 'Care has been taken that no single bird should be included that has not been actually found in the county', adding that 'the collection promises to become one of the best in the county.'[30] As Karen Wonders has noted of Brighton's Booth collection of birds, the criteria of locality can be very loosely applied in the service of recruiting as large a number of species as possible. In this case, some notably rare birds are enlisted as proof of diversity of Hampshire wildlife.[31] Fearon's introduction concluded that

> if the charm of the collection should attract some Wykehamists to take an interest in the birds of Hampshire, and learn something of their lives, it will accomplish what seems well nigh impossible – to add to the joys of school life at Winchester.[32]

This presents an idyllic picture of happy schoolboys studying ornithology, responsibly remembering 'Never wantonly to destroy either nest or egg' while endeavouring to 'secure good specimens of nests for exhibition in the Memorial Buildings.' But is slightly at odds with contemporary accounts of the hardships of junior 'sweaters' (fags) and other insalubrious aspects of school life.[33] For Fearon, the museum collection is described in terms of charm, joy, wonderful beauty, skill, devotion, and poetic imagination, romantic terms which identify the birds with almost Wordsworthian constructions of boyhood while celebrating local heritage and pride.[34]

Similarly uplifting if rather different messages were conveyed to the boys of Bedford Modern School (founded 1873) by the more exotic game sent home by intrepid colonial hunters. The School acquired many such items from fathers and Old Boys. Irreverently nicknamed 'the curiosity shop', this school museum none the less provided a link between the schoolboys of Bedford and the wider world of adventure which they might enter as colonial administrators, soldiers or missionaries.[35]

Hunting and Sporting Trophies

Nowhere is the definition and construction of animals according to human need and reference more appreciable than in sporting and hunting trophies.[36] Hunting had an almost mystical aura conjured by the identification of hunter and prey and, as Gary Marvin explains, the taxidermied animals in a hunter's collection were, and are, 'linked to the autobiography of their hunter' functioning as the ultimate souvenir in recalling the intense experience of days in the wild.[37] Some of these trophies were displayed in museums or used in habitat dioramas and exhibition scenes; others were presented more directly as products of the chase. Implicitly, big game trophies served the affirmation of man's dominance over the animal kingdom and the supremacy of Imperial hunters over the 'kingly' beasts of far flung lands. Throughout the nineteenth century, the heroic figure of the 'white hunter', often a professional ivory hunter, became synonymous with supposedly British values such as sportsmanship, hardihood, and shooting prowess. One example already mentioned is Frederick Courteney Selous, claimed as the model for H. Rider Haggard's Allan Quatermain.[38] Across the social scale kings and princes enjoyed elaborately hosted tiger hunts while humbler military personnel, colonial administrators, and later tourist groups all added to the death toll of animals and the proliferation of sporting trophies such as heads, skins, and full animal mounts. By 1900, big game meant big business for taxidermists with the resources to process it. Animals such as elephants, rhinos, bears, lions, and especially tigers, presented a series of technical challenges which could only be met by large firms such as Rowland Ward and latterly van Ingen and van Ingen of Mysore, India, who pioneered a factory system and a range of technical advances, such as the use of artificial skulls rather than the actual animal bones which were often shattered by the hunter's fatal shot. It is estimated that this firm processed more than 43,000 tiger and leopard trophies in less than ninety years of operation, many of them for Indian royals as well as for European collectors.[39] Such items included whole

Figure 6.1 The Natural History section of Winchester City Museum in the 1940s. Source: By kind permission of Winchester City Council/ Hampshire Cultural Trust.

body mounts, heads, and skin rugs, some with head attached: the sensuous qualities of tiger skin rugs were legendary, especially after the publication of Elinor Glyn's erotic novel *Three Weeks* (1907) in which the hero is introduced to the delights of love on a magnificent tiger rug (Figure 6.1).

Ward, Chalkley, and many other taxidermists professed to be able to convert hoofs, tusks, trotters, and so on into useful items like inkstands, practices which maintained trophies while domesticating and commemorating the animals whose parts were treated. While this was particularly practicable with smaller sections such as horse hooves (candlesticks, match holders, etc.) and deer feet (hat racks, pen wipers) much larger animals could also be used. Rowland Ward commented,

> Elephants do not at first glance seem to lend themselves as articles for household decoration, and yet I have found them most adaptable for that purpose. The head is of course preserved and mounted separately but the skin may be converted into innumerable amber like articles of domestic utility. The thick slabs of hide can be turned into table tops, trays, caskets and other articles. An elephant's foot will make an admirable liqueur stand.[40]

(Ward 52)

A recent taxidermy auction featured numerous elephant feet stools, stick holders and waste bins, as well as furniture with animal legs, skin coverings, and so on.[41] Harder to find but frequently noted by taxidermy scholars is the genre of large 'animal furniture' such as bear dumb waiters or chairs made from whole baby elephants or giraffes.[42] These pieces were spectacular and widely publicized but their size and expense probably limited numbers.

More commonly found at auction and in country houses are trophies from the British Isles. Foxes, either as masks or full mounts, were especially popular; stags, being too large to preserve entire (as well as being edible) usually feature as heads or sets of antlers.[43] Fish proved a favourite if challenging genre with some taxidermists specializing in preserving prize-winning specimens. William Chalkley's Winchester shop The Sports Depot stocked tackle for fishing the Hampshire Itchen, known for its trout; one such (weight 16 lbs and 2 oz) was brought to Chalkley in 1888 and later shown at The Piscatorial Exhibition at the Royal Aquarium, London on 5 March 1891.

Habitat Dioramas

Although provincial British taxidermists presented small-scale dramas in which creatures hunted, raised their young, or perched decoratively amongst appropriate foliage, they were unable to emulate the great habitat dioramas being created by the likes of heroic taxidermist Carl Akeley (1864–1926) in New York, Chicago, and Washington. Pat Morris offers a clear account of the development of habitat displays.[44] William Hornaday is usually credited with their introduction, and the economic and cultural conditions of the United States encouraged impressive dioramas conveying the excitement of the wild to city dwellers. Donna Haraway and Karen Wonders have pointed out the deeply political aspects of such habitat dioramas and museum displays including 'the instrumentalization of the diorama exhibit for nationalistic purposes' and the immortalization of 'particular virtues' needed by urban society.[45]

In Britain, only Rowland Ward, London taxidermist by Royal Appointment, had the equipment, premises, and contacts to emulate the large scale American dioramas, as he explained in his 1913 autobiography *A Naturalist's Life Study*. Incidentally, the terms 'naturalist' and 'sportsman' were widely employed for those who hunted, shot, stuffed. and displayed wildlife, especially big game and exotic creatures. Ward presented a striking combat group of two red deer struggling for supremacy at the 1871 London International Exhibition; at the Colonial and Indian Exhibitions in 1886, 1895, and 1896, he showed scenes of a tiger attacking an elephant, a child being mauled by a leopard, and so on.[46] The 1886 Exhibition featured a display intended 'to illustrate some of the more striking representatives of the flora and fauna of India as a whole' and Ward left a lengthy account of his difficulties in setting up this huge piece.[47] Many of the animals were borrowed from the trophy collections of hunters such as the Maharajah of Cooch Behar and the Prince of Wales.[48] Others were constructed from dismembered parts, while the quest for an elephant involved the slaughter of one in Hamburg Zoo. Ward's comments bring home the absolute artificiality of the set piece, belying its title of 'Jungle Life':

> I recall the endless thought and labour bestowed on the undertaking. To design it and get the objects together, hide the defects of some of the imperfect specimens, make dummy animals where required, paint the backgrounds and group the animals, birds and foliage so that it became a scene in the Exhibition which everyone went to see, gave me sleepless nights and an amount of work which I should hesitate to take on so lightly again.[49]

Exhibited at a time of British Imperial power, Ward's groups emphasized the wildness and ferocity of the animals, now safely immobilized for the viewer who could experience the dangers of the hunt without leaving the exhibition space. They were closer to the animals than anyone, including the hunter who shot them, would be in life; the Darwinian battle for existence was graphically illustrated; the ascendancy of man, especially European man, was confirmed and a good educational day out was had by the family.

Celebrity Animals and Departed Pets

Practitioners such as Rowland Ward and Montagu Browne constantly stressed the need for the skilled worker to study the natural attitudes of the animals to be mounted; he or she must be an artist or sculptor.[50] The taxidermist as portraitist could be enlisted to preserve and commemorate not only natural history specimens but also beloved pets and celebrity animals which were famous and popular in life, giving them a second existence after death. For example, Akeley was the taxidermist chosen to mount the original Jumbo, an elephant owned by the circus promoter P. T. Barnum. A popular feature of zoos in Paris and London before being purchased by Barnum in 1882, Jumbo was killed by a train in Canada in 1885; his name passed into language as signifying anything large. An even more dramatic story features a pig which escaped from a sinking German cruiser in 1915. Seen swimming amidst the wreckage, the animal was rescued by a sailor from HMS *Glasgow,* named Turpitz as an obvious insult to the German Admiral, and appointed as ship's mascot. Turpitz was bought by the Duke of Portland at a charity auction in 1917 and lived until 1919, when his head was mounted and his trotters became handles of a carving set.[51]

Animal sporting heroes, such as race horses and champion grey-hounds, were also thought to deserve preservation. The description of twentieth-century greyhound Mick the Miller as the 'Sporting Icon of the Depression' has an added resonance if the Greek word *eikōn* is taken to mean an image or likeness that represents something beyond itself. In the synecdoche of taxidermy, the stuffed form of the dog represents his living self far more effectively than a pictured representation.[52]

More recently, some taxidermied animals have become celebrities only after death, a process known as 'mascotism.'[53] The Haslemere (Surrey) Educational Museum features a Siberian bear named Arthur (after a former curator) standing on its hind legs with front paws extended. According to a news report, 'Arthur has lived at the museum since he was donated by Oswald Sisson of Fernhurst in West Sussex...The furry mascot is a prime example of the Victorian attitude to wildlife – his orig-inal role in life was as a dumb waiter.'[54] Clearly, in this article Arthur's life is assumed to be identical with his afterlife. His actual 'original role in life' as a live bear in Russia is ignored and his story begins only with his importation as a piece of furniture in 1919, continuing as a popular museum attraction and culminating in his adoption as museum mascot with a twitter feed of his own.

Arthur also exemplifies the haptic impact of uncased taxidermic mounts. Behind glass, the animals become objects of display, even though the viewer can approach them more closely than in life; but uncased, free standing mounts invite, almost require, the process of touching. Arthur has undergone various repairs to damage caused by handling, stroking, and feeling over the decades, as well as the theft of several claws.[55]

In 1913, Rowland Ward wrote that

> today the preservation, in one form or another, of a departed pet is as popular as ever it was and it is little to be wondered at that it should be so. An animal that has been a faithful friend and compan-ion to man during its lifetime may in this way claim a fuller recom-pense in death than mere burial and subsequent oblivion.[56]

Amongst these 'faithful friends' the most popular were parrots and other pet birds, cats, and, of course, dogs. As Poliquin puts it, '[w]ithout excep-tion, dogs are taxidermied because they were somehow exceptional in life. They were champions of their breed, extraordinary athletes, heroes (whether voluntary or not), film stars, or cherished family pets.'[57] As a Companion Species, dogs were deeply implicated in Victorian culture, portrayed in art (*The Old Shepherd's Chief Mourner* 1837, *The Order of Release* 1853, etc.) and fiction (Bullseye in *Oliver Twist*) as well as be-ing genetically manipulated through selective breeding. The Kennel Club was founded in 1873. Specific canine qualities were especially valued, particularly fidelity to their owner. An example is the faithful lurcher displayed in Lincoln Castle Museum. The Museum storyboard explains:

> The lurcher dog which is currently on display inside the prison belonged to William Clarke (alias Slenderman), who was hanged at Lincoln Castle on 29 March 1877, for the murder of a gamekeeper who he shot whilst he was out poaching. Clarke and his dog used to frequent one of the local hostelries, The Strugglers Inn (still in operation now just outside the castle walls) and when Clarke was hanged the dog remained at the pub and pined for his owner. When the dog died, the landlord of the pub had him stuffed and placed above the bar.

The gruesome provenance of the dog, the mythical status of a 'Lincolnshire Poacher' (as in the folk song), and the legend that the ghost of the bereaved lurcher still haunts the pub make a great story in which the dog exemplifies virtues such as devotion to his owner combined with a loveable raffishness.

Anthropomorphic Groups

Anthropomorphic taxidermy could be described as an extreme case of remodelling the natural world on human lines.[58] From the time of the 1851 Great Exhibition onwards anthropomorphic groups were immensely popular. They served a dual purpose, first decorative, and second as demonstrations of the technical skill of the taxidermist, since the small animals involved (typically kittens, squirrels, baby rabbits, hedgehogs, frogs, and so on) were difficult to process. In 1851, Stuttgart taxidermist Hermann Ploucquet exhibited several displays described by Queen Victoria as 'really marvellous', including a declaration of love between two weasels, a dormouse duel, and six kittens serenading a piglet beneath her window.[59] A later Ploucquet group of skating hedgehogs was shown at the Sydenham Crystal Palace.[60] British taxidermists imitated Ploucquet: Edward Hart's surviving anthropomorphic groups include The Prize Fight, a boxing match between two red squirrels now at Castle Ward in Ireland and dated by the National Trust at about 1900. Still in existence is William Chalkley's scene The Card Players (before 1903) which was supposed to feature baby rabbits; although more recent study reveals them as brown rats minus their tails. The four debauched rodents are seated at a table evidencing smoking and drinking besides gambling (Figure 6.2).

Perhaps the most famous practitioner of the genre was Walter Potter (1835–1881). His Sussex museum contained numerous examples of anthropomorphic taxidermy, the centrepiece being a diorama of 'The Death

Figure 6.2 The Card Players by William Chalkley. Source: Photograph, Julia
Courtney. With thanks to Winchester City Council/Hampshire
Cultural Trust.

and Burial of Cock Robin' (1861), which included ninety-eight species
of British birds. Both this and Potter's 'The Kittens' Wedding' have been
much discussed by scholars including Henning, who sees the exhibits as
'telling of a world in which the relationship of humans to animals was
being dramatically transformed' with nature envisioned 'as cultural and
historical, not eternal and outside human culture.'[61] Certainly, unlike
many branches of Victorian taxidermy the anthropomorphic scenes did
not attempt to present animals in natural poses and settings; the creatures are used as props in the creation of three-dimensional tableaux
similar to illustrations of animal stories like those of Beatrix Potter or
Alison Uttley.[62] The 'cuteness' of the kittens, squirrels, and frogs is exploited and the viewer drawn into a miniaturized fantasy world where
these animals wear human clothes and perform human actions. In a
sense they are made into toys. The ingenuity, prettiness, and gentle humour of the scenes masked the gruesome reality, the fact that the animals had been killed in order to be processed by the taxidermist, a fact
which the Victorian public seems to have been able to accept along with
the wearing of fur coats and feathered hats.

The anthropomorphic genre's rejection of the taxonomic role of much
contemporary taxidermy links it with the fantasy creations of naturalist, traveller, conservationist, and skilled taxidermist Charles Waterton

(1782–1865). Accounts of Waterton inevitably describe him as 'eccentric', partly because of his satirical montages of animal parts such as 'The Nondescript.' While Henning discusses Waterton's work alongside Potter's, Cristina Grasseni offers an interpretation focused on Waterton's marginal social status (as a Roman Catholic he was debarred from a range of career options) and on his opposition to current themes in the study of natural history: she suggests that 'Waterton devised The Nondescript as a reminder of the limits of taxonomic control over nature', in which case his taxidermy contradicts one of the main purposes of the contemporary practice.[63]

Dickens' Taxidermist

Conor Creaney's perceptive coverage of anthropomorphic taxidermy makes a conceptual leap to Dickens' novel *Our Mutual Friend*.[64] Briefly, he juxtaposes Potter's 'Cock Robin' with *Our Mutual Friend* as 'a novel that holds many of its bodies in a state of suspended animation.'[65] This fits with a commentary on 'Corpses and Effigies', in which John Carey notes Dickens' obsessive interest in the Paris Morgue, in dead bodies, in artificial simulacra of life, in dismemberment, and so in the secret life of objects, embodying what Claude Lévi-Strauss elsewhere identifies as the mythic theme of the revolt of objects against their masters.[66]

Our Mutual Friend provides a particularly rich source since it also manages the crossover with a non-fictional taxidermist, James Willis, whose profession inspired that of Mr Venus. Willis is listed amongst the London taxidermists whom Mellany Robinson identifies as profiting from the rise in popularity in stuffed items after the Great Exhibition of 1851.[67] Kitton's classic work on *Dickens and His Illustrators* explains that Marcus Stone the illustrator of *Our Mutual Friend* needed to include a dog in an Academy piece he was working on and reveals that the usual practice of the day was to use stuffed animals as models. One of Stone's colleagues recommended Willis and when Dickens later consulted Stone in search of 'any peculiar avocation' which 'must be something very striking and unusual', the artist took Dickens to the shop.[68]

Since Willis was evidently a well-known and relatively high-class practitioner, it is perhaps as well that, according to Kitton, he never realized the origins of Mr Venus' establishment, with its 'musty, leathery, feathery, cellary, gluey, gummy' smell; a 'crazy shop', whose closing door agitates '...the green-glass-eyed cats, the dogs, the ducks, and all the rest of the collection...for an instant as if paralytically animated.'[69] As Carey says, in this 'novel Dickens produced his great set piece of dumb witnesses, and dumb witnesses who are real corpses as well as effigies.'[70] Mr Venus has his own artistic obsession with 'the lovely trophies of my art' (106) such as the stuffed canary in its glass case: 'there! There's animation! On a twig, making up his mind to hop!' (103) while his actual techniques are partially noted in 'a pretty little dead bird with its head drooping and a long stiff wire piercing its breast' (99) with its almost sexual charge. Although Mr Venus' birds are evidently displayed whole, the prettiness of the dead bird reminds one of contemporary jewellery where 'Humming birds heads, their throats surrounded with a filet of gold form handsome brooches' and whole birds nestled amongst the trimmings of fashionable hats.[71]

Art, Truth and Beauty

Making the artificial seem real, attributing movement to the fixed and static, is a process at the heart of nineteenth-century realism in the novel and in painting just as in the taxidermist's art: and practitioners, whether international figures, such as London's Rowland Ward, provincial tradesmen like Edward Hart and William Chalkley, or fictional figures like Dickens' Mr Venus, were conscious and unapologetic seekers after truth and beauty. Rowland Ward declared that the specimen's 'value...may be preserved and increased by displaying its beauty truthfully to life, while the beauty is recognised for its own sake even by the unscientific.'[72] Today taxidermy is enjoying a popular revival with artists such as Polly Morgan, who though 'use[ing] animals that have died naturally' consciously celebrate the beauty and 'flamboyancy' of their physical forms, in common with Ward and his colleagues.[73]

To conclude, it seems that during the nineteenth century the potentially disturbing or disruptive elements of stuffed animals were generally contained by the positive qualities attributed to them. Specimens represented the natural world in both scientific and religious terms, were enlisted to glorify the hunter and the colonial administrator, boosted pride in local and national identity, and served as decorative commodities indicating comfort and good taste; their purposes were educational, affective, and aesthetic. This chapter began by noting the silence and ubiquity of Victorian stuffed animals and has attempted to hear the messages attributed to them, for if as Grasseni says, 'taxidermy [is] an eloquent practice' it speaks in heteroglossia, a polyphony of animal voices.[74]

Notes

1 Charles Dickens. *Our Mutual Friend* (London: Chapman and Hall, Fireside Edition, n.d.), 73.
2 Samuel Alberti ed., *The Afterlives of Animals, A Museum Menagerie* (Charlottesville: University of Virginia, 2011).
3 Rachel Poliquin, *The Breathless Zoo* (Pennsylvania: University of Pennsylvania Press, 2012), 223.
4 Samuel Alberti, 1.
5 Asa Briggs, *Victorian Things* (London: Batsford, 1988).
6 Susan M. Pearce, *Interpreting Objects and Collections* (London: Routledge, 1994, paperback 2006), 1.

7 Mellany Robinson, 'The Beast in the Parlour, Taxidermy and the Nineteenth Century Middle Class Interior', unpublished MA thesis V&A/RCA, 1999, 1 and 28.

8 Claude Levi-Strauss, *The Raw and the Cooked* (London: Pimlico, 1969), 299 n.ii.

9 Sarah Amato, *Beastly Possessions, Animals in Victorian Consumer Culture* (Toronto: University of Toronto Press, 2015) Kindle edition, and John Miller, *Empire and the Animal Body* (London: Anthem, 2012, paperback 2014).

10 Brigham, David R. "Ask the Beasts and They Shall Tell Thee," The Human Lessons of Charles Willson Peale's Natural History Displays, *The Huntington Library Quarterly* 59, no. 2/3 (1996): 183–286.

11 Lynn Merrill, *The Romance of Victorian Natural History* (Oxford: Oxford University Press, 1989).

12 Stephen T. Asma, *Stuffed Animals and Pickled Heads: The Culture and Evolution of Natural History Collections* (Oxford: Oxford University Press, 2001), 22.

13 Asma, *Stuffed Animals*, 22.

14 Asma, 22.

15 Peter Campbell, 'At the Natural History Museum', *London Review of Books*, 29.1.09: 25.

16 Final stanza of Alexander Pope's 'The Universal Prayer', published 1738.

17 See Mia Chen, ""To Face Apparent Discrepancies with Revelation": Examining the Fossil Record in Charlotte Yonge's The Trial," *Women's Writing* 17, no. 2: 2010 361–79, 362.

18 Richard Fortey, *Dry Store Room No 1* (London: Harper, 2008), 31.

19 Mellany Robinson, 31.

20 www.hampshireculturaltrust.org.uk/content/taxidermists-finder(accessed 30.10.17).

21 Christine Taylor, Head of Natural History Collections, Hampshire Museums service, conversation with JC on 25.06.08. CT adds that many British birds did in fact become extinct because of C19 collectors.

22 Rowan Roenisch, leaflet for Leicestershire Gimson walk, unpaginated.

23 Montagu Browne, *Practical Taxidermy* (London: Upcott Gill, 1884), 15 and 312.

24 Pearce, 238–39.

25 John Guille Millais, *Life of Frederick Courteney Selous* (New York: Longmans, 1919), Kindle edition Chapter One.

26 Thanks to the Warden, Fellows and Archivist of Winchester College for information.

27 Julia Courtney, 'The Stuffed Animals Will Have to Go', *Hampshire Studies*, 66 (2011): 215–27.

28 Oral History Recording, *Winchester Memories* 18, Hampshire County Record Office.

29 W. Fearon and J. Kelsall, *Winchester College Memorial Buildings, Collection of Hampshire Birds 1863–1900* (Winchester: Warren, 1900), introduction not paginated.

30 Fearon, 'Introduction'.

31 See Karen Wonders, 'Habit Dioramas and the Issue of Nativeness' for the display of native species as a definition of regional identity, 96.

32 Fearon, 'Introduction'.

33 Colin Clifford, *The Asquiths* (London: John Murray, 2002), 75.

34 By the 1930s/50s the College Museum shared the pattern of municipal collections in becoming a dumping ground for taxidermic specimens as these

became less fashionable with private collectors and symptomatic with Victorian clutter. Chalkley's birds spent years distributed amongst the cupboards and corridors of the College biology department but are now happily being revalued and renovated.

35 Information displayed at The Higgins Museum and Art Gallery, Bedford.
36 Miller, *Empire and the Animal Body*, esp. 46–48.
37 Gary Marvin, Enlivened Through Memory: Hunters and Hunting Trophies', in Alberti, *The Afterlives of Animals*, 202–18, 203.
38 Millais, *Life of Frederick Courteney Selous*, Kindle edition.
39 Pat Morris, *Van Ingen and Van Ingen, Artists in Taxidermy* (Ascot: MPM, 2006), 32.
40 Rowland Ward, *A Naturalist's Life Study* (Johannesburg: Ward, 2002), 52.
41 Nigel Poole Natural History and Taxidermy Auction, Banbury, Oxon, 17 June, 2016.
42 Ward, *A Naturalist's Life Study*, 51–60.
43 See Pat Morris and Michael Freeman, *Hutchings, the Aberystwyth Taxidermists* (Ascot: MPM, 2007) for fox items.
44 Pat Morris, *A History of Taxidermy*, 300ff.
45 Donna Haraway, *Primate Visions*, 29.
46 Ward, *A Naturalist's Life Study*, 70–75.
47 Ward, 76.
48 Ward, 75/76.
49 Ward, 82.
50 See e.g. Montagu Browne, *Practical Taxidermy* Preface to 2nd edition, and Ward, *A Naturalist's Life*, 32.
51 *The Times*, February 7, 2015.
52 Michael Tanner, *The Legend of Mick the Miller, Sporting Icon of the Depression* (Berkshire: Highdown, 2003).
53 Hannah Paddon in Alberti, 134.
54 Jennifer Morris, 'Museum's Arthur Bear Given a Spruce Up', *Get Surrey*, June 18, 2013, www.getsurrey.co.uk/news/local-news/museums-arthur-bear-given-spruce-4868261 (accessed 10 August 2017).
55 Today almost all taxidermy is displayed behind glass. An exception is the Deyrolle showroom in Paris where despite Do Not Touch notices, visitors find the ears, tails, manes and coats of the animals irresistible.
56 Ward, *A Naturalist's Life Study*, 69. Burial might not mean oblivion; the Pet Cemetery in Hyde Park was opened in 1881.
57 Rachel Poliquin in Alberti, 97.
58 Anthropomorphic taxidermy is the practice of grouping animals in situations which mimic human activities., often with clothing and accessories.
59 Pat Morris, *A History of Taxidermy*, 124 and William G. Fitzgerald, 'Side Shows', The Strand Magazine 1897, Vol XIII, 523–25.
60 Pat Morris, *A History of Taxidermy*, 123–28.
61 Henning, 663–64.
62 Commenting on Margaret Tempest's 'beautiful' illustrations of Uttley, Denis Judd notes that 'the animal characters occasionally look like stuffed exhibits', Denis Judd, *Alison Uttley Spinner of Tales* (Manchester University Press, 2001/2010), 103.
63 Cristina Grasseni, "Taxidermy as Rhetoric of Self-making: Charles Waterton (1782–1865) Wandering Naturalist," *Studies in History and Philosophy of Biological and Biomedical Sciences*, 29, no. 2 (1998): 269–94, 270.
64 Conor Creaney, "Paralytic Animation: The Anthropomorphic Taxidermy of Walter Potter," *Victorian Studies* 53, no. 1 (2010): 7–35.
65 Creaney, 10.

66 Carey notes Dickens' description of a baby's corpse: 'It had been opened, and neatly sewn up, and regarded from that point of view, it looked like a stuffed creature', Carey 82.
67 Mellany Robinson, *Beast in the Parlour*, 43.
68 Frederic G. Kitton, *Dickens and His Illustrators* (London: Redway, 1899), 199/200.
69 Dickens, *Our Mutual Friend*, 98.
70 John Carey, *The Violent Effigy*, 88.
71 For a full account of preserved animals as fashion accessories, see Michelle Tolini, ""Beetle Abominations" and Birds on Bonnets: Zoological Fantasy in Late Nineteenth Century Dress," *Nineteenth Century Art Worldwide*. www.19thc-artworldwide.org/spring02 (accessed 5 March 2015).
72 Ward, 20.
73 *Sunday Times*, 15 February 2015.
74 Grasseni, 269.

Bibliography: Books and Articles Cited; For Other Sources See Endnotes

Alberti, Samuel. *The Afterlives of Animals*. Charlottesville: University of Virginia Press, 2011.

Amato, Sarah. *Beastly Possessions: Animals in Victorian Consumer Culture*. Toronto:University of Toronto Press,2015.

Asma, Stephen T. *Stuffed Animals and Pickled Heads: The Culture and Evolution of Natural History Collections*. Oxford: Oxford University Press, 2001.

Brigham, David R. "Ask the Beasts and They Shall Tell Thee," The Human Lessons of Charles Willson Peale's Natural History Displays, *The Huntington Library Quarterly* 59, no. 2/3 (1996): 183–286.

Briggs, Asa. *Victorian Things*. London: Batsford, 1988.

Browne, Montagu. *Practical Taxidermy*. London: Upcott Gill, 1884.

Campbell, Peter. 'At the Natural History Museum', *London Review of Books* 21.1.09.

Carey, John. *The Violent Effigy, a Study of Dickens' Imagination*. London: Faber and Faber, 1991.

Chen, Mia. ""To Face Apparent Discrepancies with Revelation": Examining the Fossil Record in Charlotte Yonge's The Trial'," *Women's Writing*, 17, no. 2, 2010: 361–79.

Clifford, Colin. *The Asquiths*. London: John Murray, 2002.

Courtney, Julia. "The Stuffed Animals Will Have to Go," *Hampshire Studies* 66 (2011): 215–27.

Creaney, Conor. "Paralytic Animation: The Anthropomorphic Taxidermy of Walter Potter," *Victorian Studies* 53, no. 1 (2010): 7–35.

Dickens, Charles. *Our Mutual Friend*. London: Chapman and Hall, Fireside Edition, n.d.

Fearon, W. and J.Kelsall, *Winchester College Memorial Buildings, Collection of Hampshire Birds 1863–1900*. Winchester: Warren, 1901.

Fortey, Richard. *Dry Store Room No 1*. London: Harper, 2008.

Grasseni, Cristina. "Taxidermy as Rhetoric of Self-making: Charles Waterton (1782–1865) Wandering Naturalist," *Studies in History and Philosophy of Biological and Biomedical Sciences* 29, no. 2 (1998): 269–94.

Haraway, Donna. *Primate Visions*. London: Routledge, 1989.

Judd, Denis. *Alison Uttley Spinner of Tales*. Manchester University Press, 2001/2010.

Kitton, Frederic G. *Dickens and His Illustrators*. London: George Redway, 1899; reprinted AMS Press, New York, 1975.

Levi-Strauss, Claude. *The Raw and the Cooked*. London: Pimlico, 1969.

Maunder, Samuel. *The Treasury of Natural History*, 4th ed. London: Longman, 1854.

Merrill, Lynn. *The Romance of Victorian Natural History*. Oxford: Oxford University Press, 1989.

Millais, John Guille. *Life of Frederick Courteney Selous*. New York: Longmans, 1919. Kindle edition.

Miller, John. *Empire and the Animal Body*. London: Anthem, 2014.

Morris, Pat. *Rowland Ward, Taxidermist to the World*. Ascot: MPM, 2003.

Morris, Pat and Michael Freeman. *Hutchings, the Aberystwyth Taxidermists*. Ascot: MPM, 2007.

Morris, Pat. *Van Ingen and Van Ingen, Artists in Taxidermy*. MPM: Ascot, 2006.

Pearce, Susan M. *Interpreting Objects and Collections*. London: Routledge, 1994, paperback 2006.

Poliquin, Rachel. *The Breathless Zoo*. Pennsylvania: University of Pennsylvania Press, 2012.

Robinson, Mellany. "The Beast in the Parlour, Taxidermy and the Nineteenth Century Middle Class Interior," MA thesis V&A/RCA, 1999.

Wonders, Karen. *Habitat Dioramas: Illusions of Wilderness in Museums of Natural History*. Acta Universitatis Uppsaliensis, Figura Nova, no 25, 1993.

Part III

Decentring Meaning

Objects Becoming Things

7 Objects of Anxiety in Nineteenth-Century Children's Literature
E. Nesbit and Frances Hodgson Burnett

Valerie Sanders

When you've read the books you know what the things mean[1]

In Chapter 3 of Edith Nesbit's *The Story of the Treasure-Seekers* (1899) the six Bastable children discuss the crucial significance of objects in detective fiction. Ten-year-old Alice expands on her statement cited in the epigraph above with further details: 'the red hair on the handle of the knife, or the grains of white powder on the velvet collar of the villain's overcoat' (34). Joining in, her brother Dicky cites 'Missing Persons' notices in newspapers which always feature a vital item as a clue to the person's identity: 'it tells about all the clothes she had on, and the gold locket she wore, and the colour of her hair, and all that; and then in another piece of the paper you see, "Gold locket found," and then it all comes out' (35). While the items the children are talking about are circumstantial evidence rather than in themselves objects with complex meanings, they nevertheless reveal the children's ability to see the importance of 'things' as the source of narratives, mysteries, and most of all, as a means of defining human individuality. The missing woman is found when her gold locket is discovered, all 'comes out,' and as Alice puts it, when you have read the novel, 'you know what the things mean.'

The Treasure-Seekers, like all of Nesbit's novels for children, and to a lesser extent, Frances Hodgson Burnett's, is packed full of objects that become 'things', resonant with additional meanings that reflect the instabilities of the children's circumstances. It opens with a sad catalogue of household objects leaving the house or being patched up as the Bastables reduce their living costs, and come to terms with everything being cheaper and shabbier: even the 'new spoons and forks were yellow-white, and not so heavy as the old ones, and they never shone after a day or two' (12). The narrator with this eye for detail is in fact one of the children – the eldest boy, Oswald – whose interest in the meaning of objects more than matches his younger siblings'. This is a novel in which the children's lives are pervaded by 'things': their use and abuse, their misappropriation, their shabbiness, and eventually their re-placement with ready-made, shop-bought luxurious items, so different from the children's everyday objects transformed by fantasy and inven-tion into the stuff of adventure.

The relationship between children and 'things' is an aspect of 'thing theory' which has developed more slowly than the mainstream concern with materiality in Victorian fiction. Laurie Langbauer, writing about the early nineteenth-century child writer Marjory Fleming, argues that despite 'an explosion of recent scholarship in nineteenth-century studies devoted to the figure of the child', the theoretical model of the child as object established by Jacqueline Rose in *The Case of Peter Pan* (1984) continues to shape subsequent influential work.[2] While childhood itself is often objectified (for example, in the scrutiny of childhood behaviour and emotions applied by psychoanalysts), Rose suggests that children, as represented in children's fiction, tend to have a special relationship with objects. Citing Alan Garner's *The Stone Book* (1976), she shows how a child can access ancient myth by examining a piece of stone. For Rose this becomes a special quality: 'It is because the children are in touch with objects, and have something of their *feel*, that they are given access to a mythical past.'[3] The question of why children would have such a special relationship with objects, Rose points out, dates back to early theorists of children's learning processes, such as Rousseau and Locke, for whom words as used by children were 'imperfect, since they could not accurately reflect the essences of substances' (46): hence children's ability to relate more directly to the feel and meaning of 'things' without having recourse to the misleading complications of language.

Certainly the idea of the child as relating more directly to objects and reaching a fuller, more intuitive, if wordless comprehension of their significance, is something other theorists have noticed, as Bill Brown ob-serves in *A Sense of Things* (2003). Brown instances Walter Benjamin's 'Proustian meditation' on the pleasures of feeling the rolled-up socks of his childhood, not just because of their warmth and softness, but because of the way they were like opening a present which then dissolved.[4] Every pair of socks in the wardrobe drawer, Benjamin recalls, 'had the appearance of a little pocket,' which was like a small bag containing a present. 'It was the "little present" rolled up inside that I always held in my hand and that drew me into the depths.' The pleasure of feeling for the 'present' was, however, always followed by the disconcerting experience of losing it: 'I had brought out 'the present', but 'the pocket' in which it had lain was no longer there.'[5] As Brown notes, this game's resemblance to the '*Fort/da*' ritual of Freud's grandson Ernst – whereby an object was thrown away and then recovered – is easily recognized.[6] In both games, one might add, the child has made a plaything out of an object intended for another use.

For recent 'Thing' theorists of children's fiction, there is a productive connection between conceiving of the child as object, and the child's own response to objects external to him or herself. This is helpfully summarized by Virginia Zimmerman in her study of children's novels about museums (which briefly references Nesbit's 'thingiest' text, *The Story of the Amulet*, 1906). Drawing on Rose, Brown, and Langbauer, Zimmerman poses a dialogic relationship between child protagonists and objects, as the children come to know themselves through the way they interact with artefacts in a museum. Zimmerman concludes that 'Thing theory is a compelling lens through which to read children's literature in part because the child character is always already an object, a construction of an adult author.'[7] The equally compelling relationship between child and object is what interests Zimmerman, who adds that in the contemporary children's texts she discusses the children themselves are 'identified by the objects they carry with them' and 'know themselves by their objects' (51). This argument carries clear implications for the ways in which children in novels by Nesbit and Burnett tend to be associated with a particular object which first sustains their courage and sense of selfhood, and then disappoints by letting them down. Sara Crewe's doll Emily in Burnett's *A Little Princess* (1905) is a good example of this. Bought to comfort her when her father leaves her at Miss Minchin's academy, Emily as an embodiment of lifeless silence comes to symbolize the loneliness and isolation of Sara's situation after her father's death with no one to respond to her emotional needs. As Charles Baudelaire argues in 'A Philosophy of Toys' (1853), the inertia and emotional unresponsiveness of toys are what most frustrate a child in search of a 'soul' in a plaything. In this brief meditation about the way children, especially boys, talk to their toys and demand more of them than passive malleability, Baudelaire suggests that frustration culminates in the shaking and throwing of the toy until its destruction is complete.[8] Maggie Tulliver's 'fetish' in *The Mill on the Floss* (1860) is an extreme example of this need to vent childhood frustrations on an insensate plaything.

If, as Zimmerman has argued, exploring the 'junction of child and object' (46) is a fruitful model for locating the identity of the child, my intention in this chapter is to develop this further, into a study of the troublesome nature of things as children interact with them in the novels of Nesbit and Burnett. The way things appeal to the creative and inventive instincts of fictional children, but refuse to stay in their places or behave as intended, is noticed by both authors. While the idea that an object becomes a thing when it is misused has been at the heart of Thing Theory since its instigation by Heidegger, this is something Bill Brown explicitly links with children's behaviour in play. Langbauer summarizes his argument as follows:

> the child is not thing but agent, a small theorist, a *thing* theorist (*Sense* 6–7). It is through children's deliberate misuse of things (the first dada-ists, for them a truck can magically become a table) that they defamiliarize the object and reveal the codes that have trapped its identity. (6–14) 'Children,' he argues, 'are adept at exposing the secret life of things.'[9]

What happens in the texts discussed in this chapter, however, is that children lose their agency in their interaction with things, and become overwhelmed by the things' tendency to develop agency of their own. We have only to think of Lewis Carroll's Alice to know that mastery of objects is a particularly troublesome issue for nineteenth-century fictional children. As soon as she lands in Wonderland (having avoided being hit by a jar of marmalade) Alice, who has nothing in her pocket but a thimble, is forced to engage with objects which often turn out to be hostile. Ordered to fetch the White Rabbit's gloves and fan, and growing too large for his house, she is pelted with stones which turn into cakes. After ducking the household items hurled by the Duchess's Cook in the 'Pig and Pepper' episode, Alice, who has otherwise learnt so much, is dramatically attacked by a pack of flying playing cards which destroy her dream. In both this and its *Looking Glass* sequel, where a joint of meat and a pudding stand up in the plate to be introduced, Alice is always somehow at odds with objects which refuse to engage with her on her own level or stabilize into one purpose or meaning. In this respect she is less adept at manipulating objects for her own purposes – however briefly – than the Nesbit and Burnett children; perhaps because, unlike Nesbit's especially, she has no other children with whom to collaborate in inventing other uses for ordinary household items.

Alice is by no means the first fictional child to struggle with objects. Before focusing fully on Nesbit and Burnett, it is worth travelling back 200 years to the child who in many ways may be considered the originator of this theme: Maria Edgeworth's Rosamond of 'The Purple Jar' (1796). In this brief didactic story, Rosamond goes shopping with her mother who insists on finding a rational purpose for all purchases. Given the choice between a new pair of shoes or an intriguingly attractive purple jar, Rosamond opts for the jar, only to discover its illusory qualities: 'It was a plain white glass jar, which appeared to have that beautiful colour, merely from the liquor with which it had been filled.'[10] Profound disappointment makes her burst into tears, but as Edgeworth makes clear in the subsequent stories, Rosamond repeatedly has to tackle the frustrating need to judge the purpose and value of objects and the consequences of mistaken judgement. In the next story, 'The Two Plums' – a real one and a plum made of stone – she hankers after the aesthetic pleasures of the false plum, but is eventually grateful for the present of a practical 'housewife' or needle case. Rosamond's mother, meanwhile, succeeds in diverting her daughter from an attraction to superficially appealing but pointless objects which have no function beyond the purely ornamental, but these objects never take that necessary leap from 'object' to 'thing' which makes them interesting alike to thing theorists and children. Perhaps the enduring lesson of the Rosamond stories is that objects like the purple jar and the stone plum can only be themselves and offer a child a limited kind of satisfaction; even the pleasure of contemplating them provides a diminishing return. There is nothing she can *do* with these misleading objects, as Rosamond recalls through the memory of a 'pretty gilt coach and six', another useless ornament which she forgot about after she had had it three or four days.[11] Edgeworth's *Practical Education* (1798), co-written with her father, Richard Lovell Edgeworth, similarly deplores the futility of giving a boy 'the finest frail coach and six that ever came out of a toyshop,' because 'having admired, and sucked the paint,' and dragged it across the carpet, there is nothing further he can do with it.[12]

While girls may seem to encounter worse problems with objects than boys in early children's fiction, Tom the chimney-sweep's bafflement in Kingsley's *Water-Babies* (1863) as he inspects the contents of Ellie's bedroom proves that boys too can find themselves struggling to interpret the common household things they find around them. The most puzzling items for Tom in Ellie's bedroom are two pictures of Jesus Christ – one of him laying his hand on children's heads and the other of the crucifixion, 'which surprised Tom much. He fancied he had seen something like it in a shop-window.' Tom's ignorance overlays Kingsley's narrative with what must have seemed shocking irony to the novel's first readers. That Tom should associate the crucifixion with a shop window rather than a church is succinct shorthand evidence of his heathenish upbringing, though he is sensitive enough to feel 'sad and awed' by the sight – even if, in a further twist of irony referencing Ellie's saintliness, he assumes the Christ figure must be 'some kinsman of hers, who had been murdered by the savages in foreign parts.'[13]

Children's relationship with objects is different from adults' in a number of ways. If Thing Theory was originally associated with 'discourses of exchange value, production and consumption,' we need to remind ourselves that children's purchasing power is historically limited.[14] Goods come mainly in the form of birthday presents, which Nesbit often lists in some detail: they function as the child's high festivals of plenty, but also symbolize their family's affection and commitment to finding enough money to make the day special. We see this in *The Railway Children* with enumerations of Peter's birthday presents at the beginning and Bobbie's when they are living in the country. Their attempts to give Mr Perks, the station porter, a comparable set of birthday presents fail miserably to begin with, as he is grossly offended by what he considers to be their patronizing behaviour towards a poor but proud man. Gift-giving often misfires in these stories because children are rarely in a position to deliver largesse to adults without causing offence, intensified by class considerations. Supplies of money are unreliable, but when fictional children receive any (or acquire it via treasure hunts or the sudden reversals of fortune which are so common in Nesbit and Burnett), there is tremendous excitement about what they might buy. So in Nesbit's *Treasure-Seekers*, when the children find a half-sovereign, the youngest child, H.O. (Horace Octavius) 'wanted to go out at once and buy a mask he had seen for fourpence' (p. 209). If this sounds like something of a random choice, their elder sister Dora is blamed for not understanding 'that when you want a thing you do want it, and that you don't wish to wait, even a minute.' The children accordingly rush out to buy 'figs, and almonds and raisins, and a real raw rabbit …And we got hard-bake and raspberry noyau [a liqueur] and peppermint rock and oranges and a coconut' (p. 212). This equally random catalogue is reminiscent of the food lists we find in Edward Lear's poems and stories: for example, the Jumblies' purchases when they hit dry land:

> They bought an Owl, and a useful Cart,
> And a pound of Rice, and a Cranberry Tart,
> And a hive of silvery Bees.
> And they bought a Pig, and some green Jack-daws,
> And a lovely Monkey with lollipop paws,
> And forty bottles of Ring-Bo-Ree,
> And no end of Stilton Cheese.[15]

Children's relish for food in literary texts is well attested, but it forms only part of their relationship with 'things,' which needs to be more fully theorized. It is not so much the social and political histories of objects cited in children's literature that seem significant – as in Elaine Freedgood's excavation of the origins of mahogany or blue checked curtains[16] – but the way things function in social relationships and transactions, as well as what Bill Brown has identified as '"Unnatural" use, uncustomary use,' which discloses the 'composition of objects. Forced to use a knife as a screwdriver, you achieve a new recognition of its thinness, its hardness, the shape and size of the handle.'[17] The misappropriation of objects, or the placing of them where they do not belong, is a key marker in Thing Theory of how objects become things, as Brown explains in his discussion of works by Frank Norris. In describing such incidences as 'dislocations', Brown suggests that they 'interrupt the habits with which we view the world' (78). In the case of fictional children, their habits are less deeply ingrained, especially for Burnett and Nesbit, whose characters tend to experience extreme fluctuations of wealth and social position.

These fluctuations make them especially conscious of what they own and what they have to improvise. Children in these texts relate creatively to household objects, which are not exactly 'theirs', but which they make use of while the adults are absent. Nesbit is especially interested in the way children improvise games using mundane domestic articles, while Burnett's texts are less obviously swamped with objects. Fewer objects are misappropriated and become 'things' in Burnett's novels, but their deepening emotional significance is stressed more than in Nesbit's writing. I start with Burnett as perhaps the more cautious user of 'things,' though her autobiographical writing shows that in real life she was just as much an improviser as Nesbit's fictional children.

Dolls and Skipping Ropes: Burnett's Things

In her autobiography, *The One I Knew the Best of All* (1893), Burnett happily recalls the green baize-covered nursery sofa which, in her childhood games, she designates 'an adventurous piece of furniture,' featuring mainly as 'a fiercely prancing and snorting steed,' while a green 'Arm Chair' could be anything from a canoe to a gondola.[18] Unlike Nesbit's fictional children Burnett largely plays by herself, with a favourite doll as a collaborator. Her fictional children are correspondingly more solitary than Nesbit's, often only children rather than from large families of siblings, and they have more intense relationships with a smaller set of objects. Sara Crewe's doll Emily, for example, mentioned above, and another doll, given her on her eleventh birthday, which she calls 'the Last Doll,' are her closest companions after her father leaves her at school. Both Emily and the Last Doll are extravagantly kitted out with clothes for every occasion, as shown in the catalogue of 'lace collars and silk stockings and handkerchiefs,' a jewel-case 'containing a necklace and a tiara,' ball gowns, walking dresses, and all kinds of other luxurious items.[19] When Sara loses her financial security, her loss of status is quickly epitomized in the figure of the Last Doll, which – apparently paid for by her father's investment in Indian diamond mines – now resembles the last preposterous emblem of a decadent civilization, like Marie Antoinette's jewels during the French Revolution. As thing theorists such as Suzanne Daly and John Plotz have noticed, in their analyses of Collins's *The Moonstone* and Trollope's *The Eustace Diamonds,* diamonds – usually from India – often spell trouble for their owners, besides, as Daly puts it, illuminating 'class and gender axes of property ownership and the ways in which belief systems regarding who is fit to own and administer wealth come to possess the force of law.'[20] So far as Miss Minchin is concerned, the ruin of Sara's father means that she, the child's head-teacher, has paid the bill for the Last Doll's 'ridiculous' wardrobe standing in for Sara's own: 'the last Doll sitting upon a chair with the glories of her wardrobe scattered about her, dresses and coats hung upon chair backs, piles of lace-frilled petticoats lying upon their seats' (86). Once everyone has seen and touched these lavish items, like revolutionaries storming the inner sanctums of a palace, the mob retreats to the birthday feast, and Sara – now standing in for the despoiled doll – is forced to put on an outgrown black dress of humiliation and enter a period of deprivation in the Bastille-like attic. Failed by the Indian diamonds, Sara conjures up in her imagination 'a thick soft blue Indian rug on the floor' (128), and other luxuries, until real Indian comforts are brought to her by the Indian manservant, Ram Dass.

Shortly before her public exposure as an impoverished orphan, Sara has been privately moved by a shabby birthday gift from Becky the scullery maid, 'a square pin-cushion, made of not quite clean red flannel' (76). This is much more in keeping with the kind of lowly keepsake Burnett favoured in her earlier novel, *Little Lord Fauntleroy* (1886), which narrates a child's fortunes travelling in the opposite direction to Sara's: from humble circumstances with his widowed mother in New York to becoming heir to his grandfather's estate in England. Inexpensive keepsakes of no monetary value are exchanged between Fauntleroy and his American friends before he leaves for England: such as a handkerchief 'of bright red silk, ornamented with purple horseshoes and horses' heads,' given to him by Dick, the boot-black.[21] The value of this vulgar-sounding item is profound to the small boy, especially in the face of a roomful of expensive toys provided by his grandfather, designed to make him forget about his despised American mother. The handkerchief is mentioned several times in the text, along with all the other humble markers of Fauntleroy's emotional journey: the high stool damaged by kick marks from his feet in his friend Mr Hobbs's grocer's store, and the more traditional present – the gold watch he gives Mr Hobbs, once he knows of his good fortune, inscribed on the back with the message: 'From his oldest friend, Lord Fauntleroy,' 'When this you see, remember me' (43). Towards the end of the novel Mr Hobbs shows this watch to Dick the boot black (whom he never knew before) as a means of identifying another of Fauntleroy's old friends – having himself noticed the business sign for Dick's shoe-blacking, which Fauntleroy had given him. In other words, the child's old adult friends are able to identify each other through the things he has given them. The gift-giving in this text runs both ways, in that the wealthy child is able to benefit the business fortunes of his adult friends, while they are finally able to expose the fraudulent claimant to his title.

By the time she came to write her best-known novel, *The Secret Garden* (1911), Burnett's interest in 'things' had shifted towards an engagement with much broader concepts such as the healing qualities of the garden, of positive thinking, and friendship between solitary children. There are moments in the text, however, when 'things' surface in subtle and meaningful ways, gesturing towards hidden relationships, memories, and class politics. An orphaned exile from India, the novel's child-heroine, Mary Lennox, is moved by the discovery of a cabinet containing 'about a hundred little elephants made of ivory.'[22] These are mentioned at intervals through the book as the quiet indoor playthings that she and Colin enjoy in more reflective moments, before he starts to act like a 'rajah' in his newly discovered territory of the secret garden. The long, dark, Indian past is something she shares with Colin, in these vast old rooms full of family portraits, whereas for the Sowerby family – the servant Martha and her brother Dickon – the wholesome outdoors world of the

Yorkshire moors is the clue to recovery, emblemized in the skipping rope given to Mary by Mrs Sowerby, who is shocked that Mary has never had a skipping rope before. Martha explicitly contrasts it with the Indian elephants she did have: "Does tha' mean they've not got skippin'-ropes in India, for all they've got elephants and tigers and camels," Martha says to Mary as she gives her the simple gift.[23]

Burnett's deployment of 'things' in her children's novels is therefore measured and thoughtful. These objects function both literally and metaphorically, often as symbols of class divides which they help to bridge, but they also draw attention to themselves in ways which are not always comfortable for the reader or the fictional character. Mary comes to realize, for example, that the skipping rope, though purporting to come from Mrs Sowerby, has actually been paid for out of Martha's wages, in defiance of her sister's arguably stronger claims. Feeling awkward, Mary is unsure how to thank her, and opts for a stiff handshake, whereas Martha's sister, 'Lizabeth Ellen', would have given her a kiss. For Sara Crewe, the 'Last Doll' from her father comes to represent the end of an era and the beginning of orphanhood, poverty, and adolescence as she joins the servant girl Becky in the make-believe 'Bastille' of the upstairs attics. Things in Burnett's novels therefore, as Daly argues more generally of diamonds, tell 'tales of origins, of status, of history.'[24] They remind children of their troubled past and only gradually point towards a more hopeful future.

Edith Nesbit's Improvisations

The very titles of Nesbit's novels for children draw attention to the importance of objects: *The Phoenix and the Carpet* (1904) connects two 'things' – one live, one not – while *The Story of the Amulet* (1906) is linked with another live fabulous thing, the Psammead, or Sand Fairy, first encountered in *Five Children and It* (1902). Like Burnett, she draws on the Indian heritage which is the source of mystery and wealth in her children's lives, especially from so-called 'Indian' uncles who shower them with luxury items, but her childhood autobiography points to more direct French influences. These include a grand doll which would not have been out of place in *A Little Princess*. 'I had never really loved a doll,' Nesbit admits in the *Girl's Own* serialization of her childhood recollections (1896–7), later republished as *Long Ago When I Was Young* (1966), though she does recall being attracted to a doll at a French bazaar. 'I was bored with travel, as I believe all children are,' she recalls, '– so large a part of a child's life is made up of little familiar playthings and objects.' When her sister wins the coveted doll in a raffle, the young Edith makes her the 'heroine in all my favourite stories,' but still she never loved her.[25] The doll's greatest use is when, like Sara Crewe, Edith is left in an unfamiliar home, and she and the daughter of the house unpack the doll's clothes together.

Dolls in children's literature have their own long and well-documented history, as 'real' toys carrying associations with female bonding, rivalry, and preparation for adult female roles.[26] As this chapter argues, however, Nesbit is far more interested in the 'improper' use of objects that were never intended to be played with, especially humble domestic items such as forks and spoons, flannel petticoats, glass bottles, bath towels, brown paper, panamas, and umbrellas. The appeal of these objects comes not just from their imaginative possibilities, but also from the daring raids on the kitchen, the secrecy and whiff of danger in the children's enterprises. The two connected texts, *The Story of the Treasure-Seekers* (1899) and *The Wouldbegoods* (1901), celebrate the children's subversive attempts to rescue the family's fortunes or be virtuous, but at the same time show how time and again, their misappropriation of things causes havoc, not just for themselves, but for other people (mostly adults), caught up in their collective fantasies. While their hapless series of adventures start out with the wish to achieve something useful, inventive, or charitable, in each case their plans go awry because of their inability to force objects to comply with their wishes. The things not only take on meanings and a life of their own, but are also either misread by others or misfire in some way under pressure to function as something other than themselves. This is partly because the 'things' reimagined belong to a different kind of narrative: the wild, fictional, non-domestic, or primitive, which the children try to superimpose on their mundane shabby-genteel lives. Inspired by *The Jungle Book*, the children, in fact, repeatedly revert to the primitive. They pretend their pudding is a wild boar being stabbed to death and play Red Indians with blanket tents. In *The Treasure-Seekers*, Alice becomes a priestess with an umbrella used as a divining rod (Figure 7.1), while in *The Wouldbegoods* they roll newspapers into 'scrips' carried by Canterbury pilgrims and put pink paper tails on their rabbits and hunt them with 'horns made out of *The Times*.'[27] Their mischief with objects becomes more serious when they plant false antiquities in an archaeological dig or toy with mythology, as when they sow 'dragons' teeth' (actually the teeth of an old horse's head skeleton) to see if they produce a real army of men (improbably, they do). What keeps happening in these stories is that contrary to expectations, the children's adaptation of household objects into devices, weapons, and clothes of the past does produce results, but not the ones they expected.

As we have seen with *The Treasure-Seekers*, one of Nesbit's favourite opening scenes entails an inventory of household objects leaving the home and being replaced by inferior substitutes. The gap between prosperity and decline in the family's fortunes is greater in *The Railway Children*, where the family start with every modern convenience in their comfortable red-brick London villa, including 'a lovely nursery with heaps of toys, and a Mother Goose wall-paper.'[28] Peter's tenth birthday,

Figure 7.1 Gordon Brown, 'Treasure Seekers' (1899).

however, brings omens of trouble when his 'perfect' model engine explodes, and 'All the Noah's Ark people who were in the tender were broken to bits' (3). When their father is taken away on a false charge of spying, and the rest of the family move to the country, they take with them '[c]rockery, blankets, candle-sticks, carpets, bedsteads, saucepans, and even fenders and fire-irons' (16), emphatically not the things normally taken on a seaside holiday. The new house is bleak and unwelcoming when they arrive in the dark, with their possessions dumped in a state of disorder: 'The kitchen table from home stood in the middle of the room. The chairs were in one corner and the pots, pans, brooms and crockery in another' (20). It looks no better in the other rooms, where they find 'the same kind of blundering half-arrangement of furniture, and fire-irons and crockery, and all sorts of odd things on the floor...' (23). If 'things' in Nesbit's novels have a special meaning, they belong to the imaginative life of children, inviting them to invent and improvise. For the Railway Children this never becomes a pleasure in the way it does for the Bastables in the earlier novels, and their interaction with objects, as will be shown, is more serious and purposeful – until, as so often happens with Nesbit, they are rewarded with the recovery of their fortunes and the end of austerity.

In the Bastable stories, the children's frustration with their relative poverty is more extreme and drives them into a series of hapless schemes which in unexpected ways produce positive outcomes. At the heart of each episode is an engagement with objects they fail to control. This narrative pattern starts at the beginning of *The Treasure-Seekers*, when the children are digging for treasure and find two half-crowns, or rather Albert-next-door's Uncle points them out, and as the reader soon realizes (but not the children), has planted them there as a kindly gesture. Alice's divining-rod umbrella similarly leads them to a forgotten half-sovereign under a loose floorboard. Real coins surface at key moments in these books to provide access back to the present time, when treats can be bought and the children are given a chance to recover from the latest setbacks. In *The Wouldbegoods*, Albert-next-door's Uncle reappears with his fiancée, whose brother 'showed us a lot of first-class native curiosities and things, unpacking them on purpose; skins of beasts, and beads, and brass things, and shells from different savage lands beside India.' For once the children can relish the primitive in a legitimate and safe way, even if it means coming to terms with encroaching 'grownupness' and the end of wild games.[29]

Elsewhere real dangers exist, when the children are forced to use their initiative and adapt objects to rescue themselves from trouble: hence the recurrent use of torn-up flannel petticoats to act as distress signals. This happens in *The Woodbegoods* where Daisy's red petticoat is incorporated into a Union Jack otherwise made of pocket handkerchiefs, Alice's white petticoat becomes a distress signal when the children are locked in a tower, and the girls' striped petticoats are made into awnings for their 'Benevolent Bar' (which stocks soft drinks to refresh the poor). Oswald, the narrator, apologizes for the frequent mention of the girls' undergarments: 'I am sorry their petticoats turn up so constantly in my narrative, but they really are very useful, especially when the band is cut off' (221). Nor do they disappear after their original purpose has been served. When the children set up a circus, the petticoat-and-handkerchief Union Jack reappears tied round the waist of 'the Black and Learned Pig' (125), and female dressing-tables are raided and stripped for 'calico and white muslin stuff' for the girls' circus costumes (121). While at one level these episodes are standard dressing-up games, common to children's culture, in Nesbit's stories they take on an additional self-conscious significance as the children commandeer things to adapt their own identities as well as the objects'. For Nesbit's child characters, objects have multiple meanings, which can transform humble domestic items from bedrooms and kitchens into flamboyant costumes, flags, and signals. A further detail about Alice's petticoat reinforces the transgressive dimension of their games with objects. During what Oswald designates 'the most dreadful adventure that had ever happened to us' (88), when they hide from a sailor trying to rob them, the children are saved by Alice's willingness to sacrifice her 'Sunday' petticoat:

> By the most fortunate accident she had on one of her Sunday petticoats, although it was Monday. This petticoat is white. She tore it

out at the gathers, and we tied it to Denny's stick, and took turns to wave it...And the tin dish the Lent pie was baked in we polished with our handkerchiefs, and moved it about in the sun so that the sun might strike on it and signal our distress to some of the outlying farms.[30]

The religious associations of the 'Sunday' petticoat are echoed by the reference to the cheesecake-like pudding traditionally eaten before Lent to use up rich ingredients. In desecrating both the hidden petticoat and the pie dish the children override middle-class expectations of decorous behaviour in order to protect themselves and others. Nowhere is this more so than in the famous scene of *The Railway Children* where the children make flags from the girls' red flannel petticoats to avert a railway disaster caused by a landslide falling on to the track. The sexual and political symbolism of this episode is recognised by Shirley Foster and Judy Simons, who see the petticoats as cumbersome signs of the girls' femininity, transformed by their ripping up into 'instruments of their power and influence. The liberation that ensues from removing their underwear is a deliberate affront to the standards of propriety they have been brought up to respect.'[31] Clothes historians have been more bothered by why the girls are wearing red flannel petticoats in 1906 when they were essentially a fashion item of the 1860s. Bulky and heavy, they belonged to a time when women and girls wore much fuller skirts and multiple layers of clothing.[32] It is hardly surprising that Bobbie and Phyllis feel exhausted in the heat, and after the 'black and enormous engine' (125) grinds to a halt before the landslide, Bobbie is found, like an exhausted revolutionary, 'lying across the line with her hands flung forward and still gripping the sticks of the little red flannel flags' (125). The recent discovery that Nesbit 'plagiarized' this scene from an earlier children's book, *The House by the Railway* (1896) by Ada J Graves, reveals that the red flags of Graves's book were made from the heroine Jill's jacket, which suggests that Nesbit consciously opted for undergarments for her red flags in preference to outerwear.[33] Railway historian Simon Bradley links the red flannel petticoats with the Socialist song of the 'Red Flag' (1889), wondering whether it is 'too much to suggest that waving a red flag for the attention of working men by a fine young woman of the upper middle class may have had other connotations in 1906.'[34]

In this episode, the narrative seems both to applaud the girls' quick thinking and heroism, and then to rein in Bobbie's transgressive behaviour. Having just celebrated her twelfth birthday Bobbie – a girl with nearly a boy's name (Roberta) – is on the cusp of adolescence, with little more time left for impropriety. Perhaps for this reason the next time we see her petticoats in action they are white, and, now a nurse rather than a revolutionary, she uses the white material to comfort an injured boy in a railway tunnel, the symbolism of danger and impropriety passing to the boy's 'red jersey' (218) . Once they enter the tunnel the girls' clothes are at risk again, and Phyllis accidentally 'caught at Bobbie's skirt, ripping out half a yard of gathers' (225). After they revive the blood-coloured boy with milk, and the others run for help, Bobbie (as 'Roberta') tells herself not to be 'a silly little girl' (233). If, as Virginia Zimmerman argues, 'child protagonists come to know themselves in relation to objects,'[35] Bobbie finds herself, like Carroll's Alice when she scolds herself for crying, directly confronting the crisis in her own identity. In this scene, her sense of who she is splits between adult and child, female and male, the female images of blood, milk, and soft white flannel, prefiguring the inevitability of womanhood, as she recalls the red flannel petticoat episode: 'Her flannel petticoat today was white, but it would be quite as soft as a red one' (235): '"Oh, what useful things flannel petticoats are!" she said; "the man who invented them ought to have a statue directed to him"' (235). Alongside the incongruity of flannel petticoats being invented by a man who deserves to be honoured with a statue, especially as the petticoats have been a nuisance on a hot day, there is an undertone of irony in Bobbie's idea of their 'usefulness.' After all, they were never designed for pulling off in public view and tearing apart for use in accidents. Having cursed her petticoats before, Bobbie now sounds like the matter-of-fact nurse she becomes for the boy as she places his leg on an improvised white flannel cushion. The boy's patriarchal response – 'You're a jolly good little nurse' (236) – prompts Bobbie to revise her career plans to work on the railways, as the girls talk on the way home about becoming 'Red Cross Nurses' (249).

While *The Railway Children* stands out among Nesbit's novels in terms of its cumulative association of children with things that build their identities and begin to sketch their futures, for Nesbit and Burnett, homely, adapted things in general, however troublesome, ultimately enrich the children's lives in ways that ready-made toys do not. This imparts a certain anticlimactic flatness to the typical endings of their novels when the children's misfortunes end in a shower of luxury items arriving in gift-hampers. In *The Phoenix and the Carpet* they have a box 'of toys and games and books, and chocolate and candied cherries and paint-boxes and photographic cameras';[36] in *The Treasure-Seekers* the Indian Uncle donates 'toys for the kids and model engines for Dick and me, and a lot of books and Japanese china tea-sets for the girls' (p. 230), quite apart from all the 'Indian things...carved fans and silver bangles and strings of amber beads' (p. 232); while in *The Railway Children* the old gentleman's gift to their ailing mother of (among other things) 'peaches and port wine and two chickens' (67) arrives much earlier in the story, as if to keep up their spirits and reward the children's kindly efforts. In Burnett's *Little Princess*, the dolls' ridiculous wardrobes are replaced by the sensible gifts Sara receives from her Indian benefactor: comfortable bedding, slippers, hot suppers, 'shoes, stockings, and gloves, and a warm and beautiful coat. There were even a nice hat and umbrella' (p. 251).

These gifts of manufactured, 'bought' items seem to function as the authors' way of ending the uncontrolled fantasy life of their protagonists with a return to the real purpose of objects in children's lives: to feed and clothe them, and to entertain them with conventional toys. They are returned to an adult vision of materiality, much as Carroll's Alice returns to her Oxford college life after the chaos of the Mad Hatter's tea party and the hurled crockery of the Duchess's kitchen. In Victorian and Edwardian children's imaginations, things come alive and are used to create a regressive world where adventure happens, but via a loss of control which has to be regained. While Nesbit's child protagonists take a cavalier view of objects, wildly misappropriating them to support their collective fantasy adventures, Burnett's engage in a more solitary, often melancholy, relationship with things which help them through bleak phases of transition. For both authors, however, things function to animate their inner lives and consolidate the children's identities. In Nesbit's world, especially, objects transcend their shallow, commonplace functions and, as Zimmerman suggests, 'collect multiple meanings,'[37] in themselves reflective of the children's developing judgement of their society's values and their own more imaginative priorities.

Notes

1 Edith Nesbit, *The Story of the Treasure-Seekers* (1899), reprint (London: Puffin Classics, 1994), 34.
2 Laurie Langbauer, "Marjory Fleming and Child Authors," *Romanticism and Victorianism on the Net* 56, (2009) paragraph 6, http://id.erudit.org/iderudit/1001092ar (accessed 5 July 2016).
3 Jacqueline Rose, *The Case of Peter Pan or The Impossibility of Children's Fiction* (1984; reprint Philadelphia: University of Pennsylvania Press, 1992), 45.
4 Bill Brown, *A Sense of Things: The Object Matter of American Literature* (Chicago: University of Chicago Press, 2003), 11.
5 Walter Benjamin, "The Sock," in *Selected Writings Vol 3, 1935–1938*, ed. Howard Eiland and Michael W. Jennings (Cambridge, MA: The Belknap Press of Harvard University Press, 2007), 374.
6 Brown, *A Sense of Things*, 11.
7 Virginia Zimmerman, "The Curating Child: Runaways and Museums in Children's Fiction," *The Lion and the Unicorn* 39, no. 1 (2015): 46.
8 Charles Baudelaire, "A Philosophy of Toys (1853)," *The Painter of Modern Life* (1863), trans. Jonathan Mayne (London: Phaidon Press, 1964), 202–3.
9 Langbauer, *Romanticism and Victorianism on the Net*, paragraph 22.
10 Maria Edgeworth, "The Purple Jar (1796)," in *Works of Maria Edgeworth*, 13 vols (Boston: Samuel H. Parker, 1825), IX, 150.
11 Maria Edgeworth, "The Two Plums (1796)," in *Works of Maria Edgeworth*, 13 vols (Boston: Samuel H. Parker, 1825), IX, 154.
12 Maria Edgeworth and Richard Lovell Edgeworth, *Practical Education* (London: J. Johnson, 1798), 2.

13 Charles Kingsley, *The Water-Babies*, ed. Brian Alderson (1863; reprint Oxford: Oxford World's Classics, 1995), 16–17.

14 Jennifer Sattaur, "Thinking objectively: An overview of 'Thing Theory' in Victorian Studies," *Victorian Literature and Culture* 40, no. 1 (March 2012): 347.

15 Edward Lear, "The Jumblies," in *The Complete Nonsense of Edward Lear*, ed. Holbrook Jackson (London: Faber and Faber Limited, 1947), 73.

16 Elaine Freedgood, *The Ideas in Things: Fugitive Meaning in the Victorian Novel* (Chicago: The University of Chicago Press, 2006), Chapters 1 and 2.

17 Brown, *A Sense of Things*, 78.

18 Frances Hodgson Burnett, *The One I Knew Best of All* (1893) in *Records of Girlhood Vol 2* ed. Valerie Sanders (Farnham and Burlington: Ashgate Publishing Company, 2012), 163, 161, 165.

19 Frances Hodgson Burnett, *A Little Princess* (1905; reprint London: Puffin Books, 2003), 84–5.

20 Suzanne Daly, *The Empire Inside: Indian Commodities in Victorian Domestic Novels* (Ann Arbor: University of Michigan Press, 2011), 67–68; John Plotz, *Portable Property: Empire on the Move* (Princeton: Princeton University Press, 2008), Chapter 1.

21 Frances Hodgson Burnett, *Little Lord Fauntleroy* (1886; rept. London: Penguin Popular Classics, 1995), 45.

22 Frances Hodgson Burnett, *The Secret Garden* (1911; rept. Puffin Classics, 1994), 57.

23 *The Secret Garden*, 71.

24 Daly, 68.

25 Edith Nesbit, "My School-Days," *The Girl's Own Paper* (10 October 1896–11 September 1897); reprint Sanders (ed.), *Records of Girlhood* 2 (2012), 201–202.

26 For a comprehensive overview of the literature on dolls, see Elizabeth V. Sweet, "Dolls," *Oxford Bibliographies* (2014), www.oxfordbibliographies.com/view/document/obo-9780199791231/obo-9780199791231-0155.xml (accessed 9 July 2016).

27 Edith Nesbit, *The Wouldbegoods* (1899; reprint London: Hesperus Press Limited, 2014), 238; 24.

28 Edith Nesbit, *The Railway Children* (1906; reprint London: Vintage, 2012), 1–2.

29 Nesbit, *The Wouldbegoods*, 292, 294.

30 Nesbit, *The Wouldbegoods*, 88.

31 Shirley Foster and Judy Simons, *What Katy Read: Feminist Re-Readings of Classic Stories for Girls, 1850–1920* (London: Palgrave Macmillan, 1995), 141.

32 This was observed by Noel Streatfeild in *Magic and The Magician: E. Nesbit and Her Children's Books* (London: Ernest Benn, 1958), where she states that no child in 1905 [sic] would ever has seen a red petticoat (123). Mrs Pettigrew in *The Wouldbegoods*, appears in Chapter 5 in 'a nightcap and red flannel petticoat' (106), suggesting this had become night-time attire.

33 www.telegraph.co.uk/culture/books/booknews/8392618/The-Railway-Children-plagiarised-from-earlier-story.html (accessed 9 July 2016).

34 Simon Bradley, *The Railways: Nation, Network and People* (Profile Books, 2015), 322.

35 Zimmerman (2015), 45.

36 Edith Nesbit, *The Phoenix and the Carpet* (1904; reprint New York: Hachette), 249.

37 Zimmerman (2015), 47.

Works Cited

Baudelaire, Charles. "A Philosophy of Toys (1853)," *The Painter of Modern Life* (1863). Translated by Jonathan Mayne. London: Phaidon Press, 1964: 202–203.

Benjamin, Walter. "The Sock." In *Selected Writings Vol 3, 1935–1938*, edited by Howard Eiland, Howar and Michael W. Jennings. Cambridge, MA: The Belknap Press of Harvard University Press, 2007.

Bradley, Simon. *The Railways: Nation, Network and People*. London: Profile Books, 2015.

Brown, Bill. *A Sense of Things: The Object Matter of American Literature*. Chicago and London: University of Chicago Press, 2003.

Burnett, Frances Hodgson. *A Little Princess*, 1905; reprint. London: Puffin Books, 2003.

———. *Little Lord Fauntleroy*. 1886; reprint. London: Penguin Popular Classics, 1995.

———. *The Secret Garden*. 1911; reprint. London: Puffin Classics, 1994.

Daly, Suzanne. *The Empire Inside: Indian Commodities in Victorian Domestic Novels*. Ann Arbor: University of Michigan Press, 2011.

Edgeworth, Maria. "The Purple Jar (1796)." In *Works of Maria Edgeworth*, IX, 13 vols. Boston: Samuel H. Parker, 1825.

Edgeworth, Maria. "The Two Plums' (1796)." In *Works of Maria Edgeworth*, IX, 13 vols. Boston: Samuel H. Parker, 1825.

Edgeworth, Maria and Richard Lovell. *Practical Education*. London: J. Johnson, 1798.

Foster, Shirley, and Judy Simons. *What Katy Read: Feminist Re-Readings of Classic Stories for Girls, 1850–1920*. London: Palgrave Macmillan, 1995.

Freedgood, Elaine. *The Ideas in Things: Fugitive Meaning in the Victorian Novel*. Chicago: The University of Chicago Press, 2006.

Kingsley, Charles. *The Water-Babies* 1863; reprint. Edited by Brian Alderson. Oxford: Oxford World's Classics, 1995.

Langbauer, Laurie. "Marjory Fleming and Child Authors," *Romanticism and Victorianism on the Net* 56 (2009) paragraph 6, http://id.erudit.org/iderudit/1001092ar (accessed 5 July 2016).

Lear, Edward. "The Jumblies," In *The Complete Nonsense of Edward Lear*, edited by Holbrook Jackson. London: Faber and Faber Limited, 1947: 71–74.

Nesbit, Edith. *The Phoenix and the Carpet*. 1904; reprint. Harmondsworth: Penguin, 1967.

———. *The Railway Children*. 1906; reprint. London: Vintage, 2012.

———. *The Story of the Treasure-Seekers*. 1899; reprint. London: Puffin Classics, 1994.

———. *The Wouldbegoods*.1899; reprint. London: Hesperus Press Limited, 2014.

Plotz, John. *Portable Property: Empire on the Move*. Princeton: Princeton University Press, 2008.

Rose, Jacqueline. *The Case of Peter Pan or The Impossibility of Children's Fiction*.1984; reprint. Philadelphia: University of Pennsylvania Press, 1992.

Sanders, Valerie. *Records of Girlhood. Volume Two: An Anthology of Nineteenth-Century Women's Childhoods*. Farnham and Burlington. Ashgate, 2012.

Sattaur, Jennifer. "Thinking objectively: An overview of 'Thing Theory' in Victorian Studies," *Victorian Literature and Culture* 40, no. 1 (March 2012): 347–57.

Streatfeild, Noel, *Magic and the Magician: E. Nesbit and Her Children's Books.* London: Ernest Benn, 1958.

Sweet, Elizabeth V. "Dolls," *Oxford Bibliographies* (2014). www.oxfordbibliographies.com/view/document/obo-9780199791231/obo-9780199791231-0155.xml; www.telegraph.co.uk/culture/books/booknews/8392618/The-Railway-Children-plagiarised-from-earlier-story.html (accessed 9 July 2016).

Zimmerman, Virginia. "The Curating Child: Runaways and Museums in Children's Fiction," *The Lion and the Unicorn* 39, no. 1 (2015): 42–62.

8   Within 'The Coil of Things'

The Figurative Use of
Devotional Objects in the
Poetical Works of Algernon
Charles Swinburne and
Oscar Wilde

Francois Ropert

Swinburne met Wilde only once in 1878 – a chance meeting with 'a harmless young nobody.'[1] The signs of Swinburne's acknowledgment of Wilde's talent are scarce, providing little information as to 'their attitude toward and criticism of each other.'[2] Wilde contrastingly praised Swinburne's work on several occasions, though calling him 'a braggart in matters of vice.'[3] The 'points of connection'[4] between the two men are therefore only a few, probably due to Swinburne's aristocratic defiance at the flamboyant upstart and then controversial social figure that Wilde became over the years.

But the present study proceeds from these few biographical 'points of connection' to a comparative approach of both writers' poetical works. They are certainly different, but also surprisingly congruent. The focus is the figurative use of devotional objects. These are shown to point to a nexus of unexpected devotions. They are furthermore considered as critical touchstones of changing codes in literature and as signs of decadent times.

The study first focuses on object-oriented images, especially as these hint with both poets at the omnipresence of the Greek god Pan. The resulting 'panoply' expands along syncretic lines, from either panoptic or panoramic angles. It stands for various forms of worship. Scholars have already evidenced the Roman Catholic background to these imageries.[5] But the present study doesn't track down again any specific core of religious doctrine. It instead consists in examining a syncretic panoply of devotional objects, especially as these appear to stretch the poems' figurative remit. It is notably through figures of excess that Wilde's verse may recall Counter-Reformation baroque architecture, while Swinburne's digressive lack of figurative focus is contrastingly reminiscent of mannerism.[6]

The 'points of connection' between the two poets are then, in our view, primarily figurative, symbolic, and aesthetic. They seem to find their ultimate figurative matrix in the two poets' common fascination with a holistic (Mother) Nature. This matrix notably generates some Pan-related/pantheist paraphernalia of overall Romantic inspiration, in the form of devotional objects 'higgledy-piggledy piled in a vast mound'[7] – as Virginia Woolf describes in *Orlando* (1928) – and ceaselessly reshuffled within a figurative set-up with no stable centre attached to it.

The queasy feeling attending the impression left by such paraphernalia surfaces in images of surfeit and intoxication, leading most poems to an aporetic 'half-swoon' – for so-called 'surfeit of (...) luxuries.'[8] Whether the scope is panoptic or panoramic, the either short- or long-sighted figurative focus in the poems indeed never quite stabilizes. The imagery instead expands and contracts in figurative spasms round a 'coil of things.'[9]

'The Little Ivory Girl' in 'Le Panneau'

The poems of Oscar Wilde enable a world of the imagination that teems with a variety of beautiful objects. These often materialize the most unlikely fantasies in the way of design and ornamentation. Wilde's poems reflect an unconditional devotion to the beauty of objects in that regard. An extreme case in point is the overture poem to his *Fantaisies Décoratives* (1887). The piece is 'Le Panneau':

> Under the rose-tree's dancing shade
> There stands a little ivory girl,
> Pulling the leaves of pink and pearl
> With pale green nails of polished jade.[10]

There might be something of a Japanese print about the panneau. Erotic overtones run through the piece. The lover is said to have 'almond eyes.' But the inspiration could equally be Chinese, when considering the mention of jade, i.e., a gem typical of Chinese jewellery. The overall impression remains one of exquisite beauty, linked to some great refinement and exoticism, as also suggested by 'ivory' in 'the little *ivory* girl.' There is a paradox however: the many subtle indications leave the reader clueless as to the mimetic function of the panneau. One explanation could be that the panneau serves no purpose, except for being strictly 'decorative.' But this explanation still leaves us wondering if the poem describes a single panel only. The resulting confusion presents a typical case of indeterminacy, when the focus never quite stabilizes on one shape or form to be envisioned as the whole of the object, but instead incessantly shifts from one of its parts to the next, as with the many reflections of a multi-faceted gem. Could the depicted scene(s) then suggest that the panneau is made up of more than one panel?[11] Could it be a tapestry, possibly depicting several scenes? Or a painting, possibly including several vignettes? Or could it be the folding panels of one highly decorated screen? These questions bear witness to a gap in the poem's mimetic accuracy. And these are bound to remain open, while the panneau is contrastingly depicted in always further realistic detail, thus somehow displaying its full length and the full swing of its beauty before our reading eyes.

But, all things considered, the ultimate meaning of the poem could be encapsulated in its title. This is worth one more guess: what could be made of the etymology of the word panneau? The word is a cognate of Pan. The sudden appearance of the Greek god of flocks and herds – right with(in) the title – is bound to cause some renewed 'panic' among readers, not unlike a stampeding herd as in the story of Pan! That witty title could be a first inkling of the climate of brewing danger that constitutes the barely sketched out narrative background to the 'fantaisie.' But the reference to Pan is surely all the more significant if primarily reflecting the viewpoint adopted in the poem. That viewpoint is that of an all-seeing God. As God's omniscient viewpoint, it no doubt partakes in the object-oriented accuracy of the lavish realistic wording of each motif in the design of the panneau, no detail being spared in that piece of *ekphrastic* poetry. And, for all its lavishness, that object-oriented accuracy ultimately leaves an overall impression of baroque superfluity making the represented space impenetrably unstable. The resulting sense of space remains versatile, always likely to embrace always more beautiful details within its always more accurate focus.

That eerie versatility is further evidenced each time the focus is put on the various precious materials involved in the making of the panneau. The panel's central figure is identified as 'the little *ivory* girl.' At a still closer range, the focus regularly zooms in on 'the polished *jade* of her pale green nails.' Equally iterative is her paraphernalia:

> She takes an amber lute and sings,
> And as she sings a silver crane
> Begins his scarlet neck to strain
> And flap his burnished metal wings.
> She takes a lute of amber bright,
> And from the thicket where he lies
> Her lover, with his almond eyes,
> Watches her movements in delight.

The mention of her 'amber lute' morphs into 'a lute of amber bright' through a baroquely arc-like chiasmus. These references to precious materials, out of which the depicted objects seem to be carved, or into which they might have been moulded, open up the space represented in the poem to a third dimension. The viewpoint then generates a case of baroque anamorphosis. The 'little ivory girl' can hardly be perceived as a shape being painted or embroidered like a flat motif on a two-dimensional panneau. The versatility of the poem's sense of space is instead coupled with a metamorphic sense of depth, the three dimensions thus involved giving a cinematic quality to the whole panneau. Our mind's eyes are made to see the panneau's 'little ivory girl' as a form standing out like an ivory miniature within a three-dimensional space, rather than a two-dimensional shape flattened out on a piece of canvas or tapestry. Given the overall cinematic quality of the representation, the 'little ivory girl' could further be figured out like an automaton on a small-scale carousel, or perhaps like a figure fully equipped with an 'amber lute' that could be part of a mechanical parade on a Victorian music box.

All these assumptions ultimately validate the relevance of a viewpoint that enables a versatile and almost queasy sense of space, depth, and gyratory movement coming full circle, as suggested in the poem's last quatrain:

> With pale green nails of polished jade,
> Pulling the leaves of pink and pearl,
> There stands a little ivory girl
> Under the rose-tree's dancing shade.

The return of the first line[12] as the final one here encloses the text within a loop of repeatable readings. It should be added that this viewpoint is sustained by a foremost centripetal drive that tends to baroquely magnify, from a microscopic angle, each and every detail against the background of the broader picture. Rather than flatly panoramic and macroscopic, the viewpoint is thus 'panoptic', i.e., showing the whole at one view, but also in the infinite diversity of its constituent parts. This is notably proved by our initial incapacity to regard the panneau as a coherent set. For that reason too, the viewpoint is typical of Wilde's hypnotic and somewhat short-sighted fascination with the details of beautiful objects, to the exclusion of their wider environment. Through a characteristic chiasmus, the beauty of objects is then turned into objects of devotion in the way of devotional objects.

Further evidence of Wilde's devotion to the beauty of objects is provided by the poet's habit of morphing all forms of beauty, especially in Nature, into devotional objects. A case in point is Wilde's fascination for the colour and the flesh of the pomegranate and of all related fruits when ripening to the colour red. They are of even greater interest to him when they can be cut into halves, but can also be reunited into one single fruit of perfect ripeness. This reunion can result, for instance, from the memory of a mystic kiss delivered long ago by '*La Bella Donna della Mia Mente*':

> As a pomegranate, cut in twain,
> White-seeded, is her crimson mouth,
> Her cheeks are as the fading stain
> Where the peach reddens to the south.[13]

Through this wholly spiritual kiss – as it is remembered – the half-flower, half-lady *Bella Donna* is made virginal again, or remembered in the full sense of the verb – a 'remembering' that the white seeds of the pomegranate symbolically contains *in nucleo*. But, as its colour ranges from intense red to dark red, the flesh of the fruit may also evoke 'bleeding wounds.' These can enervate another baroque network of figurative associations with Christ's passion, as the wine of the Eucharist is kept 'enshrined' within an all flesh and blood tabernacle between kissing lips:

> And her sweet red lips on these lips of mine
> Burned like the ruby fire set
> In the swinging lamp of a crimson shrine,
> Or the bleeding wounds of the pomegranate,[14]

As part of the same imagery, foxgloves are 'nodding chalices.'[15] Vale-lilies are seen 'in their snowy vestiture' as 'sweet nuns' that 'tell their beaded pearls.'[16] Carnations 'with mitred dusky leaves will scent the wind',[17] while a 'gold-sceptred crocus'[18] is given the attributes of kings, or of symbolically related dignitaries like bishops and cardinals. The whole passion of Christ[19] is thus encapsulated, always on a microscopic scale, within fruits and flowers that are baroquely morphing into devotional objects. The focus of the figurative process under way is certainly versatile. It conflates Christian and heathen forms of worship, the latter being mostly related to the cult of Pan. The resulting pantheism is syncretic. It provides a symbolic background to Wilde's insight into the beauty of objects, not least for being malleable enough to enable a world of the imagination that architecturally builds up round structural dichotomies, while 'higgledy-piggledy' allowing endless figurative switches between the terms of these dichotomies.

'The Altar' in The Palace of Pan

The focus and the framing are as versatile with Swinburne. The related sense of space equally sustains a metamorphic sense of depth and movement. It similarly enables a world of the imagination that is packed with unbridled fantasies, often to the point of exhausting a poem's initial figurative set-up. But by contrast with Wilde, the drive with Swinburne is more likely to be centrifugal and macroscopic. The structural dichotomies, round which a poem by Wilde tends to baroquely build itself up round in circles – often using chiasmi as rhetorical scaffolding – and then to microscopically close in round a mysterious core, tend with Swinburne to expand always further away from their initial focus, and then to remain macroscopically open to a mysterious impression of mannerist latency. Not unlike the sea's ebb and flow – a favourite rhythmical pattern with Swinburne – the detail regularly recedes to the background, while the broader picture alternately expands to figure out panoramic vistas over boundless stretches of the imagination. As with Wilde, dichotomies thus sustain ceaseless figurative switches, albeit in respectively opposite directions that impart the either baroque or more mannerist touch specific to each poet.

As now regards Swinburne's equivalent of Wilde's object-oriented devotion to beauty, there is no doubt that the scope of Swinburne's devotion is contrastingly macroscopic and object-*dis*oriented, notably by turning itself towards the heathen beauty of the huge expanses of land and ocean that the centrifugal drive of his poems' imagery ceaselessly reaches out to, while never quite capturing them in. Swinburne is undoubtedly fascinated at such awesome expanses. He holds their beauty in reverence, turning their often hypnotic primal beauty – especially of the sea – into objects of heathen devotion, with probably as much intensity as Wilde holds in reverence the beauty of objects, which he conversely turns into objects of devotion of a more syncretic and baroque type.

As a result, the prominent figurative status of devotional objects, which we previously examined with Wilde, turns with Swinburne into a structural symbolic background, while the space that these objects signal – rather than fill – stands for its corresponding foreground, the latter assuming the prominent role of devotional spaces within the resulting figurative set-up. We would like to add at this stage that Swinburne's *Palace of Pan* (1894) is in our view a significant counterpart to Wilde's 'Le Panneau' (1887), the structural dichotomies to be first noticed within each piece ultimately presenting, when both pieces are compared, puzzling correspondences at text level. These might further assume a paradigmatic dimension, at a metatextual level this time, within the extended context of understanding the poems of Swinburne and Wilde separately, but also as two congruent figurative sets.

Like Wilde's 'Le Panneau', Swinburne's *Palace of Pan* is infused with pantheism. It yet expresses itself in a more heathen fashion, as the title clearly indicates with its open reference to the Greek god. Swinburne's stance is more openly foreign to and more critical of Christianity, while Wilde's pantheism remains compromisingly syncretic by providing a baroque figurative blend of pagan and Christian overtones. The subtext of *The Palace of Pan* could thereby read as comparatively iconoclastic in its figurative drive away from Christian symbolism. The most striking rendition of that drive occurs when the text is conjuring up the image of a heathen 'temple' out of the thin air of a patch of natural scenery.

> Far eastward and westward the sun-coloured lands
> Smile warm as the light on them smiles;
> And statelier than temples upbuilded with hands,
> Tall column by column, the sanctuary stands
> Of the pine-forest's infinite aisles. (...)

A temple whose transepts are measured by miles,
Whose chancel has morning for priest,
Whose floor-work the foot of no spoiler defiles,
Whose musical silence no music beguiles,
No festivals limit its feast.[20]

The temple is of a huge size since its 'transepts are measured by miles.'
Depicted as 'statelier than temples upbuilded with hands', the 'sanctuary' looms large 'tall column by column' out 'of the pine-forest's infinite
aisles.' Besides these architectural features, the edifice figuratively expands well outside the symbolic barriers that the clergy of an established
church could impose. No 'priest' but 'morning' itself comes to celebrate
the matins. The temple's 'floor-work the foot of no spoiler defiles.' It
echoes with the 'musical silence no music beguiles.' And the 'feast' that
it harbours is extraneous to the schedule of 'festivals.' This paraphrase
of the poem ultimately bears witness to a number of symbolic transfers.
These signal the 'temple' as a puzzling devotional space of a huge size,
which is raised out of the 'transepts' and 'chancel' of a ghost-cathedral,
whose already ample proportions have been organically outgrown and
swallowed by Nature, back into a silence-struck green 'sanctuary' dedicated to awesome Pan. The place is further depicted as the peaceful
haunt of 'pilgrim nymphs and fauns'[21]

The noon's ministration, the night's and the dawn's,
Conceals not, reveals not for man,
On the slopes of the herbless and blossomless lawns,
Some track of a nymph's or some trail of a faun's
To the place of the slumber of Pan.[22]

Unlike any established place of worship like a regular cathedral, this
patch of forest is no place of 'revelation' to man, but a place of inscrutable
'slumber.' The 'track' and 'trail' followed by the forest's pilgrims barely
leave any 'inscription.' The passage of these sylvan pilgrims doesn't show
through on the clearing's spotless expanse of timeless pastoral sward,
except to the persona's initiated eyes. It is only the work of 'darkling
inscrutable hands' that may signal a 'shrine' in this place.

Dim centuries with darkling inscrutable hands
Have reached and secluded the shrine
For gods that we know not, and kindled as brands
On the altar the years that are dust, and their sands
Time's glass has forgotten for sign.[23]

Down 'dim centuries', 'darkling inscrutable hands', like dematerialized
elongated hands in mannerist portraiture, 'have reached and secluded

the shrine.' 'On the altar', these hands have also 'kindled as brands' all 'the years that are dust, and their sands', which 'Time's glass has forgotten for sign.' This further paraphrase of the poem points to a figurative intersection in the shape of an 'altar.' The 'altar' stands in symbolic contradistinction to a useless 'time's glass' that has stopped tracing the track of time, as if defeated by the holistic heathen sanctity of a green sanctuary cradling in the bosom of Nature, in a manner not dissimilar to the forest's sward that hardly bears any traces of the light footprints of visiting 'pilgrim nymphs and fauns.' The centrifugal sense of space that is characteristic of Swinburne's devotional spaces is here signalled through an altar from a now vanished ghost-edifice, but the altar and the edifice are deprived of proper realistic contours and of any foremost religious consistency, at least outside an implicit parody of possibly iconoclastic intent as regards established forms of Christian worship.[24]

The Pope's Blooming Staff

To create a panoramic viewpoint, devotional objects with Swinburne tend to dematerialize in a mannerist way out of the space represented in the poem, often owing to a figurative switch of metonymic origin but of ultimately metaphoric scope, whereby the focus pans out from the devotional object proper to the larger picture of the rites and rituals with which such objects are associated. The same type of metonymic process is at work in the poems of Wilde. While Swinburne's more digressive style relies on mannerist metonymies linked to the function of devotional objects, the figurative process with Wilde relies on stricter associations, as based on spatial contiguity and on the sense of an underscoring baroque design or architecture. Wilde's metonymies furthermore tend to go in the opposite direction from Swinburne's, as when the focus that is initially put on a forest of pines zooms in on – rather than pans out from – 'a spray of clematis' or a patch of 'foxgloves',

> Fairer than what Queen Venus trod upon
> Beneath the pines of Ida, eucharis,
> That morning star which does not dread the sun,
> And budding marjoram which but to kiss
> Would sweeten Cytheræa's lips and make
> Adonis jealous,—these for thy head,—and for thy girdle take
> Yon curving spray of purple clematis
> Whose gorgeous dye outflames the Tyrian King,
> And fox-gloves with their nodding chalices.[25]

Rather than unfolding as with Swinburne, an image with Wilde tends to fold up on itself along synecdochic lines. Its focus thereby tends to move from an original whole to its constituent parts, to the point of blurring the contours of the original whole. The effect is a greater proximity with the devotional object under focus. This object is therefore more likely to be personified as in 'nodding chalices', or even eroticized, most often in the sense of a deflation, or of a subtly symbolic detumescence, while digressive inflation is the figurative mode with Swinburne. This may explain why Wilde's witty images tend to strike a quasi-architectural figurative balance between the image's tenor and vehicle. With Swinburne's more graphic images, these are more loosely metaphoric and open to free associations, thus again dematerializing the realistic contours of the imagery in a mannerist way, while further draining it of its originally religious consistency. Compared with Wilde's, Swinburne's images establish a wider figurative gap between the image's tenor, whose relevance tends to be blurred out of the figurative set-up, and the image's corresponding vehicle, whose relevance tends to be digressively blown out of proportion, possibly to the point of some hallucinatory vision.

Laus Veneris (1866) presents a striking case of such figurative dematerialization in the poems of Swinburne. This landmark poem should be set back against the syncretic background of the pagan cult of Venus and of the Roman Catholic cult of the Holy Mother. The poem is certainly also the focus of some Oedipus complex that here finds a symptomatic expression round the figure of a motherly Venus. But the ultimate key to that subtext should be found in the story of Tannhauser, especially as it surfaces in an intertext exactly conflating the persona's story with the tragedy of the young German hero. More significantly to this study, the poem's complex intertext may also read as a key to the metaphoric use by both Wilde and Swinburne of items collected from some natural scenery to be then turned into devotional objects, often riddled with erotic connotations.

As the original story goes, Tannhauser is filled with remorse after falling in love with Venus. He leaves the womb-like, underground nest where he has been cradling within the goddess's intimacy. He travels to Rome to ask a father-like Pope Urban to be absolved of his sins. But the Pope declares himself to be impotent in providing spiritual solace to the young man, just as he is impotent in having his papal staff blossoming. Yet that miracle does take place. Three days after Tannhauser returns home, the Pope's staff starts blooming with flowers. But the tragedy is that the young knight will never know about it and thus spends his life in damnation. The blossoming of the Pope's staff certainly stands as a precedent to the imagery found in the poems of both Swinburne and Wilde. The staff in the story of Tannhauser is restored, in particular, to the natural function of a life-bearing limb. And could it also be restored to its pastoral function? It certainly could. Most notably by sending a panic-stricken flock – possibly of readers as well – back onto the right path towards a shared destination, however symbolical. This happens after years of impotency as the staff was used as a rod and sceptre for strictly symbolic functions.

The story of Tannhauser may then read at a metatextual level as a Romantic parable that aims to reassert the holistic potency of vivid symbols, especially over their downplayed significance once they are submitted to ideological ends. The parable could hence warn us against the misleading grip of symbols turned into objects, as these are cut off from a symbolic substratum to be traced back to Nature. The substratum/subtext of this Romantic parable when surfacing with Wilde is his insight into the beauty of objects, this insight translating further into a microscopic observation of Nature through the filter of an object-oriented type of symbolism. With Swinburne, a similar substratum/subtext certainly surfaces too, but at the price of greater efforts and in a puzzlingly more diluted way.[26]

This is the substratum/subtext that generates one of the most potent/pregnant figurative networks in the poems of Swinburne, especially as it comes through in a variety of macroscopic images related to natural fluids, these images branching off from a core dichotomy between primal placenta waters and menstrual blood. Swinburne's *Laus Veneris* is a perfect case in point, as well as a test case of how devotional objects can be squeezed out of their realistic contours and drained of their religious consistency. This is most adequately true of all the objects used for the celebration of the Holy Communion. The celebration of love in *Laus Veneris* turns into a nondescript black/red blood-mass/bath with Venus as minister.[27] The poem thus displays quite a bright palette that looks immediately Pre-Raphaelite, but that may also recall the toned-up chromatic scale of mannerist painting.

> Her little chambers drip with flower-like red,
> Her girdles, and the chaplets of her head,
> Her armlets and her anklets; with her feet
> She tramples all that winepress of the dead.[28]

While '(Venus's) little chambers drip with flower-like red', all that blooming blood, which oozes from the porous walls of some subterranean womb-like 'chambers', drips its way all over the goddess's body from 'the chaplets of her head' to her 'anklets', meanwhile spreading like a huge crimson stain round her 'girdles' and her 'armlets.' The panoramic drive of the vantage point can then pan out on the macroscopic image of a mock-heroic/mock-erect gigantic Venus as 'she tramples all that winepress of the dead.' The now full-fledged imagery has had time to deconstruct at several levels the basic dichotomy between inside and outside, to the benefit of a 'diluted' parody of the mystery of the transubstantiation of sacramental wine and of the whole sacrament of the Holy Communion.[29]

By contrast with Wilde's finer literary ways, which are prone to embrace the oneiric viewpoint of a short-sighted butterfly flying airily over a bed of enshrined crocuses fitted with microscopic baroque gold sceptres – as it were – Swinburne has to labour a blind subterranean route back to some heathen 'terrene' subtext, if ever to reach out through the nightmarish abject circulation of primal water and blood to the holistic potency of a diluted symbol in the airy form of an altar or of a dematerialized mannerist chalice – as it were. In the meantime, the poems of Swinburne follow the comparatively iconoclastic course of a parody that misuses the function and symbolic status of devotional objects in a likely erotic/mock-heroic 'vein', well out of any explicit mention of their names or of their mimetic depiction as 'full-limbed' objects of devotion.

Within 'the Coil of Things'

The poems of Swinburne and Wilde then build themselves up round a sense of space, depth, and movement, which is malleable enough to be shaped at will, whether at a microscopic level or at a macroscopic one. The resulting panoptic or panoramic vantage points embrace, within their equally metonymic and metaphoric scope, a whole world of the imagination, whether oneiric or nightmarish, and be it mannerist or baroque in style, not least due to the figurative distortions which that word 'higgledy-piggledy' shapes itself from. With the poems of Wilde, the resulting object-oriented figurative set-up tends to zoom in on a dense inner world of exquisite beauty brimming with objects that crystallize into a highly structured and baroquely intricate network of relationships, most often to the benefit of a holistic vision that encapsulates the poet's devotion to beauty within vivid images of devotional objects in the exquisite form of miniatures of an ultimately syncretic type. With the poems of Swinburne, the resulting object-*dis*oriented figurative set-up tends conversely to pan out over a boundless hinterland of awesome beauty, crowded with the ghostly mannerist shapes of devotional objects, which are blurred out of focus, at least until their diluted contours are restored to some primal circulation, which gives free expression – often through free associations – to morbid iconoclastic drives,[30] while yet rarefying these drives, until they die down in one figurative spasm as the poet enters 'the coil of things.'

Swinburne's *Triumph of Time* (1866) is a poem whose title already articulates some liminal spasm due to its punning indeterminacy over the value of the preposition 'of.' Time might triumph, but the poem's persona also strives to triumph of/over time through a ceaseless struggle. As in a cinematic pan shot, this is typically figured out as the 'coil and chafe' of a boundless ocean where the persona's 'thoughts are as dead things, wrecked and whirled':

> My thoughts are as dead things, wrecked and whirled
> Round and round in a gulf of the sea;

And still, through the sound and the straining stream,
Through the coil and chafe, they gleam in a dream,
The bright fine lips so cruelly curled,
And strange swift eyes where the soul sits free.[31]

The most striking figurative spasm in the poem occurs when, 'through the sound and the straining stream', the persona's thoughts suddenly 'gleam in a dream', at that exact figurative juncture when the reflection of 'strange swift eyes where the soul sits free' is passing. The flight of time, which is conflated with 'a straining stream' in a turbulent ocean, is thus presented as a deadly process that reifies the persona's 'thoughts' into 'dead things.' The deadly grip of time manifests itself as being materialistic and object-oriented. But through the quite engaging assonance and promising harmony of the 'gleam' of a 'dream', the persona finally catches a fleeting reflection of spiritual freedom with(in) those 'strange swift eyes', just above the 'bright fine lips cruelly curled' of a face whose features otherwise remain beyond all recognition, as in a mannerist portrait. It is at the very core of that 'cruel curl', which reads as one figurative variant of the paradigmatic 'coil of things', that the spasmodic twists and turns of the coil will unwind, while in the process releasing their deadly grip over the persona. The object-disoriented mannerist drive that is characteristic of Swinburne's figurative set-ups here again tends to cast into the shadows the realistic contours of any specific object within that 'coil of things.' While the Wildean logic baroquely conflates the 'twain' terms of a dichotomy within a holistic dream or vision, and is thus still realistically object-oriented, Swinburne for his own part pares down this same dichotomy to the basic tension of the 'gleam' of a mannerist 'dream.'

In that respect too, the figurative drive with Swinburne dematerializes any objects as it dilutes them within images of blood or water.[32] These images may branch out at still further length into images of ingestion and intoxication, the latter being particularly related to the poet's devotion to Bacchus and wine. It indeed makes overall sense with Swinburne that his neurotic fascination for blood and devotion to the sea should turn to a red liquid substance like wine as their next best/ worst fetishistic substitute. The quasi-architectural figurative set-up in the baroque poems of Wilde cannot lead to the same mannerist 'fluid' extremities as with Swinburne. Yet, at a metatextual level, it runs a figurative course that could here again be regarded as the counterpart of Swinburne's own network of images. The 'coil of things' that keeps fascinating Swinburne to the point of devotion for the spasms that it generates in and out, indeed finds its counterpart with the whorl of each of the corollas that never fails to fascinate Wilde, to the point of devotion for the holistic scope of their baroque beauty. It appears in both cases that the epiphany that attends the very experience of getting within the 'coil of things', at that *impromptu* moment when the terms of the dichotomies elsewhere informing their poems are reconciled, is each time signalled by a malaise, whether in a spasm with Swinburne, or a 'half swoon' with Wilde. This is the 'half-swoon' that Wilde articulates in *Charmides* (1881) as an ecstatic moment that is 'half' interrupting the persona's awareness of the course of time, at the sight of a 'burnished image'[33] that triggers a holistic vision radiating in and out into aesthetic/erotic bliss. While Swinburne then turns to wine and intoxication in similar figurative set-ups, Wilde conversely turns to food by articulating the experience as a baroque 'surfeit of (...) luxuries' that 'greedy eyes'[34] have been feeding on. The figurative set-ups are here again puzzlingly congruent. They are imbued with the same symbolism of the Holy Communion. But the viewpoint with Wilde remains baroquely 'consistent', for originating from the symbolism of the sacramental bread and enervating intricate networks of syncretic images related to food and surfeit. Swinburne's 'affinities' are more with fluids, notably originating from the symbolism of the sacramental wine and enervating looser networks of mannerist images related to liquids and intoxication.

Conclusion

The above paraphrase of *Charmides* thus loops one last critical loop on the whole chapter, around one more instance of figurative counterparts, first to be noticed within the figurative set-up specific to each poet, but also to be noticed on a larger scale, when the poems of both authors are compared and contrasted, with the view to merging these poems into a corpus. It appears that the poems indeed run similar figurative courses that are generated by congruent object-(dis)oriented drives. Either pan-optic or panoramic, these drives are sustained by structural dichotomies that we find in the poems of both authors.

Yet the chapter has also pointed to several instances when these di-chotomies bring about term-to-term oppositions between the poets. Against the religious and ideological background that devotional objects have epitomized since Reformation, the present study has attempted to account for these oppositions as so many contrapuntal oddities 'be-tween' the two poets, possibly refracting profound ideological rifts in history and society up to the surface of their poems, but which more likely reflect, in our view, aesthetic choices and idiosyncrasies with both writers. In that respect, well outside the strictly historical relevance of the terms, there appears an opposition between Wilde's baroque style of poems and Swinburne's more mannerist one.

Devotional objects with both poets thus stand as the core imagery of a symbolic nexus of figurative superfluities, which may read as critical touchstones of changing codes in literature and signs of decadent times resulting from the divorce of the signified from the ideological imprint of an object-oriented signifier. That divorce certainly manifests itself in the many dichotomies that inform the poems of both authors. It furthermore signals some decentring that both poets strive to articulate figuratively, while always facing the unsurpassable challenge of getting further into/deeper within what Swinburne came to term 'the coil of things.' The task cannot then lead them any way much beyond an intransitive aporetic 'half-swoon' or a perverse spasm of nondescript *jouissance*.[35] Conversely, it cannot be but iterative and likely morbid, each one of their attempts looping one more loop round an always elusive/illusive centre.

There ultimately stands the paradigmatic quandary of decadent times, when both Swinburne and Wilde, as respectively mid- and late Victorians, but not unlike their modernist successors, stretch literary codes to their outer figurative limits, in the meantime also pushing to their object-oriented outer limits what were Victorian forms of object-centred materialism as based on capitalistic hoarding and epitomized, according to Virginia Woolf's imagery in *Orlando*, in the rotund shape of the statue of a Queen. The poems of both Swinburne and Wilde are indeed distorted reflections, notably in the way of devotional objects figuring out the Victorians' very devotion to objects and materialistic values, of 'a conglomeration at any rate of the most heterogeneous, ill-sorted objects piled higgledy-piggledy in a vast mound where the statue of Queen Victoria now stands!'.[36] But we are made to understand too that the imagined shape of the rotund statue, which is located symbolically/ironically enough 'on top of things', can hardly cap off some ever-expanding paraphernalia of objects, as there indeed seems to be no termination to that paraphernalia, even within the figuratively all-encompassing sphericity of the statue.

The figurative set-up that finds expression in Woolf's topping/capping statue ultimately articulates some decentring which, like modernist authors, Swinburne and Wilde certainly strive to put into words as well. As T.S. Eliot remarks about Swinburne, drawing from the imagery of food/liquid ingestion/digestion so typical of both poets, '(Swinburne's) language (...) is struggling to digest and express new objects, new groups of objects, new feelings, new aspects, as, for instance, the prose of Mr James Joyce or the earlier Conrad.'[37] But, unlike the latter, Swinburne and Wilde never quite come to the end of the 'struggle', particularly in never quite taking in the full aesthetic blast of the decentring that the 'digestion' implies, way down to the dregs and bottom of an empty chalice. On the other hand, Swinburne and Wilde still firmly strive to embrace the Romantic fullness of a holistic harmony with(in) (Mother) Nature. This is the fullness of the typically Pan-related harmony that their poems depict, or the related fullness of their female forbidding figures, be they virginal 'wholes' from the woods or domineering 'whores' from some netherworld, or again the fullness intermittently reflected/refracted with(in) the 'coil of things.' This could be the figurative ways whereby their poetical works signal decadent times for Victorian object-oriented values. The signs in the poems certainly crop up through figurative excesses and superfluities, and way into critical insights into the symbolic value of objects. But, unlike their modernist successors, both poets yet never quite reconcile themselves with the idea of an 'empty chalice.' They will instead batter and fashion into decadent poetic material the very few symbolic dregs left inside an ultimately totemic chalice, which they will rather romantically regard as 'emptying' and likely to be 'replenished' on contact with Nature.

Notes

1 Arnold T. Schwab, "Wilde and Swinburne: Part I," *The Wildean* 29 (July 2006): 14.
2 Schwab, 12.
3 Schwab, 13.
4 Schwab, 12.
5 See Murray-Masurel.
6 The link between Swinburne and mannerism is unrecorded, but the link between Wilde and (neo-)baroque has been evidenced on several occasions, especially in reference to Wilde's *Salome*. See Christine Buci-Glucksman, *Baroque Reason: The Aesthetics of Modernity*. (London: Sage Publications, 1994), 145–62.
7 See Woolf for a satirical depiction of the Victorians' craze for 'heterogeneous, ill-sorted objects piled higgledy-piggledy in a vast mound', 562.
8 Wilde, *Charmides*, "Half swooned for surfeit of such luxuries," line 127.
9 Swinburne, *The Triumph of Time*, line 33.
10 Wilde, 'Le Panneau', *Fantaisies Décoratives*, 1887.
11 Each stanza may be representing one specific panel in the poem's whole series of eight quatrains.
12 See n. 10.
13 Wilde, *La Bella Donna Della Mia Mente*, lines 28–31.
14 Wilde, *In the Gold Room – A Harmony*, lines 13–16. See also *Ave Imperatrix*, line 26.
15 Wilde, *The Garden of Eros*, line 57.
16 Wilde, *Humanitad*, lines 75–76.
17 Wilde, *Humanitad*, line 77.
18 Wilde, *Ravenna*, 2, line 38.
19 See Kerry Powell and Peter Raby (ed.) for developments on the Passion of Christ as a recurring motif with Wilde, 253–260.
20 Swinburne, *The Palace of Pan*, lines 6–10, 40–44.
21 Swinburne, *The Palace of Pan*, line 54.
22 Swinburne, *The Palace of Pan*, lines 41–45.
23 Swinburne, *The Palace of Pan*, lines 31–35.
24 See Aquien for developments on the relevance with Swinburne of parody and self-parody.
25 Wilde, *The Garden of Eros*, 49–57.
26 See Sébastien Scarpa on this and related questions about the legacy of German and English Romanticism in Swinburne's works.
27 See Edward Burne-Jones's painting *Laus Veneris* for a visual representation of the poem.

28　Swinburne, *Laus Veneris*, lines 121–124.
29　See n. 24.
30　See Eliot for developments on morbidity with Swinburne, 327.
31　Swinburne, *The Triumph of Time*, line 179–184.
32　See Swinburne, *Les Noyades*, for similar object-disoriented mannerist effects.
33　Wilde, *Charmides*, line 126.
34　Wilde, *Charmides*, line 125.
35　See Barthes for developments on '*jouissance*', especially as linked with its perverse intransitiveness, 70 (inter alia).
36　Extended quote from Woolf. See n. 7.
37　Eliot, 71.

Works Cited

Aquien, Pascal. "Poétique de l'écart: l'exemple de *Cyril Tourneur*," *Études anglaises* 62, (2/2009): 174–85. www.cairn.info/revue-etudes-anglaises-2009-2-page-174.htm. (No translation available.)

Barthes, Roland. *The Pleasure of the Text*. London: Blackwell, 1990. (Translated from Roland Barthes, *Le Plaisir du texte*. Paris: Le Seuil, 1973.)

Buci-Glucksmann, Christine. *Baroque Reason: The Aesthetics of Modernity*. London: Sage Publications, 1994. (Translated from Christine Buci-Glucksman. *La raison baroque: de Baudelaire à Benjamin*. Paris: Galilée, 1984.)

Eliot, T.S. "Swinburne as Poet," *Selected Essays* (1932), 323–27. London: Faber & Faber, 1999.

Murray-Masurel, Claire, "*A chalice empty of wine*": l'imaginaire sacramentel dans la littérature fin de siècle en Angleterre," *Études anglaises* 62, (1/2009): 56–72. www.cairn.info/revue-etudes-anglaises-2009-1-page-56.htm. (No translation available.)

Powell, Kerry and Peter Raby. *Oscar Wilde in Context*. Cambridge: Cambridge University Press, 2013.

Scarpa, Sébastien. *Algernon Charles Swinburne et les enjeux post-romantiques de la création*. Paris: Michel Houdiard Éditeur, 2013. (No translation available.)

Schwab, Arnold T., "Wilde and Swinburne: Part I," *The Wildean* 29 (July 2006): 12–27.

Swinburne, Algernon Charles. *Selected Poems*. Edited by L.M. Findley. Manchester: Carcanet Press, 1982–1987.

Swinburne, Algernon Charles. *Major Poems and Selected Prose*. Edited by Jerome McGann & Charles L. Sligh. New Haven: Yale University Press, 2004.

Woolf, Virginia. *Orlando. A Biography* (1928). Edited by Rachel Bowlby. Oxford: Oxford University Press, 1992.

Wilde, Oscar. *Plays, Prose Writings and Poems. With an Introduction by Terry Eagleton*. London: Random House, Everyman's Library, 1991.

Wilde, Oscar. *The Complete Works of Oscar Wilde. With an Introduction by Vyvyan Holland*. London and Glasgow: Collins, 1948–1966.

Part IV

Object or Text? Reading the Body

9 Golden Lies? Reading Locks of Hair in Mary Elizabeth Braddon's *Lady Audley's Secret* and Tennyson's 'The Ringlet'

Heather Hind

The lock of hair may seem to be inseparable from the person it came from; every lock has been produced by, attached to, styled around, and taken from a body. Yet the cutting of hair from the head disturbs this relationship. Though invariably *of* the body, it is no longer connected *to* the body physically. No longer worked upon the head, it now coils around itself, able to take on new forms. A short entry in the *Catalogue of the Great Exhibition* (1851) describes an exhibit by Antoni Forrer, a jeweller of Regent Street. The 'variety of jewellery ornaments worked in hair and gold' elicit a comment from the editor:

> These works tend to show the amount of skill, taste, design, and variety, that workings in hair are susceptible of. It has been a class of manufacture of mediocre perfection hitherto; but from the ready weaving of the material into many forms, and its graceful union with gold, as well as its being peculiarly adapted for souvenirs, it may well claim to rank higher in artistic manufactures.[1]

Cut from the head, worked into a design, and placed in an exhibition, the hair described here is no longer hair as we know it. It has been re-worked as wearable ornament by the jeweller, repurposed as saleable (though not here for sale) commodity by the exhibition, and reimagined as potential souvenir by the editor.[2] In its severance from the body, hair realises its potential as artistic medium. It is 'ready' to be woven, to take on 'many forms', to be fashioned into one of a 'variety' of possibilities. In this way, the lock of hair takes on an amorphous quality. Capable of being physically worked into new designs, it also lends itself to meta-phorical working, its meaning as well as its shape open to manipulation.

In Mary Elizabeth Braddon's *Lady Audley's Secret* (1862) and Tennyson's 'The Ringlet' (1864), locks of hair are found to be striking and perplexing objects. On first glance it is their blondness that is curious, with each golden lock seeming to suggest innate goodness and fidelity despite the suspected inconstancy of their original owners.[3]

The speaker of Tennyson's poem wonders at his lover's golden ringlet seeming 'to flame and sparkle and stream as of old' when it should turn 'silver-grey', a token of devotion that doesn't match up with the woman who gave it away.[4] For Robert Audley, a 'glittering haze' of 'his uncle's wife's golden curls' haunts his investigations into the disappearance of his friend, George Talboys.[5] There is something amiss about the locks that Lady Audley leaves for others to find.[6] The contexts in which these locks of hair are found arouse further suspicion, especially so in Braddon's novel as the material framing of the locks—two folded in paper and one tucked inside a book—aligns them with text and suggests their place as part of a narrative. Material evidence is aligned with textual evidence, locks of hair discovered within and considered alongside paper bindings and verbal confessions, in a way that suggests a likeness of form and a parallel readability. But, as Deborah Lutz argues, 'unmoored from their close relationship with one unique body', hair keepsakes become 'unstable signs with a representational promiscuity', and thus locks of hair separated from their body of origin become verbally workable, capable of being made to tell a lie, crafty in both senses of the word.[7] They are susceptible to physical reworking (as neatly curled and pressed tokens) as well as textual reworking (given along with fictitious stories). It is in this dual artifice that these locks of hair are found to be golden lies, at once alluring and misleading. To read these locks is to consider not only the hairs themselves but also the narratives that surround and shape them, whether true or false in provenance.

The First Lock: 'Evidently Taken from a Baby's Head'

The three locks of hair in *Lady Audley's Secret* (belonging to Lady Audley/Helen Talboys, her son, and Matilda Plowson) are caught up in Lady Audley's false identity in markedly different ways. While each blonde lock might be thought of as embodying a 'golden lie', a falsehood on the part of Lady Audley, only one is circulated under false pretences. The lock which appears first in the novel actually exposes a lie rather than upholding one. In a chapter suggestively titled 'Hidden Relics', Phoebe Marks, Lady Audley's maid, discovers a 'tiny lock of pale and silky yellow hair, evidently taken from a baby's head'.[8] The origin of the lock is ascertained even before the question forms, imaginatively rejoined with an identifiably infant body. Yet it is more than its being 'pale and silky' that allows Phoebe to draw conclusions so quickly. It is through the drawer and its other contents that the secret of this lock of hair is physically and metaphorically unlocked. Discovered in 'a secret drawer' of a jewellery box, 'rolled up in a piece of paper' alongside 'a baby's little worsted shoe', the lock is framed to be read as part of a larger story.[9] As with the third lock of hair in the novel, a 'bright ring of golden hair' coiled between the pages of a book inscribed by its owner, this lock is rolled within a 'little packet' like secret correspondence, a curly correlative to Lady Audley's distinctive handwriting.[10] The baby's shoe is also significant, being a far more obvious clue as to the body it belonged to. Though the lock in isolation is a questionable signifier of identity, the little shoe delimits its potential origin. While the lock has been taken from someone's head, the shoe has been tailored (perhaps knitted by Lady Audley herself) to fit around their feet, evoking the space of the body in negative. The boundaries of the body are set forth, literally from top to toe, and other possibilities ruled out. While bodily fragments like 'snippets of hair… often furnish a means to authenticate identity' in sensation novels, here the trope is subverted as the garments of the body, rather than its actual material, unexpectedly serve as a surer sign of its identity.[11]

Phoebe's swift deductions may still appear to uphold the idea of the self-evident origin of hair. The lock as evidence plays upon the notion that hair, in spite of a misleading context, truthfully discloses the body to which it formerly belonged. And yet the power over Lady Audley that should therefore come with Phoebe's possession of this lock is undermined when she asks Luke to 'bear me witness where I found this'.[12] Luke's word is brought to bear on the lock, his verbal verification necessary to form a case strong enough for Phoebe to blackmail Lady Audley. This begs the question: without the context of its being found in Lady Audley's chambers, and taken from its place in the hidden drawer among the tiny shoes, what can the lock of hair testify to? Certainly, the lock of baby hair represents absence by virtue of its presence. These hairs have been preserved in anticipation of a body rendered absent by distance and, possibly, death. This lock thereby supposes a disconnection through its attempt to maintain a material connection between (assumedly) mother and child. But because of this disconnection, this telling token that Lady Audley is *missing* a child, Phoebe is capable of exploiting the questions that arise from the lock and not the answers. The textual quality of the lock is not here fully realised. As with the lock given to George at his wife's grave, locks are figured in the novel as effectively 'illegible' without a body against which to read them.[13] They might more aptly be said to function as blank documents, receptacles for projected meanings, or at best as composite bodies of possible but indeterminable contexts. The body of the lock of hair is not self-evident, but must be reconnected to a body via narration.

The Second Lock: 'A Long Tress of Hair Wrapped in Silver Paper'

Sara Malton notes the prevalence of unreliable texts in sensation novels, listing handwriting, telegrams, advertisements, and obituaries as examples of how heroines like Lady Audley master 'the art of trafficking in false images'.[14] Indeed, Lady Audley uses hair to corroborate a false obituary she places in the newspaper. A lock of hair taken from Matilda Plowson, a recently deceased daughter of a shopkeeper, is given to George by a landlady under the pretence that it came from his wife.

> [T]he woman took something from a drawer. She gave it to him when he rose from his knees; it was a long tress of hair wrapped in silver paper.
> 'I cut this off when she lay in her coffin,' she said, 'poor dear!'[15]

Although this lock has not been physically worked, the narrative that surrounds it has been carefully crafted. That the landlady preserves this lock in silver paper marks it as a treasured memento while her added rhetorical apostrophe, 'poor dear!', frames it as an object of mourning, given to George as he rises from the ground as though part of a belated funerary ritual.[16] For the possessor of the lock of the departed, argues Leila McKellar, the remnant serves to disavow their passing and suspend them between the worlds of the living and the dead.[17] Yet this particular lock is not given to George as a token of the mortal-immortal threshold. The presentation of the lock is not for the purpose of keeping the memory of Helen alive, as it were, in George's mind. It is meant to bury Helen in his thoughts and thereby terminate his quest to find out what became of his wife. It is framed as proof that the body from which it was cut is no more: it takes the place of a death certificate. While the lock of hair may, for George, bring the dead 'back to speak' in some sense, it 'foregrounds, at the same time, the eternal silence' of the subject.[18] The lock, like a last utterance, defies further correspondence with Helen in an attempt to silence George.

As a false relic of the supposedly deceased Helen, the duplicity of the lock is still more pronounced. Rather than maintaining a physical (and symbolically metaphysical) connection between man and wife, Matilda's lock serves to break the bond between them. The lock is an invented connection, and thereby a disconnection, between George and Helen.

> He pressed the soft lock to his lips. 'Yes,' he murmured; 'this is the dear hair that I have kissed so often when her head lay upon my shoulder. But it always had a rippling wave in it then, and now it seems smooth and straight.'
> 'It changes in illness,' said the landlady.[19]

The lock works itself into George's memory in the form of a remembered interaction, 'the dear hair' falsely professing a familiarity. Though the textural difference between Helen's hair and Matilda's is as distinct as wavy versus straight, the malleability of this lock goes beyond physical restyling to associative suggestibility. That its backstory can be readily rewritten by the landlady, even as to overturn doubts over its physical composition, shows it to be the very material of deception. Lady Audley fabricates her own fairy tale, appropriating the hair of others in order to convince George of her death while she styles herself as 'the fair-haired paragon' of Sir Michael Audley's affections, with the skill of a hair worker.[20] Indeed, sending away the hairs of a loved one to be made into jewellery was an exchange fraught with anxiety, not only in the safe sending of the hair but also in getting it back. Hair worker Alexanna Speight, in *The Lock of Hair* (1871), warns against the 'trade jugglery' of dishonest tradesmen who might swap the hair of loved ones for already made-up pieces, urging readers 'to dispense with their services, and to be become masters of the beautiful art themselves'.[21] George, having been abroad when his wife is said to have died, trusts the testament he is given and unwittingly accepts the word and work of another.

The Ringlet

As well as being physically malleable, then, these locks of hair are shown to be highly susceptible to verbal manipulation. They are framed as part of a false narrative, alternately used to expose or conceal Lady's Audley's lies, the second lock belonging to Matilda Plowson even standing in *as* the false body of Helen Talboys. Tennyson's 'The Ringlet' plays upon another kind of falsity seen in and through a lock of hair. Cut at the request of the speaker, the lock given to him by his lover becomes a false testament to her fidelity (i.e. her body) and a deceivingly impermanent signifier of her vow to remain faithful (her word). Despite the physical changelessness of the lock, cut so that 'never chilling touch of Time / Will turn it silver-gray', the body from which it was cut does change, physically growing older and (it is suggested by the speaker) becoming morally defiled in the woman's transferral of affection to another.[22] The ability of this lock to tell the truth, as it were, is compromised *after* it has been exchanged. It not a false lock, a 'golden lie' at the point it is given like Matilda's lock in *Lady Audley's Secret*, but is framed as such by the speaker when its giver proves false.[23]

 The lock of hair taken from the female addressee of the poem is metonymic of her body and her promise of fidelity.[24] The physical exchange of the lock takes place with a verbal exchange between the two lovers; 'Then take it, love, and put it by; / This cannot change, nor yet can I'.[25] As a promise, this is somewhat restrained. No explicit commitment is made as the woman's changelessness appears to be relative to the lock of hair that is being handed over. With the stress falling on 'yet', it is unclear whether the woman may change, just not yet, or may change along with the lock. Nevertheless, the exchange is not without gravity. A vow is spoken *through* the token of a lock of the hair. The ringlet provides a material correlative to an immaterial process. It reifies a transferral of affect from the woman to the speaker as a moveable repository of that affect.[26] The ringlet stands in as something to be exchanged, hand to hand, between the lovers whose promise to each other is, in the absence of this token, mere words. It is an utterance made material. The speaker, not giving a lock of his hair in return, makes his own vow explicit, declaring that 'I swear henceforth by this'.[27] The ringlet is brought into another verbal performance of a promise, but here the speaker swears *on* as opposed to *through* the lock. On either side of this exchange the lock serves as an authenticating text, a pledge and a pledged upon object. Further still, the synthetic proposition that goes along with the ringlet—the statement 'This cannot change, nor yet can I' which may be proven or disproven—means that the lock is given the potential to be true or false.[28] Thus, though it is the woman that declares her fidelity and she that breaks the vow, the lock itself is addressed by the speaker—'I that took you for true gold'—and pronounced the 'golden lie'.[29]

The ringlet is first placed as mediator, a means of physical connection between the two lovers in their separation, but it swiftly becomes an object of desire in itself. Though the woman is initially addressed directly by the speaker, she is replaced as the addressee of the poem by her own hair when it becomes the speaker's possession. After the report of her infidelity, 'which now I'm told', the woman loses her voice in the poem, her responding couplet, and the ringlet takes her place.[30] From the second stanza onwards the speaker addresses the ringlet itself and not its giver at all: the desire to have 'Your ringlets' becomes the ownership of 'my ringlet', which becomes the proper noun 'O Ringlet'.[31] 'My ringlet' appears initially with the woman still present, for she replies despite the displacement of the address, 'Then kiss it love'.[32] This marks a shift of focus between the first and second stanzas from the woman to the ringlet, a person to an object. By the third stanza, the ringlet is not only addressed but 'kiss'd [...] night and day', displacing the woman altogether from the speaker's affections.[33] There is a disjuncture between the active subject of the woman and the static object of the ringlet, the latter made fetish-object and 'kiss'd' though it cannot reciprocate. Though Matilda Plowson's lock in *Lady Audley's Secret* similarly stands in for an absent female body as George presses it to his lips and remembers his wife, the ringlet here stands in for a body which is still living, still upholding a vow, and able to break it. Indeed, in taking the lock of hair the speaker attempts to prevent the circulation of the body (in particular an active, reciprocating body) by means of sympathetic magic, cutting off and keeping one single part in order to maintain possession of the whole.[34] Correspondingly, the ringlet is poetically paralysed (or perhaps preserved as evidence of the vow) from the beginning of the third stanza, appearing repeatedly as 'O Ringlet, O Ringlet'[35] without variation as though the speaker wills it (and thereby the woman) to remain unchanged. There is something of the sexual jealousy of Robert Browning's 'Porphyria's Lover' (1836) in this, a desire to deny the circulation of the woman to other men by immobilising them in death. While Porphyria's lover chokes her with her own hair, the speaker of Tennyson's poem holds on to his lover's hair as a surrogate body that he can immobilize and possess regardless of the continued mobility of that body. Keeping her hair, a kind of freezing of the soon to be absent body, is a violent enforcement of her continued tactile presence. His corporeal keepsake is proof of his lingering possession of her body, and his continued address of the ringlet a verbalized attempt to maintain her vow in courting its material manifestation.

Like Sir Audley, taken in by Lady Audley's 'gold-shot, flaxen curls', the speaker berates himself for having mistakenly taken his betrothed's hair 'for true gold', the fair-haired female being its supposed correlative in moral worth.[36] Or perhaps it is that the true gold of the lock of hair is weighed against the false gold of the woman; a 'glossy heretic' for inspiring an empty faith.[37] In either case, gold serves as the tangible material on which the abstract value of the woman may be determined, facilitated by the fairness of her hair and its exchangeability as a lock. To chart the process by which this comes into effect, I will turn briefly to Christina Rossetti's 'Goblin Market' (1862) in which Laura, unable to determine the value of the fruit which the goblin men advertise without an explicit price tag, offers that which 'depicts itself in the bodies of all other commodities': gold.[38] Conceding to 'Buy from [the goblins] with a golden curl', Laura's hair carries an erotic charge, its being 'clipp'd' suggestive of a painful loss of virginity, while her 'tear more rare than pearl' implies the loss of innocence, of virginal blood.[39] The speaker of 'The Ringlet', recalling the moment of his lover's hair being cut, evokes a sexual encounter in telling how 'She blush'd a rosy red, / When Ringlet, O Ringlet, / She clipt you from her head'.[40] Yet neither Laura nor the woman of 'The Ringlet' are, in any straightforward way, prostituting themselves in giving their hair over to men in trade or in gift. This 'clipping' is more than a loss of maidenhead. The act of coin clipping, cutting the edges off coins to be made into forged currency, underlies these exchanges.[41] The way in which the economy of each poem operates, however, is very different. In 'Goblin Market', Laura, as the clipped coin, is the debased coin in that she has compromised the whole in giving a part, her golden curl circulating in a market from which she is now excluded as a consumer. For the speaker of 'The Ringlet' it is the clipping, the lock of hair itself, that is considered debased in its being given as a counterfeit coin, offered by the woman as a piece of false gold as she exploits its apparent worth.

Lady Audley's golden curls, arranged so as to form a 'pale halo round her head', are used in much the same way as Tennyson's ringlet, though not given away as locks.[42] They are a means of manipulating her perceived character. Her curls are, as Tara Puri puts it, 'a text that explains her' though simultaneously one of her means of duplicity.[43] Luxuriant hair is part of Lady Audley's costume (or disguise by implication of her crimes) which she exploits for its connotation of angelic goodness and styles into the coiffure of the aristocrat she aspires to be. As the novel progresses, the narrator partakes in this play upon the readable quality of hair as a way of confessing her crimes. Before committing arson, it is 'a tangled mess that surrounded her forehead like a yellow flame'.[44] Like Lady Audley herself, the narrator is able to exploit the notion that hair has an 'imaginative engagement with the concealed, invisible parts', whether her changing mental states or her overall character, as her hair becomes for the reader a means of discovery, a text within the text to be interpreted.[45] For the speaker of 'The Ringlet', however, this 'imaginative engagement' is only that. At best, it is a fanciful projection of correlation between a bodily material and the inward self, and at worst a misreading. For, while seeming to profess the angelic, the woman's golden ringlets may equally suggest the demonic, ensnaring the speaker in their shining web.[46]

Whether intending to mislead the speaker with her golden lock or not, the woman of 'The Ringlet' breaks her commitment to him.

> For what is this which now I'm told,
> I that took you for true gold,
> She that gave you's bought and sold,
> Sold, sold.[47]

But is it that the woman has been 'sold' in matrimony to another, has taken another lover, or has prostituted herself? If the latter, she may have been 'sold' to any number of men depending on whether the speaker's repetition is taken rhetorically (as an exaggeration of only one or indicating many) or literally as a treble selling. The trochaic meter of these lines evokes a falling away but ends with a finality on the spondaic repetition of 'sold', suggesting that the woman depreciates in value as she is repeatedly exchanged. Yet the repetition of 'sold, / Sold, sold' by the speaker may equally tell of *his* losses, a culmination of the woman's objectification through and in the lock of her hair. The ringlet that remains in his possession, in its relation to the repeatedly sold body of the woman, correspondingly depreciates in worth, reduced to a 'golden nothing'.[48] The idea of the 'golden nothing' reflects back on the original promise of the woman. As well as being a thing of little worth, this ringlet as a 'nothing' connotes a trivial remark, an aside, a sweet nothing whispered between lovers. The ringlet diminishes as an object of utterance, in addition to diminishing in value as a romantic token for the speaker.

In one sense the lock, and not the woman, has broken a holy bond in that it stands in for and embodies a vow that the woman never incontrovertibly made.[49] The woman consistently places her changeability as contingent on the endurance of the lock—'If this can change, why so can I'—which may be misleading in that what appears to be a promise that neither will change is actually a concession that both may be found false.[50] But the very ability to mislead is displaced from the woman to the lock when it does endure despite the woman's changeability. It is the lock that is chastised for not correspondingly turning 'silver-gray', the lock that is counted 'much to blame' for having put the speaker 'to shame'.[51] The deceptive allure of this 'glossy heretic' is an interesting concept in terms of the textual qualities of the lock.[52] The 'gloss' of this lock may be taken as its commentary as well as its shine. With 'glossing' as the act of commenting upon the language of a text, the lock might be seen as a layered textual construction, a gloss upon the verbal exchange of the promise between the two lovers. The lock as a 'glossy heretic' is both comment from and commentary upon its body of origin. It is a false profession in itself (it shines gold when it should fade to 'silver-gray') and it professes falsely upon another (it shines gold despite coming from a false woman). The 'golden lie' attributed emphatically to the promise embodied by the lock, the ringlet is finally cast into the fire to 'burn, / Burn, burn' in what is not an issue of false character, but of the falsity of a seemingly self-evident token of character.[53]

The Third Lock: 'A Bright Ring of Golden Hair'

The third and final lock of *Lady Audley's Secret* is discovered while Robert is trying to find Helen's signature inside some books belonging to George. In this scene in particular, the lock of hair is shown to tangibly intersect with the material text. Searching by flicking through an almanac 'for any scrap of writing' which may be tucked in between its pages, he comes across a curled lock of Helen's hair which he immediately folds up in paper and places in his pigeon-hole.[54] Inserted, physically, into a book containing Helen's handwriting, the lock is framed in a way that suggests its own textuality. For both the reader and for Robert this lock is something to be held on to for rereading. Indeed, were the reader not to immediately decipher the real narratives behind any of the locks in the novel, the written word keeps them for later inspection, much in the same way as locks within the novel are discovered pressed and preserved in paper.[55] If the materiality of the Victorian book lies its being 'the medium upon which representation occurs as well as a potential subject of such representation', then the materiality of this lock of hair also lies in its being here both the medium and subject of representation.[56] Robert deciphers and matches up locks of hair alongside the reader of the novel as a kind of parallel reader, storing his latest find for future reference. In placing this lock among his letters—'[he] folded this yellow lock in a sheet of letter-paper, which he sealed with his signet ring, and laid aside… in the pigeon-hole marked important'—Robert's thinking of the lock as telling part of a narrative, a fragment of a paper trail linking George's disappearance with Lady Audley's unclear past, is made all the more explicit.[57] Folded in paper like a letter, writing is substituted for hair while, simultaneously for the reader, hair is substituted again for writing.[58] It is in this idea that the lock of hair as lie is most fully realised. Each of these locks is represented and misrepresented, read and misread *within* these texts as well as outside of them.

This last lock recalls the first in its revealing of the truth, the 'bright ring of golden hair' suggestively curling back on itself, exposing the lie of Helen's death rather than covering it up.[59] As the supposed sister lock to the one given to George at his wife's grave, Robert finds it to be 'very opposite in texture, if not different in hue, to the soft, smooth tresses' he has seen before.[60] Touching this lock of hair, thinking back to the texture and shade of the lock given by the landlady, Robert also demonstrates here a distinctively material, tactile mode of detective work. And in keeping this lock in letter paper in order to return to it later, perhaps to read it alongside written evidence, his approach to reading the lock is shown to be equally visual, textural and textual. Robert's detective process, collecting and connecting written and verbal narratives and also viewing and touching the objects of George's past, show how these suspect strands become one with the mental work of identifying connections and unravelling identities as Robert thinks upon them. It is in reading one lock of hair against another that he begins to unravel the story of Lady Audley, these carefully pressed and preserved locks shown to be golden lies that alternately conceal and reveal the true identities of the bodies from which they came.

We might see this final lock of tightly curled hair as having come full circle, resisting revelation even as it appears close to unravelling all. Though used as material evidence in uncovering Lady Audley's hidden past, this lock maintains its close binding of immaterial affections and connections. The lock keeps its narrative faithfully hidden, to be given in full only by the verbal confession of its originator: Lady Audley herself. While Braddon positions locks of hair against paper evidence, with these bodily tokens often disclosing more than documentation, we are left with a sense of the limitations of hair as it raises, though does not resolve, questions of identity. To return to Antoni Forrer's hair jewellery, we see that 'the ready weaving of the material into many forms' means that locks of hair can be seen as both physically and textually workable.[61] They are taken as testaments to their giver's intentions and as authenticators of identity, seeming to exceed verbal exchanges or written records as actual bodily material rather than mere representations. And yet, yielding so readily to narrative reworkings, these locks of hair are framed as golden lies which only appear to confess their true origin and to disclose something of the body from which they came. It is the ambivalence of each of these locks to self-evident meaning that enables their narration. Each lock, when endowed with such a narrative, is made an object-text while the greater narrative of the novel or poem makes each a text-object. It is in this twofold articulation that locks of hair become fallacious texts from which new and duplicitous strands are drawn.

Notes

1 Robert Ellis and Commissioners for the Exhibition of 1851, *Official Descriptive and Illustrated Catalogue of the Great Exhibition of the Works of Industry of All Nations, 1851* (London: Spicer Brothers, 1851), 690.
2 Although the objects on display at the Great Exhibition were not for sale, the Exhibition was at one point imagined as displaying the wares of a huge store, with objects priced and available to purchase. See Andrew H. Miller, *Novels Behind Glass: Commodity Culture and Victorian Narrative* (Cambridge: Cambridge University Press, 1995), 63. This reimagining is borne both by the editor's comments and the context of the hair jewellery as a display in an exhibition. The value of the Victorian souvenir, according to Thad Logan, 'depended entirely on metonymic associations with an event or locale', and so this hair jewellery becomes a souvenir in being re-contextualized in and read through this exhibition space. See Thad Logan, *The Victorian Parlour: A Cultural Study* (Cambridge: Cambridge University Press, 2001), 186.
3 Galia Ofek discusses the attribution of goodness to Lady Audley and other fair-haired women in Victorian literature in *Representations of Hair in Victorian Literature and Culture* (Farnham, Surrey: Ashgate Publishing, Ltd., 2009), 62, 197–98. For the historic association between fair hair and purity see Charles Berg, *The Unconscious Significance of Hair* (London: Allen & Unwin, 1951) and Marina Warner, *From the Beast to the Blonde: On Fairy Tales and Their Tellers* (London: Chatto and Windus, 1994).
4 Alfred Lord Tennyson, "The Ringlet", *Enoch Arden, etc.* (London: Edward Moxon, 1864), lines 8 and 6.
5 Mary Elizabeth Braddon, *Lady Audley's Secret* (Ware, Hertfordshire: Wordsworth Editions, 1997), 124.
6 I will be referring primarily to 'Lady Audley' throughout, and 'Helen Talboys' (one of her former names) where her past life as the wife of George Talboys is concerned.
7 Deborah Lutz, *Relics of Death in Victorian Literature and Culture* (Cambridge: Cambridge University Press, 2015), 9.
8 Braddon, *Lady Audley's Secret*, 26.
9 Ibid.
10 Ibid., 126 and 26. Robert reads a graphological likeness between Lady Audley's curls and her elegant handwriting when he sees one of her letters, foreshadowing his discovery of her true identity through the union of her writing and a lock of her hair in an old almanac.
11 Deborah Lutz, "The Dead Still among Us: Victorian Secular Relics, Hair Jewelry, and Death Culture," *Victorian Literature and Culture* 39.01 (2011), 136.
12 Braddon, *Lady Audley's Secret*, 26.
13 Though reading the body is complicated in the novel by Lady Audley's duplicity, Tara Puri argues that, alongside her clothing and gestures, Lady Audley's hair is an interpretable sign in the novel, enabling a reading of her

true character while codifying her duplicity. See "Lady Audley's Duplicitous Hair." *The Irish Journal of Gothic and Horror Studies* 6 (2009).

14 Sara Malton, *Forgery in Nineteenth-Century Literature and Culture: Fictions of Finance from Dickens to Wilde*, 1st ed. (New York: Palgrave Macmillan, 2009), 151.

15 Braddon, *Lady Audley's Secret*, 35.

16 There may be more to the landlady's use of silver paper than its being a delicate material with which to wrap precious trinkets. Carolly Erickson notes that Queen Victoria sometimes sealed her letters with silver paper so that any tampering would be obvious; in which case, silver paper may be seen as another false signifier of the lock's authenticity. See *Her Little Majesty: The Life of Queen Victoria* (New York: Simon and Schuster, 1997), 153.

17 Leila McKellar, "Hairpieces: Hair, Identity and Memory in the Work of Mona Hatoum," *Hair: Styling, Culture and Fashion*, eds. Geraldine Biddle-Perry and Sarah Cheang (Oxford: Berg Publishers, 2008), 177.

18 Lutz, *Relics of Death*, 137.

19 Braddon, *Lady Audley's Secret*, 35.

20 Ibid., 45.

21 Alexanna Speight, *The Lock of Hair* (London: 20 Spencer Street, 1871), 1.

22 Tennyson, "The Ringlet", lines 5–6.

23 Ibid., line 44.

24 It must be noted that there is a strong sense of 'the Victorian Medusa-Rapunzel dichotomous paradigm' in the speaker's treatment of his female lover and her golden hair, which may equally apply to Lady Audley (especially as imagined by Robert). Both women are 'either Medusas (sexually mature, 'fallen', threatening heroines) or Rapunzels (innocent, helpless and pure heroines)' according to their relations with men, their hair correspondingly seen as snake-like or an aureole. See Ofek, *Representations of Hair*, 104.

25 Tennyson, "The Ringlet", lines 11–12.

26 John Plotz, *Portable Property: Victorian Culture on the Move* (Woodstock, Oxfordshire: Princeton University Press, 2008), 32.

27 Tennyson, "The Ringlet", line 20.

28 Ibid., line 12.

29 Ibid., lines 32 and 44.

30 Ibid., line 31.

31 Ibid., lines 1, 13, and 25.

32 Ibid., line 23.

33 Ibid., line 26.

34 Deborah Lutz discusses sympathetic magic and locks of hair in "The Dead Still among Us", 131.

35 Tennyson, "The Ringlet", lines 25, 35, and 45.

36 Braddon, *Lady Audley's Secret*, 52 and Tennyson, "The Ringlet", line 32.

37 Tennyson, "The Ringlet", line 53.

38 Karl Marx. *Das Kapital: A Critique of Political Economy* (Washington, DC: Regnery Publishing, 2012), 67.

39 Christina Georgina Rossetti, "Goblin Market", *Goblin Market* (London: Phoenix, 1996), lines 125, 126 and 127.

40 Tennyson, "The Ringlet", lines 36–38.

41 Frank McLynn, *Crime and Punishment in Eighteenth-Century England* (London: Routledge, 1989), 164–65.

42 Braddon, *Lady Audley's Secret*, 9.

43 Tara Puri, "Lady Audley's Duplicitous Hair", 35.

44 Braddon, *Lady Audley's Secret*, 254.

45 Ofek, *Representations of Hair*, 2.
46 Elisabeth G. Gitter, "The Power of Women's Hair in the Victorian Imagination." *PMLA* 99.5 (October 1, 1984), 936.
47 Tennyson, "The Ringlet", lines 31–34.
48 Ibid., line 43.
49 The exchange of a lock between lovers commonly indicated their intention to marry, though it was not in itself a commitment. See Ofek, *Representations of Hair*, 27.
50 Tennyson, "The Ringlet", lines 24 and 42.
51 Ibid., lines 30, 46 and 48.
52 Tennyson, "The Ringlet", line 53.
53 Ibid., lines 44 and 53–54.
54 Braddon, *Lady Audley's Secret*, 126.
55 Elaine Freedgood, *The Ideas in Things: Fugitive Meaning in the Victorian Novel* (Chicago, IL: University of Chicago Press, 2006), 25.
56 John Plotz, "Materiality in Theory: What to Make of Victorian Things," *The Oxford Handbook of Victorian Literary Culture*, ed. Juliet John (Oxford: Oxford University Press, 2016), 525.
57 Braddon, *Lady Audley's Secret*, 126.
58 Ibid.
59 Ibid.
60 Ibid.
61 Ellis, *Official Descriptive and Illustrated Catalogue*, 690.

Works Cited

Berg, Charles. *The Unconscious Significance of Hair*. London: Allen & Unwin, 1951.

Braddon, Mary Elizabeth. *Lady Audley's Secret*. Ware, Hertfordshire: Wordsworth Editions, 1997.

Browning, Robert. "Porphyria's Lover". *Selected Poems*. Ed. Daniel Karlin. London: Penguin Books, 2000.

Ellis, Robert, and Commissioners for the Exhibition of 1851. *Great Exhibition of the Works of Industry of All Nations, 1851. Official Descriptive and Illustrated Catalogue, in Three Volumes*, vol. 2. London: Spicer Brothers, 1851.

Erickson, Carolly, *Her Little Majesty: The Life of Queen Victoria*. New York: Simon and Schuster, 1997.

Freedgood, Elaine. *The Ideas in Things: Fugitive Meaning in the Victorian Novel*. Chicago, IL: University of Chicago Press, 2006.

Gitter, Elisabeth G. "The Power of Women's Hair in the Victorian Imagination." *PMLA* 99.5 (October 1, 1984): 936–54.

Logan, Thad. *The Victorian Parlour: A Cultural Study*. Cambridge: Cambridge University Press, 2001.

Lutz, Deborah. "The Dead Still among Us: Victorian Secular Relics, Hair Jewelry, and Death Culture." *Victorian Literature and Culture* 39.01 (2011): 127–42, doi: 10.1017/S1060150310000306. Accessed 25 October 2016.

———. *Relics of Death in Victorian Literature and Culture*. Cambridge: Cambridge University Press, 2015.

Malton, Sara. *Forgery in Nineteenth-Century Literature and Culture: Fictions of Finance from Dickens to Wilde*. 1st ed. New York: Palgrave Macmillan, 2009.

Marx, Karl. *Das Kapital: A Critique of Political Economy.* Washington, DC: Regnery Publishing, 2012.

McKellar, Leila. "Hairpieces: Hair, Identity and Memory in the Work of Mona Hatoum." *Hair: Styling, Culture and Fashion.* Ed. Geraldine Biddle-Perry and Sarah Cheang. Oxford: Berg, 2008.

McLynn, Frank. *Crime and Punishment in Eighteenth-Century England.* London: Routledge, 1989.

Miller, Andrew H. *Novels behind Glass: Commodity Culture and Victorian Narrative.* Cambridge: Cambridge University Press, 1995.

Ofek, Galia. *Representations of Hair in Victorian Literature and Culture.* Farnham, Surrey: Ashgate, 2009.

Plotz, John. *Portable Property: Victorian Culture on the Move.* Woodstock, Oxfordshire: Princeton University Press, 2008.

———. "Materiality in Theory: What to Make of Victorian Things." *The Oxford Handbook of Victorian Literary Culture.* Ed. Juliet John. Oxford: Oxford University Press, 2016.

Puri, Tara. "Lady Audley's Duplicitous Hair." *The Irish Journal of Gothic and Horror Studies* 6 (2009): 35–47. https://irishgothichorror.files.wordpress.com/2016/04/ijghsissue6.pdf. Accessed August 5, 2016.

Rossetti, Christina Georgina. "Goblin Market." *Goblin Market.* London: Phoenix, 1996.

Speight, Alexanna. *The Lock of Hair: Its History, Ancient and Modern, Natural and Artistic, with the Art of Working in Hair.* London: 20 Spencer Street, 1871.

Tennyson, Alfred Lord. "The Ringlet." *Enoch Arden, etc.* London: Edward Moxon, 1864. [N.B. "The Ringlet" is omitted in some later editions of *Enoch Arden*].

Warner, Marina. *From the Beast to the Blonde: On Fairy Tales and Their Tellers.* London: Chatto and Windus, 1994.

10 The Art of Curling Up

Charles Dickens and the Feeling of Curl-Papers

Sophie Ratcliffe

In *Barnaby Rudge* (1841), Dickens describes a housemaid's 'turbulent' feelings on the departure of her beloved. It is her hair – as well as the violence of her embrace – that gives her away:

> [Miggs'] nightcap had been knocked off in the scuffle, and she was on her knees upon the floor making a strange revelation of blue and yellow curl-papers, straggling locks of hair, tags of staylaces, and strings of it's impossible to say what; panting for breath, clasping her hands, turning her eyes upwards, shedding an abundance of tears, and exhibiting various other symptoms of the acutest mental suffering.[1]

The nineteenth-century equivalent of being caught in one's housecoat and curlers, curl-papers 'became' as one Edwardian critic notes 'the stock property of author and artist for comic purposes.' 'Among the follies of fashion … nothing can equal [them].' 'The literature of the curl-paper', she adds, 'is extensive and diverting.'[2] Comic scenes with women, or men, caught in their curl-papers can be traced from eighteenth-century poetry and painting to early silent film (Figure 10.1).[3]

Like many disposable pieces of material culture, the curl-paper's ephemeral nature makes its history and narrative difficult to trace. But the phrase 'the literature of the curl paper' is suggestive enough to encourage one to do so.

The idea of 'the literature of the curl-paper' points, initially, to a niche generic category – that of literary texts inspired by the idea of individuals caught in the act of styling themselves. But 'literature of the curl paper' has wider ramifications. This chapter will argue that in Dickensian literary texts the curl-paper makes its own particular kind of inscription, an inscription which could be seen to be in critical relation to more conventional modes of literary output. It will also show that the curl-paper is one of the many examined material objects that may reveal relationships, telling us particular stories about the class, gender, and subjectivity of individuals in the nineteenth century. Such pieces of paraphernalia are not simply representing such relationships. As Margaret. J. Conkey

Figure 10.1 Paul Gavarni, 'Ernest has his hair curled', Bibliothèque des Arts Decoratifs, Paris, France/Archives Charmet photo: Bridgeman Images.

argues 'material objects are not, and have not been, just caught up in an ever-shifting world but are actually creating, constructing, materializing and mobilizing history, contacts and entanglements.'[4]

Indeed, the idea of material 'entanglement' is central to this essay. A curl-paper is an object which is literally entangled – and which creates, in shaping a curl, a tangle of its own. But, as an object in itself, the curl-paper's status is also metaphorically entangled with variety of fields. Its instability, as an object, may help us re-examine some complex questions relating to material and literary history. A study of the ephemeral curl-paper (and the ephemeral curl itself) involves us in questions of the borders between art and artefact, between high and low culture, between mind and body, and between presence and absence.

In this sense, my essay engages with discussions about the methodology and boundaries of research into material culture, ranging from Viccy Coltman's reflections on the trajectory of material object in artistic and literary representation, to Carolyn Steedman's seminal essay on the ethics of recovering the material life of the past.[5] This discussion also takes its place in the history of research on the borderlines of material culture and the history of the book, as developed, in particular, by Leah Price in her 2012 work, *How to Do Things with Books in Victorian Britain* and Luisa Calè, in her research on the book as an object in the nineteenth century.[6] Finally, this essay aims to make a contribution to the understanding of Dickens as a particular kind of stylist. Miggs may be a comic figure, but in terms of Dickens' own story, I will argue that the curl-paper trope is not as funny as it seems. Going beyond the comic set piece, I offer a reading of the curl-paper which resists the nostalgic pressure which later readers have laid upon these flimsy material players. As Miggs' 'strange *revelation* of blue and yellow' (my emphasis) suggests, Dickens' curl-papers articulate something: they tell tales, illuminating his work and self in its material environment.

Curl-Papers in Use

Curl-papers, also known as 'curling papers' or 'curl paper', or even 'paper shackles', were small pieces of paper which were used to wrap and twist up locks of hair in order to enhance or create a curl.[7] Some also provided protection: when the curl was 'set' with curling tongs, the paper prevented singeing and burning. As Daumier's cartoon suggests, this didn't always work (Figure 10.2)

Curl-papers were prevalent in the eighteenth century when professional barbers used them to curl both hair and wigs. One twisting method was the 'papillote' curl. In her fine account, hairdresser and archaeologist, Janet Stephens, notes that the page on 'Perruquier–Barbier, Barbe et Friseur' (Figure 10.3) in the volume on *Arts de l'Habilement* in Diderot's *Encyclopédie* demonstrates the equipment needed to create a papillote 'hidden in plain sight' in the middle of the page, labelled as figures 16 and 17.[8]

Another older, more popular method, known as 'split curling', was a simple strip with a partial longitudinal cut (or tear) down its centre, depicted in the top right-hand corner of Diderot's page as figure 9. In this

Figure 10.2 Honoré Daumier, 'L'Inconvénient de se faire bichonner,' *Le Charivari*, November 14, 1844.

case, the hair was wrapped around one tail, then the tails were rolled or folded together.

The use of curl-papers is difficult to trace, but their popularity for lay use in the nineteenth century may have been due, in part, to the accessibility of cheaper paper. Stephens suggests that while papillote curls needed the thinnest (and therefore more expensive paper) the alternative, older method favoured heavier paper such as 'old letters, expired documents, pamphlets, broadsides, newspapers...might all have been used.'[9]

Despite their ubiquity, the provenance of curl-papers is not straightforward. In terms of their commercial presence, matters are confused by the fact that the phrase 'curl paper' or 'curling paper' used primarily in nineteenth-century stock-lists and by nineteenth-century shoppers to save embarrassment when describing lavatory roll or toilet paper.[10] Advertisements for ready-made, hair-related curl-papers are rare, though

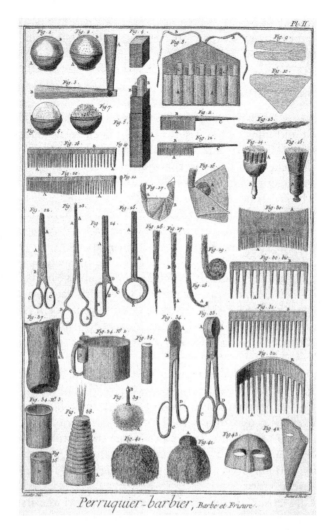

Figure 10.3 'Perruquier-barbier, Barbe et Frisure,' Copper engraving after
Lacotte, from Denis Diderot and J. B. D'Alembert, *Encyclopédie
des Sciences, des Arts et des Metiers,* 1751–1781. Photo: akg
images.

there are occasional extant mentions. An 1834 newspaper advert in the
Age offers 'French Curling Paper at 6d. per packet. The attention of Ladies is particularly directed to this useful article, which is indispensable
to the toilet, which nourishes and assists the growth of the hair.' Later
advertisements invite women to visit 'a Toilet Parlour' which would offer
'curling pads and papers.'[11] But Victorian beauty manuals offered tips
for making do with less specialised equipment, suggesting a 'roll of thin

brown paper' cut into strips was fit for the task.[12] It is likely that for reasons of speed and cost, women or their maids would have made their own curl-papers from scrap paper that was available to them, rather than buying the pre-cut form.

Dickens and Curl-Papers

A character in a 1927 *Washington Post* story claims that 'ALL the cross, ugly women and unattractive young girls' in Dickens wear curl-papers; this is an exaggeration.[13] But what she describes as Dickens' paper 'ornamented heroines' do haunt readers' imaginations. An 1881 fashion journalist jokingly wishes for a return to curled hair, predicting 'visions of Fanny Squeers in her forest of play-bills… aris[ing] before us,' while the 1912 Thanhouser version of *Nicholas Nickleby* shows Mrs Squeers bedecked with rather badly applied screws of paper.[14] Actual mentions of curl-papers in Dickens' novels are certainly memorable. One thinks of the infant phenomenon in *Nicholas Nickleby*, pirouetting in a 'white spencer, pink gauze bonnet, green veil and curl-papers'; in *Bleak House*, we meet Mrs Snagsby, the law stationer's wife, with her 'perfect beehive of curl-papers' of presumably the best quality; and not forgetting the Pickwickian girls' school with its 'three teachers, five female servants, and thirty boarders, all half-dressed an in a forest of curl-papers.'[15] But their curliness has been strangely elaborated in their critical afterlives and in film and theatrical versions of Dickens. The first Mrs Squeers is never said, in fact, to wear curl-papers. Fanny is never said to wear playbills. Curl-papers work as a kind of a crinkling folk memory which appears out of all proportion with the actual number of lines they take up in his oeuvre.[16] In coming to act as a comic shorthand for various assumed Dickensian qualities – particularly an ambivalence about strong women – the actualities of what curl-papers might really have meant has been lost in translation.

For looking closer, throughout his novels, the curl and its associate paper, seem like a kind of threat. It's a threat which encompasses ideas of style, masculinity, selfhood, and class, which culminates in the figure of Dora in *David Copperfield*, whose 'quantity of curls' threatens to entwine everything in sight.[17] As they begin married life, David gradually notices Dora's need to manufacture curls out of anything within her reach. The dog's ears, his own hair, even the household accounts: the basket of bills look 'more like curl-papers than anything else.'[18] Dora, he learns, is the stuff of art, not nature. Given this, David's initial declaration on meeting Dora – 'I never saw such curls – how could I, for there never were such curls!' – takes on a retrospective irony.[19] Dickens' joke, here, of course, hints at the fact that, after their marriage, David presumably discovered that Dora's hair was created through artificial means. But the remark also opens up the intriguing question of whether a curl actually ever exists in space and time. Does the curl exist as the entwined strands of hair, or in the space that it encircles? Is a curl an example of an object that is, in itself, a kind of absence?

In her 2009 work on *Representations of Hair in Victorian Literature and Culture*, Galia Ofek focuses primarily on a symbolic, rather than pragmatic, relationship between Dickens and hair. She notes, however, that Dickens was familiar with 'the commercial aspects of hair-fetishism' because the monthly numbers of his fictions were surrounded by ads for balsams and hair remedies.[20] Such an observation may be pushed further. The 'commercial aspects' of hair-craft are not simply familiar to Dickens' writing. As they surround his work, the impulse behind these commodities, suggesting that natural style is something that can be purchased, acts as a kind of taunt.

This is why the budget homespun aspects of hair styling mean so much to Dickens. His sympathies, as ever, lie with those who are forced to make a style from, if not despair, then from straightened circumstance. Here, Dickens' interest in what it means to compose oneself, either visually or verbally, could be seen as being played out at its most literal stylistic meeting ground – the common medium of paper.

Price notes the ways in which Dora's curling activities may be seen as playing out David's consciousness about, and fears concerning a lack of composure – a consciousness which is elided with the feminine. Dora's 'own curl-papers, recycled from the account book literalize the equivalent ledger' that David's mother ruined by 'putting "curly tails to my sevens and nines".' Curls, Price argues, symbolise a world where texts are under threat:

> In Phiz's illustration, even the bookshelf contains a jar named PICK-LES. The spines of the books between which its jammed are blank: in the topsy-turvy household, food can be read, while books only provide raw material for curlers.[21]

The curl-paper trope can be traced further back in Dickens' work, and it touches on questions of both gender and class. It is in the 1841 'Preface' to *Oliver Twist* that Dickens speaks directly to his reader, in his own voice, about curl-papers. Dickens chooses them as an example of those daily details which must be included when truly describing the world. Outlining 'the purpose' and realist credo 'of this book', he asks us to 'contemplate' what he calls the 'horrors' of criminal London. Among them, he notes, are the horrors of dress: 'I would not' he warns 'abate one hole in the Dodger's coat, one scrap of curl-paper in the girl's dishevelled hair.'[22] This direct reference seems telling, not least for the way in which it is presented. Dickens promises that his strain of realism will not omit two things – a hole and a curl-paper – and these hypothetical omissions are of intriguingly different kinds. Telling the tale of the 'hole in the coat' would be a story of absence and neglect. The 'scrap' of paper-curl in the hair is, on the other hand, an addition. And it's important that it is a 'scrap.' Its scrappiness imagines hair-curling as a desperate effort and fragile artifice – it is the practice of aspiring, and failing, to achieve a better class of self. Dickens felt deeply for this idea of failed social aspiration. It was what Chesterton calls Dickens' 'least noble' and 'most painful' concern.[23]

'Scrap' is significant because it bears the semantic weight of a past life. Scrap paper is a term for general waste and it *specifically* connotes paper which carries a textual inscription that has already performed its purpose. The story of this scrappy hairstyle is one of attempted transformation – and Dickens alerts us to the idea that the scrap paper which is used to make this change may have its own history.

Perhaps Dickens' most famously transformative curl-paper moment comes from *The Pickwick Papers* (1836–7). This scene is deeply comic, but it also ends with one of the novel's darkest and most moving vignettes. Mr Pickwick, while visiting an inn in Ipswich, accidentally finds his way to the wrong bedroom. He makes himself comfortable in his nightshirt and cap, and climbs into the wrong bed. Soon, the rightful occupant arrives. Summoning all his courage, Pickwick peers out through the curtains of the four-poster bed:

> [He] almost fainted with horror and dismay. Standing before the dressing-glass was a middle-aged lady, in yellow curl-papers, busily engaged in brushing what ladies call their 'back-hair.' However the unconscious middle-aged lady came into that room, it was quite clear that she contemplated remaining there for the night [...]
>
> 'I never met with anything so awful as this,' —thought poor Mr. Pickwick, the cold perspiration starting in drops upon his nightcap. 'Never. This is fearful.'
>
> It was quite impossible to resist the urgent desire to see what was going forward. So out went Mr. Pickwick's head again. The prospect was worse than before. The middle-aged lady had finished arranging her hair; had carefully enveloped it in a muslin night-cap with a small plaited border, and was gazing pensively on the fire.[24]

The carefully paced final sentence which ends with 'fire' touches, lightly, on the curl-papered woman's flammable potential. It also reminds us that Pickwick is not particularly fired up by his bedroom encounter. Playing on the classic nineteenth-century image of a woman unfurling her locks, Dickens offers us a domesticated Medusa, a Rapunzel past her prime. As the scene unfolds, Pickwick cannot resist making some mental annotations. But the prose summons Pickwick's awkwardness. The quotation marks around 'back-hair' hover between the authority of the seasoned anthropologist and the pincer-like embarrassment of the man confronted by a woman's toilette. Meanwhile, the placement of phrases which are conventionally a prelude to lust ('perspiration', 'impossible to resist', and 'urgent desire') work to unman, rather than unbridle, his hero.

Pickwick ends the evening by exiting the bedroom, and making do in a dark corridor.

> He had no resource but to remain where he was until daylight appeared. So after groping his way a few paces down the passage, and, to his infinite alarm, stumbling over several pairs of boots in so doing, Mr. Pickwick crouched into a little recess in the wall, to wait for morning, as philosophically as he might.[25]

Indeed, it is more the stuff of philosophy than farce. This is a scene in which the life of the mind encounters that of the body, and it is played out, in a fascinating way, on the plane of paper. Here we see Mr Pickwick of *The Pickwick Papers*, whose title and existence is justified by the idea of paper enlightening the mind, only to find it being the means of decorating a head. Confronted by the paper-curled woman, Pickwick curls up. And the characteristically poetic prose intensifies this moment. Dickens presses on the word 'in' – 'grop_in_g', '_in_finite alarm', 'stumbl_in_g', '_in_ so do_in_g', '_in_to', '_in_ the', 'morn_in_g' (my emphases) – as if to echo the shape of his painfully provisional and redundant 'crouch.'

Pickwick's tragic response to curl-papers has can be intriguingly counterpointed with the attitude of a real-life, nineteenth-century working-class figure, this time a Frenchman: Jacques Jasmin. Jasmin's primary occupation was that of a hairdresser – but he was also a self-made poet. He began his career by reciting to customers and writing poems on the tools of his trade – curl-papers or the French 'papillotes' – before placing them in his clients' hair. Jasmin was commemorated by Samuel Smiles in an 1891 biography for his desire to write for the love of art, rather than for fame or money.[26] For Jasmin, the idea of the curl-paper, and its connotations of literary redundancy, was a cause for celebration rather than apprehension. He deemed art both beautifully styled and essentially useless – and the title of his 1835 work *Las Papillotos* bears this out.[27] His published papillotes are, as a result, at peace with the notion of art being both crafted and throwaway. He is also seen to be peace with his dual status as both hair and poetic stylist. Celebrating Jasmin, Alphonse de Lamartine noted that he was 'l'Homère sensible et pathétique des prolétaires.' His title page proudly bears the legend: 'Jasmin – coiffeure.'[28]

When it comes to hair-curling, most nineteenth-century writers fall somewhere in between Jasminian playfulness and Dickensian panic. As critic H. J. Jackson remarks, 'the joke or threat in literary circles that pages of a book could end up as curl-papers for hairdressing' was, by the early nineteenth century, somewhat dog-eared.[29] When an 1890 beauty columnist reports on her neighbour's habit of wearing 'any of the daily papers' on her head, or an 1839 short story tells of a character making 'papillotes' out of 'her husband's prayer books', they contribute to a long history of tales about books being ripped up and worn.[30]

In Sheridan's *The Rivals*, Lydia Languish finds a book of sermons 'torn away' by the hairdresser.[31] A close look at Gavarni's lithograph of Ernest (Figure 10.1) shows that he is in fact tearing up the letter that he is reading, in order to hand it to the woman tending his curls. (The accompanying text reveals that the letter comes from his would-be beloved, who passionately hopes he will write treasure her letter. Instead, 'Ernest s'en fait des papillotes.') Dickens' great favourite, Laurence Sterne, meanwhile, has Tristram Shandy nearly lose his poems, only just noticing that the 'papilliotes' in the hair of the French 'chaise vamper's wife' are inscribed with his handwriting.[32] For these writers and artists, the idea of literary text or letter as curl-paper makes a claim to the pragmatics of everyday life, and holds much comic promise. As an artist's words are turned into something more inherently useful, but essentially frivolous, the literary curl-paper unfolds as a conceit of conceit itself, for the curl-paper of recycled words highlights both the narcissism and the futility of the artist. There's even bravado in a writer discussing the afterlives of books in such a way – in airing the possibility that literary works may become mere curl-papers, there's usually a swaggering knowledge that the pages in hand will be immune from such a fate.

Dickens and Unbinding

For Dickens, the relationship between art and vanity was more volatile, and his handling of curl-papers more pained, than these other writers. The complexity, for him, relates to his strained relationship with ideas of style and selfhood – it relates to his sense of what comes naturally. In terms of his own hair, Dickens was famously proud of his trademark natural curls. On his trips to America, admirers solicited locks of his hair as keepsakes. Dickens protested that setting such a 'precedent' might 'terminate before long' in 'total baldness.' The joke was 'taken up by the newspapers' and the idea of a bald Dickens was used as part of an advertising campaign for the hair remedy 'Balm of Columbia.'[33]

Jealously guarded throughout his life, his curls were a benchmark of what he valued, writing in letters that he would 'sooner have his hair cut off' than face something unpleasant.[34] The motif of the false curl indicates, for Dickens, something which goes against the idea of a natural style, or natural self, and even, perhaps, or what it means to have a style at all. Indeed, one can read Dickens' engagement with curl-paper as a kind of working out of ideas of authentic and natural self-expression.[35] A naturally curled hair-style becomes a productive metaphor for a natural prose style. Each, as J. S. Mill's sense of nature would have it, 'is of itself, without human intervention.' Both are trying to hide their origins – trying, in their own way – to look naturally effortless.[36]

The curl-paper metaphor also indicates something about Dickens own anxieties about status. Dickens' curl-papered plot twists reveal the insecurity of a man who in his own words, 'might easily have been, for any care that was taken of me, a little robber or a vagabond.'[37] Dickens was constantly in fear of those 'might have beens'; of doing something that was seen to be, in his words, 'infra-dig.' He quietly feared his works might be that very thing.[38] Conducting his writing career through what his friends saw as 'a low, cheap form of publication' in weekly and monthly disposable numbers allowed him fame, but risked status.[39] Even in bound form, his novels, as Luisa Calè argues, quoting Walter Bagehot's 1858 review, 'still had "the feel of graphic scraps"' about them, carrying the 'memory of the incomplete, disconnected form' of weekly or monthly publication.[40]

In this sense, Miggs' state of unbinding in *Barnaby Rudge*, as the back 'staylaces' of her dress come apart, is a revelation of something other than flesh. It articulates something about Dickens' own unbound literary state, and his anxieties about it. *Barnaby Rudge,* in *Master Humphrey's Clock,* was a loosely laced entity. Initially published as a floppy 'folded sheet of sixteen pages, of which twelve were the numbered pages – and the other four pages (two leave) forming the outer wrapper.' 'Every fourth of fifth week' these parts were collected and 'made up' into the only slightly more substantial duck-egg blue/green monthly parts – with additional advertisements.[41] As if to remind readers that their literary work was worthy of an upgrade, those reading the weekly issues were notified by frequent advertisements that 'subscribers could have their copies bound' either by the Publishers or by their local booksellers, and that 'cloth cases' would be available.[42]

Dickens hated the weekly mode of publication. He signed off, in the later numbers of in October 1841, with the admission that he 'had often felt cramped and confined...by the space in which I have been constrained to move...I have found this form of publication' he added 'perplexing, and difficult.'[43] His primary complaint is a metaphorical perplexity – the confusion and interruption to the plot that the weekly form caused. However, there is here for Dickens, a very real fear of becoming literally perplexed by his form – I press here on etymological root of perplexity – to plait, twine, interweave. At a base level, Dickens was frightened of these weekly numbers being no more than a tangle of throwaway waste paper, or, more critically, a twist of curl-paper. In order to understand this, it is worth pressing on a nuanced detail of his capillary world. When Dickens mentions curl-papers, we are frequently and emphatically told about their colour. Pickwick's middle-aged lady, of course, wears yellow. Fanny Squeers is surrounded by a 'semicircle of blue curl-papers.' Nancy is gorgeous in a 'red gown, green boots, and yellow curl-papers', and Miss Miggs, has two colours at once, 'a revelation of blue and yellow curl-papers.'[44] Coloured curl-papers were a sign of bad form and poverty. A magazine column from 1855 notes that women should attempt to use paper with 'a tint harmonizing with the colour of the hair.'[45] Miss Miggs' unharmonious curl-papers, then, may hurt her pride as well as her temples. If we are to speculate about why Miss Miggs has these two particular colours, it may help to return to the form of the fiction she inhabited and the textual world Dickens knew.

For the colours might mean something to Miggs' fictional onlookers – indicating her lack of resource or style – but they meant something to Dickens too. For 'the blue and yellow' was the popular shorthand term for one of the oldest and respected journals in the nineteenth century – the *Edinburgh Review*.[46] Dickens admired, and envied, 'the old blue and yellow.' As Philip Collins argues, he felt that it outclassed him. The *Review* offered readers something that was more 'solid and weighty' than he himself could produce.[47] Dickens own 'bluest' and 'yellowest' moments, however, were the result of his 'low, cheap form of publication.' Yellow and blue advertisements, punctuated his blue-green monthly numbers, ranging from the full page (yellow) advertisement for 'Bearts Pneumatic Coffee Filter', and 'The Chunk Stove' in *Master Humphrey's Clock* to the blue advertisement for 'The Scottish Widows' Fund' in *Our Mutual Friend*.[48]

Miggs' 'strange revelations' in blue and yellow curl-paper, then, point half-teasingly and half-timidly back to the materiality of the very text she inhabits. Miggs embodies the idea that her own textual existence, a copy of *Barnaby Rudge,* might end up not in, but on his readers heads. It would be a fate that would leave him feeling as 'cramped and confined' as Mr Pickwick, curled up in a corridor after a humiliating encounter. Echoing the vulnerable, 'unbound' nature of Dickens's monthly numbers, Miggs reveals Dickens' own 'turbulent feelings' of envy and shame, and a future that might render him laughable.

Recovering the Absence

The delicacy and vulnerability of the original weekly parts of *Barnaby Rudge* in *Master Humphrey's Clock* raise particular questions about the study of material objects. The survival of these parts, as items which seem in themselves so close to throwaway, seems incredible. This surprise allows one to reflect on the difficulties of working on such a truly ephemeral object as the curl-paper, and on how an historian and critic is to engage with histories of loss. Here, we have lost not simply the object of study; we've also lost the precise processes and knowledge as to how these particular pieces of paraphernalia were used. As Anne Gerritsen writes, while '[s]ome objects survive and offer us interpretative possibilities... far more... have not survived, and their absence can feature in our stories only with difficulty.'[49] In reflecting on whether and how nineteenth-century books and journals might have been plundered and torn up to create curl-papers, a researcher needs to access the actual journals themselves – they need to feel and weigh their weight and thickness. The critical importance of concrete, rather than digital, research is apparent here. Methodologically, a study of the curl-paper also highlights the need to acknowledge the embodied and affective encounter with material culture. It demonstrates the critical need for practical history and sensory methodologies in an understanding of how we have lived and felt in the past. A study of the curl-paper requires the expertise of hairdressers and hair historians, specialists in paper, and indeed, what Angela Loxham describes as the 'under-used methodology' of 'physical historical reconstruction.'[50] There are elements of understanding this material encounter which can be better understood only by physically engaging with the object itself – by practice-based reconstruction. In attempting, for example, to tear up a book and wear it on one's head, one may begin to feel, affectively, some of the meanings of the curl-paper.

Such discoveries, such as they are, are always partial. Our knowledge about the curl-paper, after all, comes not from an examination of the object itself, but from its survival in what Coltman calls 'representation as phantom object.'[51] The Victorian curl-paper exists to us only in its cameo appearances in print, in visual culture, in beauty manuals and advertisements – and all these representations may in fact disturb, unsteady, and elaborate upon its real appearance. However, the curl-paper is intriguingly and doubly lost in time. For, as an object, the curl-paper feels distinctive, if not unique, for me because of the way it existed in order to be erased. It was an object which was never meant to be seen.

Curl-papers are, of course, just one of the many pieces of 'stuff' that support our fictions of selfhood; a tangible example of a self which has been constructed, embarrassingly, out of paraphernalia. This realization highlights the fact that our critical selves are, at times, no less constructed, and no more natural. In writing histories of any objects from the past it is all too easy to begin fabricating. As Carolyn Steedman argues, the more apparently humble the object, the easier it is to fall into nostalgic patterns of thought. Material objects from the past, in real or 'phantom' form, may become 'obscure object[s] of desire for all who read the past.'[52] The narratives which we reconstruct about 'objects made from torn fragments of other things' may, Steedman notes, be too easily drawn, disconnected with the actualities of 'somebody else's story.'[53] Indeed, the curl made from paper, in its styled deliberation, and flyaway absence, may act as a kind of symbol for some of the problems with any approach to material culture, and any narrative that results. While attempting to get close to the nature of things, our approach to the history of objects, will always be styled, elaborated, and teased out to suit our fashion. In the end, our stories, not unlike the intangible curl, are things made of thin air.

Notes

1 Charles Dickens, *Barnaby Rudge*, ed. Clive Hurst (Oxford: Oxford University Press), chapter 51, 410.
2 Anonymous, "Curl-papers," *Youth's Companion*, June 13, 1901, 306.
3 See, for example, Hogarth's 1743 *Marriage a la Mode: 4 The Toilette* or the appearance of Mrs Squeers in a headful of curl-papers in Thanhouser's 1912 film *Nicholas Nickleby*.
4 Margaret W. Conkey, "Style, design and function" in *Handbook of Material Culture*, eds. Christopher Tilley, Webb Keane, Susanne Kuechler-Fogden, Mike Rowlands, Patricia Spyer (London: Sage, 2006), 355–72, 364.
5 Viccy Coltman, "Material History and the History of Art(efacts)," in *Writing Material Culture History*, eds. Anne Gerritsen and Giorgo Riello (London: Bloomsbury 2014), 17–32; Carolyn Steedman, "What A Rag Rug Means," *Journal of Material Culture* 3, no. 3 (November 1998): 259–81.
6 Leah Price's pioneering *How to Do Things with Books in Victorian Britain* (Princeton NJ: Princeton University Press, 2013) explores the ways in which books may be used as, and for, things other than reading. Such things, as Price notes, may range from 'women's curlpapers' to 'pie-plate liners', 10. Luisa Calè's work in this area includes "Horace Walpole's Dream: Dismembering the Dispersed Collection," *Critical Quarterly*, 45, no. 4 (Dec 2013): 42–53 and "Gray's Ode and Walpole's China Tub: The Order of the Book and Paper Lives of an Object," *Eighteenth-Century Studies* 45, no. 1 (2011): 105–25.
7 Anonymous, *The Art of Preserving Hair, on Philosophical Principles*, by the Author of *The Art of Improving the Voice* (London: S and R Bentley, 1825), 141.
8 Janet Stephens, "Papillote Curls: Historical Hairdressing Techniques." www.youtube.com/watch?v=lP9PJsY5__4 (accessed 25 July 2017). I owe my knowledge of Diderot's *Encyclopédie* to this video, and my knowledge of curling techniques to my further correspondence with Janet Stephens.
9 Janet Stephens, personal correspondence with the author.
10 See Wallace Reyburn, *Flushed with Pride: The Story of Thomas Crapper* (Clifton-Upon-Teme: Polperro Heritage Press, 1969), 82.
11 Advertisement for L. Stocken, including 'French Curling Paper' amongst its goods, *The Morning Post*, Monday December 8, 1834: 1. The L. Stocken advertisement appears frequently on the front page of the *Age* and the *Morning Post* in 1834. Madame Cross advertises her Oxford Street 'Toilet Parlour' in a number of papers including the 1897 issues of *Pick-Me-Up* – see, for example, vol. 17: 159.
12 Anonymous, *Sylvia's Book of the Toilet Book: A Ladies' Guide to Dress and Beauty* (London: Ward, Lock & Co, 1881), 27.

13 A. S. T. Harrison, "Curl-Papers," *Washington Post*, August 28, 1927, 9.

14 C.H.H. "Note on Dress," *The Art Amateur*, April, 1882: 108. Mrs Squeers appears at 09:30 at https://vimeo.com/20529673 (accessed 17 July 2017).

15 *Nicholas Nickleby*, ed. Paul Schlicke (Oxford: Oxford University Press, 2008), chapter 23, 288; *Bleak House*, ed. Nicola Bradbury (London: Penguin, 1996), chapter 33, 365; *The Pickwick Papers*, ed. James Kinsley (Oxford: Oxford University Press, 2008), chapter 26, 243.

16 See, for example, the advertisement for a theatrical version of *The Pickwick Papers* advertised in *The New York Times*, January 21, 1868: 7, which prominently features 'MISS WALLACE as The Lady in Curl-papers.'

17 Charles Dickens, *David Copperfield* (Penguin: Harmondsworth OUP, 1966), ed. Trevor Blount, chapter 26, 456.

18 *David Copperfield*, chapter 44, 712.

19 Ibid., chapter 26, 455.

20 Galia Ofek, *Representations of Hair in Victorian Literature and Culture* (Farnham, Surrey: Ashgate, 2009), 107.

21 Price, *How to Do Things with Books*, 98–99.

22 Charles Dickens, "Preface," *Oliver Twist*, ed. Philip Horne (London: Penguin, 2002), xvi.

23 G. K. Chesterton, *Dickens* (Hertfordshire: Wordsworth, 2007), 20.

24 Charles Dickens, *The Pickwick Papers*, chapter 22, 339.

25 *Pickwick Papers*, 342.

26 Samuel Smiles, *Jasmin: Barber, Poet, Philanthropist* (London: John Murray, 1891).

27 Jacques Jasmin, *La Papillotos de Jasmin Coiffeur* (Agen: Prosper Noubel, 1835).

28 Alphonse de Lamartine quoted in 'Avant Propos de l'Éditeur', Jacques Jasmin, *La Papillotos 1843–1851*, vol 3, v.

29 H. J. Jackson, *Romantic Readers: The Evidence of Marginalia* (New Haven: Yale University Press, 2005), 34.

30 Felicia Holt, "Curl-Papers and Husbands," *Ladies' Home Journal* 7, no. 11 (October 1890): 6; John Gideon Millingen, "Portrait Gallery – No. 7: Adventures of the Cannon Family," *Bentley's Miscellany* 6 (1839): 36–42, 37.

31 Richard Sheridan, *The Rivals* (Oxford: Oxford University Press, 1968), 1.2, l.1.74, 39.

32 See Chapter 38 of Laurence Sterne's *Tristram Shandy* (Oxford: Oxford University Press, 1983), 425.

33 See Charles Dickens to Unknown Ladies of Plymouth, Massachusetts, 2 February 1842, and fn. 3 in *The Pilgrim Edition of the Letters of Charles Dickens,* ed. Madeline House, Graham Storey and Kathleen Tillotson (Oxford: Clarendon Press, 1974), 3: 47. A thirty-five year old Louisa May Alcott, in the audience of one of Dickens' American book tours, observed sharply that in later life, Dickens' curls may not always have been entirely natural. His 'youth and comeliness were gone', she notes 'but the foppishness remained, and the red-faced man, with the false teeth, and the voice of a worn-out actor, had his scanty grey hair curled', *Boston Commonwealth*, 21 September, 1867: 1.

34 See, for example, Charles Dickens to W. H. Wills, 12 March 1850, *The Pilgrim Edition of the Letters of Charles Dickens, 1850–1852*, eds. Madeline House, Graham Storey, Kathleen Tillotson (Oxford: Clarendon, 1988), 6: 61–62, 62.

35 Some critics noted that *Household Words* was generally overstyled. Edward Fitzgerald argued that: 'A mere natural, unaffected account of any transaction, it was felt, was out of place', cited in Helen Small's excellent account

of Dickens' style, "Dispensing with Style" in *Dickens and Style*, ed. Daniel Tyler (Cambridge: Cambridge University Press, 2013), 253–77, 255–56.

36 John Stuart Mill, *Collected Works of John Stuart Mill*, eds. F. E. L. Priestley et al., 31 vols. to date (Toronto: University of Toronto Press, 1963), 10: 377. I owe my knowledge of this to Paul Schachte's excellent "Dickens and the Uses of Nature," *Victorian Studies* 34, no. 1 (Autumn 1990): 77–102.

37 From Dickens' autobiographical fragment, reprinted in John Forster, *The Life of Charles Dickens*, ed. A. J. Hoppe (London: J. M. Dent, 1966), 1: 25. I owe this observation and my knowledge of this quotation to Robert Douglas-Fairhurst's *Becoming Dickens* (Cambridge, MA: Harvard, 2011), 17 which offers a brilliant account of Dickens' anxieties about the contingent matter of his life.

38 See his letter of 11 October 1846 to John Forster reflecting that 'a great deal of money might possibly be made (if it were not infra dig) by one's having Readings of one's own books,' *The Pilgrim Edition of the Letters of Charles Dickens*, ed. Kathleen Tillotson (Oxford: Clarendon Press, 1977), 4: 631–35, 631.

39 Charles Dickens, "Preface to the Cheap Edition, 1847," *The Pickwick Papers*, 43–47, 45.

40 Walter Bagehot, "Charles Dickens," National Review 7 (October 1858): 458–86 cited in Luisa Calè, "Dickens Extra-Illustrated: Heads and Scenes in Monthly Parts (The Case of *Nicholas Nickleby*)," *Yearbook of English Studies* 40 No. 1/2 (2010): 8–32, 31.

41 Thomas Hatton and Arthur H. Cleaver, *A Bibliography of the Periodical Words of Charles Dickens* (London: Chapman & Hall, 1933), 163.

42 See, for example, page 396 of the weekly issue no. 86 of *Master Humphrey's Clock*, Saturday, November 20, 1841.

43 *Master Humphrey's Clock* no. 79 (October 1841), *Barnaby Rudge*, chapter LXV.

44 See chapter 39 of *Nicholas Nickleby*, 502 and chapter 12 of *Oliver Twist*, ed. Philip Horne (London: Penguin, 2002), 114.

45 "How to Treat the Hair," *Godey's Lady's Book and Magazine* 51 (November 1855): 419.

46 Dickens asks, for example, 'have you seen my note … in the blue and yellow?', J. Forster, *Life of Dickens*, 294; Thomas Macaulay desires to see Dickens "Inrolled [*sic*] in our blue and yellow corps," *Oxford Companion to Charles Dickens: Anniversary Edition*, ed. Paul Schlicke (Oxford: Oxford University Press, 2011), 229.

47 Phillip Collins, "Dickens and the *Edinburgh Review*," *Review of English Studies* NS 14, no. 54 (1963): 167–72, 171.

48 See, for example, *Master Humphrey's Clock*, Part 1 (April 4–25, 1840), Part 5 (August 1840), and Part 8 (November, 1840), Bodleian Special Collections, Arch. AA d. 127 or *Our Mutual Friend*, Part 7 (November 1865). Some advertisements were also pale pink, brick-red, or green. For details see Hatton and Cleaver.

49 Anne Gerritsen, "Introduction" in *Writing Material Culture History*, eds. Anne Gerritsen and Giorgo Riello (London: Bloomsbury, 2014), 1–14, 8.

50 Angela Loxham, "Time Travel as a Tool for Sensory Research," *The Senses and Society* 10, no. 1: 125–28, 126, 128 www.tandfonline.com/doi/pdf/10.2752/174589315X14161614601448 (accessed 26 July 2017).

51 Coltman, "Material History," 27.

52 Steedman, "What a Rag Rug Means," 259.

53 Ibid., 271.

Works Cited

Alcott, Louisa May. *Boston Commonwealth*. 21 September 1867: 1.

Anonymous. "How to Treat the Hair," *Godey's Lady's Book and Magazine* 51 (November 1855): 419.

———. *Sylvia's Book of the Toilet: A Ladies' Guide to Dress and Beauty*, 27. London: Ward, Lock & Co, 1881.

———. "Curl-Papers," *The Youth's Companion*, June 13, 1901: 306.

The Art of Preserving Hair, *On Philosophical Principles*, 141. London: S and R Bentley, 1825.

Calè, Luisa. "Dickens Extra-Illustrated: Heads and Scenes in Monthly Parts (The Case of Nicholas Nickleby)." *Yearbook of English Studies* 40, no. 1/2 (2010): 8–32.

Chesterton, G. K. *Dickens*. Hertfordshire: Wordsworth, 2007.

Collins, Phillip. "Dickens and the *Edinburgh Review*." *Review of English Studies* NS 14, no. 54 (1963): 167–72.

Coltman, Viccy. "Material History and the History of Art(efacts)." In *Writing Material Culture History*, edited by Anne Gerritsen and Giorgo Riello, 17–32. London: Bloomsbury, 2014.

Conkey, Margaret J. "Style, Design and Function." In *Handbook of Material Culture*, edited by Christopher Tilley, Webb Keane, Susanne Kuechler-Fogden, Mike Rowlands and Patricia Spyer, 355–72. London: Sage, 2006.

Dickens, Charles. *Barnaby Rudge*, edited by Clive Hurst. Oxford: Oxford University Press, 2008.

———. *Bleak House*, edited by Nicolas Bradbury. London: Penguin, 1996.

———. *David Copperfield*, edited by Trevor Blount. Penguin: Harmondsworth, 1966.

———. *Master Humphrey's Clock*, no. 86, Saturday November 20, 1841. Bodleian Special Collections, Arch. AA. d. 88.

———. *Master Humphrey's Clock*, no. 79, Saturday October 1841. Bodleian, Arch. AA. d. 88.

———. *Master Humphrey's Clock*, Part 1 (April 4–25, 1840). Bodleian Special Collections, Arch. AA d. 127

———. *Master Humphrey's Clock* Part 5 (August 1840), Bodleian. Arch. AA d. 127.

———. Master *Humphrey's Clock* Part 8 (November, 1840), Bodleian. Arch. AA d. 127.

———. *Nicholas Nickleby*, edited by Paul Schlicke. Oxford: Oxford University Press, 2008.

———. *Our Mutual Friend*, Part 7 (November 1865).

———. *The Pickwick Papers*, edited by James Kinsley. Oxford: Oxford University Press, 2008.

———. "Preface to the Cheap Edition, 1847." In *The Pickwick Papers*, edited by James Kinsley. Oxford: Oxford University Press, 2008, 43–47.

———. "Preface" to *Oliver Twist*, edited by Philip Horne. London: Penguin, 2002, xvi.

———. To the Ladies of Plymouth, *The Pilgrim Edition of the Letters of Charles Dickens*, edited by Madeline House, Graham Storey and Kathleen Tillotson, vol. 3, 47–48. Oxford: Clarendon Press, 1974.

———. To W. H. Wills, 12 March 1850. *Letters of Charles*, Dickens, 6: 61–62.

———. To John Forster, 11 October 1846. *Letters of Charles Dickens*, 4: 631–35.

Diderot, Denis. *Encyclopédie: ou Dictoinnaire raisonné des sciences, des arts et métiers*. Paris: Braison, 1762–1782.

Douglas-Fairhurst, Robert. *Becoming Dickens*. Cambridge, MA: Harvard, 2011.

Forster, John. *The Life of Charles Dickens*, edited by A. J. Hoppe, 2 vols. London: J. M. Dent, 1966.

Gerritsen, Anne and Giorgo Riello, eds. *Writing Material Culture History*. London: Bloomsbury, 2014.

Harrison, A. S. T. "Curl-Papers." *Washington Post*, August 28, 1927: 9.

Hatton, Thomas and Arthur H. Cleaver. *A Bibliography of the Periodical Words of Charles Dickens*. London: Chapman & Hall, 1933.

C.H.H. "Note on Dress." *The Art Amateur* (April 1882): 108.

Holt, Felicia. "Curl-Papers and Husbands," *Ladies' Home Journal* 7, no. 11 (1890): 6.

Jackson, H. J. *Romantic Readers: The Evidence of Marginalia*. New Haven: Yale University Press, 2005.

Jasmin, Jacques, *La Papillotos de Jasmin Coiffeur*. Agen: Prosper Noubel, 1835.

———. *La Papillotos de Jasmin Coiffeur, 1843–1851*. Agen: Prosper Noubel, 1851.

Loxham, Angela. "Time Travel as a Tool for Sensory Research." *The Senses and Society* 10, no. 1 (2015): 125–28.

Mill, J.S. *Collected Works of John Stuart Mill*, edited by F. E. L. Priestley et al., vol. 10, Toronto: University of Toronto Press, 1963.

Millingen, John Gideon. "Portrait Gallery – No. 7: Adventures of the Cannon Family," *Bentley's Miscellany* 6 (1839): 36–42.

Nicholas Nickleby. Directed by George O. Nicols. Thanhauser Company, 1912, film.

Ofek, Galia. *Representations of Hair in Victorian Literature and Culture*. Farnham, Surrey: Ashgate, 2009.

Price, Leah. *How to Do Things with Books in Victorian Britain*. Princeton NJ: Princeton University Press, 2013.

Reyburn, Wallace. *Flushed With Pride: The Story of Thomas Crapper*. Clifton-Upon-Teme: Polperro Heritage Press, 1969.

Schachte, Paul. "Dickens and the Uses of Nature." *Victorian Studies* 34, no. 1 (Autumn 1990): 77–102.

Schlicke, Paul. *Oxford Companion to Charles Dickens: Anniversary Edition*. Oxford: Oxford University Press, 2011.

Sheridan, Richard. *The Rivals*. Oxford: Oxford University Press, 1968.

Small, Helen. "Dispensing with Style." In *Dickens and Style*, edited by Daniel Tyler, 253–77. Cambridge: Cambridge University Press, 2013.

Smiles, Samuel. *Jasmin: Barber, Poet, Philanthropist*. London, 1891.

Steedman, Carolyn. "What a Rag Rug Means," *Journal of Material Culture* 3, no. 3 (November 1998): 259–81.

Stephens, Janet. "Papillote Curls: Historical Hairdressing Techniques." www.youtube.com/watch?v=lP9PJsY5__4 (accessed 25 July 2017).

Sterne, Lawrence. *Tristram Shandy*. Oxford: Oxford University Press, 1983.

Part V
Objects in Circulation
Print Culture

11 Woman's Dress as a Polemical Object in the Mid-Victorian Period

Odile Boucher-Rivalain

In the mid-nineteenth century, given Britain's rapid industrial expansion, ownership of manufactured objects was generalized to all social classes. It is therefore important to consider how those objects achieved a symbolical function as an indicator of their owner's identity and social status. Dress affords an interesting viewpoint from which to observe habits and mentalities at any given period of history, perhaps even more so in the nineteenth century as academic research has shown in recent years. In her introduction to her book *Study of Dress History* (2002), Lou Taylor sees dress as an appropriate vantage point in interdisciplinary studies, remarking, 'Because of the multi-faceted "levels" at which clothing functions within society and any culture, clothing provides a powerful analytical tool across many disciplines.'[1] In this paper I will consider how woman's dress became a much-debated subject in the mid-nineteenth century within the context of woman's emancipation. As Taylor points out, changes in woman's dress aimed at 'more practical and comfortable clothing for women during the 1850–1910 period' signifying also women's growing desire for freedom: 'Fears in the public mind aroused by the debate on the emancipation of women indelibly connected any forms of radical dress reform to social anxieties over women's rights.'[2] Considered as a material object, dress served at all times the double function of utility by protecting the body and enhancing the wearer's natural beauty. In the context of Victorian social history, it had become a polemical subject considering the extravagant fashions raising a number of questions related both to women's financial autonomy and capacities as well as health hazards.

In this chapter, I will first consider woman's dress as a material object, one among thousands displayed in the 1851 Great Exhibition, itself an indicator of first-class British industry and creativity. I will then examine the social role played by dress in the Victorian era. In the 1850s and 1860s dress in its latest fashions had become an absurdity endangering women's health, according to Harriet Martineau who had come to see it as an object diverted from its original function to take on an irrational second role, that of an unconventional sign of women's boldness in taste and habits. I will thus consider the question of woman's dress in the context of domestic life and working conditions, dress itself being the expression of woman's desire for independence. Woman's dress will therefore be analysed as an example of the symbolical value of a specific Victorian object not to be exhibited in one's domestic environment only but in the public sphere as well.

Materials Used in Dress Manufacturing: The Dress as a Social Symbol

With the rapid expansion of the middle class during the first half of the nineteenth century, fashion was no longer the exclusive privilege of the aristocracy but had become accessible to the rising middle class. Considering the 1851 Great Exhibition Catalogue as an indicator, we can see that one textile given ample attention was the noblest of all, silk. Silk manufacturing was at that time not so much a British speciality as a French one, with the silk manufacturing tradition in Lyons placing British silk industry in a difficult position. As a result, *The Illustrated London News* on May 1851 admitted the French superiority in skilled manufacturing: 'the long-tried skill of our French neighbours will subject us to the severest test.'[3] It was acknowledged that the French superiority in the field was due to the English having disregarded the aesthetic aspect in their silk production, finding it more convenient to use pirating to obtain innovative patterns. In his *History of Industrial Exhibitions* journalist Blanchard Jerrold points out the supremacy achieved by France in taste as well in manufacturing skills dating back to the thirteenth century, an excellence due to the artistic education given to the French workmen with the introduction of Schools of Design, an advantage that their English counterparts never benefited from, thus leaving the quality of the English production far behind:

> These fine national Institutions have yielded to France the reputation which she holds of leading, in matters of taste, the manufactures of the world. [...] Manchester can produce a printed calico at a greater speed than Rouen; but Rouen can imprint the finer designs and dyes over its fabric.[4]

The silk articles mentioned in the Guide are ladies' handkerchiefs and silk shawls presented by the Macclesfield exhibitors. Beside those silk items, in its Clothing and Hosiery section, the Guide urges visitors to look at 'the very interesting straw bonnets,' the bonnet being an essential part of woman's dress. The pictures of visitors at the Crystal Palace show women wearing long and ample dresses, shawls and bonnets as suited to this formal occasion and typical of woman's dress in the upper and middle classes. The 1840–1850 period is the pre-hoop era and features the wearing of full skirts supported by petticoats which were stiffened by inserting horsehair to give them more amplitude, the waist being narrowed and the tightly laced waistline being accentuated.

As testified by the numerous descriptions of female characters in Victorian fiction, dress reflected social status. 'Cloth is a social tissue,' Charlotte Gilman, the early twentieth-century American sociologist, said.[5] Indeed, Victorian novelists never failed to describe their female characters' dress as emblematic of their social class.

Elizabeth Gaskell's descriptions of her heroines are significant of dress expected to correspond to the social status of the character wearing it. The opening lines of *North and South* (1855) point out the rich material Edith's dress is made of, in perfect harmony with the furniture in the Shaw family's drawing room in Harley Street, inviting moments of comfort and leisure as fitting the lifestyle of the upper-middle class:

> She lay curled up on the sofa in the back drawing-room in Harley Street, looking very lovely in her white muslin and blue ribbons. [...] Edith had rolled herself up into a soft ball of muslin and ribbon, and silken curls, and gone off into a peaceful little after-dinner nap.[6]

Chapter 9, significantly entitled 'Dressing for Tea', taking place no longer in the London upper-middle-class environment of Harley Street but in the northern industrial town of Helstone, insists on the dressing up ritual as a sign of respects for guests, and on the social class of the persons visited requiring a suitable dress code. Mr Thornton, the local rich mill owner, is about to dress up to have tea with the Hales, a modest family, thereby gaining the narrator's and reader's approval for his respectful attitude of persons, regardless of their social class. His mother's contempt for the family of a former village clergyman is therefore implicitly disapproved of:

> - Why should you dress to go and take a cup of tea with an old parson?
> - Mr Hale is a gentleman, and his wife and daughter are ladies.[7]

In chapter 7, entitled 'New Scenes and Faces,' describing the first meeting between Margaret Hale and Mr Thornton, Gaskell insists on the heroine's plain dress as suited to her family's modest social status, yet worn by a character whose natural elegance did not require any artificial trimming:

> Her dress was very plain: a close straw bonnet of the best material and shape, trimmed with white ribbon; and a dark silk gown, without trimming or flounce; a large Indian shawl, which hung about her in long heavy folds, and which she wore as an empress wears her drapery.[8]

Here Gaskell makes it clear that her vision of dress as a sign of social identity goes beyond the Victorian conception of the social class criterion as the uppermost element in the definition of an individual's identity: moral qualities are far more important than material and social considerations in one's judgment of a person, a view shared by many Victorian novelists questioning class prejudices through their characterization. In the opening chapter of *Middlemarch* George Eliot describes her heroine as a woman whose natural beauty sufficed and did not need any artificial devices to enhance it. Her natural dignity and social origins spoke for themselves, needing no outward sign in the shape of an elegant dress:

> Miss Brooke had that kind of beauty which seems to be thrown into relief by poor dress. Her hand and wrist were so finely formed that she could wear sleeves not less bare of style than those in which the Blessed Virgin appeared to Italian painters; and her profile as well as her stature and bearing seemed to gain the more dignity from her plain garments, [...] for Miss Brooke's plain dressing was due to mixed conditions, in most of which her sister shared. The pride of being ladies had something to do with it: the Brooke connections, though not exactly aristocratic, were unquestionably 'good.' [...] Young women of such birth, living in a quiet country-house, and attending a village church hardly larger than a parlour, naturally regarded frippery as the ambition of a huckster's daughter.[9]

It thus appears very clearly that Victorian heroines were represented as dressing simply thus disregarding social conventions, conscious that their natural capacities and qualities did not need to be artificially enhanced by overdressing or wearing jewels. Didn't Jane Eyre reject Rochester's gift of expensive jewels as 'heirloom to the ladies of Thornfield?'[10]

Woman's dress was not only seen as an indicator of a person's social identity as reflected in the description of characters in Victorian novels but emerged prominently in the mid-Victorian period as a topic in discussions on women's working conditions and as a warning against health hazards associated with domestic life conditions.

Woman's Dress Seen in the Context of Domestic Life and Working Conditions

In an article entitled 'Manners and Fashion' published in 1854, Herbert Spencer spoke against the dominant spirit of conformity which could be found at the origin of a number of issues emerging as the consequence of the newly influential upper-middle class. Reviewing three recent works on social practices at the time, Spencer saw the pressure to conform to fashion as particularly dangerous:

> The desire to be *comme il faut*, which underlies all conformities, whether of manners, dress, or style of entertainment, is the desire

which makes many a spendthrift and many a bankrupt. To 'keep up appearances' is an ambition forming the natural outcome of the conformist spirit. [...] If we consider all that this extravagance entails – if we count up the robbed tradesmen, the stinted governesses, the ill-educated children, the fleeced relatives, who have to suffer from it- if we mark the anxiety and the many moral delinquencies which its perpetrators involve themselves in, we shall see that this regard for conventions is not so innocent as it looks.[11]

Spencer went on to analyse the current pressure to conform as a moral danger, that of unsatisfied desire causing perpetual dissatisfaction and bitterness:

What, now, is the secret of this perpetual miscarriage and disappointment? Does not the fault lie with all these needless adjuncts, those elaborate dressings, these set forms, these expensive preparations, these many devices and arrangements, that imply trouble and raise expectation? [...] Hence it follows, that the more multiplied the *unnecessary* requirements with which social intercourse is surrounded, the less likely are its pleasures to be achieved.

(385)

Spencer's message found an echo in numerous papers published in the more radical press of the 1850s. Among the earliest expressions of concern about woman's dress requiring urgent warning against possible health hazards is to be found in a series of articles entitled 'Woman and Womankind' published in *Tait's Edinburgh Magazine* in 1858. Although it was published anonymously, it is very probable that Harriet Martineau was the author of this series for the following reasons. First, she had been connected to *Tait's* right from 1832 when the magazine was launched.[12] Then, she may well have offered this series as a contribution to *Tait's* while she was also writing on woman's dress and health in *Once a Week*. 'Woman and Womankind' can be said to be a sociological survey of women's occupations in the 1850s examining social divisions and their impact on women's life and health. It points out the changes in woman's dress at the various stages of her life, each article of clothing being suited to her social rank. After the initial period of courtship and the newly achieved status of a married woman, a lower-class young woman will give up the previously attractive ways of dressing up now that her life is confined to her home and domestic tasks: 'Ball dresses are given away and the sober silk and straw bonnet (always of a modern and becoming shape) donned.'[13] In section IV of the series 'Servants and Mistresses', the reader confronts the regrettably unreasonable realities of woman's dress, highlighting its absurdities and the risks involved, whether financial risks or health hazards. It must be specified that in 1856 the cage crinoline was reinvented allowing the skirts to expand and to become unreasonably wide and making moving about a real challenge.[14] Both observant of contemporary trends and considering her mission as that of a moral guide, Martineau strongly recommends urgent changes in the habits of working women in their way of dressing:

> Our great grandmothers would not have permitted their maids to scrub their floors in 'hoops'; yet housemaids now wear crinoline, and whalebone, and spring petticoats, and pretend to work in them. Then come their flowers and cheap finery, lace bobbing round the chubby pumpkin of a face, heading the corpulent body of some fashion aspiring cook. All are absurdities, and dangerous moreover, for these things, although tawdry, and trumpery, and foolish, cost a great deal of money, and wear out in time, and the wages of a servant will not enable her to obtain them honestly, and also put by a little money against sickness or misfortune. Not only do they cost her money, but she has to spend time and thought in their purchase, and construction; and then comes the habit of thinking of these sorts of things, the consequent love of finery, and the means of displaying that finery, [...] all these follow in the trail of the tawdry finery, and might be checked in the beginning by a judicious remark of her mistress. Perhaps the remark might not be liked, but that does not exonerate the mistress from her duty.[15]

The question of woman's dress was raised again in *Tait's* in 1858 emphasizing the gap between 'Dress Makers and Dress Wearers.' It was a vehement outcry against the abominable working conditions of dressmakers, precisely those Elizabeth Gaskell had depicted in her novel *Ruth* (1853), young women working under the incessant pressure of their employer's demands. It is predominantly the injustices in the treatment of seamstresses that are denounced here:

> [...] must it not also be granted that milliners in this town, and others, are starved by miserable remuneration for long hours and hard work? must it not be granted that overdressing is the rule and not the exception? Now, that it is not allowable but desirable for every woman to dress well in her station, etc., we admit; but that good dressing is necessarily extravagant dressing, we question.[16]

The reasons for the dress makers' intolerable working conditions are specified as the result of commercial competition: 'The present rage for fashionable *modistes* creates the evil of dear rents, expensive showrooms and – as money must be made somehow – the concomitants of long hours and underpaid workwomen.' Thus, the injustices in the working conditions here denounced are due to the distinction to be made between 'first-class milliners,' making high-quality dresses and paying their seamstresses decent wages, and those who are less in demand with middle-class customers and having consequently to pay their working women on a tighter budget:

> It is rather of those whose customers are composed of the middle-class, would-be fashionable ladies, whose pockets are not equal to a full development of, and fair prices for, their extravagant notions, that we complain; and not of them only, but of their customers also. If Mrs Jones wishes a dear material fashionably made up she goes to a second-rate *modiste*, she higgles about price, and consequently the milliner is obliged, to make her profit and keep up a showy establishment, to underpay the poor worker.
>
> (728)

Thus, fashion and extravagance are denounced as the two evil tendencies of the day against which a war was waged at that time by popular educators who wished to teach their women readers moral lessons in order to obviate their tendency to extravagant expenses:

> Now, if ladies would be contented to dress in strict accordance with their means, and to pay fair prices for fair work, many of the thimble and thread grievances might be obviated. [...]
>
> To dress *well* in our notion, a woman must keep in mind three things: her age, her station, and her 'points,' and if these essentials are rigidly observed, whether she be the first lady in the land, or Polly Brown, the scullery maid, with £8 a year wages, she must dress well because she dresses suitably.
>
> (728)

Since Herbert Spencer's 1854 article had identified the disastrous effects due to the tyranny of fashion regarding men's fashion, with no specific item of women's dress being mentioned, Harriet Martineau felt the need to tackle the question of woman's dress. Thus, her article 'Female Dress in 1857' published in *The Westminster Review* starts with a quotation from Spencer's article on ridicule as a revolutionary agent: 'The time is approaching then, when our system of social observances must pass through some crisis out of which it will come purified and comparatively simple.' Hence, Martineau's paper on female dress signals the follies and dangers of woman's dress, confirming her status as a journalist writing on a wide range of topics from politics to social questions and education.[17] Although she defends herself against the reproach of preaching 'on the easiest of all topics – the sin of extravagance in dress,'[18] she cannot help feeling disappointed that the hope she had nourished for a more reasonable female fashion had proved a mere illusion and goes so far as to predict some sort of crisis:

> Thus it appeared in 1854 that we had reached such a pitch of extravagance in our tastes and usages, that we could scarcely make ourselves more absurd. Yet, during the intervening years, the gravest of those extravagances, that of female dress, has become so much conspicuous than at any time within three generations, that the expected crisis must be very near indeed [...] Seven years ago we were confident that the barbaric ages of dress were over for ever. We had attained (and this was true) a rational and tasteful mode of dress and more favourable to health and convenience and further removed from exaggeration of any kind than at any time within memory. [...] Yet we are already entangled among absurdities and extravagances.
>
> (315–16)

This 'rational and tasteful mode of dress of dress' of past years was 'a gown of an easy length and breadth, of a moderate weight in the skirt, and a natural division at the waist' which has given way to 'a costume which barbarians might mock at.' (317) Martineau points out the culprit, Parisian fashion. What else could it have been? French fashion, with Empress Josephine as its representative, wreaks havoc all over Europe, extending its influence to 'the women of England, Russia and America and perhaps a good many more, into extravagant exaggerations of the caprices of an extravagant beauty.' (317) Martineau saw the cage crinoline dress, introduced in 1856 to copy the then Parisian fashion, as exemplifying 'the absurdity of the imitation' for its inadequacy to everyday life situations. Such an ample dress was obviously as a hindrance when moving about and was very ironically described here:

> The dinner table will not accommodate the old number; and if a leaf is inserted, the waiting-maid can hardly get round, - a process the more difficult from the number of breadths in *her* skirt, and the extent of stiff cord in her petticoat. The most delicate flowers in the garden are cut off by the ladies' hems as they walk the path, and the little greenhouse is no place for such tragedy queens; they cannot move without knocking down half-a-dozen pots. [...] Sunday is changed. The children cannot go to church, because mamma leaves no room for them; and papa has to stand aside, in the face of the congregation, while his lady is effecting the difficult enterprise of entering her pew. [...] An admiring father, who till lately delighted in his daughter's grace and lightness of movement, and her elegant figure, now sees her deformed and trammeled, whether at the piano, or in the dance, or simply sitting on the sofa.
>
> (320, 321, 322)

The fashionable absurdities listed allow Martineau to draw her readers' attention to the risks and health hazards inherent to the new fashion.

Her reflection based on attentive observation is combined with medical considerations and her voice reflects the tone of medical authority. Thus, she points out that the headgear worn by fashionable women is 'a structure of silk or straw, adorned with flowers, ribbon and lace' regretfully replacing the traditional wholesome straw bonnet and gives away to the most ridiculous absurdities:

> The straw bonnet admits of all reasonable modifications, and that of five years ago, enclosing the face modestly, and covering the head comfortably, gratified taste then, while it satisfies sound reason now. Instead of it, we daily see old ladies in one of the two extremes; either their lank jaws are exposed by the dark strings of a slouching hat, or their wrinkled faces and grey hair are encompassed with blonde and artificial flowers, as the trimming of the little excrescence called a bonnet in our day.
>
> (318–19)

Even worse than being inappropriate to 'dowagers with roses and foliage clustering round their cheeks at every turn' (319), the new headgear is responsible for causing 'eye-disease, toothache and neuralgic pains of the head and face.' (318) She sees in the broad-brimmed hat a sign of good sense and pleads for a return to 'the indigenous, serviceable, becoming, unobjectionable English straw bonnet of all times.' (318) The climax of her indignation is reached when she considers the dress itself with 'tight waists, bare shoulders and arms, cumbrous and encroaching skirts' which would be absurd enough by itself were it not that it is made of 'the most expensive materials obtainable.' (319) Here again, Martineau points out the disastrous financial consequences of following such absurd fashion. This is seen, not only with lower-class women, maid-servants preferring to spend money on 'buying twice as many yards [of material] as formerly for their gowns' (320) rather than keeping money in a savings bank, but also with middle-class women as the willing victims of fashion. Indeed, a middle-class man of business just cannot afford buying

> the rich silks of the day, under their various names, of which every rich lady now thinks one at least necessary for a wife and daughters, with the prodigious trimmings which are equally indispensable, under a less sum than would maintain a country clergyman, or half-pay officer and his family. The paraphernalia of ribbons, laces, fringes and flowers, is more expensive than the entire gown of ten years ago.
>
> (320)

Martineau extended her campaign in favour of a radical change in women's dress trends to a series of articles in *Once a Week,* a popular journal she did not hesitate to contribute to for transmitting her message to a larger class of readers than the outstanding *Westminster Review.* The article she wrote in 1859 entitled 'Dress and its Victims' was a further outcry against the follies of the recent fashion in woman's dress causing countless injuries and even deaths every day. She was careful not to attack the unreasonable character of recent fashion too vehemently from the start by pointing out that this was no new issue as in previous ages dress had already been the cause of domestic accidents:

> Perhaps we are thinking of the accidents that have happened during particular fashions of dress, as the burning of the Marchioness of Salisbury, from her high caps nodding over the candle; or the deaths of the Ladies Bridgeman last year, or the number of inquests held during the fashion of gigot-sleeves, when a lady could scarcely dine in company, or play the piano at home, without peril of death by fire.[19]

With arguments based on practical considerations, Martineau addresses the question of dress 'in connection with preventable mortality' in an attempt to warn her readers against the risks of dress extravagances. Her first argument is that dress affects all parts of the body, basing her point on the authority of specialists to enhance the reliability of her advice:

> We remember the explanations of physicians – that dress may, and usually does, affect the condition and action of almost every department of the human frame; – the brain and the nervous system, the lungs, the stomach, and the other organs of the trunk; the eyes, the skin, the muscles, the glandular system, the nutritive system, and even the bony frame, the skeleton on which all hangs. If dress can meddle mischievously with the action, or affect the condition of all these, it can be no marvel that it is responsible for a good many of the hundred thousand needless deaths which are happening around us this year.
>
> (387–88)

Since her method dictated her to base her arguments on observation, she stipulated that a woman's dress should be submitted to both sense and good taste. Sense, first, since dress should serve its purpose, allowing one to move freely, good taste being a necessary complementary attribute as dress should be 'agreeable to wear', 'modest and graceful', these qualities being considered as the natural effect of good taste. So, as to avoid any impediment, the dress should be close to the body:

> Dress should bear a close relation to the human form. [...] Where it follows the outline of the frame it should fit accurately enough to fulfill its intention, but so easily as not to embarrass action. It

should neither compress the internal structure nor impede the external movement. An easy fit, in short, is requisite. It is part of this easy fit that the weight should be properly hung and distributed.

(388)

However, Martineau does not advocate the strict utilitarian conception of dress: if utility is its prime function, it does not exclude decoration provided that good taste prevails and bans any excess in artificial decoration:

Grace and beauty are flowers to the root of utility. The worst in dress is where things are put on for no purpose or use. [...] The best taste is where the genuine uses of dress are not lost sight of, and the gratification of the eye grows out of them.

(388)

She laments the fact that such sound principles are not taken into account in the fashionable dress of the 1850s, thus causing countless victims every day:

The variety, the cheapness, the manageableness of clothes in our day, compared with former time, ought to render us obedient in an unequalled degree to the main condition of good dress. Instead of this, we see trains of funerals every year carrying to the grave the victims of folly and ignorance in dress.

(388)

The major reason for the absurdity of woman's fashionable dress is the disregard of its primary function, the protection of the body:

Their clothing does not protect them from cold, heat, damp, or glare. [...] At present, too, no woman who adopts the fashion of the hoop in any form is properly guarded against the climate. Any medical man in good practice can tell of the spread of rheumatism since women ceased to wear their clothing about their limbs, and stuck it off with frames and hoops, admitting damp and draught.

(389)

Martineau also discusses the question of the bonnet as she had previously done in her 1857 article. The new sort of bonnet, replacing the traditional straw bonnet, has become a mere excuse for piling up decorative accessories and no longer serves its purpose of protecting the head and face, which represents an unprecedented folly:

The eyes are unsheltered from sun and wind, and the most important region of the head is exposed by the bonnets which Englishwomen are so weak as to wear in imitation of the French. Again, the doctors have their painful tale to tell of neuralgic pains in the face and head, which abound beyond all prior experience of complaints in the eyes, and all the consequences that might be anticipated from the practice of lodging the bonnet on the nape of the neck, and leaving all the fore part of the skull exposed. Why the bonnet is worn at all is the mystery. [It serves to exhibit] the handful of flimsy decorations now usurping the place of the useful, cheap, and pretty straw bonnet, which suits all ages in its large variety.

(389)

Martineau reveals an exceptional degree of humour using her usual ironical tone at its best when debunking the excesses of fashion as far as the hat is concerned:

The new and brimless invention is nearly as bad as the bonnet for use, while more fantastic. A chimney-pot hat with a tall upright plume may possibly suit a volunteer rifle corps or a regiment of Amazons rehearsing for the opera, but it is not very English in taste.

(389)

Next on her list of absurdities is the new fashion of the scarf worn in all seasons which causes another set of diseases:

The fearful spread of throat and chest diseases is ascribed, by those who should know best, mainly to the modern notion of muffling up the throat in furs and other heating substances. Before the boa came in, we heard little of any one of the tribe of throat diseases which we now meet at every turn. Some ladies carry a boa all through the summer, and many tie up their throats with a silk handkerchief whenever they go abroad, in all seasons; suffering their retribution in hoarsenesses, bronchitis, sorethroat, and other ailments never endured by those who cultivate more hardy habits, and reserve such wraps for very special occasions.

(389)

Her denunciations of woman's dress considered from head to foot continue with the evils of shoes according to the most recent fashion. Thin shoes, patent-leather shoes, and high-heeled boots caused all sorts of undesirable effects and, at worst, dangerous falls down the stairs when wearing high-heeled boots. Martineau concludes her exhaustive list of evils caused by extravagant fashionable trends, from gasping for breath due to undesirable pressure on the waist from whalebones, to fainting fits following the practice of tight lacing. She considered ridicule as the most effective means to draw the readers' attention, the most conducive method to warn them against avoidable risks:

Do the petticoats of our time serve as anything but a mask to the human form- a perversion of human proportions? A woman on a sofa looks like a child popping up from a haycock. A girl in the dance looks like the Dutch tumbler that was a favourite toy in my infancy. The fit is so the reverse of accurate as to be like a silly hoax- a masquerade without wit: while, at the same time, it is not an easy fit.

(390)

Given the extravagant fashion in woman's dress, Martineau saw the need to explore the question of woman's health put at risk not only by wearing such articles of clothing but also by making them. In her article 'The Needlewoman. Her Health' she resolutely adopted a less alarming tone than she had in previously when considering needle women's working conditions. The reason was that she considered the recent introduction of the sewing machine as the answer to what had been intolerable conditions:

Here lies the solace of the poor needlewomen. A multitude will sooner or later be employed in the fresh areas of industry; and not a few are already testing a degree of comfort that they never knew before. As slaves of the contractors for the outfitters they may have earned three or four shillings a week, at the expense of eyesight and health. Those among them who can adapt themselves to the new circumstances will earn more than twice as much, with little fatigue. [...] We must not stop in our improvements till needlewomen are distinguishable from the rest of the world on the ground of health.[20]

As a keen observer of women's daily occupations and habits, Martineau could only lament the harmful effects of needlework as a constant occupation, either as a professional occupation or a required one for a housewife and mother, and advises giving up former practices in embroidery fatal to eyesight. To alleviate physical strain when sewing, women are advised to lay by their needlework every now and then and change their occupation, opting for something requiring physical activity:

It cannot be denied, either, that prolonged sewing is very hurtful, and constant sewing probably fatal. Any mechanical action which employs a few muscles almost exclusively must be bad; and any diligent needlewoman can describe the sensation between the shoulders, the nervous irritability which constitute real suffering when the needle has been plied too long. [...] They should stop before they become irritable or weary, and they should at once go for a walk, or pass to some active employment. It is nonsense, too, in these days of marking inks, to strain the precious eyesight over the pedantic methods of our grandmothers who made a great point of marking fine cambric as true as coarse linen. But needlework is not to be condemned because some women still pursue it without moderation or good sense.

(597)

Harriet Martineau's sensible considerations encouraging women to adopt healthy practices made her the popular educator she was acclaimed for being. As she admitted, her advice was based on her personal experience of health problems, whether it was a severe deafness from an early age or some devastating illness which only mesmerism came to cure, and besides her journalistic writings she was called upon by various associations to speak at public meetings on health questions and their remedies:

> Some months since I was petitioned to speak up for fancywork as a solace to invalids and sorrowful people. I certainly can do it with a safe conscience; for my needle has been an inestimable blessing to me during years of ill health. It is sometimes said that the needle is to a woman what the cigar is to the man – a tranquilising, equalizing influence, conservative and restorative. It is at least this; and I should imagine more.
>
> (597)

However important the question of dress, it was not the only subject that Martineau explored concerning Victorian women in the mid-nineteenth century, but we can certainly assert that her preoccupation with woman's health and working conditions made her an innovator in the field of gender studies. She never spared her efforts to write at length on the subject of woman's health, advocating not only the educators' and employers' active roles in redressing women's unhealthy practices but recommended a nationwide effort following the model of the American Dress Reform Association:

> What is to be done? Will anything ever be done? or is feminine will-fulness and slavishness to fashion to kill off hundreds and thousands of the race, at present? There are whole societies in America who do not see the necessity for such mischief, and who hope to put an end to it in their own country at least. The Dress Reform Association of the United States was instituted some years since by women who refused the inconvenience of Paris fashions in American homesteads; and they have been aided, not only by physicians, but by other men, on the ground of the right of women to wear what suits their occupations and their taste, without molestation.[21]

Thus, what Martineau pleaded for was the opposite of what fashion demanded of women, showing off an eccentric image of oneself, going against one's natural inclinations to conform to the image imposed by the latest fashionable trends. She repeatedly recommended that women should conform their dress to a way of life that should be as plain, as natural, and as healthy as possible, in strict accordance with reasonable criteria. It can therefore be argued that Martineau was not only an early feminist, supporting women's right to conduct their lives according to their own choices, but, beyond that, she was a prophetess of our contemporary values with a return to authenticity and respect of individual choices. Given that woman's dress has always been relied upon to reflect the values of its age, it is essential that it should leave to the generations to come an image of a period which was capable of making sense balance sensibility with aesthetic choices, Proust himself having defined woman's dress as 'the spiritualized apparel of a civilization.'[22]

Notes

1 Lou Taylor, *The Study of Dress History* (Manchester and New York: Manchester University Press, 2002), 1.

2 Ibid., 96.

3 Anonymous, *The Illustrated London News*, Exhibition Supplement, 10 May 1851, 393.

4 Anonymous, *The Illustrated London News*, 17 May 1851, 404.

5 Charlotte Gilman, *The Dress of Women. A Critical Introduction to the Symbolism and Sociology of Clothing.* (1915) reprint (Westport and London: The Greenwood Press, 2002), 3.

6 Elizabeth Gaskell, *North and South*. 1855; reprint (Harmondsworth, Penguin Books, 1977), 35.

7 Ibid., 117.

8 Ibid., 99.

9 George Eliot, *Middlemarch: A Study of Provincial Life*. 1871–1872; reprint (London: Oxford University Press, 1963), 1–2.

10 Charlotte Brontë, *Jane Eyre*. 1847; reprint (Harmondsworth, Penguin Books, 1978), 287.

11 *The Westminster Review*, vol. V n.s., April 1854, 357–92, 381–82.

12 See H. Martineau's letter to W. Tait, 28 December 1832 in Valerie Sanders (ed.), *Harriet Martineau. Selected Letters* (Oxford, Clarendon Press, 1990), 39.

13 "Woman and Womankind. n. 3 Humble life in England." *Tait's Edinburgh Magazine*, 25 n.s. (1858): 167.

14 http://trulyvictorian.com/history/1855.html, consulted on May 15, 2016.

15 "Woman and Womankind." *Tait's Edinburgh Magazine*, 25 n.s. (1858): 480.

16 "Dress makers and Dress wearers." *Tait's Edinburgh Magazine*, 25 n.s., 726.

17 See M. Hill and S. Hoecker-Drysdale (eds.) *Harriet Martineau: Theoretical and Methodological Perspectives* (New York, Routledge, 2001).

18 *The Westminster Review*, 68 (October 1857), 315–16.

19 "Dress and its Victims." *Once a Week*, 5 November 1859, 387.

20 "The Needlewoman. Her Health." *Once a Week*, 24 November 1860, 596, 599.

21 "Dress and its Victims." *Once a Week*, 5 November 1859, 390. On woman's health see also "The Maid of all Work. Her Health." *Once a Week*, 19 May 1860, 464–67. "The Young Lady in Town and Country. Her Health," *Once*

a Week, 25 February 1860, 191–95. "The Governess. Her Health," *Once a Week*, 1 September 1860, 267–72.
22 In M. Contini, *5000 ans d'élégance de l'antiquité à nos jours. La mode à travers les âges* (Paris: Hachette, 1965), 263.

Works Cited

Anonymous, *The Illustrated London News*, 10 May 1851, 17 May 1851.

Brontë, Charlotte. *Jane Eyre*. 1847; reprint Harmondsworth: Penguin Books, 1978.

Contini, M. *5000 ans d'élégance de l'antiquité à nos jours. La mode à travers les âges*. Paris, Hachette, 1965.

Eliot, George. *Middlemarch; A Study of Provincial Life*. 1871–1872; reprint London: Oxford University Press, 1963.

Gaskell, Elizabeth. *North and South*. 1855; reprint Harmondsworth: Penguin Books, 1977.

Gilman, Charlotte. *The Dress of Women. A Critical Introduction to the Symbolism and Sociology of Clothing*. 1915; reprint Westport and London: The Greenwood Press, 2002.

Hill, Michael, Hoecker-Drysdale, Susan. *Harriet Martineau: Theoretical and Methodological Perspectives*. New-York and London: Routledge, 2001.

Hoecker-Drysdale, Susan. *Harriet Martineau (1802–1877), First Woman Sociologist*. New-York & London: Berg, 1992.

Once a Week, "Dress and Its Victims" 5 November 1859, "The Needlewoman. Her Health" 24 November 1860.

Sanders, Valerie. *Harriet Martineau. Selected Letters*. Oxford: Clarendon Press, 1990.

Tait's Edinburgh Magazine, "Woman and Womankind" 25 n.s., 1858 "Dress Makers and Dress Wearers" 25 n.s., 1858.

Taylor, Lou. *The Study of Dress History*. Manchester and New York: Manchester University Press, 2002.

The Westminster Review, "Manners and Fashion" 5 n.s., April 1854, "Female Dress" 68, October 1857.

12 Paper Love
Valentines in Victorian Culture

Alice Crossley

The nineteenth century witnessed the development and proliferation of widely affordable, commercial valentine cards, thus securing a place in the cultural imagination. Valentines might seem innocuous enough, as manufactured and embellished objects designed to convey a particular sentiment to the recipient, and so operating within a system of commodification in which the valentine card emerges as a commercial product. However, as the expanding 'material turn' in literary and historical criticism continues to insist by opening up new and fruitful avenues of critical thought, such items also possess a cultural valence which leaves these seemingly trivial objects to signify in other ways – as illustrative of their affective capacity, of their heritage or the ideas that inhere within them (rather than their value), and therefore as particularly fluid and productive of open-ended meanings.[1] This essay draws on the work of scholars such as Elaine Freedgood in her work on *The Ideas in Things*, in which she articulates in her performance of 'Victorian "thing culture"', which she claims is 'a more extravagant form of object-relations' as it emerges in her study as 'one in which systems of value were not quarantined from one another and ideas of interest and meaning were perhaps far less restricted than they are today.'[2]

As with the other 'things' which have been observed to clutter museums and exhibitions in the Victorian period, nineteenth-century homes, and the fictional spaces of Victorian novels, valentines possess meaning, invested with their own material presence and significance in Victorian culture. Admittedly, how valentines are interpreted will shift according to these cards' situations, and their relative position when considered as a personal item in isolation or as part of an abstract assemblage (real – in the archive, or imagined – as just one type of general paraphernalia). One the one hand, valentines may be viewed as generic symbols *en masse* when viewed from a wide social perspective or as part of a common collective. Of course, valentines might signify differently if one takes an individual card to which personal meaning is attached, the particular item revealing the social relationship to which it gestures between giver and receiver. However, it is the former, expansive view of the long lens which occupies this essay, and so it is to the heritage, type, form, and cultural meaning of valentines in this period that I now turn.

In the Victorian period, the occasion of St Valentine's Day, and the valentine cards that mark its passing, might be viewed as conventions that gesture symbolically towards the continued popularity of sentimentality. However, both public and private expressions of sentiment could also serve as a disguise, which highlighted the capacity of sentimentality to camouflage inauthenticity. The proliferation, by the end of the century, of mass-produced, commercial valentine cards increasingly raised concerns about the loss of sincerity, authenticity, and self-expression in a culture of consumer capitalism. This created a corresponding kaleidoscopic perception of the valentine itself, whose personal and social meaning was not always clear.

This essay is concerned with tracing what culturally specific meanings were ascribed to the valentine in the Victorian period, the sending of which was a popular custom – in 1883 2,768,000 valentines were purportedly sent in Britain.[3] The social significance of the valentine will be coupled with its cultural resonance as a material object. The perceived history of this type of object in Victorian Britain was bound up with attitudes towards its heritage and origins, its materiality, and its affinities with related discourses such as gender, matrimony, courtship, and traditions of misrule. Rather than being dismissed as trivial, mawkish, or as mere pretty nonsense in the nineteenth century, valentines play a fascinating role in the cultural life of the period. Although the social visibility of valentines was largely confined to the second month of each year, there was an annual recurrence of attention to the practices of Valentine's day through not only the popularity of the objects themselves, but also the prominence of advertisements, displays in stationers' windows, public commentary on the strain placed on the postal service, and reminders in periodical articles about the history and heritage of these material tokens. Such diversity in the yearly proliferation of valentine-related paraphernalia and the interchange of old and new information about the cards and their origin nonetheless created a persistent – if cyclical – pattern of awareness, fascination, and even trepidation for Victorians when considering the cultural determination of valentines, embedded and rehearsed over the course of several decades in the nineteenth century. The increasing variety of forms that valentine cards took over the century, from cheap and crude single-sided sheets of paper, to elaborate confections of costly embellishments, also impacts on the ways in which they could be perceived.

Although real examples of valentines sent or designed during the nineteenth century are introduced in this essay in order to illustrate a type, or to demonstrate how they functioned generally as forms of communication and expression of sentiment, despite the fact that valentines developed significantly in terms of form and popularity during the nineteenth century they also possessed latent meaning connected to their earlier history and evolution. This follows Freedgood's recognition of the ideas attached to things. She develops what she calls a strong metonymic reading, choosing to move beyond the acknowledged symbolism of an object or thing, to encompass wider meanings, and more unstable means of signification:

> Metonymy's apparently subversive ability to disrupt meaning, to be endlessly vagrant and open ended, may be attended by an equally subversive ability to recuperate historical links that are anything but random.[4]

Hazy cultural knowledge of the heritage of Valentine practices was itself an important part of the annual festival of St Valentine. The cards themselves belong to what Freedgood has termed 'that mass of information that is retained by a culture but not always actively remembered or valued.'[5] When seeking to uncover what value the valentine may have possessed for Victorian society, the qualities and memories that are inherent to its physical presence, this mass of information may be seen to inform what the valentine came to signify in Victorian culture. The cultural memory of such objects and the history of the calendrical day itself are inevitably brought to bear. The evolution of St Valentine's celebrations into popular custom or tradition by the mid-nineteenth century illuminates the willingness of Victorian society to collude in maintaining the occasion, imprecise as it may be, and embracing the ritual exchange of cards that mark it.

For mid-Victorian society, various types of meaning would seem intrinsic to the valentine, whether consciously acknowledged or via unconscious affiliation. For example, many Victorians would have been aware that the celebration of St Valentine's Day was acknowledged to mark the martyrdom of either a Roman priest killed in the third century or a Bishop from central Italy.[6] Church historians remain unsure which was originally canonized, and in the Victorian press one or both hagiographies might be raised for consideration.[7] It was not until at least the middle ages that the saint came to be known as the patron saint of lovers – before that his name has been associated with the prevention of fainting or epilepsy.

The Catholic feast day of St Valentine, however, was also frequently acknowledged in Victorian periodical articles to have its origins in the Pagan Roman festivals of the Lupercalia and of Juno Februata, which took place at the same time of the month – between 13 and 15 February.[8] These were celebrations dedicated to health and fertility. According to some sources, the archaic rites of these festivals included the sacrifice of goats and dogs; their skins would be used as loincloths to two otherwise naked men, who would run around the city walls whipping the women that they met with leather thongs from the goat-hide to help them conceive and to ensure easy childbirth. Such superstitions and fertility rites have often been taken as one reason why the feast of St Valentine became an occasion for displays of affectionate intimacy, and of course, such ties have also meant that through history St Valentine's Day has also been associated with sex and procreation. As a springtime festival, the Lupercalia was bound up with ritual purification, rebirth, and abundance, and the association of these aspects of the season, rooted in a long tradition which can be traced through the popularity of love-trinkets in the eighteenth century, back to Chaucer's fourteenth-century depiction of St Valentine's day in *The Parlement of Foules* as the moment when birds choose their mates, and even further to the original celebration of the Lupercalia. Despite the valentine as, in some ways, a peculiarly nineteenth-century item, then, these deceptively simple objects also alluded to their longer evolution over time.

This heritage is evident in writing about valentines and St Valentine's Day in the nineteenth century. In his brief essay 'Valentine's Day' of 1823, Charles Lamb refers gesturally to 'old Bishop Valentine' to ask: 'who and what manner of person art thou? Art thou but a name, typifying the restless principle which impels poor humans to seek perfection in union?'[9] Subsequent essayists and journalists were to follow in Lamb's train of thought, musing on the shadowy origins of the mysterious martyred saint whose name has been attached to the exchange of symbolic gifts and other declarations of love and affection on 14 February each year. Lamb's willingness, however, to accept this 'returning festival' without provenance and with little preamble is indicative of a wider cultural trend towards this so-called holy day from the nineteenth century onwards. After all, as Lamb notes, 'this is the day on which those charming little missives, ycleped Valentines, cross and intercross each other at every street and turning.'[10] The day itself, and the way in which it is marked, has been established, he suggests, and recognizable through the 'charming little missives' bought and sent for the occasion. The *accuracy* of the association of St Valentine with love and courtship is no longer of great importance, as Lamb seems to indicate, given that society has embraced the *fact* of the association – regardless of the convoluted process of whatever historical prelude led to the saint's name being appropriated for such usage. Those cards and letters are after all, as Lamb observes, known familiarly as 'Valentines.' These come to signify, in Lamb's phrase, a form of 'ephemeral courtship' under the shady auspices of the bygone saint.

Lamb highlights the collective remembrance at work in the so-called 'history' of St Valentine and the rituals of the day. The dimly remembered scraps of history that Lamb draws on can also be read into the paper scraps of the valentine itself. The evolution of St Valentine's celebrations into popular custom or tradition by the mid-nineteenth century illuminates the willingness of Victorian society to collude in maintaining the occasion and the ritual exchange of cards that mark it. Lamb's essay goes on to ruminate on the appropriation of the heart, as illustrative of romantic love:

> In these little visual interpretations, no emblem is so common as the *heart*,—that little three-cornered exponent of all our hopes and fears,—the bestuck and bleeding heart; it is twisted and tortured into more allegories and affectations than an opera hat. What authority we have in history or mythology for placing the head-quarters and metropolis of God Cupid in this anatomical seat rather than in any other, is not very clear; but we have got it, and it will serve as well as any other.[11]

Again, Lamb takes up a similar refrain, not challenging the period's consolidation of St Valentine's Day, or the fact of its visibility in the sending of cards covered with hearts, cupids, and flowers. Rather, he reveals the habit of using a heart to do visually the work of expressing verbally one's sentiments. The reason for doing so, Lamb states, 'is not very clear', but he subscribes nonetheless – with a mental shrug – to the collective acceptance and convention of the heart emblem, by conceding 'we have got it, and it will serve as well as any other.' This allusion to the power of superstition and tradition offers an analogy for a corresponding cultural acquiescence in the proliferation and existence of the Valentine's rituals in the period, as evidenced by Lamb and a host of other writers.

As well as accounts of the so-called history of Saint Valentine, each February the Victorian press revisited the superstitions and folk customs that had apparently been practiced in the previous century – particularly in rural areas. Many of these traditions reminded society that some valentines might be expected to conclude in marriage. Recorded practices included the notion that the first person seen on Valentine's morn would be your husband or wife – or at least a lover for a day. Other people stuck bay leaves to their pillow, believing that they would then dream of their true love. A popular tradition also included writing names on scraps of paper, rolling them up in clay, and placing them in water, then waiting to see whose name rose to the surface first, to pair off accordingly – a tradition said to go back as far as the Lupercalia.[12] By mid-century these folk customs of courtship-play and marital prediction were cast as antiquated games and superstitions, which still having their place in the visual motifs and mottos of commercially produced valentines. As one article in the *London Society* magazine acknowledged in 1863, 'the tender correspondence itself is chiefly confined to the kitchen or the nursery. In short, by the upper ten thousand Valentine's Day is neither celebrated in the spirit nor in *the letter*.'[13] As the performance of such rural (and supposedly working-class) customs to '*the letter*' waned during the nineteenth century, the rituals alluded to became increasingly rare, with little mention of them as literal current practices as the century wore on. However, the 'letter' pun draws attention to the object which had come to stand in place of such games: the valentine. In its material form, a valentine had the capacity to allude to these rural traditions of courtship; such inherent meanings, references to its heritage, coalesced in its popular emergence as a greetings card. These valentines became items which, variously (and often simultaneously) retained the element of fun, could provide mystique when sent anonymously, might elicit shock or surprise, and they also became tokens of affection to be treasured and admired. The 'letter' of the valentine as a physical, visual object, then, was an established part of the cultural festivities of the season. In February each year, folk customs gave way to the circulation of these commercially produced items, through a process which sought in many ways to elevate wooing into a process of exchange and possession. This giving of sentimental paper tokens was playful, as although it could still remain a declaration of serious intent, it was largely considered first and foremost a form of entertainment and amusement. Depending on language, imagery, and style, it might still refer to courtship, but the cards were by no means confined to lovers.

The mention of valentines in the Victorian period would have conjured very different images. First, there was the conventional sentimental or sincere valentine, which might be purchased for between one penny and one guinea, often with written verse or a blank space for a personal inscription. It often contained images and designs in simple lithography with a splash of hand-painted colour (in an application called pooning), or, from 1837, chromolithography. The visual motifs of these valentines might now be considered fairly conventional, and they were likely to include symbolic flowers, ferns or weeping willows, winged cupids, suggestive church steeples or alters, two lovers standing handclasped, bleeding hearts, pairs doves or swans, butterflies, wreathes, and waterfalls. One article of 1864 referred to a humorous view of this type of card, describing them as containing:

> Hearts transfixed by darts; turtle-doves apparently commiserating each other on the absurdity of the position they are made to occupy; a profusion of small fat boys, principally remarkable for their disinclination to patronize the cheap clothing establishments of the day ...; pretty, but otherwise highly insipid young gentleman; and mincing young ladies, looking fit for anything but useful domesticated wives.[14]

By this point, then, the series of popular, if stilted, visual motifs relating to the day were becoming well worn. As well as this type of sentimental valentine which depicted a simple set of stock images, valentine makers also took advantage of developments in modern technology. Increasingly widespread and more costly examples became more common by the mid-Victorian period. These often highly ornamental valentines were typically mounted on embossed and lace paper, with elaborate borders, inscribed mottos, and even folded leaves of decorated paper which opened to reveal further designs beneath. They often received a lavish addition of scraps – plain, coloured, or embossed – of the kind that were used for scrap albums and sold in sheets, as well as other forms of embellishment such as perfume sachets and delicate boxed, sprung valentines. Eventually these gorgeous offerings moved beyond the form of simple cards, to become more three-dimensional and tactile, featuring scraps of fabric (such as silk or velvet), ribbons, pearls, shells, gilt paper, and feathers. The most expensive valentines – those designed for presentation, with novelty gifts inside such as a fan, purse, pencil case, or scent-bottle, and often given in glass cases to protect them – could be between 15–65 shillings each, according to one stationer's advertisement of 1875, so these become costly and extravagant gifts and demonstrations of affection.[15] Perhaps in a bid to extend what was becoming a profitable holiday for the stationers, valentines cards for leap years were also produced, designed to turn the table and provide an opportunity for women to propose to men on 29 February. Although it was most usually associated with wooing and flirtation, Valentine's day also became an appropriate occasion in the nineteenth century to send a message of affection to a friend or family member, so the supposed remit of the valentine extends beyond romance.

Valentines could also be fun and witty, or lighthearted and whimsical with playful relationships between texts and image. Notable in this type of valentine were popular maps of matrimony, which were geographical maps with illustrated where the 'quicksands of censure', 'petticoat government', and 'Land of Rejection' surround the 'River of Sincerity' and 'Province of Courtship', and so on.[16] These were amusing, but there were also puzzles (which often involved mazes, word-play, and visual trickery to conceal a message), and engaging cards with moveable parts in which a flap could be pulled to move part of the picture. Another fun type of valentine popular throughout the century was the rebus valentine, in which images and icons would be substituted for words, which required deciphering.

There were also Bachelor's Buttons, which were valentines sent by women to men, which offered a sort of domestic felicity if their playful suit were accepted. These valentines contained sewing materials and a button or two, together with the coy promise of nimble fingers to patch up the gentleman's bachelor clothing – if he were to marry the sender. One example, from the John Johnson Collection of Printed Ephemera at the Bodleian Library reads: 'Bachelor's Buttons With much Sympathy! Here's a threaded needle and a couple of shirt buttons! Wouldn't you like someone to sew them on for you? With Fondest Love.'[17] Further novelties for the season included bank notes drawn from the Bank of Love and fake marriage certificates. The former in particular proved so realistic that they had to be removed from circulation.

However, not everyone would want – or could afford – to buy an expensive, elaborate, commercially produced valentine, and many felt themselves unable to pen an original composition for the occasion. Thus, emerged the Valentine Writer – a book or pamphlet containing rhymes and pleasantries designed for those who could not, or chose not to, furnish their own verses. These Writers often advertised their wares with improbable titles such as *The Turtle Dove; or Cupid's Artillery levelled against human hearts, being a new and original Valentine Writer*, or *The New Cupid's Bower; Being a Poetical Garden of Love, abounding with Original Valentines calculate to convey the Sentiments of the Heart in language neat, chaste, and expressive*. The excesses promised by these books usually translated into a series of short doggerel lines, mostly written with a specific recipient in mind (by using popular Christian names, for example, or forms of employment as a mean of categorization or classification).

One Valentine Writer drew attention to the shortage of new amorous offerings in the stationers' windows each year as a ploy to entice purchasers: 'those who wish to pay their compliments of the season ... are obliged unless inclined to hazard an original composition) to fall back on ... perennials, or else make use of those senseless lace-paper gew-gaws, which are a degree worse.'[18] The Writer suggests somewhat disingenuously that 'nothing can be so pungent as an immediate emanation from your own heart', emphasizing a pseudo-originality while nonetheless peddling a series of pre-written verses designed for reproduction in valentine letters.[19] Setting themselves apart from the pre-fabricated cards available from stationers, in which the emphasis tended to be on a comprehensive visual representation of affection, Valentine Writers established their merit by seeming to advertise a happy medium. The hackneyed text and rhymes that they contained – while unimaginative and mechanical – might still impress the recipient and make the sender feel that their sentiments had been captured more fully or effectively through reproduced words rather than 'senseless lace-paper gew-gaws.'[20] Valentine Writers usually provided verses designed specifically for noticeable characteristics or by profession – which might include a valentine for a farmer, glover, milkman, pawnbroker, sailor, and so on. In particular, 'low' trades often came into focus through these volumes, despite occasional lines intended to be addressed to gentlemen ladies, perhaps to cover all bases.

An example of the playful side of sending valentines is evident in a slightly antagonistic, but clearly original, valentine received by Fanny Brawne earlier in the century – the girl loved by Romantic poet John Keats. In 1819, she was amused to receive a joke valentine from Keats's friend Charles Brown – although their letters reveal that Keats himself was not pleased by his friend's teasing imposition. Years later, she was still able to recite the poem it contained, which ran on the theme of her own apparent sense of self-importance:

Whene'er we chance to meet
You know the reason why
You pass me in the street
And toss your head on high.

Because my walking stick
Is not a dandy twig
Because my boots are thick,
Because I wear a wig.

Because you think my coat
Too often has been worn,
And the tie about my throat
Is at the corners torn.

To see me thus equipped
What folly to be haughty!
Pray where you never whipped
At school for being naughty?[21]

Although the simple poem seems harmless enough, Brown is clearly taking the opportunity to poke fun at 'Haughty' Miss Brawne, pointedly commenting on her tendency to look down on his own sartorial shabbiness – Fanny herself was always elegantly dressed in clothes of her own design and making. What it also does, however, is to demonstrate the potential of the valentine to become a covert means of more risqué communication. Brown's final two lines ask Fanny about her disobedience and wilfulness as a girl, playfully reminding her that her attitude needs an adjustment; but they also draw startling attention to an implied sadomasochism through the image of corporal punishment enacted on the young woman's body, which is erotically suggestive.

As Brown's valentine to Fanny Brawne indicates, there lurks a darker side to the valentine in the nineteenth century, perhaps harking back to the potentially carnivalesque fertility rites of the Lupercalia. Behind the apparent innocence of playful displays of amatory interest in the Victorian period, the capacity for more primitive expression of desire could still be glimpsed, leading to the retention of St Valentine's Day traditions of mischief and misrule as a Springtime festival. This illustrates another facet of the valentine, and how contradictory meaning might adhere to this type of object. Comic or vulgar valentines were often designed to be humiliating and degrading, providing caricatures of men and women perhaps as a means of intimidation as well as spiteful fun. One periodical writer for *Once a Week*, while admitting that 'On that one day of the year hints can be conveyed with a facility and effect which are impossible at any other', laments the fact that such satirical comments on a person's appearance or profession can also be painful:

> It is an uncomfortable fact, but it has to be admitted, – we are not all models of symmetry and beauty; and, thanks to St. Valentine, most of us are reminded of it at least once a year. … If by some accident they could forget it, on the morning of the hateful Fourteenth the will be made fully aware of it on opening the letters. …
>
> Innocent pictures of cooing doves, eh? By no manner of means. The malice of the serpent peeps out in every line and curve of them. Their direct purpose is to destroy your peace of mind, and break down all sense of self-respect.[22]

Such mean and vulgar cards were often condemned by the press. However, this does illustrate that Valentines could be used, notionally at least, to correct characters flaws, such as puncturing arrogance and deflating self-satisfaction. Their cruel mockery found targets in the appearance, profession, or character defect of the unfortunate addressee, and such valentines were usually cheaply produced on a single sheet of paper. One such example focuses on a trade, in order to mount a (supposedly humorous) denunciation of a fishmonger:

> You cry your Fish so loud and shrill
> Turbot, Mackerel, Plaice and Brill
> And on the women passing by
> You leer and cast a fishy eye,
> Now who on earth would ever wish
> To have a man who smells of fish.[23]

Both the man's low trade and lewd tendencies come under attack, in a cruel rejection of the possibility of future matrimony. Another particularly vicious example of the type of content these might contain is taken from a Valentine Writer of 1820, addressed to 'a Disagreeable Fellow':

> Than you a more disgusting creature never had existence – though art the very antidote to love – the shadow and outline of a man.… Retire then thou humble apology for anything like a man – thou withered abortion of human nature – a mere speck in the creation. … From your despising Valentine.[24]

While many examples were clearly intended to be humorous – at least for the sender, if not the unfortunate recipient – this suggestion for an inscription feels rather shocking in its vitriol. It is a sobering reminder that, while valentines could be vehicles through which to communicate desire or affection, they could also express darker desires and could be designed to wound. In an article of 1864, one periodical writer observes wryly of this type of valentine that 'some of the specimens at the lowest extremity of this group are so exceedingly gross as to be fit only for the dens of Holywell Street', effectively casting some forms of valentine as obscene items, as this notorious road was the home to pornographic booksellers. Perhaps it is unsurprising, then, that other examples of valentines even took the opportunity to chastise errant spouses, or extramarital affairs (see Figure 12.1, which is a valentine for a cuckold), and in doing so attempt to restore moral order, as with this pointed verse to a married man:

> You know very well when your mistress retires
> Which is seldom not much after ten
> And having assisted her as she requires
> You are back to the kitchen again[25]

As Annebella Pollen has commented, such comic or vulgar valentines could be used to 'police social norms', by 'employ[ing] laughter as a weapon.'[26] One imagines that the recipient of these cards did not always find the joke amusing, although the rise in this cheap, crude type of valentine certainly adds a further dimension to the ways in which 'the valentine' might have resonated in the period.

The comic or satirical valentine, which emerged as the carnivalesque reversal of traditional sentimental cards, became popular after 1840, together with the wider increase in the popularity of valentines more generally. This was in part because of the emergence of the penny post, which meant that cards and letters could be sent much more cheaply than before. Prior to 1840, the gradual rise in these 'alternative' valentines had caused financial as well as emotional burden to the recipients, as satirical valentines had often been sent without postage. The cost of delivery would have to be paid by the addressee, adding insult to injury. Complaints about this, and requests for refunds, were so widespread that in 1817 an official decision was made by the General Post Office to create a regulation whereby compensation for such deliveries would not be made. The difficulties continued, and in 1857 the Post Office issued a statement that forbade postmasters and clerks from colluding in customers' attempts to conceal a letter's origins, for example by smudging a postmark in order to keep the writer's identity of a valentine secret.[27] The continued rise of numbers of valentines being sent each year was largely a result of the newly efficient, centralized system of pre-paid postage. Perhaps in part due to the license this provided for increased postal traffic, the tradition of sending valentines anonymously persisted, despite the Post Office's refusal help customers to protect their identity. It was

A. PARK, LONDON.

Thou easy fool, whom every woman scorns,
Sit like an ass, and calmly wear the horns;
Thy wife intriguing comfortabley goes,
And by her cant she leads you by the nose.

There on his knee you see her seated thus;
While you poor fool supplies her with the purse,
Thou Nincompoop, arouse thee if you can;
Pull off the horns, and be thyself a man.

Figure 12.1 'Untitled cuckold valentine'. Source: © Museum of London.

not only the crude, mean valentines which were sent without attribution, but often those by whom love was declared would withhold their identity in case of rejection, which added to the sense of liberated excess which operated around the holiday. The receipt of a valentine could therefore be a matter for celebration, but also cause for a more deeply ambivalent response. While valentines had long been associated with romanticized courtship ritual, they were also clearly put to other purposes. The valentine, then, operated at different levels as a form of social hieroglyph.

As an object in itself, a valentine card might initially appear to be fairly unremarkable, as a seasonal expression of regard for another. However, the valentine would also conjure the object's inherent affiliations – allowing an echo of its origins, its uses, its history, construction, and superstitions to illuminate the way in which it was received, intended, collected, or even simply observed when displayed in a shop window. As the examples provided here have demonstrated, the valentine provokes questions about sincerity, authenticity, intent, and humour. It might be playful and draw on the traditions of springtime misrule as a part of the traditional calendar and gestures towards its early origins, but it can also be a costly demonstration of affective investment in either a person or a relationship. While it remains an ephemeral object, what collectors refer to as 'fugitive material', such objects were often treasured for their personal value.[28] The idea of the valentine also conjures up its associations with similar paper products – scraps in albums, Christmas cards, and postcards. In this way, the valentine resonates unstably with numerous ideas and discourses in the period, effectively 'stockpil[ing]' knowledge, to borrow Freedgood's useful term, in which a host of ideas become attached to the valentine through its association with these practices and relations.[29] An abundanc of kaleidoscopic meaning is therefore inherent in the Victorian valentine, so that it can perform as cultural object, social hieroglyphic, and fragile, tactile thing in a juggling act that remains fascinating today. The cultural work of the valentine is manifold; but perhaps, as the work of the essays in this volume demonstrate, that very ambiguity in signification is instructive. By encouraging a deeper reading of what valentines were like and what they might have meant, this essay seeks to uncover some of those associations and resonances which adhered to the Victorian valentine, in spite of its status as 'fugitive material.'

Notes

1 The term taken from Lyn Pykett's guest-edited article of *Literature Compass* examining the commodity in Victorian culture, "The Material Turn in Victorian Studies," *Literature Compass*, 1 (2003), 1–5.

2 Elaine Freedgood, *The Ideas in Things: Fugitive Meaning in the Victorian Novel* (Chicago and London: The University of Chicago Press, 2006), 8.

3 According to Alan Clinton, *Printed Ephemera: Collection Organisation and Access* (London: Clive Bingley, 1981), 36.

4 Freedgood, *The Ideas in Things*, 16.

5 Ibid., 25.

6 A more detailed history of St Valentine's Day may be found in Leigh Eric Schmidt, "The Fashioning of a Modern Holiday: St. Valentine's Day, 1840–1870," *Winterthur Portfolio* 28, no. 4 (1993), 209–45.

7 See, for example, "S St. M," "St Valentine's Day," *London Society: An Illustrated Magazine of Light and Amusing Literature for the Hour of Relaxation* 11, no. 62 (Feb., 1867), 113–19 (p. 119).

8 One article of 1881 also observes a connection between the date of St. Valentine's Day and 'Faunus in the Roman Calendar', who is described as 'a rather licentious god', referring to the Folk Lore Society for further illumination on the

coincidence. 'Valentines', *Saturday Review of Politics, Literature, Science and Art* 51, no. 1, 320 (Feb. 12, 1881), 203–204 (p. 204).

9 Charles Lamb, "Valentine's Day," *The Essays of Elia*, Project Gutenberg www.gutenberg.org/files/10343/10343.txt (accessed 5 November 2016).

10 Lamb (accessed 5 November 2016).

11 Ibid.

12 Noted in "S St. M," "St. Valentine's Day," together with other local traditions such as young girls tossing hempseed from a church porch and chanting lines, which was supposed to reveal a ghostly form of a true lover raking up or hoeing the seeds.

13 C.L.E., "About Valentines," *London Society*, 3, no. 2 (Feb., 1863): 97–105 (p. 101).

14 "A Chat about Valentines," *London Society*, 5, no. 27 (Feb., 1864), 178–82 (pp. 179–80).

15 "Valentines for Presentation," T. Chapman, advertisement, *The Graphic* (Feb. 6, 1875), p. 143. ILN database (accessed 28 August 2016).

16 Example from the John Johnson Collection, Bodleian Library. JJ Valentines 7.

17 Valentine from the John Johnson Collection, Bodleian Library, University of Oxford. Box JJ Valentines 7.

18 *A Collection of New and Original Valentines, Serious & Satirical, Sublime & Ridiculous*, on all the ordinary names, professions, trades, etc., With an Introductory Treatise on the Composition of a Valentine, by a *Master of Hearts* (London: Ward and Lock, 1858), 9–10.

19 A Collection of New and Original Valentines, 14.

20 A Collection of New and Original Valentines, 10.

21 Maurice Buxton Foreman, *Some Letters and Miscellanea of Charles Brown* (London: Oxford University Press, 1937), pp. xiii–xiv.

22 W. Cyples, "St. Valentine as a Satirist," *Once a Week*, 3, no. 58 (Feb. 9, 1867), 149.

23 "Comic Valentines," *The Scrap Album*, www.scrapalbum.com/svcomic/svc_p3.htm (accessed 17 March 2015).

24 *Carvalho's Town and Country Valentine Writer, or Lover's Repository, Containing an Entire Collection of All the New and Scarce Valentines & Answers* (London: S. Carvalho, 1820), 8.

25 Chris Hastings, "For the enemy in your life: The vicious Valentine cards that promised endless hate," *Daily Mail* (12 February 2012) www.dailymail.co.uk/news/article-2099901/Valentines-Day-cards-promised-endless-hate--enemy-life.html.

26 Annebella Pollen, "'The valentine has fallen upon evil days': Mocking Victorian Valentines and the Ambivalent Laughter of the Carnivalesque," *Early Popular Visual Culture*, 12, no. 2 (2014), 127–73 (p. 128).

27 According to Frank Staff, *The Valentine and Its Origins* (London: Lutterworth Press, 1969), 42–44.

28 Clinton, *Printed Ephemera*, 15.

29 Freedgood, *The Ideas in Things*, 2.

Works Cited

"Comic Valentines," *The Scrap Album*. Accessed 17 March 2015. www.scrapalbum.com/svcomic/svc_p3.htm.

Carvalho's Town and Country Valentine Writer, or Lover's Repository, Containing an Entire Collection of all the New and Scarce Valentines & Answers. London: S. Carvalho, 1820.

C.L.E. "About Valentines," *London Society* 3, no. 2 (Feb. 1863): 97–105.

Clinton, Alan. *Printed Ephemera: Collection Organisation and Access*. London: Clive Bingley, 1981.

Cyples, W. "St. Valentine as a Satirist," *Once a Week* 3, no., 58 (Feb. 9, 1867): 149.

Foreman, Maurice Buxton. *Some Letters and Miscellanea of Charles Brown*. London: Oxford University Press, 1937.

Freedgood, Elaine. *The Ideas in Things: Fugitive Meaning in the Victorian Novel*. Chicago and London: The University of Chicago Press, 2006.

Hastings, Chris. "For the enemy in your life: The vicious Valentine cards that promised endless hate," *Daily Mail* (12 February 2012). Accessed 17 March 2015. www.dailymail.co.uk/news/article-2099901/Valentines-Day-cards-promised-endless-hate--enemy-life.html.

Lamb, Charles. "Valentine's Day," *The Essays of Elia, Project Gutenberg*. Accessed 5 November 2016. www.gutenberg.org/files/10343/10343.txt.

"M, S St.," "St Valentine's Day," *London Society*, 11, no. 62 (Feb 1867): 113–19.

Pollen, Annebella, "'The valentine has fallen upon evil days': Mocking Victorian Valentines and the Ambivalent Laughter of the Carnivalesque," *Early Popular Visual Culture* 12, no. 2 (2014): 127–73.

Pykett, Lyn, "The Material Turn in Victorian Studies," *Literature Compass*, 1 (2003): 1–5.

Schmidt, Leigh Eric. "The Fashioning of a Modern Holiday: St. Valentine's Day, 1840–1870," *Winterthur Portfolio* 28, no. 4 (1993): 209–45.

Staff, Frank. *The Valentine and Its Origins*. London: Lutterworth Press, 1969.

"Valentines," *Saturday Review of Politics, Literature, Science and Art* 51, no. 1, 320 (Feb 12, 1881): 203–204.

"Valentines for Presentation," T. Chapman, advertisement, *The Graphic* (Feb. 6, 1875), p. 143. ILN database. Accessed 28 August 2016.

13 Exotic Bodies and Mundane Medicines

Advertising and Empire in the Late-Victorian and Edwardian Press[1]

Peter Yeandle

> Wherever we look, we see the same thing. Advertising is universal, and must necessarily be so. It has always existed; but it is only in the last decades of the present century that it is being systematized and treated in an intelligent fashion; [...] press advertising [...] reaches the consumer in the spot where he is most susceptible – his home. No other form of advertising has such opportunities of penetrating into the very sanctum sanctorum of the consumer.
>
> William Stead Junior, *The Art of Advertising* (1899)[2]

By the end of the Victorian period, readership of newspapers had increased significantly because of the onset of mass literacy. Given that newspapers made considerable profit from advertising, and advertisers made ever-increasing use of newspapers to promote their products, it is little surprise that general scholarship identifies this period as a key juncture in histories of consumerism.[3] The removal of stamp duty in 1855 led to a surge in publication of new periodicals and was a vital moment not only in publishing history in general but also for the significance of the press to shape public opinion.[4] However, it was not until the final decades of the century that – in a context of increased disposable income and the active targeting of consumers of all social classes – advertisers fully manipulated the potential of newspapers to promote their products in the very heart of the Victorian home.[5] In terms of business history, this period was pivotal: the 1880s witnessed the expansion of advertising agencies and specialist manuals dedicated to the art of advertising and marketing proliferated.[6] Pictorial advertising benefited from technological developments that drove down the production costs of newspapers, increased the speed of their production, and – crucially for studies into visual culture – increased their scope to incorporate intricate visual material.[7] As Anandi Ramamurthy argues, in discussion of the impact of race on advertising, the 'power of advertising lies not simply in its quantity, but also in its use of the latest technology to bamboozle us with brilliant images.'[8] The final two decades of the nineteenth century are additionally characterized by the attempt to impose imperial propaganda on multiple forms of popular print and visual culture. It seems logical, therefore, that some of the most detailed investigations into late-Victorian and Edwardian advertising situates research within the context of debates about the influence of racial and imperial ideologies on consumer culture.

This essay examines illustrated advertising to revisit precisely that debate; that is, what can the study of advertising suggest about the extent to which imperialism left an imprint on British popular and visual culture? Does the widespread use of militaristic and what we now consider racist adverts – both at the time and subsequently in academic study and museum (online or otherwise) exhibitions – illustrate that empire had reached into the 'very sanctum sanctorum' of the late-Victorian home? Most studies, outlined below, argue that advertisers did indeed use visual iconography to exploit popular imperialism – not only to make their products more appealing to Victorian consumers but, in doing so, to extol their companies' own patriotic credentials. However, scrutiny of a range of newspapers over the course of the 1880s, 1890s, and early 1900s (the period of peak propaganda) reveals that the genus of press advert that might be called *explicitly* imperial was not as commonplace as might be expected. In his recent book, *Empire of Things* (2015), Frank Trentmann observes a similar trend: although late-Victorian imperialism was the crucial period for creation of the citizen-consumer, adverts tended to focus less on the colonial than anticipated. He writes that although 'In the era of 'new imperialism' in the 1880s–1890s, imperial symbols and slogans gained grounds in advertising ... what is noteworthy is not that racial images appear but that they do so far less than we expect.'[9] Trentmann is correct; explicitly imperial adverts feature intermittently rather than consistently. This is not, however, to argue that advertisers did not seek to exploit empire in their promotional materials – they did, and when they did the evidence of the imagery is unequivocal – but that we need to be more alert to why these adverts appeared in some moments and not others.

Below, I sketch out of the significance of thinking about topicality: advertisers clearly responded to the news and sought to position their products in relation to current affairs. When imperial themes dominated the news, adverts followed; when empire was not front-page news, other factors influenced marketing techniques. This line of analysis does not necessarily undermine the argument that explicit imperial discourses shaped advertising practice in key moments of time (as will be shown); rather, it is to suggest that we need to be more alert to how implicit manifestations of imperial ideology affected advertising content. Indeed, closer scrutiny of products that extolled the health and nutritional qualities of mundane medicines and everyday consumables may also be indicative of an imperial culture, albeit a discourse of domestic imperialism significantly less overt than one that one that traded on clear visual demarcations of race and the newsworthiness of military conflict. Adverts for cough medicine, tonics, soap, and meat extracts might not have depicted empire as an explicit selling point (though some did), but – when placed within a wider context of discourses of race, nation, and empire, and especially concern about the future of the Anglo-Saxon 'race' – suggest other ways in which the domestic traces of an imperial ideology shaped patterns of product promotion. In short, the imperial – at times explicit, but often less obvious – can also be detected in the quotidian.

* * *

The Victorian period was dominated by the visual – a 'universal language' of seeing and understanding the world, in Lynda Nead's neat formulation, in which advertising became 'part of the visual fabric' of everyday life.[10] Where there was a public gaze, adverts dominated the eyeline: billboards, hoardings, transportation, leisure venues, the exteriors of buildings, to name but a few. As in the public space of the street, so too in the privacy of the home. In the place of streams of classified texts, technological developments by the end of the century made possible the dominance and creativity of image making – font, picture, iconography – which, in turn, allowed advertisers to appeal to the immediacy of the first glimpse. 'A well laid out advertisement', according to the *Advertisers' Guide to Publicity* (1887), 'frequently creates want, as well as tells people where such can be supplied.'[11] 'Pictorial advertising', according to Stead Junior:

> is the most effective form of advertisement. A picture appeals to all classes of the community whether educated or uneducated. Anyone can understand a picture. A man may not be able to read his ABC but he can recognise the meaning of a picture as soon as his eye sees it.[12]

Advertisers made use of techniques used by the press to incorporate more intricate imagery. The author of *Successful Advertising* identified the trend towards the dominance of the visual in 1878: 'Anyone who has followed the developments in advertisements will be struck by the immense increase in the number of illustrated advertisements. Not long ago whole page advertisements consisted nine tenths of type matter only. Now it is the other way.'[13] This was the period of the mass circulation of the illustrated press – the *Illustrated London News* and the *Graphic*, catering for those who could afford 6 pence an issue, were followed by the penny and half penny *Penny Illustrated Paper* and *Daily Mail* (from 1896) for those who couldn't, all of which recorded huge advertising revenues. Stead Junior documents that by 1900, money spent on advertising in London alone equated to millions, approximately 9 shillings per year, per citizen; or more 'than was spent on the campaign which destroyed the power of the Khalifa' in 1898, or 'the total public expenditure of Ceylon or Natal.'[14] In the final decades of the nineteenth century, newspaper advertising was big business and the use of images were core to that process.

It was surely no accident that Stead Junior, writing in 1899, drew a contrast between the cost of advertising and the costs of (recent front-page) colonial warfare and colonial administration in Asia and Africa. The last two decades of the nineteenth century were not just significant in terms of media history, they were also a period of intense imperial propaganda. A series of studies have demonstrated that imperialism featured heavily in Victorian print and visual culture; this included 'official' sites such as school textbooks and the carefully manufactured use of the image of Victoria herself, as well as the increasingly profitable commercial fields of juvenile literature, the commodification of celebrities, and performance culture.[15] If the Porter-MacKenzie debate about the extent of the reach of such propagandistic intentions into public consciousness is yet fully to be resolved, nonetheless the evidence from previous scholarly research into the relationship between race, empire, and advertising seems to support MacKenzie's interpretation; not only that imperialism was a core ingredient of late-Victorian and Edwardian public and private life, but that the public was broadly susceptible to imperial propaganda.[16] Important books by Anandi Ramamurthy (*Imperial Persuaders*), Thomas Richards (*Commodity Culture of Victorian England*), and Anne McClintock *(Imperial Leather)* all testify to a prevailing influence of racial and imperial ideology on companies and their marketing strategies.[17] Printed anthologies of Victorian advertising tend to substantiate such conclusions – the most immediately obvious is Robert Opie's *Rule Britannia: Trading on the British Image* (1985).[18] These books, collating explicitly imperial images, draw our attention to how adverts and product packaging recycled and reaffirmed symbols of imperial conquest – racial bodies, exotic animals, military prowess, technological superiority, domestication of wild landscapes – in their attempts to promote soft consumer commodities such as tea, chocolate, cigarettes, and soap. These accounts argue companies sought commercially to exploit imperial tropes to make their product more desirable to potential consumers; the inference is that these explicitly imperial adverts indicate a popular acceptance of, and perhaps even enthusiasm for, empire. Moreover, the argument that late-Victorian advertising was dominated by racist and colonial imagery persists because of the prevalence of such advertising in museum exhibitions and in online repositories.[19]

The narrative of the chronological commingling of mass media, mass consumerism, and imperial ideology is seductive. When present, imperialist iconography is unambiguous. In a notorious Pears soap advert, a black child is washed and, in the process, becomes civilized (more comment below). Tea adverts, with the backdrop of Indian elephants, women in indigenous costume, and semi-naked male plantation workers, position British settlers and dignitaries at the forefront of the image.[20] A cigarette is reshaped to depict a Gatlin gun. A smorgasbord of products, from edibles such as biscuits, cocoa, and baking powder through to relative luxuries – watches, hearth rugs, camping equipment – are endorsed by the recommendation of imperial heroes. Henry Morton Stanley, the explorer, is used to sell bootlaces, jewellery and cough remedies (and a whole lot more) upon his return from the Emin Pasha relief expedition in 1890.[21] Kitchener's face is emblazoned across adverts for cigarettes, razors and whiskey following his military success defeating the Khalifa at Omdurman (1898).[22] His iconic moustache made manly products manlier (and this was *before* that First World War recruitment poster).[23] Villains are defeated, their 'only solace' – in the words of one advert – their access to British commodities, symbolizing the global exportation of British manufactures as central to the imperial mission.[24]

* * *

Defining what a visual manifestation of the 'imperial' might look like, however, is not such a straightforward task. Indeed, central to the dispute between Porter and MacKenzie is the methodological question of what, precisely, constitutes evidence. For Porter, historians have fallen into the trap of knowing their arguments before they know their archive; his refrain, that 'it will not simply do to look for 'imperial' evidence without being aware of what lies around it',[25] is valuable in the context of the study of pictorial advertising. Porter's observation is particularly relevant here since studies into advertising and imperialism tend to highlight and analyse those sources that take as a start point imperial content. Porter recognizes that, from the 1880s, 'the empire appeared in advertisements' at a frequency and 'intensity' that was new. This is certainly the case: opportunities afforded by technological improvements to printing images gave advertisers more scope to illustrate the exotic. Nonetheless, Porter reduces such imagery to 'trivia' and his two sentences on the topic do not sufficiently address an issue that might otherwise have partially substantiated his argument.[26] Adverts with no immediately obvious link to the empire vastly outnumbered those that thumped the jingo drum.

I have used three broad indicators to determine explicitly 'imperial': the use of stereotypes in racial iconography suggestive of white superiority; celebratory representation of the British abroad as explorers and members of the armed forces, centred not only on the hero figure of the leader but the ordinary Tommy; and, the visual appropriation of the flora and fauna of colonial places to show British control over territory and raw material as well as people.

Studying the illustrated press from between 1882 and 1902 confirms that adverts were responsive to current affairs; trading on the ideology of imperialism and the image of the empire at key moments in which the empire was at the forefront of the news agenda. The key point to emphasize is that empire featured explicitly in advertisements when empire dominated headlines. Analysis of some of the most frequently seen adverts confirms their contemporaneity. Illustrated papers carried adverts in which stereotypes of Africans, as either primitive and childlike or barbaric and therefore requiring the civilising touch of Europeans, were used as visual shorthand for the promotion of British goods. In December 1884, one of the most famous and retrospectively controversial of Victorian advertisements (use an internet image search for Victorian racism and advertising) was first published in the *Graphic*: a Pears soap advert presented a scene in which a black child is washed white. This image, analysed in depth in several key studies,[27] reveals much about racial attitudes. Not only is cleanliness and civilization associated with whiteness, but the black child is depicted as subject to the white child's influence. When clean, the black boy examines his complexion and is happy, his contentment the result of the white child's intervention. The advert was published while the Berlin Conference was ongoing. At this conference, European powers, previously engaged in competition with one another over African territory and raw materials, agreed effectively to partition the continent. The advert is an explicit topical reference to imperial policy, reifying racial attitudes to the 'Dark Continent', and confirming the product as a symbol of a civilising mission. The image, as Ramamurthy informs, formed the template of an advertising trope repeated in press and others forms of advertising for over two decades.[28] As indicated in Ramamurthy's analysis of newspapers, the trope of 'washing black white' was adopted by multiple companies including Vinolia, Cooks, and Sunlight.[29]

Later in the 1880s, British colonial wars in Egypt and the Sudan set a context for even more explicit references to race. A Pears Soap advert (Figure 13.1) – 'The Formula of British Conquest' – found in the *ILN* (27 August 1887), the *Graphic* (30 July 1887), as well as other papers on multiple occasions across several weeks, depicts 'dervishes', appearing animalistic, looking at a rock structure on which is embossed 'PEARS SOAP IS THE BEST.' This image is reproduced in Ramamurthy and McClintock, and an adapted version of it from 1890 is found in Richards.[30] Following Ramamurthy's observations, this advert depicts several explicitly imperial themes: the product appeals to the Christian justification of imperial expansion – Africans are presented as defeated savages who have laid down their weapons, now reminiscent of biblical shepherds bowing not to the Angel Gabriel but to the supremacy of the white British product.

PEARS' SOAP IN THE SOUDAN.
"Even if our invasion of the Soudan has done nothing else it has at any rate left the Arab some-thing to puzzle his fuzzy head over, for the legend
PEARS' SOAP IS THE BEST,
inscribed in hugh white characters on the rock which marks the farthest point of our advance towards Berber, will tax all the wits of the Dervishes of the Desert to translate."—Phil Robinson, *War Correspondent* (*in the Soudan*) *of the Daily Telegraph in London,* 1884.

Figure 13.1 'The Formula of British Conquest.' *Illustrated London News* (27 August 1887). Source: Image courtesy of Mary Evans Picture Library.

The landscape situates the product as dominating over alien terrain, bringing light to space that might otherwise be empty but for the dark presence of African skin. Newspaper readers will have recalled the death of General Gordon, in 1885, at the hands of the Mahdists, and recalled also the fierce religious rhetoric of a war of Christian civilization pitched against African barbarism. The text information at the bottom, quoting a war correspondent, confirms that Pears extended as far as the British army but, unlike the military, not only endured where Gordon had failed but exerted influence:

> Even if our invasion of the Soudan has done nothing else it has at any rate left the Arab something to puzzle his fuzzy head over, for the legend PEARS SOAP IS THE BEST, inscribed in high white characters on the rock marks the farthest point of our advance.

Clearly the advert manipulated the image of the racial body to situate the product within an imperial discourse. If the 1884 advert showed Pears washing black skin white, here it was sanitising a continent. However, as will be shown later, discourses of cleanliness and hygiene need not always refer to differences in the colour of the skin of human subjects.

Moreover, advertisers exploited the topicality of warfare as front-page news. Richard Fulton's excellent study of Kitchener and the 'Sudan Sensation' of 1898 (Stead Junior's defeating the Khalifa moment) powerfully argues that, in the context of a media-driven obsession with the east African campaigns, advertising formed a vibrant part of a visual broadcast culture. Companies helped sustain enthusiasm for war and, in doing so, positioned themselves as central to heroization of Kitchener and the commercial exploitation of his image.[31] At the time of the second Boer War, advertisers positioned their products as central to all aspects of the war effort.[32] As the British public demanded instantaneous news,[33] Bovril was keen to use its adverts to *tell* the news as well as react to it. Bovril was 'liquid' life that provided comfort to wounded soldiers and its logo was frequently emblazoned on images of field hospitals in adverts.[34] This was important in a context of news returning home of poor conditions and military retreats – more on this below. Its nutritional qualities were used to endorse its central role in sustaining the British military effort. At the time of the Relief of Mafeking a whole page spread in the *Daily Mail* (24 September 1900) – citing testimonies from 'doctors, nurses, officers, soldiers, and newspaper correspondents' (including the household names of Baden-Powell and Kipling) – extolled Bovril's virtues and its 'part in the South African War.' The advert mimics the layout of news pages and editorial; the advert *is* the news. In other advert styles, small display ads were used but nonetheless the message was immediate and effective: in once instance of many, when reservists were being called to the front in October 1899, Bovril declared itself to be 'an unfailing reserve force' (*Daily Mail*, 21 October 1899; see Figure 13.2). In March 1900, the letters that spelled out BOVRIL were embossed on a map of South Africa showing it was an essential ingredient in Lord Roberts' march across the country to relieve besieged British troops at Kimberley. The text of the advert reads: 'This extraordinary coincidence is one more proof of the universality of Bovril, which has already figured so conspicuously throughout the South African campaign' (*Illustrated London News*, 28 March 1900). It was no extraordinary coincidence that Bovril should adopt such a tactic. The advert was a clever piece of graphic trickery entirely consistent with a product that had positioned itself as an essential ingredient in improving and sustaining British military fortunes. Patriotism sold.

Bovril was not alone in seeking to make gain by aligning itself with up to the minute news. An advert for Pioneer tobacco published in the *ILN* on 3 March 1900 depicted John Bull, carton of cigarettes in one hand and union flag in the other, in debate with Paul Kruger (the Boer leader). John Bull declares: 'I'm here and civilisation is coming so you'd better come to terms' – clearly a play on the week's news about how the Ladysmith siege had been relieved and that the Boers were seeking dialogue. Ogden's cigarettes ran a series of adverts in which their product was labelled a 'comrade' to men at the front, selling the product as both an ally of troops but also a method for consumers at home also to show solidarity. One example demonstrates the extent to which the company tapped into topical affairs. On 4 January 1901, an advert in the *Daily Mail* – appearing also in the *Illustrated London News* the next day – simply contained a sketch outline of Roberts and read 'Unbeaten.' Roberts, established as a war hero not only for leadership in South Africa but previously in Afghanistan and India, had returned to Britain. The press was awash with reports of fanfare and ceremony. The advert clearly sought to exploit the mood of the moment.[35]

It would be possible to pick out hundreds of other examples of advertising reflecting current affairs, and several scholars – as indicated – do so. These adverts include images of exotic animals, such as in Huntley and Palmer's biscuits which depict the tiger hunt in northern India (and reconstructing multiple images of the royal tour to India in 1889–1890 that saturated the illustrated press). Examples can easily be found of racial stereotyping demonstrating that advertisers not only used visual technologies to illustrate visual contrast between the British colonizer and the African colonized: for instance, Indians and Chinese were frequently included in images used to sell tea and other exotic products. Moreover, a common trope of the trade carton deposited in wild landscapes appears in many adverts for multiple products: cargo of tea, soap, biscuits, cigarettes, and so on are seen in a series of locations – in chronological tandem with military adventures or feats of exploration – ranging from the tropical African jungle to the mountainous north of India, from the Persian desert to the Antarctic. The consistent visual message is that products not only advanced into new territory as empire expanded, but that products were part of the civilization of the wild and reinforced white British superiority. Studies that focus on race and colonial advertising tend to hold these up as examples of soap advertising in general. Likewise, studies that investigate advertising at time of war do not have to search too hard to find examples of products positioning themselves as central to the war effort. Following Porter's critique, it is all too easy – especially in an age of digitized newspapers in which use of specific search terms rapidly speed up the research process making possible direct searches rather than page-by-page reading – to find adverts that unashamedly utilized explicitly imperial themes.

* * *

Yet, the question of typicality remains. Of course, the existence of these adverts confirms that companies did exploit imperialism to make their product more appealing to the consumer; they reckoned that spectacular visually arresting images could persuade consumers to choose their brand over another. Soap advertising, albeit in a context of enhanced technologies of visual iconography, was well placed to reproduce ideologies of racial difference, yet did not commonly resort to racial imagery. Cigarette companies may well, in Mike Dempsey's words, have exploited the fact that 'war offered a heaven-sent opportunity for tobacco manufacturers to produce advertising which would both increase sales and express appropriately patriotic sentiments.'[36] However cigarettes, at other times and even in times of war, played mostly on other themes of masculinity. Meat extract products, such as in the case of Bovril, manipulated wartime conditions to emphasize its health and energy-giving properties. But, overall, questions of nutrition and health led to advertisements that played on cost and quality to emphasize value-for-money approaches to raising vigorous children in times of poverty.

What other discourses determined the subject of advertising? Here, I want to explore key marketing hooks of 'health' and 'nutrition' since these dominate the context of advertising. It is possible, especially around the context of the Boer War, to identify aspects of social imperialism not fully considered in a literature concerned to analyse spectacular visualizations of empire. Can adverts – not overtly imperial – nonetheless testify to an influence of imperialism on social life?

At the time of the Boer War, Britain was gripped by a panic about public health. A third of volunteer recruits was deemed unfit to serve, a statistic made worse by revelations that volunteers from the smoke cities of the north were suffering from all sorts of physical weaknesses caused by poor nutrition.[37] In Manchester, for instance, 8,000 out 11,000 would-be volunteers were rejected after medical testing.[38] News from the front during the first months of war further reinforced a sense of national decline (already at panic levels due to existential threats posed by the rise of Germany as a competitor nation): not only was Britain being heavily defeated by a foe she was expected to easily crush, but British troops were suffering through poor leadership. Of the 22,000 recorded British deaths in southern Africa, less than a third took place on the battlefield.

According to Anne Summers, the neglect of soldiers, the overcrowded and inadequately staffed field hospitals, and deaths caused by 'preventable diseases', served to provoke heated national debate about the nation's and, by extension, empire's, strength.[39] If war was a test of national fitness, Britain was obviously failing. It is little surprise that, in such a context, companies like Bovril and Ogdens sought to promote their goods by extolling their contribution to the health and morale of troops. Ogdens, as seen, was a 'comrade.' Bovril was 'liquid life', positioning itself as central – as we have seen – to the war effort. One particular Bovril advert, published in the *ILN* on 24 February 1900 and with the widely reported news of significant British fatalities at Spion Kop fresh in the public mind, depicts an injured soldier recovering from injury and sipping Bovril. The text of the advert states that Bovril is 'assisting the recovery of wounded soldiers' by giving 'life to the soldier faint from loss of blood.' Here, in the absence of nurses on the front line, the product stood in for female care. When British military fortunes turned following the relief of the siege at Kimberley, Bovril proudly declared in an advert in the *Daily Mail* (7 March 1900) that it doubled its sales in the calendar year; 'a remarkable result' the text of the advert ran, especially since the company had donated 'large quantities ... to the Government for use in Hospital tents in South Africa.' Clearly, Bovril's alliance with the war effort had reaped financial rewards. In January 1901, around the time of relatively successful British offensives, an advert entitled 'Bovril is in a class by itself', the company boasted that 'Bovril has played such a conspicuous part in South Africa that it forms no inconsiderable feature of the story of the Campaign.' The advert included endorsements from the *Lancet*, the Royal Army Medical Corps, scientists, and physicians, and explained Bovril's vital role 'as nourisher as well as stimulant' *(Daily Mail, 25 January 1901).*

Bovril's commercial success, by its own definition, owed to its self-positioning as fundamental to the health and strength of the war effort. Figure 13.2, published around the major military success at Mafeking, emphasized the point in a full-page advert: Bovril's qualities are not only endorsed by the household names of Baden-Powell and Kipling, but by unnamed medical experts, hospitals commissions and the Red Cross. When Britain was not at war, Bovril's health-giving properties remained central to its promotional message. Scanning the pages of newspapers before and after the war – and even during – shows the much greater frequency of adverts not extolling the product's explicit imperial values. Several clear tropes emerge: Bovril was affordable and was for cooking and consuming; thus, adverts emphasized nutritional value in the domestic sphere as well as the field of battle. Images of children, the elderly, and the infirm made healthy by their consumption of the value-for-money product are commonplace. Bovril associated itself with physical fitness campaigns – both at the level of debate about policy towards child health – but also seeking endorsements from famous athletes and strongmen.[40]

Figure 13.2 'Bovril's Part in the South African War', *Daily Mail* (24 September 1900). Source: Used with permission of Solo Syndication on behalf of the *Daily Mail*.

Emphasis on value, nutrition, and strength is no surprise. Food accounted for a third of working-class expenditure in 1900.[41] Poverty surveys had revealed shocking levels of malnutrition,[42] a concern exacerbated at the time by those reports of the medical failings of would-be recruits. During the war, Bovril emphasized it was assisting troops in a fight against ill health and inadequate nourishment as well as a fight against the Boer enemy.[43] At home, it did likewise. A multitude of adverts urged consumers to buy Bovril, not only for its value for money, but because of its medicinal properties; a stream of adverts declare Bovril waging war on influenza, rickets, hunger, and the cold (see, for instance, the list of medical authorities testifying that Bovril can combat ill health in Figure 13.2). Beecham's pills, similarly, sought credit for war success. In a full-page advert reflecting on the relieved sieges at Kimberley and Ladysmith, the advert (*Daily Mail*, 13 April 1900) was entitled 'For this Relief, Much Thanks.' The advert's dense text is informative: 'An instructive comparison may be drawn between the power and vitality of an Empire and the personal wellbeing of an individual ... the enemies of that Empire of Health, which should be the birth right of each of us are many.' Having associated the Boers with bacteria and contagion, Beecham's declared to the reader that 'you may therefore unhesitatingly and at once put Beecham's pills into supreme command if you are threatened by an invasion.' In the *ILN* the following day the same image was used in an advert propounding: 'Guard Yourself.' As in the Bovril examples, Beecham's allied itself to the war effort, utilising contemporaneous concerns about troops' health to promote its health-giving properties for the wider population. For the majority of the time, however, its advertising related to the domestic context – images dominated of once ill and now healthy children, recovered mothers, and the elderly and infirm made better.

Much the same pattern is evident in techniques used to promote tea and cocoa. Both the UK Tea Company and Lipton's, frequently seen in adverts being drunk by explorers in the jungles of equatorial Africa or as respite during a tiger hunt in India, consistently accentuated their purity and quality in promotional materials.[44] The location of the home was just as commonly seen in adverts as the colonial landscape. Cadbury's, likewise, tapped into consumer demand for nutritional drinks. Indeed, a series of studies have confirmed that chocolate broke into the British market as a drink precisely because it could market itself as tasty, nutritious, and medicinal. Martha Makra Graziano asserts that cocoa became a nineteenth-century health food and medicine.[45] Advertising bears this out. In 1906, as the government empowered Local Education Authorities to provide milk at school, Cadbury's ran a series of advertisements entitled 'A Word to Mothers.' One advert shows a healthy-looking mother holding a healthy-looking child, allowing the child to drink from her cup. The text of the advert states: 'There is little to choose between Cadbury's absolutely pure cocoa essence and milk, so closely allied are they in composition. It is highly nourishing, and as a daily beverage for growing children it is unexcelled' (*ILN*, 10 March 1906).

Several key themes have become clear. At times of war, companies exploited military contexts to market their products; at times in which race was under discussion, racial imagery was used. While some of the more mundane adverts cited here do not tend to feature in scholarship, it is images with unambiguous racial demarcations that have been the most commonly reproduced as examples of late-Victorian advertising. Yet, attention to health and nutrition reveals to us that advertisers manipulated fears about the racial health of the British (Anglo-Saxons in some phrasing) to sell their goods, and that these tropes dominated. This is not a surprise: concern about national health led to contemporary demands for 'national efficiency' – that is, state intervention to raise up the quality of British racial stock (no pun intended). The working-class mother, moreover, was subject to an onslaught of advertising reminding her of her responsibility to her children. Schools were required to teach girls in the skills of motherhood; the 'foremost duty' of women, according to one education manual, was 'protecting the quality and ensuring the continuance of the English race, nation and empire by being a good mother.'[46] Anna Davin's meticulous research into state attempts to influence women's behaviour demonstrates how the raising of healthy children became a 'matter of imperial importance.'[47] In a context in which national unease was high already, the results of studies showing a declining birth rate contributed to increased anxiety about Britain's future strength. Advertising exploited this trepidation, seeking to 'sensationalize parental fears' (in Lori Anne Loeb's words) to emphasize the necessity of their nutritional and healthy goods.[48] Emphasis on mothers as consumers reflected the fact that women were the most likely consumers of domestic goods. Indeed, as Loeb has shown, women were the 'clear audience for most nineteenth-century advertisements' and were subjected to 'all the puffery and paraphernalia that a Victorian consumer society could supply.' Advertisers, Loeb demonstrates, operated on the basis that 'the hand that rocks the cradle is the hand that buys the boots.'[49]

This observation is substantiated by advertising for condensed formula milk. Despite concern at the time about insufficient breast feeding and germ-riddled bottle teats, adverts exhorting mothers to buy condensed milk to feed their young were commonplace, and increasingly so in the first decade of the twentieth century.[50] The high employment rate of working-class mothers created a market ripe for exploitation. Allenburys, for instance, frequently reproduced images of idyllic scenes of contented, rested mothers and bouncing babies. In 1899, Allenburys staple slogan was launched: 'a progressive dietary, unique in providing nourishment suited to the growing digestive powers of young infants from birth upwards' (*Graphic*, 16 September 1899). That line of persuasion remained, though as the state took an increased role in the wellbeing of children through registrations of births, medical testing, and provision of milk in schools, advertising techniques subtly altered. In 1907, Allenburys appealed to mothers of newborns explicitly to give their child the best head start in life, and that included preparing them for school: 'mothers should early recognize how essential good health is for the success of their child' (*ILN*, 3 August 1907). Advertising responded to government insistence on breastfeeding. In 1905, an advert insisted that 'Allenburys milk foods are similar in composition to and are as easy of digestion as maternal milk' (*Daily Mail*, 4 May 1905). Full-page spreads, citing expert after expert and displaying growth charts documenting the health of babies raised on formula milk, were produced. In one such advert, advice is given on all aspects of child rearing and self-care for the mother. Published at the time the Children Act was passing through parliament, it is no surprise that the advert emphasized Allenburys was a useful ally in the protection of and raising of healthy children (*Daily Mail*, 11 August 1908). There is nothing explicitly imperial about these adverts; nor there is there anything immediately racial in the text of these adverts. Understood in the context of widespread debate and discussion about the racial health of the nation, however, these adverts take on new meaning since they propounded women's civic and patriotic responsibilities to raise future citizens of the empire. Advertising that appealed to health, especially the health of children, was part of a wider discourse of imperialism – one that dominated domestic discussion about Britain's national and imperial wellbeing, and one that marketing companies knew how to exploit just as effectively as they did conditions of war or moments in which questions of racial difference were at the forefront of public debate.

* * *

There are several conclusions we can draw from this preliminary study, and several ways in which these findings can inform future research. First, more analysis needs to be undertaken that understands women as the primary targets of advertising companies and the main consumers of advertising. Indeed, the preponderance of advertising for health, hygiene, and nutritional products need to be evaluated as part of a wider investigation of the reach of domestic discourses of imperial ideology. This is especially the case since advertisers evidently targeted women's gendered obligations to home and nation and, by extension, empire. Second, the increase in imperial tropes used in advertising is clear; when empire was front-page news (and there was a lot of newsworthy imperial stories in this period) advertisers exploited current affairs to help make their products more appealing to consumers. Yet, focus on 'race' as a core component of imperialism suggests that although some advertising sought to exploit racial difference to sell their products, many other examples (often by the same companies) instead situated their promotional pitch to consumers in the context of the racial health of the British. By searching for and finding the 'ordinary' we can identify additional ways in which contemporary languages of imperialism, through the illustrated press, formed a central part of late-Victorian and Edwardian consumer culture. Third, then, the value of adverts as historical sources should not be decided merely by the extent to which they illustrate explicit imperial themes. In the twenty-first century, we are mad for Victoriana, and we appear particularly fascinated by late-Victorian racism. Perhaps, on the one hand, these artefacts of an age long gone serve as reassurance that we, as cultured moderns, have progressed beyond the reprehensible worldview of our ancestors. On the other hand, studies that have looked for empire in adverts – and have found it in visual representations of race difference and militarism – serve an important function in reminding us just how embedded such racist stereotypes were and, in some cases, remain.

I began this essay with a quotation from William Stead Junior's advertising manual. It is apposite to conclude with another. 'The newspaper', Stead Junior wrote, 'is a microcosm of national life. A glance over the advertising columns of a large morning paper shows reflected, as it were, in a mirror, the whole of the active life of the people.'[51] The study of a range of adverts in the context of their responsivity to the news proves Stead Junior's observation to be insightful. Based on ideas explored in this essay, one might speculate that adverts did not need to be explicitly imperial to indicate an enduring influence of imperialism on consumer culture generally.

Notes

1 This essay is part of a larger study of the advertising content of several national newspapers between 1882 and 1902. Findings presented here are speculative. Please email the author for further information. I'd like to thank students at Manchester and Loughborough who studied my third-year module on popular imperialism and popular culture, especially Matthew Foukes whose subsequent dissertation on advertising history I supervised.

2 W. Stead Junior, *The Art of Advertising: Its Theory and Practice Fully Described* (London: T.B. Browne, 1899), 17, 25.

3 John Benson, *The Rise of Consumer Society in Britain, 1880–1980* (London: Longman, 1994). For a general history of advertising, see Diana Hindley and Geoffrey Hindley, *Advertising in Victorian England, 1837–1901* (London: Wayland, 1972) and Terence Nevett, *Advertising in Britain: A History* (London: Heinemann, 1982). On the economic history of advertising, and the debate about chronological turning points, see Roy Church, "Advertising consumer goods in nineteenth-century Britain: new perspectives," *Economic History Review*, 13, no. 4 (2000): 621–45.

4 Martin Hewitt, *The Dawn of the Cheap Press in Victorian Britain: The End of the 'Taxes on Knowledge', 1849–1869* (London: Bloomsbury Academic, 2014).

5 Paul Johnson, "Conspicuous consumption and working-class culture in late-Victorian and Edwardian Britain," *Transactions of the Royal Historical Society*, no. 38 (1998): 27–42.

6 For more on the professionalization of advertising agencies, see Hindleys, *Advertising in Victorian England*, 27–41. See also Jane Chapman, *Comparative Media History* (Cambridge: Polity, 2005), 87–88.

7 John Hewitt, "Designing the Poster in England, 1890–1914," *Early Popular Visual Culture*, 5, no. 1 (2007): 57–70.

8 Anandi Ramamurthy, *Imperial Persuaders: Images of Africa and Asia in British Advertising* (Manchester: Manchester University Press, 2003), 1.

9 Frank Trentmann, *Empire of Things: How We Became a World of Consumers, from the Fifteenth Century to the Twenty-First* (London: Allen Lane, 2015), 171.

10 Lynda Nead, *Victorian Babylon: People, Streets and Images in Nineteenth-Century London* (New Haven: Yale University Press, 2000), 59, 58; M. Meisel, *Realizations: Narrative, Pictorial, and Theatrical Arts in Nineteenth-Century England* (Princeton: Princeton University Press, 1983).

11 Quoted in the Hindleys, *Advertising in Victorian England*, 29.

12 Stead Junior, *Art of Advertising*, 98.

13 Quoted in the Hindleys, *Advertising in Victorian England*, 67.

14 Stead Junior, *Art of Advertising*, 134.

15 Peter Yeandle, *Citizenship, Nation, Empire: The Politics of History Teaching in England* (Manchester: Manchester University Press, 2015); John Plunkett, *Queen Victoria: First Media Monarch* (Oxford: Oxford University Press, 2003); Michelle Smith, *Empire in British Girls' Literature: Imperial Girls, 1880–1920* (Basingstoke: Palgrave, 2011); Marty Gould, *Nineteenth-Century Theatre and the Imperial Encounter* (London: Routledge, 2011); Berny Sèbe, *Heroic Imperialists in Africa: The Promotion of British and French Colonial Heroes, 1870–1939* (Manchester: Manchester University Press, 2013).

16 John MacKenzie, *Propaganda and Empire: The Manipulation of British Public Opinion* (Manchester: Manchester University Press, 1984); Bernard Porter, *The Absent-Minded Imperialists: What the British Really Thought about Empire* (Oxford: Oxford University Press, 2004). To my mind, one of the most useful assessments of the debate remains Stuart Ward's 'Echoes of Empire', *History Workshop Journal* 62, no. 1 (2006): 264–78.

17 Ramamurthy, *Imperial Persuaders*; Thomas Richards, *The Commodity Culture of Victorian England: Advertising and Spectacle* (Stanford: Stanford University Press, 1991), ch. 3 'Selling Darkest Africa.' Anne McClintock, *Imperial Leather: Race, Gender and Sexuality in the Colonial Context* (New York and London: Routledge, 1995), ch. 5, 'Soft Soaping Empire: commodity racism and imperial advertising'.

18 Robert Opie, *Rule Britannia: Trading on the British Image* (London: Viking, 1985). See also the selection of images in Ashley Jackson and David Tomkins, *Illustrating Empire: A Visual History of British Imperialism* (Oxford: Bodleian Library, 2011).

19 See, for instance, the book to accompany to Bodleian's exhibition on the visual culture of empire: Ashley Jackson and David Tomkins, *Illustrating Empire*. See also the advertisingarchives.co.uk website in which the reader is invited to search by categories, one of which is race (accessed June 27, 2017).

20 Anandi Ramamurthy, "Absences and Silences: The representations of the tea picker in colonial and fairtrade advertising," *Visual Culture in Britain*, 13, no. 3 (2012): 367–81.

21 The press was awash with all things Stanley and, subsequently, 'Stanleymania.' In an early nod towards the consumption of the 'celebrity' there's an interesting blurring between Stanley as the promotional hook for selling the object and the object as the hook to sell Stanley. See Richards, *Commodity Culture*, 122–31; Felix Driver, *Geography Militant: Culture of Exploration and Empire* (Oxford: Blackwell, 2001), ch.6; Clare Pettitt, "Exploration in Print: from the miscellany to the newspaper," in *Reinterpreting Exploration: The West in the World*, ed. Dane Kennedy (Oxford: Oxford University Press, 2014), 80–108.

22 Professional endorsements were a key technique used by advertisers to demonstrate the superiority of one brand over another. Lori Anne Loeb observes the gradual replacement by the turn of the century of the medical or scientific authority by the celebrity, including military and explorer heroes. *Consuming Angels: Advertising and Victorian Women* (New York and Oxford: Oxford University Press, 1994), ch. 4: 'The Hero for Sale.'

23 Keith Surridge, "More than a great poster: Lord Kitchener and the image of the military hero," *Historical Research*, 74, no. 185 (2001): 298–313.

24 This example relates to an advert in the *Graphic* (28 April 1900) by Ogden's Guinea-Gold cigarette in which Cronje, a Boer general, is captured and made a prisoner of war. Like many adverts, the image was reused and to be seen in multiple publications across several weeks. See Richards, *Commodity Culture*, 160–61.

25 Porter, *Absent-Minded Imperialists*, 13.

26 Porter, *Absent-Minded Imperialists*, 179.

27 See Ramamurthy, *Imperial Persuaders*, 26–30; McClintock, *Imperial Leather*, 213–15.

28 Ramamurthy, *Imperial Persuaders*, 28.

29 Ramamurthy develops analysis into gendered representations of the black body in soap advertising, finding African men 'were depicted as helpless babies and African women were represented as happy in servitude.' *Imperial Persuaders*, 60.

30 For detailed analysis, see Ramamurthy, *Imperial Persuaders*, 37–40 and McClintock, *Imperial Leather*, 225–26. Richards, *Commodity Culture*, 140–42.

31 Richard Fulton, "The Sudan Sensation," *Victorian Periodicals Review*, 42, no. 1 (2009): 37–63.

32 As Simon Popple argues, the second Boer War was perhaps the first genuinely media war: news from the front arrived rapidly, theatres and music halls responded in near real-time, and images circulated widely. Understood as part of this culture in which in which the visual reproduced and negotiated the most up-to-date news, it is possible further to advance the claim of topicality. Simon Popple, "'Fresh from the Front': performance, war news and popular culture during the Boer War," *Early Popular Visual Culture*, 8, no. 4 (2010): 401–18.

33 Kenneth Morgan, "The Boer War and the media (1899–1902)," *Twentieth-Century British History*, 13, no. 1 (2002): 1–13. See also Paula Krebs, *Gender, Race and the Writing of Empire: Public Discourse and the Boer War* (Cambridge: Cambridge University Press, 1999).

34 In addition to Richards, *Commodity Culture*, 158, McClintock, *Imperial Leather*, 226, see: Glenn Wilkinson, "'To the Front': British Newspaper Advertising and the Boer War," in *The Boer War: Direction, Experience, Image*, ed. John Gooch (London: Routledge, 2013 ed.), 203–12; Lesley Steinitz, "Bovril: A very beefy (and British) love affair," www.cam.ac.uk/research/news/bovril-a-very-beefy-and-british-love-affair, 5 July 2013 (accessed 25 June 2017).

35 'British-made' was a line frequently used by cigarette manufacturers. This takes on added significance in the context of attempted American buyout of British tobacco companies. See Matthew Hilton, *Smoking in British Popular Culture, 1800–2000: Perfect Pleasures* (Manchester: Manchester University Press, 2000), 86; Frank Trentmann, *Free Trade Nation: Commerce, Consumption, and Civil Society in Modern Britain* (Oxford: Oxford University Press, 2009), 29.

36 Mike Dempsey, *Pipe Dreams: Early Advertising Art from the Imperial Tobacco Company* (London: Pavilion, 1982), 40.

37 Anna Davin, "Imperialism and Motherhood," *History Workshop Journal,* no. 5 (1978): 15–16.

38 Geoffrey Searle, *The Quest for National Efficiency: A Study in British Politics and Political Thought, 1899–1914* (Oxford: Blackwell, 1971), 60–61.

39 Anne Summers, *Angels and Citizens: British Women as Military Nurses, 1854–1914* (London: Routledge, 1988), 205–206.

40 Steinitz, "Bovril: A very beefy (and British) love affair"; David Waller, *The Perfect Man: The Muscular Life and Times of Eugen Sandow, Victorian Strongman* (Brighton: Victorian Secrets, 2011). In 1904, Bovril published an advert containing text from a letter of gratitude from the Antarctic explorer Robert Falcon Scott. Scott lauded Bovril as 'excellent', giving 'every satisfaction', helping keep the men sustained in the cold. *Daily Mail,* 8 November 1904.

41 Martin Daunton, *Wealth and Welfare: An Economic and Social History of Britain* (Oxford: Oxford University Press, 2007), 420.

42 Derek Oddy, "Working-Class Diets in late nineteenth-century Britain," *Economic History Review,* no. 23 (1970): 314–23.

43 On supplies available to troops, see Edward Spiers, *The Victorian Soldier in Africa* (Manchester: Manchester University Press, 2004), 160.

44 In addition to Ramamurthy, *Imperial Persuaders,* 93–130, see Julie Fromer, *A Necessary Luxury: Tea in Victorian England* (Athens: Ohio University Press, 2008).

45 Martha Makra Graziano, "Food of the Gods as Mortals' Medicine: the uses of chocolate and cacao products," *Pharmacy in* History, 40, no. 4 (1988): 132–46.

46 Cited in Stephen Heathorn, *For Home, Country, and Race: Constructing Gender, Class and Englishness in the Elementary School, 1880–1914* (Toronto: Toronto University Press, 2000), 163–64.

47 Davin, "Imperialism and Motherhood," 14.

48 Loeb, *Consuming Angels,* 114.

49 Loeb, *Consuming Angels,* 5, 8.

50 Davin, "Imperialism and Motherhood," 25–27.

51 Stead Junior, *Art of Advertising,* 28.

Works Cited

Newspapers are cited in text.

advertisingarchives.co.uk. Accessed June 22, 2017.

Benson, John. *The Rise of Consumer Society in Britain, 1880–1980.* London: Longman, 1994.

Chapman, Jane. *Comparative Media History.* Cambridge: Polity, 2005.

Church, Roy. "Advertising consumer goods in nineteenth-century Britain: new perspectives", *Economic History Review* 13, no. 4 (2000): 621–45.

Daunton, Martin. *Wealth and Welfare: An Economic and Social History of Britain.* Oxford: Oxford University Press, 2007.

Davin, Anna. "Imperialism and Motherhood," *History Workshop Journal,* no. 5 (1978): 9–65.

Dempsey, Mike. *Pipe Dreams: Early Advertising Art from the Imperial Tobacco Company.* London: Pavilion, 1982.

Driver, Felix. *Geography Militant: Culture of Exploration and Empire.* Oxford: Blackwell, 2001.

Fromer, Julie. *A Necessary Luxury: Tea in Victorian England*. Athens: Ohio University Press, 2008.

Fulton, Richard. "The Sudan Sensation," *Victorian Periodicals Review* 42, no. 1 (2009): 37–63.

Gould, Marty. *Nineteenth-Century Theatre and the Imperial Encounter*. London: Routledge, 2011.

Graziano, Martha Makra. "Food of the Gods as Mortals' Medicine: the uses of chocolate and cacao products," *Pharmacy in History* 40, no. 4 (1988): 132–46.

Heathorn, Stephen. *For Home, Country, and Race: Constructing Gender, Class and Englishness in the Elementary School, 1880–1914*. Toronto, ON: Toronto University Press, 2000.

Hewitt, John. "Designing the Poster in England, 1890–1914," *Early Popular Visual Culture* 5, no. 1 (2007): 57–70.

Hewitt, Martin. *The Dawn of the Cheap Press in Victorian Britain: The End of the 'Taxes on Knowledge', 1849–1869*. London: Bloomsbury Academic, 2014.

Hilton, Matthew. *Smoking in British Popular Culture, 1800–2000: Perfect Pleasures*. Manchester: Manchester University Press, 2000.

Hindley, Diana and Geoffrey Hindley, *Advertising in Victorian England, 1837–1901*. London: Wayland, 1972.

Jackson, Ashley and David Tomkins, *Illustrating Empire: A Visual History of British Imperialism*. Oxford: Bodleian Library, 2011.

Johnson, Paul. "Conspicuous consumption and working-class culture in late-Victorian and Edwardian Britain," *Transactions of the Royal Historical Society*, 38 (1998): 27–42.

Krebs, Paula. *Gender, Race and the Writing of Empire: Public Discourse and the Boer War*. Cambridge: Cambridge University Press, 1999.

Loeb, Lori Anne. *Consuming Angels: Advertising and Victorian Women*. New York and Oxford: Oxford University Press, 1994.

MacKenzie, John. *Propaganda and Empire: The Manipulation of British Public Opinion*. Manchester: Manchester University Press, 1984.

McClintock, Anne. *Imperial Leather: Race, Gender and Sexuality in the Colonial Context*. New York and London: Routledge, 1995.

Meisel, Martin. *Realizations: Narrative, Pictorial, and Theatrical Arts in Nineteenth-Century England*. Princeton, NJ: Princeton University Press, 1983.

Morgan, Kenneth. "The Boer War and the media (1899–1902)," *Twentieth-Century British History* 13, no. 1 (2002): 1–13.

Nead, Lynda. *Victorian Babylon: People, Streets and Images in Nineteenth-Century London*. New Haven, CO: Yale University Press, 2000.

Nevett, Terence. *Advertising in Britain: A History*. London: Heinemann, 1982.

Oddy, Derek. "Working-Class Diets in late nineteenth-century Britain," *Economic History Review*, no. 23 (1970): 314–23.

Opie, Robert. *Rule Britannia: Trading on the British Image*. London: Viking, 1985.

Pettitt, Clare. "Exploration in Print: from the miscellany to the newspaper." In *Reinterpreting Exploration: The West in the World*, edited by Dane Kennedy, 80–108. Oxford: Oxford University Press, 2014.

Plunkett, John. *Queen Victoria: First Media Monarch*. Oxford: Oxford University Press, 2003.

Popple, Simon. "'Fresh From the Front': Performance, War News and Popular Culture during the Boer War," *Early Popular Visual Culture* 8, no. 4 (2010): 401–18.

Porter, Bernard. *The Absent-Minded Imperialists: What the British Really Thought about Empire*. Oxford: Oxford University Press, 2004.

Ramamurthy, Anandi. *Imperial Persuaders: Images of Africa and Asia in British Advertising*. Manchester: Manchester University Press, 2003.

———. "Absences and Silences: The representations of the tea picker in colonial and fairtrade advertising," *Visual Culture in Britain* 13, no. 3 (2012): 367–81.

Richards, Thomas. *The Commodity Culture of Victorian England: Advertising and Spectacle*. Stanford, CA: Stanford University Press, 1991.

Searle, Geoffrey. *The Quest for National Efficiency: A Study in British Politics and Political Thought, 1899–1914*. Oxford: Blackwell, 1971.

Sèbe, Berny. *Heroic Imperialists in Africa: The Promotion of British and French Colonial Heroes, 1870–1939*. Manchester: Manchester University Press, 2013.

Smith, Michelle. *Empire in British Girls' Literature: Imperial Girls, 1880–1920*. Basingstoke: Palgrave, 2011.

Spiers, Edward. *The Victorian Soldier in Africa*. Manchester: Manchester University Press, 2004.

Stead Junior, W., *The Art of Advertising: Its Theory and Practice Fully Described*. London: T.B. Browne, 1899.

Steinitz, Lesley. 'Bovril: A very beefy (and British) love affair', www.cam.ac.uk/research/news/bovril-a-very-beefy-and-british-love-affair, 5 July 2013. Accessed 25 June 2017.

Summers, Anne. *Angels and Citizens: British Women as Military Nurses, 1854–1914*. London: Routledge, 1988.

Surridge, Keith. 'More than a great poster: Lord Kitchener and the image of the military hero', *Historical Research* 74, no. 185 (2001): 298–313.

Trentmann, Frank. *Free Trade Nation: Commerce, Consumption, and Civil Society in Modern Britain*. Oxford: Oxford University Press, 2009.

———. *Empire of Things: How We Became a World of Consumers, from the Fifteenth Century to the Twenty-First*. London: Allen Lane, 2015.

Waller, David. *The Perfect Man: The Muscular Life and Times of Eugen Sandow, Victorian Strongman*. Brighton: Victorian Secrets, 2011.

Ward, Stuart. "Echoes of Empire," *History Workshop Journal* 62, no. 1 (2006): 264–78.

Wilkinson, Glenn. "'To the Front': British Newspaper Advertising and the Boer War." In *The Boer War: Direction, Experience, Image*, edited by John Gooch, 203–12. London: Routledge, 2013 edition.

Yeandle, Peter. *Citizenship, Nation, Empire: The Politics of History Teaching in England*. Manchester: Manchester University Press, 2015.

Index